Gypsies and Orientalism in German Literature and Anthropology of the Long Nineteenth Century

LEGENDA

LEGENDA, founded in 1995 by the European Humanities Research Centre of the University of Oxford, is now a joint imprint of the Modern Humanities Research Association and Routledge. Titles range from medieval texts to contemporary cinema and form a widely comparative view of the modern humanities, including works on Arabic, Catalan, English, French, German, Greek, Italian, Portuguese, Russian, Spanish, and Yiddish literature. An Editorial Board of distinguished academic specialists works in collaboration with leading scholarly bodies such as the Society for French Studies and the British Comparative Literature Association.

MHRA

The Modern Humanities Research Association (MHRA) encourages and promotes advanced study and research in the field of the modern humanities, especially modern European languages and literature, including English, and also cinema. It also aims to break down the barriers between scholars working in different disciplines and to maintain the unity of humanistic scholarship in the face of increasing specialization. The Association fulfils this purpose primarily through the publication of journals, bibliographies, monographs and other aids to research.

Routledge
Taylor & Francis Group
LONDON AND NEW YORK

Routledge is a global publisher of academic books, journals and online resources in the humanities and social sciences. Founded in 1836, it has published many of the greatest thinkers and scholars of the last hundred years, including Adorno, Einstein, Russell, Popper, Wittgenstein, Jung, Bohm, Hayek, McLuhan, Marcuse and Sartre. Today Routledge is one of the world's leading academic publishers in the Humanities and Social Sciences. It publishes thousands of books and journals each year, serving scholars, instructors, and professional communities worldwide.

www.routledge.com

Gypsies and Orientalism in German Literature and Anthropology of the Long Nineteenth Century

❖

Nicholas Saul

Routledge
Taylor & Francis Group
LONDON AND NEW YORK
2007

First published 2007 by Modern Humanities Research Association and Routledge

2 Park Square, Milton Park, Abingdon, Oxfordshire OX14 4RN
52 Vanderbilt Avenue, New York, NY 10017

Routledge is an imprint of the Taylor & Francis Group, an informa business

First issued in paperback 2020

ISBN 978-1-900755-88-7 (hbk)
ISBN 978-0-367-60405-9 (pbk)

CONTENTS

PREFACE

❖

This book has been seven years and more in the writing, and I would like heartily to thank my family, especially Veronika, for their love, support and patience. I would also like to thank the British Academy. That remarkable institution assisted my research with the award of both a Small Research Grant in 2002 and a Senior Research Fellowship in 2004–05. Gratitude is due additionally to Dr Kornelia Küchmeister and the Landesbibliothek Kiel for generous assistance in exploring the Jensen–Heyck and Petersen papers and for permission to cite from them; also to Dr Wolfgang Trautwein of the Literaturarchiv, Akademie der Künste, at Berlin for permission to explore and cite the Carl Hauptmann papers held there. I am also grateful to the editors and publishers concerned for permission to republish here in different form material which has appeared previously as 'Keller's *Romeo und Julia auf dem Dorfe*', in *Landmarks in German Literature*, ed. by Peter Hutchinson (New York, Munich, and Bern: Peter Lang, 2003), pp. 125–40, and as '". . . die schönste Menschengestalt": The Nature, Culture and Ethnography of Stifter's Gypsies', in *History, Text, Value. Essays on Adalbert Stifter. Londoner Symposium 2003*, ed. by Michael Minden, Martin Swales and Godela Weiss-Sussex, *Jahrbuch des Adalbert-Stifter-Institutes des Landes Oberösterreich*, 11/2004 (2006), 129–40. Earlier versions of material published for the first time in the following pages were given in the form of lectures at Vancouver in 1995 and Glasgow in 1996 (Brentano), Manchester in 2001 (Wolzogen), Sydney in 2004 (Raabe), and Lancaster in 2005 (Jensen). I thank the discutants at these venues for their valuable comments. Jonathan Long, Frank Möbus, Roger Paulin, Ritchie Robertson, and Susan Tebbutt gave tips and provided helpful criticisms on individual chapters. Patrick Zuk explained Liszt's music. Last but not least, thanks are due for further financial support to the Institute of Germanic and Romance Studies of the University of London, the Faculty of Arts and Humanities at the University of Durham and the School of Modern Languages at the University of Durham.

Nicholas Saul
Durham, September 2006

CHAPTER 1

❖

Stations in Gypsy Cultural Anthropology from Jacob Thomasius to Liszt

Even that most generous, relativist, and cosmopolitan of German Enlightenment anthropologists, Johann Gottfried Herder, wanted to put them in the army. The 700,000 or 800,000 Gypsies present in Europe, he wrote in his *Ideen* (1794), were a strange, heathen, subterranean nation, alienated by birth from everything godly, decent and *bürgerlich*, committed even after centuries to this demeaning destiny, and thus good for nothing but a dose of military discipline.[1] In his brief adversion Herder encapsulates the fascination and frustration which, since their appearance in Europe in the twelfth century (and Germany in the early fifteenth), the Romany nation has retained for the occidental and especially the German mind. The strange charisma of the Romanies plainly attracts Herder's philanthropic gaze. But their complete indifference to the heritage of German Enlightenment humanist values incites even in Herder's most elastic of minds something close to contempt and far from understanding, and invites from this most tolerant of spirits something equally close to punishment and far from justice. There is no direct link between the exemplary humanist Herder and the criminal racial hygienists who later formulated the ideology of National Socialism. And yet even Herder, with the failure of understanding and elusive hostility to the Romany presence typical of his age, represents a chapter in the long story of Germanic anti-Gypsyism which reached an unspeakable nadir in the *Porrajmos*[2] or Romany Holocaust under National Socialism. In that inferno from 500,000 to 750,000 Gypsies are estimated to have been murdered. Despite official gestures to the contrary, anti-Gypsyism still dominates popular attitudes in German-speaking lands.[3]

Of course the context in which Herder, who was not a professional ethnographer, made his judgement, was by today's standards unsophisticated. Today, as documented in the work of Thomas Acton, Angus Fraser, Donald Kenrick, Ian Hancock, Leo Lucassen, David Mayall, Judith Okely, Susan Tebbutt, Rüdiger Vossen, Wolfgang Wippermann, and many others,[4] Romany ethnography is a well-defined, critically orientated, highly differentiated and controversial sub-discipline of cultural anthropology. Perhaps the Romany presence is now better understood (if not better received), than in Herder's day. After a flowering of research over the last twenty years the story of Gypsy anthropology in Germany in the eighteenth and early nineteenth centuries is a reasonably well-mapped road, as is the era of Romany

Holocaust itself. But what path led the Gypsies from Herder's cosmopolitan (if flawed) epoch through the age of high German nationalism and nascent imperialism in the latter half of the long[5] and difficult[6] nineteenth century to the threshold of genocide?[7] If the last century brought us National Socialism and the Holocaust it is in this only the heir of the nineteenth. It was the nineteenth century which bred the energies that, under German conditions, made these disasters possible: industrialization and technologization, urbanization and mass society, nationalism, imperialism, Social Darwinism, racism. The nineteenth century divided Germany almost irrevocably from its thousand-year beginnings. It was the age of Germany's slow transition to nation- and statehood under Prussian hegemony, of its incipient imperialism under Bismarck and the Kaiser after 1884,[8] its transformation from largely rural-agrarian to mainly urban-industrialized modern economy,[9] of its railway and technology boom,[10] and last but not least its intellectuals' cultural shift (in the categories of David Friedrich Strauss), from a traditional, theocentric, 'old' religion to a largely monist, post-Darwinian, 'new' religion.[11] The literature of this epoch brought all that into meaningful focus for the German collective mind and laid the ideological foundations for what followed. To give an account of the Gypsy story in that crucial period by reconstructing the shifts in the representation of the Gypsy in German culture through the medium of literature and the discipline of anthropology from around 1850 to the First World War is the goal of this book. This chapter will describe the stations of official Romany anthropology in its deeply ambiguous relation to the Gypsy nation over that period.

The tone for what follows is already set by the seventeenth century. One of the earliest responses to the Gypsy presence is Jacob Thomasius's *Dissertation de Cingaris*, his Leipzig doctoral dissertation of 1652, later published in German as the *Gründliche Historische Nachricht von denen Ziegeunern*.[12] Why are they called *Zigeuner*? Where are the Gypsies from? are the key questions of Thomasius's rudimentary account (Thomasius, 10). He can answer both in one move. They are called *Zigeuner* not because they wander in from abroad ('Ziehe einher', 17), but because this is a corruption of the term *Egyptianer* (13), connoting their claimed provenance from Egypt (31–38), or Nubia — or possibly elsewhere in this general area (35–36). Expelled from their homeland on some account — perhaps because they abandoned their Christian faith (50) — they may return only when their penance, a period of exile, has been endured. These Egyptians, he records (22), entered Germany in 1417 and spread rapidly through Germany and the rest of western Europe. Horse traders, fortune tellers and beggars, they were 'garstig und schwarz von Farbe', 'unrein in der Kleidung' and 'in ihrer gantzen Lebens Art unflätig' (29). Today they have the reputation of thieves and tricksters (29). But the letters of protection issued for them by Emperor Sigismund suggest this was not always so (29–30, 32). Thomasius, who as a rule claims to have experienced the Gypsies only 'aus Büchern' (63; compare 9), notes that their language, which exists only in spoken form, is not identical with thieves' cant (*Rotwelsch*, 39). *Rotwelsch* is merely a veneer of esoteric verbs and nouns spread over a comprehensible German substratum. But he has been unable to understand the language the Gypsies spoke among themselves in his presence (39). True, they do in fact still speak thieves' cant (39–40). But the grouping today known as Gypsies in Germany also, in part, comprises all manner of idle and disreputable travelling folk: 'allerley Schelmen-Pack' (53), 'ein zusammen gelauffener Schwarm von müßigen Leuten, der aus allerley Völckern sich gesammlet, [. . .] und von denen ersten Ziegeunern gar weit unterschieden' (52). Masters of disguise (55–56) and of language (56–57), they are at home everywhere and nowhere in Europe (57–58). Whatever their moral probity in the past, today these 'so böse Buben' (63) earn their living not only by honest chiromancy but by begging, theft, and highway robbery (59). Indeed, says Thomasius, warming to his task at the close of his dissertation, they are today cunning horse traders, cheating gamers, lubricious disdainers of religion, poisoners, murderers, magic bespeakers of fire, betrayers of Christians, and spies of the Turks (60). They should be banished across the furthest oceans to the end of the earth (63).

The characteristic ambiguity of all occidental utterances on the Romanies is painfully evident in Thomasius's remarkable amalgam of apology and denunciation, fact and invention, critique and credulity. He has seen the Gypsies and heard their incomprehensible tongue. But he has also only used books as his source for the dissertation. The Gypsies are from Egypt, or possibly not. Their skin is naturally dark, or perhaps only dyed (55–56). The Gypsies are criminals, who should be expelled; or perhaps they have merely been slandered. The Gypsies in Germany today are members of the Gypsy nation; or possibly a motley crew of thieves and vagabonds, with or without Gypsies admixed. It is tempting to abandon Thomasius's work as unconsciously self-destructive. And indeed it possesses for the literary reader an irritant subtext, strangely reminiscent of two other well-known unreliable narrative improvisers — Sterne's Shandy and Hoffmann's Kreisler biographer — in the form of Thomasius's constant reminders that he is writing an improvised dissertation with inadequate resources against the clock (Thomasius, 9, 63), and we shall just have to make do with his results. But irrespective of truth content it has its own significance and authority as one of the very few early, uncontradicted testimonies to the Gypsy presence in the *gadjo* (non-Gypsy) world. Some of it recognizably belongs even in a modern account: the legend of Egyptian origin, the palm reading, the claim of magic powers, the imputation of criminality, the (disproved, 55) claim of child stealing. In this context it is equally notable that other features which the popular mind today thinks of as typifying Gypsy culture — the flamboyant dance, the improvised violin music, the physical beauty and sexual allure — at this stage of the Gypsy story told in the *gadjo* voice make no appearance in Thomasius's compilation. Most significantly, he leaves us in doubt as to whether a clear racial attribution can be made to today's 'Gypsies'.

The article *Ziegeuner* in *Zedlers Großes vollständiges Universal-Lexikon aller Wissenschaften und Künste* (1749),[13] the most widely read source of general scholarly knowledge in the eighteenth century, positively institutionalizes the tendency inaugurated by Thomasius in early German Romany cultural anthropology — the habit of uncritical compilation from written sources — by largely compiling from Thomasius himself. All of Thomasius's substantive, 'ethnographic' points are reproduced approvingly in one form or another (Zedler, 520–24), with Zedler adding to the debate on the riddle of Gypsy provenance only the further, helpless theory that the Gypsies were probably 'ein umlauffendes Volck [. . .], so nirgends zu Hause gehöret' (524), identical with the fakirs in Muslim lands. Today they are merely 'zusammen gelauffenes böses Gesindel, so nicht Lust zu arbeiten hat, sondern von Müßiggang, Huren, Fressen, Saufen, Spielen u.s.w. Profession machen will' (525). But to this Zedler does add something useful, namely a sketch of the desperate legal situation of the Gypsy in the eighteenth-century Holy Roman Empire. For by now Sigismund's letter of protection has long since been revoked, and Thomasius's wishes have come true. The criminalization of this ethnic (or mixed) group of wanderers has progressed so far as officially to sanction its outlaw status:

> Da nun dieses Zigeuner-Volck [. . .] mancherley Unheil anzurichten pflegt, so ist gar eine billige und gerechte Straffe für diese Leute, daß man sie, wie fast allenthalben in Deutschland angeordnet ist, aller Orten, es sey in Städten, Flecken, Dörfern, Büschen und Wäldern, mit gewaffneter Hand aufsucht, und mit Gewalt aus dem Lande verweiset; sie auch bey verspürten Widerstande so gleich tod schiessen läst, und diejenigen, so man ergreifft ohne einige Gnade und Nachsehen, und ohne allen weiteren Proceß blos und allein um ihres verbotenen Lebens-Wandels und bezeigten Ungehorsams halber, mit Leib- und Lebens-Strafen belegt, die Weiber und Kinder aber in die Zucht- und Arbeit-Häuser auf ewig verdammt. (527)

Gypsies are thus by law banished from most constituent states of the Empire — and from most other states too (527). This is no mere claim. In the rest of the article Zedler pedantically reproduces long extracts from draconian Imperial, Saxon, Prussian, Bavarian (and other) Gypsy ordinances designed to cleanse the lands of this dissolute riff-raff ('das Land von dem liederlichen Gesindel rein zu halten', 537) from 1500 to the present (527–43), deploring only their relative inefficacy or untoward mildness (527, 543) against the 'Zigeuner-Geschmeiss' (543). An Imperial mandate of 1 July 1720 prescribed for example that anyone might kill a Gypsy who resisted arrest and eviction (531). A Prussian edict of 24 November 1724 commanded that Gypsies and robbers caught red-handed should be hanged without question or shot if they resisted (537).

Only in the work of the comparative linguist Johann Rüdiger and in particular the Göttingen scholar Heinrich Grellmann[14] did Romany ethnography at the end of the eighteenth century take a step forward. Grellmann, who applied a popularized version of Rüdiger's etymological insights into the family tree of the Romany language[15] in order to solve the riddle of Romany provenance, was by today's standards, and even by the standards of his near-contemporary Georg Forster,[16] still a very inadequate ethnographer. He seems not to have conducted any fieldwork at all, relying instead — far more efficiently and effectively than Thomasius, it must be admitted — on the time-honoured tradition of the collation and critical evaluation of information obtained by others. Herder's source,[17] he was unashamedly a man inoculated against any flavour of the anthropological latitudinarianism we know so well in Goethe, Herder, Alexander von Humboldt or Georg Forster, a man from the rationalist wing of the German Enlightenment, a believer in both its uniformitarian view of human nature and one-dimensional concept of historical progress. Yet in

1783 this armchair anthropologist published a book, the *Historischer Versuch über die Zigeuner,*[18] which remained the standard work on Romanies in Europe for most of the nineteenth century.[19] It received a second edition in Germany within four years, was translated into English in 1787, French in 1788, Dutch in 1791, and went into second English and French editions in 1807 and 1810 respectively.[20] All other works, including the ethnographic section of August Friedrich Pott's ample linguistic study *Die Zigeuner in Europa und Asien* (1844–45),[21] whilst they accept Grellmann's (and Rüdiger's) results, nevertheless return methodologically to the older tradition of Gypsy cultural anthropology, in that they merely reproduce the substance of Grellmann.[22] Even the wandering poet-scholar George Borrow, who lived for years among the Gypsies of Spain and England, who established the presence of the Gypsy in English letters with *The Zincali*, *Lavengro*, *The Romany Rye*, and *Romano Lavo-Lil*, and whose work in turn became well-known in Germany, can be found deferring to Grellmann's authority.[23]

Grellmann's strengths were three: the vast amount of information he compiled, which is intended to be comprehensive, indeed offers an intimidatingly systematic survey of Gypsy life, and yet is cast in a well-analysed, highly readable form; the fact that he provided a definitive, positivistically irrefutable answer to the endlessly fascinating riddle of the Gypsy nation, its provenance, and so fixed them immoveably on the map of human knowledge; and, equally important, the fact that he constructed an image of the Romanies, based in ethnographic fact, which has stayed put in the occidental imagination until our day. In terms of information Grellmann covers every conceivable point of Romany life, from economics to diet, dress, sexuality, manners, religion, language, arts, physiology and physiognomy, character, population distribution, legal history, and so forth. In the matter of provenance, he at last demolishes the legend propagated since Thomasius of the Gypsies' Egyptian origin[24] and then, using Rüdiger's work,[25] correctly identifies the mysterious outsiders who had wandered western Europe for 400 years (or more) as genuine Orientals,[26] originating from north-western India. The Gypsies, he further theorizes, can on the basis of similarities in mode of life be named as descendants of the lowest, despised, constitutionally abject, Indian Pariah caste (327–42). They are thus *authentic* outcasts, and their extraordinary existence in the Occident is in truth comprehensible as merely the continuation of their original way of life (328).

Just as important is the image Grellmann creates of the Gypsies. Inevitably, this further occidental twist to the Gypsy story is also marked by ambivalence. On the one hand they are frankly abject. In this context Grellmann, to an extent, speaks the pathetic language of high Enlightenment philanthropy. He insists on the Gypsies' human dignity and deplores the injustice of their centuries-long outlaw status (10). He is outraged at abuses of their human rights, such as the unspeakable practice of Gypsy hunting (11–13). He defends them against the charge of cannibalism and child theft (54–55). He insists on the talents Gypsies possess (15, 84), which will one day make them good servants of the Enlightenment state, and praises the ruthlessly rationalistic, assimilatory measures of Maria Theresia and Joseph II in their Eastern provinces (13–15, 187–94).[27] But Grellmann is by the same token of Enlightenment philanthropism also mercilessly dismissive in his evaluation of the Gypsies' actual status and way of life. The Gypsies are a pre-civilized, infantilized, illiterate *Naturvolk* (1), guided in their behaviour by sensual inclination rather than the intellect (155). They are — in this a horror to the Protestant German Enlightenment mind — constitutionally lazy (80, 159–60). They prefer any easy and dishonourable labour or huckstering and prostitution to any form of hard-won craft- or tradesmanship. The men will even let themselves be supported by the women (92). This mindset is the chief cause of their poverty. They are untrustworthy, except to other Gypsies, cowardly, proud, and yet always satisfied with their abject condition (157–62). They dress in dirty, barely decent, bizarrely coloured rags, and leave their children naked until the age of ten (66–69). They live in tents entirely lacking in civilized amenities (70–79). They are addicted to brandy (the men) and tobacco (the women) (46–47). They love nothing better than to eat carrion (42). With their amulets and prophecies, they are irredeemably superstitious (95–99). Yet they have no positive religion, beyond a respect for divine fate (141–45) and an intense love of life, and no belief in an afterlife (128). Despite their innate need to travel, they remain always the same. Culturally isolated from European nations, they are, he says, proudly unchanged, unmixed, even after so many centuries (1), since their tradition forbids them to marry outside of the race (119–20).

On the other hand, Grellmann also, paradoxically, makes the Gypsies for the first time in their story glamorous, or at least available for glamorizing treatment by others. They are, despite everything, and in fact probably because of their physical privations (41), aesthetically beautiful. Their bodies are slim, lithe, regularly formed, and athletic (36–38). The darkness of their skins will, he concedes, repel some and attract others. That apart, however, their physical attributes — 'ihre weißen Zähne, ihr langes schwarzes Haar, auf das sie sehr halten, [. . .] ihre schwarzen lebhaft umher rollenden Augen' — are all 'allerdings Stücke, die der Geschmack des Europäers, mit ziemlicher Einmüthigkeit, unter die Eigenschaften leiblicher Schönheit setzen wird' (36). In this context Grellmann — the first of many German writers to do so in the nineteenth century — devotes considerable energy to defending the beauty of the young Gypsy women's usually barely concealed breasts (37).[28] Even the aesthetic defects are only apparent. Their skin pales when exposed to European conditions for a number of years (40). But not only are their women sensual and licentious (159), the Gypsies as a nation are unusually artistically talented, producing gifted, erotically tantalizing dancers among the young women (94) and brilliant, improvising musicians of both sexes (103–04, 153). In particular Grellmann hails their virtuosity on the violin, singling out for special mention the renowned 'Magyar Orpheus' (103) Barna Michaly, patronized by the Hungarian nobility and even commemorated by a portrait.

Grellmann's Gypsy book, far more informative and sophisticated than any of its predecessors, is thus obviously an expression of Germany's particular Orientalist tradition.[29] In this it can be taken as in Foucault's sense the inaugurator of the modern discourse on Gypsies. A textbook example of occidental knowledge-power over the eastern other, it hermeneutically appropriates the facts of the Gypsy story as then known, smoothly controlling the lettered presentation of an illiterate other to their occidental hosts, the very model of a modern master narrative. In classic Orientalist style it emphasizes Gypsies' sensuality over their rationality, their immaturity and passivity, their lack of agency, and inability to progress. It emphasizes their common humanity at the same time as their abject dependence on the white races for that humanity's full realization. But it also, in compensation, emphasizes their erotic and aesthetic attributes, on the one hand concealing the power exercised over the represented Oriental other, but on the other hand 'excessively' revealing the repressed power of the *Orient* over the Occident. The Gypsy girl's erotic dance and the Gypsy man's virtuoso violin improvisation will henceforth remain compensatory dominants of the Gypsy image in German (and European) culture, always co-ordinated with its equal and opposite image of the Gypsy's shocking abjection. Grellmann's beautiful artist Gypsy is of course the prototype of the Romantic poetic outsider,[30] of *Zigeunerromantik* and *Naturpoesie*, found especially in the writings of Clemens Brentano, who took his beautiful Gypsy pair, the dancer Mitidika and the violin virtuoso Michaly in *Die mehreren Wehmüller* (1817),[31] directly from Grellmann's pages. The Romantic Gypsy, emphatically idealized as a missionary from the land of poetry, the Oriental homeland of the human race, features with startling frequency in German Romantic and other literary discourse, from Wolzogen to Schiller, Goethe, Kleist, Lenau, Eichendorff, and many others,[32] but with equal prominence in French (Victor Hugo's *Notre-Dame de Paris*, Prosper Mérimée's *Carmen*, Henri Murger's *Scènes de la vie de Bohème*) and English literature and art (John Clare's Gypsy lyrics, Sir Walter Scott's *Guy Mannering*, George Eliot's *The Spanish Gypsy*, Wilkie Collins's *The Moonstone*) of the epoch.[33] Our next chapter will chart the course of literary *Zigeunerromantik* over the first half of the nineteenth century. In the story of Gypsy cultural anthropology, however, Grellmann's main legacy for our cognitive interest lies elsewhere. In Thomasius and Zedler the contemporary *Zigeuner* had always been presented as a mixed bag of ethnic Romanies and vagrants of many other groupings. In Grellmann and henceforth in German cultural anthropology — in stark contrast to German specialist legal discourse — the Gypsies are always considered as a *race*.

If we look for innovation after Grellmann, the cultural anthropology of the Romanies in nineteenth-century Germany is for long periods virtually a desert. Grellmann's auratic presence is the one great constant. Grellmann, says Theodor Tetzner respectfully in 1835, is 'Meister' of this anthropological terrain.[34] In that tug of the forelock he is followed by every other writer,[35] the sole difference being the extent to which they acknowledge their indebtedness to Grellmann or are attacked by others for not doing so.[36] Conversely, very few other writers on the Gypsies, even Pott (who mentions having encountered them fleetingly once or twice),[37] claim to have studied them at first hand or, still less, consider this lack of direct experience a disadvantage. Unsurprisingly, most of those few who exceptionally claim first-hand experience of the Gypsies do so from the perspective of an expressly criminological cognitive interest.[38] No less surprisingly, an account of fictive literary sources treated as fact is a regular feature of most early Gypsy anthropologies,[39] and Tetzner, indeed, unselfconsciously features extracts from Goethe's *Zigeunerlied* and Pariah ballad (1822–24),[40] as the *motti* and cognitive guiding lights of each chapter. Thus

Grellmann's conclusions are endlessly reaffirmed, rarely or never challenged. His major conclusion, that the Gypsies are Pariahs, is repeatedly attested,[41] as are his other observations, from the legendary beauty and musical talent of the wandering race[42] to its savage or infantile, constitutional incapacity for civilization,[43] often supplemented by would-be informative contrasts with the Jewish nation,[44] allusions to the Austrian acculturation experiments and their Prussian equivalents at Friedrichslohra,[45] and sagely balanced by regretful philanthropic comments on the nation's inhumane treatment by their *gadjo* hosts[46] or emphatic conjurings of the Gypsy mystery.[47] Why were such shameless compilations as those of Tetzner, Michael von Kogalnitchan, or Carl von Heister ever published? One can only speculate that they satisfied a need for ritualized affirmations of received judgements on the Gypsy race.

Even so, one move of the official Gypsy discourse after Grellmann does mark a significant tectonic shift in the structure of the paradigm. Grellmann had testified to the large numbers of Gypsies living in Europe. But around 1830 even the armchair Gypsy anthropologists who followed him — recalling perhaps Thomasius's notion that the real Gypsies had long departed from Europe — were no longer quite so sure. In one of his few notable observations Tetzner records 'daß in unserm Norden die schwarzgelben Gesichter immer mehr verschwinden, und wir vielleicht nach zwanzig Jahren blos den Namen nach kennen, was uns schon jetzt nur einzeln vor Augen liegt [. . .] in einigen Jahren möchte es vielleicht zu spät sein' (Tetzner, vii–viii). The lyrically minded Carl von Heister, writing in 1842 at the belated dawn of the German industrial revolution, echoes him. He for his part sees in the Gypsies 'in der That ein höchst poetisches Motiv' (Heister, 4). They are now poetic because they represent the last picturesque relics of another age in today's prosaic epoch (6) of steam and iron. Following the introduction of convenient mass travel and emancipation a tendency to cultural uniformitarianism now threatens to level the old characteristic differences (6). The Jews, he thinks, will eventually become fully assimilated — a desirable outcome, yet regrettable for the loss of visibility of 'diese so höchst interessanten Orientalen' (6). Something similar is in store for the poetic Romanies. The ongoing Romany–German cultural assimilation experiments will, he speculates, soon lead to their disappearance (in this, aesthetic sense) too: 'Schade, Schade um die Zigeuner!' (6). Having sketched a picturesque Gypsy camp à la Callot, Heister calls all armchair Gypsy portraitists to arms: 'Man muß sich beeilen, solche Bilder als Gegenwärtiges fest zu halten, da sie nur zu bald erlöschen und der Vergangenheit angehören werden' (6). Thus his and Tetzner's and Gypsy ethnography add to the bad old tradition a new strain of Romantic sentimentalism — indebted, no doubt, to Fenimore Cooper.

Now the cognitive interest of the German Gypsy ethnographers could so far be described as a kind of received Enlightenment humanism. It is the humanism of Alexander von Humboldt or his brother Wilhelm, whose theory of infinitely varying language as the manifold dwelling place of the universal human spirit, for example, motivated the otherwise uninterested Pott's study of the Romany language.[48] Compared with this, however, Emil Reinbeck, writing in 1861 (after Gobineau,[49] the founding father of racial cultural theory, and Darwin,[50] the author of natural selection in its application to survival of the races), embodies a different spirit. He of course notes the 'abenteuerliche Romantik dieses Stammes' (Reinbeck, 36). But his otherwise decidedly post-humanistic ethnography places the Gypsies squarely in the context of a racial theory of cultural development. Europe, he notes, is the continent of culture and civilization (1). But the study of the less intellectually advanced 'Racen' (2) is a duty of humanity. This is all the more necessary given the process of natural attrition to which races are subject over history. For just as many kinds of wild animal are now extinct, 'so gehen auf ähnlich naturgemäße Weise die uncultivirten wilden Racen des Menschengeschlechts ihrem Untergang entgegen; denn es scheint im Plane der Vorsehung zu liegen, daß in einer von ihr voraus bestimmten Periode alle Menschen der bewohnten Erde sich einer gleichen Cultur und Bildung erfreuen sollen' (2–3). In particular — Reinbeck has the Red Indians in mind (3–4) — the entry of the white race as bearer of culture seems, as a prime example of the dialectic of Enlightenment philanthropy, to entail the extinction of the native population: 'denn es ist eine bekannte, auf Erfahrung beruhende Thatsache, daß da, wo die Kultur der weißen Race ihren Fuß hinsetzte, die farbige Bevölkerung allmählich abnimmt und zuletzt dem decimirenden Hauche der eingedrungenen fremden Elemente aussterbend erliegt' (4). This fate awaits the Gypsies (4–5). They have rigorously avoided all civilizing influences (5–6). Hence they have regressed to the status of Pariahs and animals (5). They now form a kind of missing link between the human and the animal kingdom: 'Unter solchen Erscheinungen nahm dieses Volk gewissermaßen den Uebergang oder den vermittelnden Standpunkt zwischen Thier und Mensch ein, denn unverkennbar existiren zwischen ihnen und den Thieren bis zur Kröte hinab, intime Bande der Verwandtschaft, denn nach ihrer Meinung waren sie unter Beiden primi inter pares' (12). There may be around 600,000 in Europe. But they are becoming ever rarer in Germany, France, and Italy, and bands of Gypsies are only seldom seen (39). We shall later see much evidence of the racial theory being applied to understand the state of the Romany nation.

That said, another near-contemporary of Reinbeck, who is today much passed over in accounts of Romany anthropology,[51] and who did not espouse any modern version of racial theory, merits in the context of this conspectus rather more attention than he has traditionally received. The image of the Romanies in Franz Liszt's *Die Zigeuner und ihre Musik in Ungarn* (1859; German 1861),[52] a work originally intended as the preface of the *Hungarian Rhapsodies* (1851–54), builds on Grellmann in particular — a fact he readily acknowledges (Liszt, 60–61). However Liszt's cognitive interest is deeply opposed to the easy, monolithic Orientalism that precedes him.

Liszt's book has a conventional and an unconventional part. In the conventional part of his account Liszt acknowledges the Gypsies' uniqueness among nations, their stubborn rejection, despite abysmal living conditions, of assimilation into other cultures, their remarkable preservation of a way of life unchanged over the centuries, and their uncontrollable, 'magic' fascination for the occidental mind (3–4, 43, 75). He has no hesitation in categorizing the Gypsies as a pre-civilized *Naturvolk* of Oriental provenance and cast of mind (120). Nomadic 'Outcasts' (35),[53] they despise organized labour or trade (21) and live by instinct and opportunity on the margin of the settled peoples' world. Like children they are constitutionally incapable of letters, formalized social and legal relations, archival history of their own origins (3), hopeful projections of the future, indeed even the structuring of time (34) and abstract thought *per se* (20–21, 42).

Having delivered this set of wholly conventional observations, Liszt then, however, in his unconventional part, shifts gear and applies for the first time a characteristically sophisticated, philosophical register of his own to the discourse on Gypsies. As children of nature the Gypsies, he argues, ultimately reject 'jene [. . .] Königswürde der Intelligenz' (33) — the highest attribute of humanity — in favour of an occasionalistic mode of life driven by the spontaneous impulse of reactive affect (32–33). Consequently the structure of their consciousness inversely mirrors the civilized nations' norm. In the latter case impressions are concentrated by the intellect into a singular order of representations, just as a convex lens focuses light in one intense point. Precisely this act of distancing abstraction elevates humanity to a rank of being distinctly different from nature. In the Gypsies, however, that sovereign, ordering consciousness evaporates under the power of the sensual impression, like water in the sun, into the endless, chaotic rhapsody of identity (or sameness, or indifference) with nature (33). Thus where the occidental mind is constituted by a centripetal energy, Gypsy consciousness is one constant, centrifugal ebbing of intellect into the discontinuous sensual moment, sustained only by a dull substrate of habit (34). Only this 'intellectual somnambulism' has carried the Gypsy identity, such as it is, across the generations (35).

On this basis Liszt then becomes the first Gypsy anthropologist (if we may so describe him) explicitly to attack Grellmann's stance. Grellmann's problem, says Liszt with the authority of one who over a period of years has spent many weeks and months living with the Gypsies,[54] is his antipathetic attitude. Grellmann contemplates the Gypsies 'mit dem frostigen Blick des Naturforschers, der ein unsauberes Tier beobachtet und dabei seinem Ekel aus wissenschaftlicher Aufopferung Gewalt antut' (61). He may defend them against the worst popular prejudices. But he can never quite repress 'einen geheimen Abscheu vor ihnen' (61), still less discover in them 'auch nur die verwittertsten Spuren eines Vorzugs, das leiseste Zeugnis ehemaliger Noblesse in ihnen' (61). It is this, new, apologetic — but not quite Romantic, and no longer conventionally Orientalist — note which Liszt introduces into the tradition of Gypsy anthropology. We have already noted that Liszt adopts a markedly more sophisticated philosophical tone than is usual among the professional anthropologists when addressing the Gypsy problem. What Liszt really attempts in *Die Zigeuner und ihre Musik* — and this is intimately linked with the project of the *Hungarian Rhapsodies* — is a philosophically based recuperation of the Gypsies as then known beyond Grellmann's horizon from their frankly presented abjection[55] into the dignity, the 'Noblesse' (as he calls it) of the human family. He uses Hegel — then of course still the dominant force in the German philosophical tradition — to do it.

Reflection on art, and on music in particular, is inevitably Liszt's means to this end. In his *Vorlesungen über die Ästhetik*, given between 1820 and 1829, first published in 1835 and then again in a corrected, definitive edition of 1842,[56] Hegel had argued that art, along with religion and philosophy, follows the formation of the state as an objective, concrete form of the self-expression of *Geist* (mind or spirit) on its way to the full self-realization which is the result of history. Art precedes religion and philosophy in the ascending hierarchy of the spirit's self-knowledge, in that it (unlike the state) presents the harmonious unity of the idea and the world for the first time in a form adequate to the essential inwardness of spirit. The representation of the naked human body in Greek classical art is thus the ultimate example of the aesthetic ideal. Art's limit of course is for Hegel precisely the sensual form in which this inwardness is presented. This contradiction leads to the intrinsically less sensual but still subjective and emotionally charged modality of religion's contemplation of spirit, and thus ultimately to the pure objective self-transparency of philosophy. In this framework the art history of the nations represents each culture's particular sensual grasp of the relation between idea and world, from the symbolic (of the ancient and Oriental cultures), to the classic (of Greece) and romantic (of modernity), as logically driven stages in the historical process. Thus, given Liszt's presentation of the Gypsy intellectual orientation — as a primitive nation's determinedly centrifugal flight from all the cultural structuring possibilities of the logocentric mind — Hegel's philosophy of art, as one of three highest expressions of the human spirit in its engagement with the absolute, might surely be dismissed as the most unlikely basis for the redemption of Romany cultural dignity. And yet this is precisely how Liszt attempts to deploy Hegel.

For this he turns to Hegel's notion of epic literature[57] in its relation to national identity. In Hegel's view of the historical process the epic is the earliest form of literature. The epic presents above all the rounded, objective totality of a conflictual event or series of events behind which the emotive, individual subjectivity of the author recedes into invisibility (*Ästhetik*, XV, 321–22). The lyric by contrast foregrounds precisely the poet's personal inwardness, the drama synthesizes both of these poles into a new totality representing both the full complexity of the inner person and that person as fully engaged in the conflicts of external reality (322–23). Now, in that the epic strives to depict the totality of its event with the greatest possible degree of elaborated objectivity it also, despite its attempted elimination of all traces of the personal, inevitably acquires a characteristic signature: that of the national culture whence it springs and which it paints (330). Thus the 'gesamte Weltanschauung und Objektivität eines Volksgeistes' (330), crystallized *as* the epic event, constitute in this sense both the form and the content of the authentic epic. Every characteristic aspect of a national culture, from religious consciousness to laws, customs, domestic life, and so forth, belongs intrinsically in this capacious and hospitable form. As Hegel's ideal, Homer's *Iliad* and *Odyssey*, demonstrates, the epic loves naturally to dwell on the episodic and the particular, and progresses to its inevitable end only at a typically stately pace; but it nevertheless also, like the other, smaller genres, always possesses the characteristic inner unity of all authentic art which binds together every seemingly disparate element (331). In its role as totalizing mirror of a culture the epic, as Hegel makes plain, is thus nothing less than a national Bible, the first, absolute book which expresses a nation's originary spirit (331). Every great and significant nation possesses such a book, which provides nothing less than 'die geistige Grundlage für das Bewußtsein eines Volkes' (331). A collection of such national epics would provide a veritable 'Galerie der Volksgeister' (331). To appreciate the entire corpus of authentic national epics is to parade the spirits of the nations before our very (inner) eyes; all together they represent nothing less than a living spectacle of world history (345). Importantly, the epic is for Hegel only an early form of national literature. The national epic may be a classical work of art, but it differs from later, definitively modern classical works of national literature both in virtue of its totalizing achievement of representation — later works, in the fragmented context of modernity, capture only an aspect of the totality — and in respect of the author, who in the later epoch can no longer wholly share the naive mentality, 'das naive Bewußtsein einer Nation' (332), of the epic age (332).

On this basis the amateur ethnographer Liszt pulls off an astonishing move. Every nation, he claims in good Hegelian fashion at the start of his extended preface to the *Hungarian Rhapsodies*, possesses in its pre-modern phase its own 'Volksepos' (Liszt, 1). These arise, he says (again following Hegel),[58] in the shape of poetic fragments and songs which express immediately some aspect, but not all, of the national spirit, and accumulate slowly but surely over time, until at a certain point they either form a large, coherent body of their own accord or fall into the hands of a poet with a mission, who then — Liszt omits to say when — transforms the incoherent fragments into a transparent aesthetic whole (3).[59] He praises the well-known Greek, Nordic, Slavic, Arabic, Iberian achievements (2–3). Thus the Gypsy nation, he claims, is *also* 'im Besitze von Gesängen und Dichtungen' (4) and these, taken together, are also capable 'gewissermaßen eine besondere Art Epopöe zu bilden' (4). But how on earth could a disparate nation with no land, no home, no nostalgia, no writing, no religious culture, no history, and no book of laws — indeed seemingly a childlike *Naturvolk* — aspire to the production of fragments which could eventually crystallize into (of all things) an heroic epic, signature cultural production of a great, significant nation?

Liszt offers two arguments by way of answer. First, the Gypsy nation has in response to its fate in fact made an extraordinary renunciation of all those occidental, civilized values and institutions which condition the production of epic material. By the same token it cannot produce the poet who would celebrate them either (4–5). Instead this unrealized nation has withdrawn into strategic passivity and silence, so that when, inevitably, primal yearnings and dreamings — he means the compensatory foreshadowings of as yet absent heroic dignity — occupy its consciousness (5), they take the non-verbal, constitutionally indefinite form of music: 'die reine Instrumentalmusik als das geeignetste Mittel [. . .], als die Kunst, welche Gefühle ausdrückt, ohne sie auf ein bestimmtes Ziel zu lenken, ohne sich auf die von der Epopöe erzählten, im Drama dargestellten Tatsachen zu beschränken' (5). Pure instrumental music is thus for this nation 'die einzige Sprache, die es zum Ausdruck seiner Innerlichkeit ohne mühsame geistige Anstrengung gebrauchen konnte, und die ihm zugleich sinnliche Freude, vollen Genuß bot' (5). Its content of course is the essence of the Gypsy national character: 'die Verherrlichung des

Wandertriebes [. . .], welcher es unserem Verkehr fernhält, unseren Lockungen unzugänglich macht, es einzig und despotisch beherrscht' (6). Liszt acknowledges the obvious outward discrepancies between the literary epic and what he is proposing. But he insists on the validity of his postulated epic-musical aggregate, 'wegen der Analogie der Inspiration, welche in beiden dieselbe, heroische, von dem der Rasse eigenen Genius durchdrungene ist' (6). Gypsy music, he insists, expresses the same unconditional, free passion as Hegel's epic heroes (6), and he then triumphantly inserts two pages of accurately cited (if rather repetitive) extracts from Hegel's *Ästhetik* (Liszt, 7–8) — the very passages discussed above in their original context — to support the contention. Thus for Liszt the Gypsies, more or less conformable in this to Hegel's prescription, express their individual national consciousness in the naive, living, collective immediacy of a pre-literary, pre-institutional age. They may lack a physical homeland, but not a spiritual one. Incapable of producing their own absolute, national book, they have nevertheless yearned for one and so (in Liszt's metaphor) had to sing where they could not say (9).

Liszt's second move is of course to present *himself* as the author whose mission it is to collect and fuse these fragments of the postulated Gypsy national epic into the dazzling musical totality that is the *Hungarian Rhapsodies*. This is not quite so plausibly Hegelian. True, Hegel insists that third-party single authorship is not only possible but also essential in order to form a single, organic epic text from the fragmented elements (*Ästhetik*, XV, 332–35). However Hegel also argues that in nineteenth-century modernity the epic, with its compendious synthesis of the concrete particular and totality, is probably dead (the novel succeeds it; XV, 342–44). Moreover, Liszt is not exactly the kind of author Hegel proposes for his act of epic integration. Hegel's epic author may, indeed must, live after the epic age. But his consciousness must also still be substantially *shared* with that age (333). Despite his well-known claimed affinity (75) and extensive lived intercourse with the Gypsies,[60] despite his conviction that Hungarian music was entirely Gypsy in origin (108–19, 170–73),[61] the same can hardly be said of the nineteenth-century German-descended, Hungarian-born, French-speaking, self-proclaimed Hungarian patriot Liszt.[62] Liszt's theory, as this exaggeration reveals, is motivated not only by an undoubted affinity with his postulated heroic age of Gypsy national culture[63] but also by a concern that authentic Gypsy culture is dying out in the age of the railway and the burgeoning culture industry.[64]

But Liszt has still added a new dimension to the monotonous history of Romany anthropology. Grellmann, the non-Gypsy armchair anthropologist, had, as we have seen, assumed the status of dominant discourse, and monopolized in Orientalist style the *authorship* of the Gypsy story. Liszt in his assumed role as modern author of the as yet unrealized Gypsy epic — the absolute book and story of Gypsy identity — uniquely offers a challenge and an *alternative* to that: to *recuperate* the authentic Gypsy voice in that other, freer, non-verbal medium, music. He wishes in short to channel Gypsy *self*-expression where — unlike the realm of letters — it can objectively be said to exist.

It is in this light that we should regard what Liszt actually says (in the monograph, not the music) on the content of the Gypsy epic, utilizing Liszt's version of the

Gypsy–Jew contrast. The Gypsies' art, by contrast with the mere simulation of occidental music offered by the assimilated Jews, draws strength from their freedom in wilfully non-adaptive isolation. Committed to the self-indulgent life of feeling, Gypsy art is both wholly egoistic and wholly original (25), conveying exclusively the self-consciousness of the nation's own inner value (25). That inner value is pain and pride (35–44). Despite his permanent flight into sensual enjoyment, the Gypsy ultimately realizes that he can claim no alternative, utopian history (36). The result is a comfortless sense of isolation and impotence, the oppression of the soul we know as pain, and the need of the proud race to express that emotion. This is the birth of Gypsy music (37). Pain, says Liszt, is the equal and opposite reaction to the pursuit of the ideal, the pledge of human greatness (38). In Gypsy art that pain is transmuted into something more powerful yet more peaceful (39). In Hungary, where the Gypsies enjoy relative liberty from oppression, that music reaches its perfection as the art of improvisational freedom and ornament (104), perhaps indeed the ideal of oriental music (131). Thus, given the impossibility of communication between Gypsy and *gadjo* in ordinary language and despite the Gypsy's constitutional lack of interest in communicating with third parties (107–08), it is only Gypsy music which at last achieves the communication of their characteristic pride and pain (42). It is, then, the revelation of this essentially noble and humane quality, 'das innere Licht, die duftige Spur eines erhabenen, edlen Gefühles' (43), as latent even in the abject, excluded Gypsy race, which for Liszt — by contrast to Grellmann — explains the Gypsy fascination for the occidental races (43). Despite their infantilization and cultural oppression, despite their reactive silence and willed separatism, despite their animalistic closeness to nature, despite their oriental otherness, *the Gypsies are like us*. They possess despite everything 'noch den Instinkt ihres Adels' — the 'unzerstörbare Größe der menschlichen Seele, ihre nicht einzubüßende Erhabenheit' (60). Gypsy music — in Liszt's would-be redemptive authorial realization — thus recuperates Gypsy culture into a musical pantheon equivalent to Goethe's (anthropologically relativistic) *Weltliteratur* (172) and therewith recalls the fractured, abject Gypsy identity into dignified membership of the human family, an individual face in the Hegelian cultural gallery of the nations. Thus Liszt can at one level unproblematically admit the Grellmann story of the Gypsy's Pariah provenance, whilst at another transcending it: 'Diese Fragmente erzählen allerdings keine Tatsachen, aber Ohren, die zu hören verstehen, werden den Ausdruck eines gewissen Sehnens aus ihnen erlauschen, nach dem Ideal eines ganzen Volkes. Was fragt die Kunst danach, ob dieses Volk aus Parias besteht?' (172).

In this way Liszt moves beyond the horizon of received Gypsy Orientalism. He avoids both uniformitarian Enlightenment philanthropy and easy aestheticist Romanticism. The Gypsy's aesthetic talent is, admittedly, their chief anthropological characteristic. But Liszt's Gypsies are not Romantic symbols of living beauty or bohemian beauty worship.[65] The content of their beautiful art is the barely mediated pain and melancholy (92, 119) of pre-reflexive, decentred illiterates beyond cultural assimilation through conventional nineteenth-century methods.[66] Their art is, moreover, *their* art, not a projection or an overwriting of an *a priori* Romantic idea. It is only as *such* that their art redeems them, and it does so for Liszt only at the level of philosophical aesthetic cosmopolitanism through admission to the pantheon of Liszt's pioneering concept of *Weltmusik*. Nor are his Gypsies seen as free, except in a self-consciously abstract and problematic, Hegelian sense. Nowhere in the official Gypsy anthropology of the nineteenth century is so sophisticated a body of thought brought to bear on the Gypsy problem, still less by professional anthropologists. Nor is so sophisticated — if at bottom still ambiguous — an answer to the Gypsy question produced as here.[67] Liszt's work is thus a unique — though ignored — response of anthropological discourse to the problem which dominates the *gadjo* reception of the Gypsy presence in Germany: how to give the Gypsy voice without appropriating authorship of the Gypsy story. Only in *literature*, as we shall see in the next chapters, in Clemens Brentano's high Romantic intercultural vision and the severely critical and sceptical, liberal texts of Keller and Raabe, does there emerge an echo of Liszt's attempt at a redemption of the Gypsy presence in Germanic culture.

Notes to Chapter 1

1. See *Ideen zur Philosophie der Geschichte der Menschheit*, in Johann Gottfried Herder, *Werke*, ed. by Martin Bollacher and others, 10 vols (Frankfurt a.M.: Deutscher Klassiker Verlag, 1985–2000), VI, 703.
2. See Ian Hancock, *We are the Romany People/Ame sam e Rromane dzene* (Hatfield: University of Hertfordshire Press/Centre de récherches Tsiganes, 2002).
3. See for a very concise overview of problems of memorialization, the author's 'Hackl's *Abschied von Sidonie* and the Romany Holocaust Remembered', *Bulletin of The Center for Holocaust Studies at the University of Vermont*, 9.2 (2005), 1–3, 8; the standard work on the Romany Holocaust is Donald Kenrick and Grattan Puxon, *Gypsies under the Swastika* (Hatfield, Gypsy Research Centre: University of Hertfordshire Press, 1995).
4. See the following general works: Thomas Acton, *Gypsy Politics and Traveller Identity* (Hatfield: University of Hertfordshire Press, 1997); Angus Fraser, *The Gypsies* (Oxford: Clarendon Press, 1992); Ian Hancock, *The Pariah Syndrome* (Ann Arbor: Karoma, 1987); David Mayall, *Gypsy Identities 1500–2000: From Egipcyans and Moon-Men to the Ethnic Romany* (London: Routledge, 2003), which contains very substantial overviews of research in most areas; see on Gypsies in Germany: Katrin Reemtsma, *Sinti und Roma: Geschichte, Kultur, Gegenwart* (Munich: Beck, 1996); *Sinti and Roma: Gypsies in German-Speaking Society and Literature*, ed. by Susan Tebbutt (New York and Oxford: Berghahn, 1998); Rüdiger Vossen, *Zigeuner: Roma, Sinti, Gitanos, Gypsies zwischen Verfolgung und Romantisierung. Katalog zur Ausstellung 'Zigeuner zwischen Romantisierung und Verfolgung — Roma, Sinti, Manusch, Calé in Europa' des Hamburgischen Museums für Völkerkunde* (Frankfurt a.M. and Berlin, Vienna: Ullstein, 1993); Wolfgang Wippermann, *Geschichte der Sinti und Roma in Deutschland: Darstellung und Dokumente* (Berlin: Pädagogisches Zentrum, 1993); on Gypsies in nineteenth-century Germany: Rainer Hehemann, *Die 'Bekämpfung des Zigeunerunwesens' im Wilhelminischen Republik und in der Weimarer Republik, 1871–1933* (Frankfurt a.M.: Haag + Herchen, 1989); Martin Ruch, *Zur Wissenschaftsgeschichte der deutschsprachigen 'Zigeunerforschung' von den Anfängen bis 1900* (Dissertation, Freiburg im Breisgau, 1986); Leo Lucassen, *Zigeuner: Die Geschichte eines polizeilichen Ordnungsbegriffes in Deutschland 1700–1945* (Cologne, Weimar, and Vienna: Böhlau, 1996); on the problematization of the concept of the Gypsy see Judith Okely's pioneering *The Traveller-Gypsies* (Cambridge: Cambridge University Press, 1983); also Wim Willems, *In Search of the True Gypsy: From Enlightenment to Final Solution* (London and Portland, OR: Frank Cass, 1997). For recent positions see *The Role of the Romanies: Images and Self-Images of 'Gypsies'/Romanies in European Cultures*, ed by Nicholas Saul and Susan Tebbutt (Liverpool: Liverpool University Press, 2004).
5. See David Blackbourn, *The Long Nineteenth Century: A History of Germany, 1780–1918* (New York, Oxford: Oxford University Press, 1998).

6. See *Das schwierige 19. Jahrhundert: Festschrift für Eda Sagarra zum 65. Geburtstag*, ed. by Jürgen Barkhoff, Gilbert Carr, and Roger Paulin (Tübingen: Niemeyer, 2000).
7. See on this in addition to Kenrick and Puxon also Joachim S. Hohmann, *Geschichte der Zigeunerverfolgung in Deutschland* (Frankfurt a.M.: Campus, 1981), esp. pp. 95–178; Michael Zimmermann, *Verfolgt, vertrieben, vernichtet: Die nationalsozialistische Vernichtungspolitik gegen Sinti und Roma* (Essen: Klartext, 1989) and Michael Zimmermann, *Rassenutopie und Genozid: Die nationalsozialistische 'Lösung der Zigeunerfrage'* (Hamburg: Christians, 1996).
8. See Hans-Ulrich Wehler, *Bismarck und der Imperialismus* (Cologne, and Berlin: Kiepenheuer & Witsch, 1969); also Wehler's *Das deutsche Kaiserreich 1871–1918* (Göttingen: Vandenhoeck & Ruprecht, 1973).
9. See Blackbourn, *Long Nineteenth Century*, pp. 175–399; also Eda Sagarra, *A Social History of Germany 1648–1914* (London: Methuen, 1977), pp. 253–401.
10. See on this Wolfgang Schivelbusch, *Geschichte der Eisenbahnreise: Zur Industrialisierung von Raum und Zeit im 19. Jahrhundert* (Munich, Vienna, Frankfurt a.M.: Hanser, 1977).
11. David Friedrich Strauss, *Der alte und der neue Glaube* (Bonn: Emil Strauss, 1873; 1st edn, 1872), esp. pp. 94–219.
12. *Gründliche Historische Nachricht von denen Zigeunern, Darinnen nebst andern Merckwürdigkeiten dieses Volcks insonderheit desselben Ursprung und erstes Vaterland, Ankunfft, Fortpflantzung und Ausbreitung in Teutschland und andern Europäischen Ländern aus bewährten Geschicht-Schreibern kürtzlich gezeiget und erwiesen wird.* Aus dem Lateinischen des hochberühmten Jacobi Thomasii in das Teutsche übersetzt (Frankfurt a.M. and Leipzig, 1748). The first German translation appeared in 1702. On this see Ruch, *Wissenschaftsgeschichte*, pp. 64–75.
13. *Zedlers Großes vollständiges Universal-Lexikon aller Wissenschaften und Künste*, 62 vols (Leipzig, Halle: Johann Heinrich Zedler, 1732–), LXII (1749), cols. 520–44.
14. Grellmann's status is contentious. Willems, following Ruch, attacks Grellmann strongly as a compiler. See Willems, *In Search of the True Gypsy*, pp. 22–91. For a defence of Grellmann, who does not conceal so much as understate his indebtedness to Rüdiger, see Günter Oesterle, '"Zigeunerbilder" als Maske des Romantischen', in *'Zigeunerbilder' in der deutschsprachigen Literatur*, ed. by Wilhelm Solms and Daniel Strauss (Heidelberg: Dokumentations- und Kulturzentrum Deutscher Sinti und Roma, 1995), pp. 47–64 (58 n. 58).
15. Johann Christoph Christian Rüdiger, 'Von der Sprache und Herkunft der Zigeuner aus Indien', in *Neuester Zuwachs der teutschen, fremden und allgemeinen Sprachkunde in eigenen Aufsätzen*, 1. Stück (1782), 37–84.
16. See on Forster's ethnography Vanessa Agnew, 'Ethnographic Transgressions and Confessions in Georg Forster's *Voyage Round the World*', in *Schwellen: Germanistische Erkundungen einer Metapher*, ed. by Nicholas Saul, Daniel Steuer, and Frank Möbus (Würzburg: Königshausen & Neumann, 1999), pp. 304–15.
17. Herder acknowledges both Grellmann and Rüdiger (*Ideen*, p. 703).
18. Heinrich Moritz Gottlieb Grellmann, *Historischer Versuch über die Zigeuner betreffend die Lebensart und Verfassung[,] Sitten und Schicksale dieses Volks seit seiner Erscheinung in Europa, und dessen Ursprung.* (2nd edn, Göttingen: Dieterich, 1787; 1st edn., Leipzig 1783). Citations are from the second edition.
19. See Willems, *In Search of the True Gypsy*, p. 24.
20. See *A Catalogue of the Gypsy Books Collected by the Late Robert Andrew Scott MacFie* [. . .] *Sometime Editor and Secretary of the Gypsy Lore Society* (Liverpool: University of Liverpool, 1936), pp. 55–56.
21. August Friedrich Pott, *Die Zigeuner in Europa und Asien: Ethnographisch-linguistische Untersuchung, vornehmlich ihrer Herkunft und Sprache, nach gedruckten und ungedruckten Quellen*, 2 vols (Halle: Heynemann, 1844–45).
22. This would apply substantively to Emil Reinbeck, *Die Zigeuner: Eine wissenschaftliche Monographie nach historischen Quellen bearbeitet. Herkommen, Geschichte und eigenthümliche Lebensweise dieses räthselhaften Wandervolkes, von seinen ersten Auftritten im fünfzehnten Jahrhundert bis auf diese Zeit* (Salzkotten and Leipzig: Sobbe 1861) and Richard Liebich, *Die Zigeuner in ihrem Wesen und in ihrer Sprache: Nach eigenen Beobachtungen dargestellt* (Leipzig: Brockhaus, 1863). Authentically new ethnographic observations derived from residence among Romanies are introduced into

the discourse on (eastern European) Gypsies only by Heinrich von Wlislocki, *Aus dem inneren Leben der Zigeuner*, in Heinrich von Wlislocki, *Ethnologische Mittheilungen* (Berlin 1892), where Grellmann is merely one source amongst others. See however, for a savage critique of Wlislocki's received latent Romanticism and prejudice, Ruch, *Wissenschaftsgeschichte*, pp. 191–261.

23. George Borrow, *The Zincali: An Account of the Gypsies in Spain* (London: Dent, n.d.; 1st edn, 1841), p. 8, n. 4.
24. Grellmann, pp. 250–79; on Thomasius, pp. 252–59.
25. Grellmann, pp. 280–326; on Rüdiger, p. 284, n. 32.
26. Grellmann regularly and self-consciously applies the tag 'Oriental' to the Gypsies (pp. 4–5, 9, 13, 45, 153).
27. On the Prussian version of the inculturation project see Heinz Mode and Siegfried Wölffling, *Zigeuner: Der Weg eines Volkes in Deutschland* (Leipzig: 1968), pp. 162–66; also Barbara Danckwortt, 'Franz Mettbach — Die Konsequenzen der preußischen "Zigeunerpolitik" für die Sinti von Friedrichslohra', in *Historische Rassismusforschung. Ideologen — Täter — Opfer*, ed. by Barbara Danckwortt, Thorsten Querg, and Claudia Schöningh (Hamburg: Argument, 1995), pp. 273–95.
28. See on this motif as a minor obsession of German Romany anthropology Ruch, *Wissenschaftsgeschichte*, pp. 155–58.
29. At the origin of this discourse Edward W. Said, *Orientalism: Western Conceptions of the Orient* (Harmondsworth: Penguin, 1985; 1st edn. London: Routledge & Kegan Paul, 1978); most recently: Todd Kontje, *German Orientalisms* (Ann Arbor: University of Michigan Press, 2004).
30. See Nicholas Saul, 'Leiche und Humor: Clemens Brentanos Schauspielfragment "Zigeunerin" und der Patriotismus um 1813', *Jahrbuch des Freien Deutschen Hochstifts* (1998), 111–66.
31. See for a brief exposition of this Nicholas Saul and Susan Tebbutt, 'Gypsies, Utopias and Counter-Cultures in Modern German Culture', in *Counter-Cultures*, ed. by Steve Giles and Maike Oergel (Zurich: Peter Lang, 2003), pp. 43–60.
32. See Claudia Breger, *Ortlosigkeit des Fremden: 'Zigeunerinnen' und 'Zigeuner' in der deutschsprachigen Literatur um 1800* (Cologne, Weimar, Vienna: Böhlau, 1998).
33. See on the French tradition Marilyn Brown, *Gypsies and Other Bohemians: The Myth of the Artist in Nineteenth-Century France* (Ann Arbor: University of Michigan Research Press, 1985); also Karl Hölz, *Zigeuner, Wilde und Exoten: Fremdbilder in der französischen Literatur des 19. Jahrhunderts* (Berlin: Erich Schmidt, 2002); on Gypsies in German and anglophone literature see Katie Trumpener, 'The Time of the Gypsies: A "People without a History" in the Narratives of the West', *Critical Inquiry*, 18 (1992), 843–84; also Nicholas Saul, 'Half a Gypsy: The Case of Ezra Jennings in Wilkie Collins's *The Moonstone* (1868)', *The Role of the Romanies*, pp. 119–30.
34. Theodor Tetzner, *Geschichte der Zigeuner; ihre Herkunft, Natur und Art* (Weimar, Ilmenau: Voigt, 1835), p. ix.
35. See Ferdinand Bischoff, *Deutsch–Zigeunerisches Wörterbuch* (Ilmenau: Voigt, 1827), pp. v–x, 1–2; H. Graffunder, *Ueber die Sprache der Zigeuner: Eine grammatische Skizze* (Erfurt: F. W. Otto, 1835), pp. 54–56; Michael von Kogalnitchan, *Skizze einer Geschichte der Zigeuner, ihrer Sitten und ihrer Sprache, nebst einem kleinen Wörterbuche dieser Sprache.* Aus dem Französischen übersetzt und mit Zusätzen begleitet von Fr. Casca (Stuttgart: J. F. Cast, 1840), pp. 3, 6–8; Carl von Heister, *Ethnographische und geschichtliche Notizen über die Zigeuner* (Königsberg: Gräse und Unzer, 1842), p. 6; Pott, I, 14–15; Reinbeck, *Die Zigeuner*, pp. 26, 28; Liebich, p. 12.
36. Compare Pott on the general tendency (Pott, pp. 14–15); Liebich on Tetzner and Heister (Liebich, pp. 12, 15); Heister on Bischoff and Tetzner (Heister, pp. 6–7).
37. Pott, I, p. x.
38. This is the declared purpose of Ferdinand Ludwig Alexander von Grolman's *Wörterbuch der in Teutschland üblichen Spitzbuben-Sprachen, in zwei Bänden, die Gauner- und Zigeuner-Sprache enthaltend*, 2 vols (Gießen: C. G. Müller, 1822), I, pp. ii–iii; see Ferdinand Bischoff's dictionary (Bischoff, pp. v, x–xii), and Criminalrath Liebich's volume, pp. vii–viii, 103–13. The exception is Graffunder, who observed Gypsy children at Friedrichslohra and Erfurt (Graffunder, pp. 5, 8–9).
39. See Tetzner (on Cervantes, Scott, Lenau, Pius Alexander Wolff), pp. 76–77, 96, 106–09); Kogalnitchan (on Cervantes, Scott, Hugo), pp. 26–27; Pott, I, pp. ix–x; Reinbeck, pp. 23–24; Liebich, p. 80.

40. For *Paria* see Johann Wolfgang von Goethe, *Werke*, Hamburger Ausgabe, ed. by Erich Trunz, 14 vols (Hamburg: Beck, 1948–1960), I, pp. 361–68; for the *Zigeunerlied* see Johann Wolfgang von Goethe, *Sämmtliche Werke*, Weimarer Ausgabe, 133 vols. (Weimar: Böhlau, 1887–1914), Section I, vol. 39, pp. 141–42.
41. See Tetzner, p. 138–40; Kogalnitchan, p. 3; Heister, p. 3; Reinbeck, p. 3, Liebich, p. 15.
42. Tetzner, pp. 88–89, 96; Kogalnitchan, pp. 22–23, 25–27; Heister, p. 4; Reinbeck, pp. 42–44, 47, 53–54; Liebich, p. 58.
43. Bischoff, pp. 9, 13; Graffunder, p. 5; Kogalnitchan, p. 10; Heister, pp. 65, 75; Reinbeck, pp. 6, 35; Liebich, pp. 22–23.
44. Tetzner, pp. 51–53; Kogalnitchen, p. 1; Heister, pp. 6, 70; Reinbeck, pp. 4–5; Liebich, pp. 18–19.
45. See on this Tetzner, pp. 117–19; Graffunder, p. 5; von Heister, pp. 114–16: Reinbeck (who thinks that the settlement project finally collapsed in 1737), p. 38; Liebich, pp. 91–92.
46. Bischoff, p. 8; Tetzner, pp. 103–20; Heister, pp. 6, 79. 104; Pott, p. ix; Liebich, pp. 4, 7, 16–17.
47. Graffunder, p. 8; Heister, pp. 4–5.
48. See Pott, I, p. xiv; also Graffunder, p. 8.
49. *Essai sur l'inégalité des races humaines* (Paris: Firmin Didot, 1853–54). Pott was an early opponent of Gobineau. See August Friedrich Pott, *Die Ungleichheit menschlicher Rassen hauptsächlich vom sprachwissenschaftlichem Standpunkte, unter besonderer Berücksichtigung von des Grafen Gobineau gleichnamigem Werk. Mit einem Ueberblicke ueber die Sprachverhältnisse der Völker. Ein etymologischer Versuch* (Lemgo and Detmold: Meyer, 1856), p. 8.
50. Darwin's *The Origin of Species* (1859) was first — unsympathetically — translated as *Über die Entstehung der Arten im Thier- und Pflanzenreich durch natürliche Züchtung oder Erhaltung der vervollkommneten Rassen im Kampfe um's Dasein.* Nach der 2. Auflage mit einer geschichtlichen Vorrede und andern Zusätzen des Verfassers für diese deutsche Ausgabe aus dem Englischen übersetzt und mit Anmerkungen versehen von H. G. Bronn (Stuttgart: Schweizerbart, 1860). The new translation of Victor Carus, initiated by Darwin himself, became the standard: *Über die Entstehung der Arten durch natürliche Zuchtwahl oder die Erhaltung der begünstigten Rassen im Kampfe um's Dasein.* Nach der 4. engl. Ausgabe übers. von J. V. Carus (Stuttgart, 1867).
51. Liszt merits but a single mention in perhaps the most ambitious work so far on the history of Gypsy ethnography, Willems, *In Search of the True Gypsy*, p. 153. Compare Trumpener, 'Time of the Gypsies', p. 859.
52. Liszt's original, *Des Bohémiens et leur musique en Hongrie* (1859), was translated by Peter Cornelius as Franz Liszt, *Die Zigeuner und ihre Musik in Ungarn* (Pesth: Heckenast 1861). Citations from *Die Zigeuner* are taken from Franz Liszt, *Gesammelte Schriften*, 4 vols (Leipzig: Breitkopf & Härtel, 1910), vol. III.
53. Liszt accepts Grellmann's location of the Gypsies as Pariahs (*Die Zigeuner*, pp. 53–60).
54. See Alan Walker, *Franz Liszt*, 3 vols (New York: Knopf, 1983–96), I (1983), 334–42, 379, 434.
55. I mean something analogous to Kristéva's well-known sense of devalued subjectivity, if without her psycho-analytic elaboration. See Julia Kristéva, *Powers of Horror: An Essay on Abjection*, trans. by Leon S. Roudiez (New York: Columbia University Press, 1982).
56. References are to *Vorlesungen über die Ästhetik*, in G. W. F. Hegel, *Werke*, ed. by Eva Moldenhauer and Karl Magnus Michel, 20 vols (Frankfurt a.M.: Suhrkamp, 1970), XIII–XV. Here especially XIII, 127–44.
57. *Werke*, XV, 325–515.
58. *Werke* XV, 325–30.
59. Hegel too insists (against the Göttingen philologist F. A. Wolf and the Schlegel brothers) on the single authorship of Homer (*Werke*, XV, 337–38) without which, he believes, no aesthetic unity could have been achieved. Wolf and the Romantics maintained however that corporate authorship, including the co-operation of poets and critics (*Diaskeuasten*), was more plausible given the work's long genesis and equally conducive to aesthetic quality. See for a brief exposition of this Nicholas Saul, 'Aesthetic Humanism: German Literature 1790–1830', in *The Cambridge History of German Literature*, ed. by Helen Watanabe-O'Kelly (Cambridge: Cambridge University Press, 1997), pp. 202–71 (pp. 228–29).

60. See the autobiographical chapters of *Die Zigeuner in Ungarn*, dealing with Liszt's Gypsy encounters in Hungary, Bucharest, and Russia (pp. 75–93).
61. Reinbeck attacks it (pp. 44–45).
62. On Liszt's self-identification with Hungary and his linguistic proficiencies see Walker, *Franz Liszt*, I, 13–14, 48–49.
63. Walker comments on the extent to which Liszt's 'Gypsy' melodies have turned out to belong to Hungarian folk music (*Franz Liszt*, I, 340–42; II, 381–83).
64. Compare Liszt, *Die Zigeuner in Ungarn*, pp. 124, 161–62.
65. He attacks *Zigeunerromantik* in literature as threadbare cliché (*Die Zigeuner*, pp. 47–48).
66. Compare the story of Jozsy (*Die Zigeuner*, pp. 93–101), treated in Chapter 4.
67. The first to acknowledge Liszt is the otherwise highly problematic Martin Block, in his *Die Zigeuner: Ihr Leben und ihre Seele, dargestellt auf Grund eigener Reisen und Forschungen* (Leipzig: Bibliographisches Institut, 1936), pp. 174–75, but then only as musicologist. Block is treated in Chapter 8.

CHAPTER 2

❖

Zigeunerromantik, Gypsy Others, and Fake Gypsies in German Literature from Wolzogen to Immermann

Scarcely had Heinrich Grellmann made the Gypsies present in the German public mind than they became almost omnipresent in German literature. The literary Gypsy can be found in more or less prominent roles in major works of high or popular literature from *Wilhelm Meisters Lehrjahre* (1795–96), Schiller's *Jungfrau von Orleans* (1801), Caroline von Wolzogen's *Die Zigeuner* (1802), and August Klingemann's *Nachtwachen des Bonaventura* (1805–06), to Kleist's *Michael Kohlhaas* (1810), August von Kotzebue's *Die kleine Zigeunerin* (1810), Arnim's *Isabella von Ägypten* (1812), Clemens Brentano's *Die mehrerern Wehmüller* (1817), and Hoffmann's *Kater Murr* (1821–22), to Pius Alexander Wolff's *Preciosa* (1820), Eduard Mörike's *Maler Nolten* (1832), and Karl Immermann's *Die Epigonen* (1835–36) — and innumerable others in all genres. In the case of Arnim and Brentano, the frequency, prominence, and significance of Gypsy figures in their entire *œuvre* suggest that these two leading late Romantic authors were, for a time, little short of obsessive self-identification with the Romany nation.[1] But it is also clear that the fascination of the Gypsy phenomenon extended for the German literary mind of that age well beyond the compass of the Romantic movement. Now in recent years the phenomenon of the Gypsy in German literature around 1800, long neglected by scholarship,[2] has received a good deal of attention, almost all of it devoted to *Zigeunerromantik*, and hence prior to our cognitive interest.[3] But it is from the age of *Zigeunerromantik* and other German representations of the Gypsy around 1800 that the literary representation of the Gypsy in German literature until the First World War develops, and against which it reacts. This chapter therefore offers a concise survey and evaluation of the Gypsy presence in key works around 1800. In Chapter 1 we saw that unsympathetic, Orientalist appropriation of the Romany voice by the master narrative of the *gadjo* host was the defining characteristic of Gypsy anthropology after Grellmann in the first half of the nineteenth century. Here it will become evident that the literary representation of the Gypsy can be seen as accompanying that phenomenon in a number of complex ways. Chief amongst them, as will be seen, is a shift in focus from pseudo-Gypsies to genuine Gypsies.

How that happens has, however, necessary limits, which should first be clarified conceptually, in terms of general Orientalist and post-colonial theory so far as it concerns literary history. Literary discourse is often regarded in this context as a mode of expression for a distorting representation of the way things are. Thus Edward Said, in his foundational book, exploited Foucault's critique of occidental rationalism to formulate the notion of Orientalism as an essentially repressive discourse. The positive identity of occidental culture, he argued, was not so much given as founded upon a negative: a discursive practice constituting the East as that which the West was not. This relation (if it can be called such) was in the nature of a cultural hierarchy. But the collective eastern subordinate other, whilst strange and attractive, was in truth, Said argued, little more than a solipsistic occidental fiction based on fantasy: the fear, exclusion, and functional silencing of whatever the East *really* was. Imperialism, then, was not only economic and political but also cultural and anthropological injustice.[4] Said focused mainly on English and French literature. But even in nineteenth-century Germany, he argued, the lack of an empire (until 1884) made no difference for cultural-critical purposes: 'what German Orientalism had in common with Anglo-French and later American Orientalism was a kind of *intellectual* authority over the Orient within Western culture' (Said, 19). We saw how Orientalism was applied in the scholarly discourse *within* German borders — with the honourable exception of Franz Liszt — to the representation of the Romany.

But literature is of course not essentially or primarily a medium of cultural oppression. It can also, evidently, *de*constitute repressive semantic orders. Both Said's authority Foucault and Paul Ricœur (to name a very differently orientated theorist) emphasize how the literary text, as autonomous and self-referential construct, can subvert the language in which reality is represented by ironic counter-discourse or the dissolution of received metaphorical reference.[5] Thus Said's Orientalism rests on an inadequate account of the literary text's function. He himself, in *Culture and Imperialism*, moved away from his former dualistic view of Orientalist discourse to allow for a degree of dialectical mixing in the literary representation of occidental self and exotic other.[6] But it was finally Homi Bhabha who in *The Location of Culture*[7] replaced Said's dualism with the developed notion of cultural hybridity: the idea that a colonial culture is enunciated not in dualistic Orientalist opposition and unmediated negation but as an uneasy, if relatively stable, ongoing discursive *negotiation* between two cultures, in which a (post)colonial 'writing back' *in* the language of the master can be practised.[8] The concept of hybridity as the space of negotiation between heterogeneous cultural voices within the once monocultural domain of the colonizer's language is today — stretching well beyond the Orientalist remit — a popular focus of research in German literary and cultural studies, from German-Jewish literature, to Prague and Czech German literature, to writing by Germans of Turkish and Italian provenance, and that of Ossis in the language of the Wessis.[9]

The implications of this rapid conspectus for the current study are clear. Bhabha's hybridity theory evidently offers an ideologically more advanced framework for the study of Orientalist literature in a (post)colonial context. But can we really talk of hybridity and writing back as modes of Romany resistance and literary presence in the nineteenth century? Of course the Gypsies, unlettered as they were, could not then, unlike German Jews, write back, produce alternative mixed discourses in this sense. There are no Romany-German literary texts in the periods of our concern. '[E]cht zigeunerisch gesprochen', says a character in one of the most sympathetic portrayals of literary Gypsies in the Romantic age, Clemens Brentano's *Die mehreren Wehmüller*, in response to a heartfelt outburst by the Gypsy Mitidika.[10] But her words are not spoken like a true Gypsy; this is only a German *simulation* of the Gypsy voice.[11] Even in literature, then, the Romany — unlike the German Jew — is still dependent around 1800 on the *gadjo* voice for the representation of his reality. It is within this limitation that all study of the Gypsy presence in literature before the twentieth century must operate.[12] And this will be our mode of operation in the pages that follow.

On the spectrum of remaining possibilities there manifest themselves two chief modalities of the Gypsy presence in literature, which we may call in conceptual shorthand Gypsies who *are* Gypsies, and Gypsies who flatter to deceive, but turn out to be counterfeit. In the first series, of Gypsies presented with some arguable degree of authenticity and decentred openness to the Gypsy voice, we find Romantics, of whom inevitably Arnim and Brentano stand out. In the latter there belong texts which exhibit opposite characteristics, stifle the authentic Gypsy voice, and refuse to authorize any manifestation of meta-Orientalist cultural difference. This tradition, inaugurated by Cervantes, includes works by a diverse collection of authors from Wolzogen to Pius Alexander Wolff and Eduard Devrient. From it, however, Romantics *stricto sensu* are notably absent. As a result the term *Zigeunerromantik* will be used here in a positive, non-standard, non-Orientalist connotation. The two different classes of literary Gypsies also exhibit strikingly characteristic, contrasting functions. The Romantic Gypsy is presented not only in a relatively authentic light, but also as aestheticized and politicized, both as the ideal of the Romantic artist and also, in their capacity as Gypsy other, the touchstone of authentic *German* identity. The fake Gypsies, even where they touch on issues of German identity, are merely an instrumentalized motif. Mörike and Immermann, we shall see, belong in the Romantic category, but in fact inaugurate a twilight of deep cultural pessimism and, for the time being, the end of *Zigeunerromantik*. Let us for structural reasons treat the fake Gypsies first.

'Gypsies', says the narrator in the opening lines of Cervantes's exemplary novella *The Little Gypsy Girl* (1613),[13] 'seem to have been born into the world for the sole purpose of being thieves' (Cervantes, 19). This foundational text sets the tone for one strand of the literary tradition not only in its frankly denunciatory imaging of the Romany, but also in its use of the foundling motif to deny the Gypsy identity of the otherwise positively presented central protagonist. The Gypsy, we know from our readings in Gypsy anthropology, is alleged to steal the *gadjo* child. Thus this strand of the literary tradition promotes the most ancient, radical, and scandalous denunciation of the Gypsy to something like the primal scene of Gypsy–*gadjo* encounter; with always the same outcome: the virtuous Gypsy who turns out not to be a Gypsy both preserves the a priori *gadjo* self-image, and, equally important, precludes the breaking of a *gadjo*–Romany miscegenation taboo.

Cervantes's tale follows the typological comic structure of loss and recuperation. A beautiful, fifteen-year-old girl has been taught all the 'gipsy arts and frauds and thieving tricks' (19) by her Romany grandmother and earns her living with the Gypsy band through dancing, improvised songs, and palm-reading. But despite this education and way of life she is both beautiful and charismatically virtuous. Her dancing is chaste (22). None of the Gypsy women dare to curse or sing lewd songs in her presence (19). She captivates the attention of Spanish and Gypsy men alike, but always protects her virtue (29–30). Indeed she also looks different. Other Gypsies are tanned (53). But Preciosa, as she is called on account of her virtues, has green eyes and golden hair (31), and, as the narrator authoritatively comments, gives 'every sign of having been born of better stock than gypsies' (19). Thus when a rich and elegant young knight of Madrid declares his love, she accepts the proposal, but sets strict conditions. He must prove himself by spending two years with the Gypsies *as* a Gypsy under the name 'Andrés Caballero' (42). But even in this period the 'free and easy' (52), patriarchal sexual conventions of the Gypsy culture will not apply. A Gypsy man, says Cervantes, does not bother with 'finicky ceremonial' (52) when choosing his mate, and has the power to dispose of her when he wishes. Preciosa, however, insists that she is not governed by this 'barbarous and shameless licence' (55). 'Andrés' may eventually possess her body, but not her soul, which is 'born free' (54). For his part 'Andrés' too, even as a simulated Gypsy, distances himself from Gypsy practices not to his taste — for example by using his money discreetly to buy things for the Gypsies rather than steal them (55–56, 58). 'Andrés' is furthermore sorely tested in love during the Gypsy trek to Murcia by an apparent rival, the poet Alonso Hurtado, who has also joined the caravan. But an adventure brings the apprenticeship in love to a premature end. The daughter of a rich widow has suddenly fallen in love with 'Andrés'. Rejected, she revenges herself by concealing jewels in 'Andrés's' possession, and has him arrested and tried. Of course, as her white complexion (78), documents secreted by the fake grandmother (77), and other sure tokens reveal, Preciosa turns out to be the daughter of the Murcian judge appointed to try the case. She had been stolen by the Gypsies when they last passed through (77). 'Andrés' — Don Juan de Cárcamo — must pass one last test, bravely facing an apparent death-sentence by his future father-in-law. That done, he is forgiven even the deception practised on his own father, and the date of his wedding with 'Preciosa' — Doña Constanza de Azevedo de Meneses — is set.

Thus Cervantes shows how the integrity of the Azevedo family, ruptured by the Gypsies, is restored. Constanza's exemplary virtue has enabled both her rescue and her marriage, and Juan too has proven himself. But what remains of the Gypsies in their lives, or in the text? Life with the Gypsies, despite their attempt at Romany acculturation, leaves as her true name implies no trace on Constanza's person, indeed it has served only as the occasion for her demonstration of non-Gypsy virtue. Preciosa always felt herself to be a cut above them (81). The same is true of Juan. As for the rest, there are no good Gypsies here. In the symbolic economy of the text, they are superfluous save only for their function as occasion for the affirmation of bourgeois virtue. As a nation of illegal immigrants, they seek not to integrate with the host nation, but — through the theft of Constanza — to assimilate it into the Gypsy body politic. Otherwise, they are presented as dishonourable (if entertaining) thieves, whose chief cultural values are the love of abstract freedom, money, and ready wit (41). As the Gypsies melt uncommemorated into the forest whence they came, they leave only one trace of their presence. Even in her true, restored identity as Doña Constanza the heroine will — at her father's wish — retain the name Preciosa (79). But this apparent gesture of recognition merely institutionalizes the *gadjo* name chosen by the Gypsies for a value they themselves do not possess, merely reaffirms her original, deeply intuited, and finally untouched identity. Nothing else of value, even poetry, is left. The poet Alonso may see Preciosa as his muse, but in fact Cervantes's Gypsies lack even poetic talent: they buy their song texts from *gadjo* poets (20, 27). His Romanies, in short, are less Gypsy Others than other 'Gypsies'.

Cervantes's anti-Gypsyist Gypsy creation had a long and successful career in the early nineteenth-century German cultural imagination. When Carl Maria von Weber set the melodramatic adaptation of Cervantes by Pius Alexander Wolff to music in 1820,[14] it was an instant popular success. We need not dwell too long on this, save to note that Wolff modifies the Cervantes original for the purposes of a four-act melodrama with enviable skill. The meta-poetic figure of Alonso is removed, which sidelines the half-hearted love-rivalry, simplifies the plot, and so intensifies the effect of the basic development. But his name is retained and transferred as Alonzo to the 'Andrés'/Juan figure, and it is this person who, under the new, Wilhelm Meister-ish pseudonym of Felix, travels with the Gypsies as Preciosa's simulant lover. Equally, the unmediated widow plot at the conclusion is replaced by a well-motivated dispute between Alonzo and a new figure, Preciosa's brother Eugenio. As a result, the two fathers, now Fernando and Franzisco, play a more collaborative and prominent role in manipulating Alonzo at the mock trial. Finally, Preciosa is aged a little, from fifteen to nineteen, in deference to Biedermeier prudishness and 'Constanza' is changed to the (even more moralizing) Anna Clara. But the salient features of Cervantes's version of Gypsy discourse are retained and intensified. The Gypsies are still, despite their self-presentation as roguish, freedom-loving innocents (27), seen objectively to be venal, and Preciosa herself attacks them for that (Wolff, 44, 48). Her own qualities as paragon of virtue (12) and aesthetic ideal are intensified. She is positively venerated by the Gypsy band (28), from whom she is as distinct as '[ei]ne Taube unter Raben' (35). She is a brilliant zither-player (6), dancer of the Zambarallo (14) and Bolero (35), and singer of beguiling improvised songs (9). She is herself dazzlingly beautiful (7). Still more significantly, she is not only blessed with the power of intuitive prophecy (13, 29), but also believes in the redemptive power of 'die heilige Kunst' (11) and possesses a very modern faith in her own feminine agency. Thus, when Alonzo is arrested by the forces of the man who turns out to be her father, she disobeys the Gypsy Captain, rounds on the cowardly band with a rifle, and enters the castle alone, determined to liberate her beloved with nothing less than the transformative power of song (41). That duly comes to pass in the *dénouement*, and confirms her divinatory intuition (57–58). Anna Clara still retains her old, Gypsy-given name 'Preciosa' at her father's request (Wolff, 63). But in Wolff the Gypsies turn out once more, despite attempts at polishing their image, to have stolen Preciosa as a child, something they have concealed as long as possible (61). As in Cervantes, then, the only good Gypsies here turn out to have been *gadje* all along.

Wolff's and Weber's work remained well-esteemed for several decades. As severe a judge as Friedrich Hebbel was amused enough by it at Munich in 1838[15] to see it again at Hamburg in 1840: 'Leben, freilich nicht das höchste, aber doch frisch und voll', he thought.[16] Indeed, 'Preciosa' seems in the course of the century to have become a sort of brand name. As late as 1895 Fontane gives Gieshübler the forename Alonzo — 'ein romantischer Name, ein Preziosaname' — in order to link him with Effi Briest's world of exotic Romantic yearnings.[17] More disappointingly, even the contemporary would-be anthropologists, for a time at least, adduced Preciosa as a manifestation of authentic Gypsyness in their supposedly learned works: 'man findet in der Moldau wie in der Walachei nicht selten Esmeralda's und Preciosa's', claims the French-Rumanian writer Michael von Kogalnitchan in 1840, and he was not alone in that.[18]

But the motif of the fake Gypsy was not limited to the Preciosa brand, even if the core motif of child theft is afterwards — ambiguously — mitigated. In *Die kleine Zigeunerin* (1810) one of the epoch's most successful exponents of popular drama, August von Kotzebue, had already offered a version which — apart from the obvious Cervantes derivations — fused the motif of the fake Gypsy with that of Romeo and Juliet in the service of then fashionable Enlightenment anti-Catholic propaganda. Here, in sixteenth-century Toledo, Francesko, and Cölestine have fallen in love. Yet their fathers, the (unnamed) Vice-King and Don Ignazio Zapata, the Grand Inquisitor, are fierce political enemies (Kotzebue, 15). Into this tricky situation emerges the beautiful, young, artistically gifted (and so forth) Gypsy girl Lasarilla. She, oddly enough, is the very personification of Enlightenment philanthropy. Well educated for a Romany, she can sing, dance, write, and read. But she prefers the wandering life, earning her keep by cynically (if harmlessly) prophesying whatever her credulous and irrational customers want to hear (6–7). Despite her youth, Lasarilla has learned much of human nature from her wise Gypsy mother and her worldly experience (10–11). With her unknown father long lost in some distant exotic land, and her mother long dead, Lasarilla now enjoys herself wandering through Spain and applying her wisdom to doing good: '*helfen, helfen*, das thät ich gern' (6, compare 11). The plot thickens as Francesko, in search of Cölestine, encounters Lasarilla before the residence of the Grand Inquisitor. Once assured that Francesko is marrying only for love (rather than political expediency), she decides to mediate. There too Lasarilla encounters still another victim in need of assistance: Don Alwares, cruelly incarcerated for the last year as a heretic by the Grand Inquisitor. Alwares had accompanied Pizarro twelve years since to the New World, there acquiring great wealth. On his return he learnt of the death of his wife and daughter. Only his son, the weak and corrupt Antonio, still lives. Dismayed at this despotic infringement of religious freedom, Lasarilla decides to save him too. Of course it turns out that Lasarilla is none other than Marie, the long-lost daughter of Don Alwares, who was unnaturally neglected by her mother in favour of Antonio and in her father's absence heartlessly given away to 'eine [. . .] Bettlerin' (120) — the Gypsy woman who has raised her. The intrigue unwinds as Francesko, disguised as the Gypsy Torsillo, and Lasarilla gain the Grand Inquisitor's confidence and with it a contract — with absolution in advance (160) — to murder the Vice-King. Thus in the final confrontation the two Gypsies denounce the Grand Inquisitor in the presence of his intended victim, so that he must flee, the lovers are joined, peace is made between Church and State, religious conscience is satisfied, and justice done. Thanks to a sure token — a Peruvian icon with a mysterious inscription (68) sent back for his daughter by Alwares — what remains of Alwares's family is restored.

Now positive things can be said about this play. Like Wolff, Kotzebue has endeavoured to present in his little Gypsy girl an image of then-modern feminine agency. Kotzebue also presents his Gypsies, it must be admitted, in a generally favourable light. Their trickery, in so far as Lasarilla has learnt it, is applied to good causes only, such as deceiving the Grand Inquisitor, or harmless exploitation of the credulous. Lasarilla offers a pleasingly cynical and latitudinarian, indeed almost Brechtian apology of Gypsy thievery: 'Zum stehlen und gestohlen *werden* | Ist alles auf der Welt gemacht; | Ein wenig gröber, ein wenig feiner, | Das gilt ja wohl am Ende gleich? | Hüner und Gänse stiehlt der Zigeuner | Und Alexander der Große ein Reich. | Auf diesem ganzen Erden-Runde | Beseelt den Menschen derselbe Trieb; | Der ehrlichste Mann ist doch im Grunde | Höchstens nur der kleinste Dieb' (126). The Gypsies are even, in a sense, exculpated from the usual charge of child-stealing. And Lasarilla's Gypsy 'mother' (by contrast to her real mother) seems little less than a saintly and philosophical figure: 'Wahrlich! ihre Lumpen deckten | Eine edle treue Brust' (9), whose spirit watches over Lasarilla in all her adventures (127). But of course: 'Schätze wurden ihr zugewogen | An Geist und Herz von der reichen Natur' (8). Lasarilla's adoptive Gypsy mother is in truth less an ethnic Gypsy (of whom not a single one is present in the text) than the familiar type of the noble savage, not the abject human but the unspoilt sovereign creation of nature, draped with some few (even in 1810) tired clichés of what then passed for Gypsy ethnography. Kotzebue's Gypsy girl at the end seems to retain two names — '*Maria* oder *Lasarilla*, gleichviel, du bist mein einziges liebes Kind' (239), cries Alwares — but here, as in the works more manifestly in the Cervantes tradition, even the good Gypsies are not really Gypsies at all, but sophisticated and philanthropic Enlightenment ideals, whose ostensible cosmopolitan humanism poses no obstacle to their taking possession of the sacred relics (the Peruvian icon) plundered by Pizarro's genocidal colonists. The last trace of the Gypsy presence on her person — her fantastic costume, tambourine, and castanets — is dedicated by Lasarilla in this anti-Catholic play's closing gesture to the altar of the nearest nunnery (240).

Our penultimate example of this type, the successful actor-manager Eduard Devrient's opera libretto *Die Zigeuner* (1832),[19] presents (by way of innovation) a sort of masculine-gendered Preciosa based loosely on the Prodigal Son motif, but — like Clemens Brentano's unpublished *Zigeunerin* fragment (c.1813)[20] — is indebted also to Goethe's *Götz von Berlichingen* (1773).[21] As Mérimée was later to do with *Carmen* (1845), Devrient accompanies his work with a little, Grellmann-derived essay explaining something of the Gypsy provenance (Devrient, 339–40), in particular that the Gypsies, in this sixteenth-century German setting, were once protected by Kaiser Sigismund but are now, after Maximilian's edict, outlawed. And so here too we find clichés recycled. A leaderless Gypsy band (346) has illegally and secretly (343) camped in the forest of Count Hohenegk. Two of them rashly kidnap a young girl, Agnes, with a view to robbery or worse. Noble Polgar, who has ambitions to lead the band and recognizes the danger posed by attacking one who is in fact the Count's daughter, defends her virtue and sacrifices all his money to buy her from the kidnappers. As he guides her back, a bond of affection is formed, and Agnes feels a mission to redeem him (354). But Polgar refuses to leave his 'primitive nation' (351) and cross to the German side. He knows the prejudice he would face; he values at least the abstract freedom of the forest (352). All that is confirmed by the ensuing encounter with Count Hohenegk. He, like his adoptive son Theobald, is pleasantly surprised yet unconvinced by Polgar's virtue: 'Was? ein Zigeuner, der das Geld nicht achtet?' (358); and has him arrested. But there is more to this situation than meets the eye, and the remainder of Devrient's plot is devoted to analytical disentanglement of the complication. For Beda, the Gypsy band's wise woman, recognizes the Count from an encounter seventeen years ago. Mysteriously she spits at him: 'Daß Du der grimme Eber bist, | Der seine eignen Jungen frißt!' (360). She insists that Polgar return to her a diamond-encrusted crucifix before he accompanies the Count (363), for it will endanger his life should the Count see it. The Count, it turns out, is the last male of his family. Worse, he himself is responsible for this impending extinction of the line. Suspecting his young wife of adultery, he many years ago heartlessly evicted her and her little boy to the forest; later only her body was found (372). Since then he has been consumed by remorse, and finds peace only in accepting the end of his line and the passing of his inheritance to his crass cousin Veit as God's judgement. It is thus only natural that Polgar, compelled to work as a servant in the family halls, is plagued by a sense of *déjà vu* (377–80), for he is indeed the long-lost son, raised by Beda with the Gypsy band. His innate sense of self-worth motivates a conflict with the Count, who however is attracted by the young man's spirit, and frees him at the price of banishment. But he is made of sterner stuff. As Beda prophesies: 'der junge Adler kommt zurück und wirft die Kukuksbrut aus seinem Nest!' (407). Polgar leads the Gypsies in a desperate attack on the castle in the knights' absence. They occupy it, but are at last beaten. As the Count, in an echo of the flight scene (417–18), is about to stab him, he recognizes the crucifix, and the play concludes with Polgar assuming his original identity, making peace between the emancipated Gypsies and the Hohenegks, preventing Agnes's marriage to Veit and his own incest with her, and triumphantly swinging the eagle banner of the restored dynasty.

As with Kotzebue, there are interesting perspectives embedded in this otherwise trivial construct. In the years following the July Revolution, it is significant that the aristocrat Hohenegk knows of his feudal estate's decadence: 'Ich habe mich überlebt' (428), he whines. As in Kotzebue, the Gypsies no longer steal, they merely come into possession of a *gadjo* child. They moreover do not disappear, but are finally tolerated in a *gadjo*–Gypsy contact zone. That said, Polgar is really just a male Preciosa. He keeps his name, but this may have been his real baptismal name all along. Without him the Gypsies are a leaderless rabble. His nobility distinguishes him from them, and one of the marks of his nobility is of course his wresting of the kidnapped Agnes from the less ethically elevated Gypsies, so that the child-stealing reproach, whilst withdrawn at one level, is reinstituted at another. His agency, in the end, is derived not from his years as a Gypsy — which as ever leave no trace on him — but from his nature as a member of the Hohenegk family, whose sin he redeems just as he overcomes his own self-misunderstanding, accepting the true freedom of his German inheritance rather than the illusory freedom of the forest. The rightfully restored aristocracy at peace with the proletarian Gypsies under neo-feudal leadership seems to be Devrient's message.

The last example from this series is one of the most fascinating in the Gypsy literature around 1800, in that it combines the writing of the Gypsy for the first time with the authorship of a woman, and so involves two kinds of denied subjectivity or agency: Caroline von Wolzogen's novella *Die Zigeuner* (1802).[22] Here the motif of encounter with the Gypsies is utilized by Schiller's sister-in-law, an experienced writer of novels and successful protégée of his, to support a polemic against the injustice of woman's situation. However, whilst Wolzogen valorizes the feminist line, she also — perhaps unexpectedly for any who might presume the immediate solidarity of the marginalized[23] — reaffirms the anti-Gypsyist tradition of Cervantes. On her beloved father's death free-thinking Aloisia faces the necessity of marriage, since her younger brother, as patrilinear German law stipulates, is to inherit all. Contracted to marry the wrong man, she places her hopes on a handsome stranger who once rescued her from a hunting fall and offered love, but unaccountably refused to accompany her back to the 'Cirkel der Edlen' (Wolzogen, 95) at the residence. The serendipitous appearance of Gypsies precipitates a solution. En route to the wedding, Aloisia is kidnapped by Gypsies under the command of Mario, a fierce, yet also deep-thinking and troubled individual. He, it turns out, is the father of Rodrigo, and of course Rodrigo is Aloisia's mysterious and glamorous lover. Mario urges her to follow the logic of her expulsion from the family home by the cruel laws of bourgeois society (104) and to live henceforth with Rodrigo in their domain of natural freedom (105). This offer Aloisia, despite her otherwise grave situation, never seriously considers. She refers to the Gypsies with impeccable political incorrectness as 'diese Bande' (106), finds their appearance unappetizingly grotesque (109), and hopes fervently if at first without foundation that Rodrigo, with his noble features and brown hair, racially speaking, is not one of them (106). Like Preciosa she is prepared to defend her virtue with her life, even if Rodrigo — unlike the others — is too noble to threaten it, and she does have Emilia Galotti-like moments when she mistrusts her own sexual self-control (108). At this point she acts. She decides '[d]urch Verstellung sich die Freiheit zu verschaffen' (110). Thus, having inwardly rejected Romany culture, she boldly allows herself, like a radicalized and feminized Andrés Caballero, to become assimilated into this culture of the Other, with the purpose of dissimulating and eventually leaving it, in the name of a woman's freedom. Hence she braids her hair, dresses in Gypsy style, and learns 'bald das ganze Betragen eines artigen Zigeunermädchens nachahmen' (111). And she is accepted by the Romanies, if only as Rodrigo's property (108).

What Aloisia in fact aims for is a third way, an alternative community of authentic love beyond both the false and oppressive patriarchy of the bourgeois world and the brutal and infantilized realm of the Gypsies. Convinced of Rodrigo's non-Romany provenance — he is too beautiful and too noble to be the offspring of so ugly and coarse a mother (Leona, 119) — she turns detective (128–29), and reconstructs his history to free him from the Romany world. Stories of her idyllic life before her father's death awaken in Rodrigo strange, anamnesic resonances (123), which function as a spontaneous call of self-recognition, in the form of the dream of his elegant and cultivated, noble childhood, spent with quite a different mother, a beautiful and glittering figure. Relics of Rodrigo's childhood preserved by Mario confirm this memory trace (125). Aloisia learns that Rodrigo was first introduced into the Gypsy band many years ago in the Apennines, chance has it that the band (134) is now in precisely that area, and Aloisia, utilizing her Gypsy skills, easily discovers the identity of Rodrigo's true mother: a widowed Countess. Mario, it emerges, *is* Rodrigo's father, but he is really the Italian nobleman Pietro Gentilesco (147). Rodrigo is the result of an illicit liaison with the (otherwise unnamed) Countess. Mario has joined the Gypsies when he thought himself betrayed by the Countess (hence his misanthropy, cynicism, and melancholy, and admiration of the pre-cultural Romany lifestyle). Rodrigo has in fact been stolen by Leona as an unasked act of revenge on Mario's part. The tale ends with a kind of Schillerian crescendo. A new community of love has been created where previously there was fragmentation and loss, as Mario/Pietro is reunited with the Countess, Rodrigo with his mother and his family, and Aloisia with her beloved.

Now this tale is an admirable performance of female agency. No-one could doubt Aloisia's subject status and agency as she single-handedly carves out a feminist new future and new community. The extent to which she exploits her acquired Gypsy skills in the service of her feminism has rightly been admired.[24] In particular she adopts the medium of the dance (one of Schiller's favourite themes, as evidenced by 'Der Tanz'). Aloisia's Gypsy dance, an utterance in a meta-language uncontaminated by phallogocentric patriarchal discourse, tactfully mediates the truth of her tale to the Countess (141–43). As an encounter with Romany alterity this text however leaves much to be desired. Wolzogen's image of the Gypsies, doubtless indebted to Grellmann, is by contrast with the later practice of the Romantics wholly unglamorized. But this realistic depiction of the Gypsy domain is negatively accentuated throughout, as nothing more than the realization of Mario's pathological critique of civilization. Aloisia is not afraid to use the term 'thierische[s] Daseyn' (117) about them. She willingly assimilates into Romany culture, but this is always with the purpose of dissimulation, to manipulate and then escape from something she considers below herself, and without utopian value. As ever in the Cervantes tradition, none of the important people she encounters in the Gypsy world are actually Gypsies, nor do any of them, Gypsies or not, exercise any agency in changing her life. Both Mario/Pietro and Rodrigo are disguised and renegade occidentals, who are however intrinsically incapable of denying their provenance. It is vital for Aloisia to establish that provenance, for it alone qualifies them for admission to the recuperated idyll. Leona, ugly, liar, and child thief, is the only real Romany, and Aloisia's kidnapping by Mario is merely the continuation of this behavioural pattern. Thus Wolzogen, despite her sympathetic feminism, in the last analysis merely reinscribes the anti-Gypsyist discourse. True, Leona and the other Gypsies are invited to stay at the castle. But they do not. In accordance with their presumed nomadic nature, no doubt, Wolzogen's narrator moves them on.

With the Romantics we enter a literary domain of very different quality with a markedly different presentation of the German–Romany cultural encounter. Gypsies may be prominent in German literature around 1800, but they are everywhere in German Romantic literature. Distinguished scholars have argued that the German Romantics, by contrast to the Cervantes-inspired tradition, wholly identified with (at least their vision of) ethnocentric Gypsyness,[25] and it is no coincidence that the literary-historical phenomenon *Zigeunerromantik* was named after the movement itself — even if, as we saw with Fontane's usage, that coinage has been devalued and misappropriated to include the *Preciosa* line. There are, as will be seen, key differences between the *Preciosa* line and the Romantic Gypsy. But the main distinguishing feature, too little acknowledged hitherto, is that Romantic Gypsies — because or despite of that self-identification — really *are* ethnic or racial Gypsies. Equally important, the Romantic Gypsy is saturated with meaning, as the self-reflexive symbol of Romantic aestheticism but also as the vehicle of Romantic political utopianism.[26] It will also be seen that whereas the products of the *Preciosa* tradition are without fail comedies, those in the Romantic tradition are at best mixed tragedies. Given the popularity of the subject in recent scholarship,[27] it cannot be our purpose to cover the entire movement. Arnim's *Isabella von Ägypten* (1812) and Brentano's *Die mehreren Wehmüller* (1817) will serve.

Arnim's poetic-historical novella[28] projects back onto the realm of Emperor Karl V a vision of the German nation's future after the first Empire's collapse in 1806. It argues that here, tragically, a chance has been lost to integrate the pragmatic philosophy of the state with the therapeutic and emancipatory energies of Romantic poetry. Consequently the state has regressed to its old condition as mechanism of functionalist, spiritless, money-centred governance by expediency. Arnim's means of symbolizing these tensions have always been contentious. Karl, symbol of the once and future ideal polity, is placed between Isabella's Gypsies, symbol of authentic poetic humanism, and representatives of the Jewish nation, negation of Gypsydom. The failure of Karl and Isabella to keep faith entails the dominance under his régime of a 'Jewish', unpoetic principle. Thus Grellmann's Gypsy–Jew opposition[29] is finally projected in literature onto the field of German national self-understanding.

But Arnim is not indebted to Grellmann here. Where Grellmann fixed the Indian identity of the Gypsies, Arnim revives and revalues the Gypsies' own story of origin. His Gypsies really do come from Egypt. But this is not some ethereal flight of fantasy. Apart from legitimating the Gypsies' own *poetic* self-understanding, it enables Arnim to foreground not only the political, but also the religious dimension of their presence in Europe. The Gypsies, who have sinned by failing to shelter the Holy Family on their Flight to Egypt, have in fact already performed the hardest part of their penance — reached the furthest borders of Christian territory — and may be considered shriven. The political resonance is further heightened by Isabella's status. She is not merely a charismatically beautiful and virtuous Gypsy girl (48, 71), she is a Gypsy princess, daughter of the Gypsy leader Duke Michael, and herself, given the lack of a male heir, its future leader. As such she is faced with completing the task of national redemption (Arnim, 36).

That said, Arnim's presentation of the Gypsies is in many respects also realistic and committedly apologetic. Arnim had personal experience of Romanies, for a band had once settled on his patrimonial estate, and his 'Von Volksliedern' (1805), the preface to his and Brentano's folksong collection *Des Knaben Wunderhorn* (1806–08), breaks a lance for the Romany cause.[30] In *Isabella*, we find the Gypsy nation after the epoch of protection under Sigismund[31] enduring the first epoch of their persecution in Europe under Karl's grandfather, Emperor Maximilian I.[32] Isabella's own family is the main victim. Once a noble and wealthy tribe (70), the Gypsies have now run out of funds (37) and must earn their living through demeaning arts — exhibiting bears and monkeys (72), acrobatics and strong-man shows (36), the hunting of ignoble beasts (36) — or theft (36). In Ghent they are obliged to live in a house otherwise shunned by the local populace (for fear of ghosts, 38), and forbidden to show themselves by day (38). Under this régime Duke Michael suffers his unjust fate. Two of his people, newly arrived from France and penniless, are caught stealing. Michael, who had been demonstrating feats of strength to earn their bread, attends as they are apprehended, but is himself taken and summarily hanged. It has been observed that this image of the leader of his abject nation, innocent yet martyred on the gibbet, postfigures Christ. Certainly Arnim's Christian Gypsies are far from the irreligious riff-raff of the anthropological tradition. But here nonetheless we also have the first militantly apologetic literary depiction of a Gypsy's judicial murder. It is henceforth Isabella's problem to lead the Gypsies home. Her solution — prompted by Braka, her old Gypsy duenna — is deeply Romantic: an alliance of the abject Gypsy nation with Karl. They have fallen in love, when he, undergoing his formation in Ghent, has dared to spend a night in the haunted house. Their child, under Karl's protection, might fulfil the mission (82). The idea, however, creates both solutions and problems, namely the need for money, which makes everything possible but also unfolds destructive energies in equal measure; and the dystopian presence of the Jews.

The Jews had already featured at the margin of the story. The narrator denounces them as having caused the persecution of the Gypsies by posing as Gypsies in the hope of being tolerated (36).[33] As Isabella's leadership plan crystallizes, the Jews emerge in the tale in three manifestations, all travesties of genuine human nature (52) and two intimately related to the acquisition of money: the mandrake Cornelius Nepos, the undead Bärnhäuter, and the Golem Bella. The mandrake, made by Isabella, possesses only the lowest qualities of soul, the ability to mimic languages (having none of his own, 78), and to sniff out money, simulacrum of value (76). The treasure he finds makes possible Bella's journey into the world by making her 'invisible' amongst the *gadje*. But it also introduces the Bärnhäuter. This old soldier of Kaiser Sigismund (63–67) sells his soul for seven years in return for a treasure. He is so attached to it, that when it is uncovered by the mandrake, he rises from the dead to claim his due. The Golem Bella (98), a well-known Jewish myth, is the product of Karl's misplaced desire for Bella: a man-made sensualized *Doppelgängerin* of the Gypsy girl, the ultimate, competing, camouflaged symbol of all the Gypsies are not. Thus whilst the 'Jewish' figures make possible the union of Bella and the future Kaiser, they also release energies in his problematic character which finally destroy it and the ideal state which they, or their heir, might create.

The exalted prince and the abject princess are therefore brought together at the carnivalesque fair in nearby Buik, they do conceive a child (99, 103), and Karl does promise to use his wealth and power to send the Romanies home (105). Karl, however, has forged an alliance with Cornelius Nepos for the sake of the money which this 'soul of the state' can provide (121, 139–41). He is distracted from Bella by the pragmatic interests of state (106) and the Golem (116–17, 122–23). In fact the marriage of Bella and Karl (142) is invalid, for she has been unable to say 'yes'. Recognizing the flaw in their relationship, she flees with her Gypsies to Bohemia. Whilst Isabella does bear Karl's child (Lrak) and lead her Gypsies home, Karl, despite having granted the Gypsies their freedom in the Netherlands (143), never sees them again. He remains committed to egoistic, ideal-free pragmatism and the 'Jewish' ethos of wealth (149), achieves what he can on this basis, but, tortured by conscience, retires early to the monastery to spend the rest of his days as a penitent; 'wehe uns Nachkommen seiner Zeit' (149) warns the narrator. Arnim grants Bella and Karl a blessed death and a reunion in heaven, but says nothing of Lrak, the fusion of German and Romany.

Thus Arnim's Gypsies are highly aestheticized figures. But this feature, although it derives from the negative Orientalist tradition, in a sense brings them closer to reality. For the aestheticized quality of these Gypsies connotes the concrete Romantic utopia of *lived* human fulfilment and — discreetly projected against the historical backcloth — is transparently linked to the great political problem of the post-revolutionary age. Karl, given the chance, fails to realize the possibility of a state which is Christian, poetic, humane, and anti-capitalist; today, says Arnim, we live with the consequences. Arnim is on the one hand keen to keep that utopia alive, in the form of Lrak, at least *as* utopia, as the story of the ideal ruler. On the other hand he is determined to anchor that vision in reality. Hence his Gypsies — in direct contradiction of the anti-Gypsyist tradition we have hitherto examined — are real, genetic Gypsies,[34] who, even if we can understand the reasons, really are morally imperfect. It is all the more unfortunate that this daring revalorization of the Romany ethos, as a desirable fiction of the ideal German identity, should be bought at the price of a denunciatory anti-semitism.

Brentano's *Die mehreren Wehmüller und ungarischen Nationalgesichter*[35] marks the Romany–Jewish contrast and dual structure of the Romantic utopia of alterity less than Arnim's story.[36] Anti-Gypsyist persecution is also hinted at only in the margin.[37] But here again we find the full-blooded Romany identity maintained against the *Preciosa* tradition, and the poeticized Romany nation, following the Congress of Vienna in 1815, is presented as the catalyst of a cosmopolitan utopia even more ambitious than Arnim's, as tailor-made for fusing the bewildering variety of individual nations that made up the tendentially centrifugal Habsburg *Vielvölkerstaat* into an organic unity.

Thus individual identity, its true and false representation, stands at the centre of this seemingly humoristic work. Wehmüller is the model of an inauthentic artist.

His art serves the market and the officer class. Worse, his art is false. He practises the old-fashioned genre of the portrait, but his officer portraits are cynical travesties of the individual they purport to depict. For Wehmüller has adopted modern mass-production methods. The portraits are pre-painted in quantity according to generalized national types, and later touched up in the presence of the individual subject. A few strokes (at no extra cost) render any physiognomic particularity not captured by the type. Rather more strokes (at great extra cost) are required to render the full individuality of the uniform. Wehmüller's competitor Froschauer has adopted an innovative variation, whereby first the uniforms and then the faces are done (Brentano, 142–43). Thus the tale, in true Romantic fashion, unfolds Wehmüller's poetic nemesis and the triumph of authentic poetry, in the shape of two Gypsies drawn from Grellmann's pages.[38]

Wehmüller's nemesis is manifold. He is separated from his beloved wife Tonerl by an outbreak of plague across the Hungarian–Croatian border. When he attempts to cross illegally, he discovers that his *Doppelgänger* (symbol of his loss of identity and a punishment to fit the aesthetic crime) has already done so. Hence he will not only lose his target customers but also his wife. Compelled to wait for the removal of the plague cordon, Wehmüller holes up in a shabby border tavern, which happens to be populated not only by a Frenchman, Devillier, but also by representatives of nearly every other Habsburg nation: Austrians, a Tyrolean, an Italian, a Savoyard, a Hungarian, a Croatian, and so forth; and of course a Gypsy, none other than the famous violin virtuoso Michaly. Here, in an ingenious strategic reversal of Boccaccio's fundamental novella situation (Brentano's characters want to *enter* the plague-infested territory), characteristic tales are told by three members of this impromptu intercultural polity. Now all these tales are not only told on a national border, they also all take place on one — Croatian–Turkish, Franco-British, and Austro-Italian — and all moreover also involve the negative consequences of crossing borders illegally. It is thus their capacity to cross borders with impunity which makes Brentano's Gypsies into the true, symbolically cosmopolitan heroes of the tale. These Gypsies, in Brentano's ultimate potentialization of the myth, are virtuoso representatives of poetry. Twice handsome Michaly, like a new Orpheus (150–51, 159–69), quells an outbreak of multi-national chaos by playing irresistibly brilliant improvisations which compel all present to dance to his tune. More significant still, his sister Mitidika is not only a captivating singer and dancer, but also, in her capacity as a border-crosser, the main agent for resolving the comic entanglement. Mitidika is not only the leading character in the last inset tale — Devillier's lost lover — but also the companion of Tonerl Wehmüller on the wrong side of the plague cordon. It is she who, as inset and framework tales merge, dons man's clothing, dresses Tonerl as a man, and leads a large band of equally impatient border-crossers — including the *Doppelgänger* — into Hungary. It is she who unmasks the false Wehmüller (Froschauer), and compels him to form a business alliance with his former competitor. Thus this cross-dressed Gypsy has a most remarkable curriculum vitae: she personifies the androgynous perfection of poetic humanity, she triumphs over the modern unpoetry of mass-production artists, makes peace in the art market, detects true individual identity behind uniformitarian illusion, reunites separated spouses (Franzerl and Tonerl, Froschauer and his bride), and restores lost lovers (herself and Devillier) across a seemingly insuperable and life-threatening border. Gypsy poetry in short is presented by Brentano as nothing less than a universal therapy and medium for the harmonization of difference across borders of any kind. As the universal language for mediating individuality with totality, Romantic-Gypsy poetry contrasts starkly with the dead lingua franca (Latin) of the soldiers manning the plague cordon (147, 182).

Michaly is the main symbol of poetry as catalyst of the Habsburg utopia. His violin is not ultimately plucked from Grellmann's Orientalist tract but is rather the mythic reincarnation of the emblematic lyre of Orpheus, Romantic instrument for awakening the song that slumbers as the inner order of beauty in all things. In this, Brentano's Michaly continues the tradition of the aesthetically generated utopia revived by Schiller in the *Ästhetische Briefe* (1794–95), but poetically realized only by Friedrich von Hardenberg. Hardenberg's *Heinrich von Ofterdingen* (1802) figures an Orphic poet, lute in hand, as ruler of Atlantis.[39] The emblematic contrast in the title of Theodor Körner's contemporaneous anthology of patriotic songs *Leyer und Schwert* (1814) marks the strength of poetry's claim to power at this time.[40]

But Mitidika too is a symbol of poetry's ability to create intercultural harmony. Like Isabella, she possesses the aura of power. Devillier is in awe of her commanding presence (179). Michaly claims that such a woman is born (messiah-like) only once in a thousand years (180). In this context, despite her Gypsy loyalty to Devillier, she also captivates the Italian Martino. Repelled at first by her blackness (174), the sympathetic Martino, having claimed a kiss, slowly imagines himself becoming black — becoming a Gypsy — and at last gives her a beautiful ebony pin box with ivory inlay (174), black-and-white emblem of an intertwined occidental–oriental union, meta-poetic symbol of the text, and surely also cryptic self-image of Brentano (Martino-Brentano) himself as artificer of cross-cultural mediation. In another extraordinary scene Brentano's irony exposes the colonialist gaze underlying the construction of Gypsy identity. Baciochi, narrator of the inset tale, watches voyeuristically as Mitidika changes her clothes for Devillier's visit (174–76). Dazzled, he wonders cynically about 'der wunderbare Schmuck in dem Besitz der kleinen braunen Bettlerin' (176), and can only conclude that she has either stolen it or is 'eine verkleidete, versteckte Prinzessin' (176). His association — Mitidika as 'eine indianische Prinzessin, welche die Geschenke eines englischen Gouverneurs mustert' (175) — betrays the colonialist structure of his imagination.

Brentano, lastly, is careful to distance his Romantic discourse on the Gypsy from less defensible varieties. It is significant at one level that the inauthentic *gadjo* artist Wehmüller, who pays a number of characters (the Vizegespan, the surgeon) in kind with a portrait, is never permitted to paint the Gypsies — despite that honour, as Grellmann (Grellmann, 103) noted, being accorded to the historical Michaly. At another level Brentano introduces the poet Lindpeindler as representative of the wrong kind of literary discourse on the Gypsy. Lindpeindler is the trivial kind of Romantic, who praises a night with one of the castle maids as 'eine der romantischsten seines Lebens' (181). He is also dim, being (in contrast to Mitidika and like all inauthentic artists) unable to tell the true Wehmüller from a false one (152). Most tellingly, he can no more render the authentic Gypsy voice than the perpetrators of vulgar *Zigeunerromantik*. After Baciochi's inset tale of Mitidika, in an obvious allusion to that tradition, he intones the familiar clichéd praise of 'das hochpoetische freie Leben der Zigeuner' (178). But after Michaly's moving improvisation he fails to understand that the true *Naturpoesie* of the authentic Gypsy voice cannot be captured in *gadjo* writing (160). This attack perhaps best documents the distance between the Romantic rendition of the Gypsy voice and the *Preciosa* tradition, and Brentano's self-conscious sense of discursive inadequacy, despite his overweening symbolism, is perhaps the most appealing feature of Romantic Gypsy discourse in the strict sense outlined here.[41] This sense of the inimitability of the authentic Gypsy voice — even if it is only an extrapolation of typically Romantic phonocentrism — is echoed in Gypsy anthropology of the period only by Liszt. It is from this vantage-point that we should emphasize the tale's final undermining of its comic *dénouement*. One of Mitidika's most significant acts of peacemaking — between Wehmüller and Froschauer — will, as she fails to grasp, merely perpetuate the divisive role of bad art in a nationalistic world, and so destroy the apparent triumph of poetry. Worse, perhaps her most significant act of reunion — her own with Devillier — can never be consummated. In Brentano's treatment of the miscegenation problem, Mitidika as a true Gypsy may unlike Duke Michael and Isabella never marry outside her race. She will therefore never bear a Gypsy–*gadjo* child, nor, since she remains loyal to Devillier, marry at all (180). The *gadjo*–Gypsy utopia is thus revealed not as sterile, but as *only* a utopia, and the comic end has a latent tragedy.

Eduard Mörike's long novella *Maler Nolten* (1832)[42] treats the problem of art itself in the Romantic tradition by projecting that problem onto a Gypsy figure. But it adds an agonizingly pessimistic twist.[43] Here two Gypsies, Loskine and her daughter Elisabeth, each incorporate an ideal of true, if wholly unconventional, 'other' and exotic beauty for a *gadjo* artist — Friedrich Nolten and his nephew Theobald respectively. But in each case, and in blank contrast to the trend of Brentano's and Arnim's earnestly cosmopolitan works, Mörike's bleak Biedermeier masterpiece reveals the attempt to integrate the cultural and aesthetic other into *gadjo* life as a disaster for both parties.

The carefully constructed perspectivist work at first locates Friedrich Nolten's encounter with the Gypsies as the mainspring of ensuing tragic complications in both his and the next generation. The painter Friedrich — presented as a 'Genie' by his philistine brother (Mörike, 180) — has enjoyed princely patronage and six years in classical Italy (181). But he is restless on his return, unwilling to marry, and seizes the chance to travel. In Bohemia of course his aesthetic–erotic yearnings are fulfilled. Different views of the Gypsies compete in his mind as he glimpses their fires in the forest on a sketching trip. Uncertain whether they will rob him, his telescopic study of their faces from a safe distance — a symbol of the pseudo-scientific *gadjo* anthropological gaze and gesture to Brentano's voyeur scene — leaves him unsure (182–83). Yet 'ein altes Vorurteil für dies eigentümliche Volk' (182) decides him to join the band for a time, and he is rewarded with a cautious welcome. He entertains them with travellers' tales, and notes in return the 'merkwürdige Gesichter [. . .] und köstliche Gruppen' (183). But in the darkness of a sudden storm a symbolic lightning flash illuminates a face which changes his aesthetic and his life: 'vor meinem innern Sinne blieb jenes Gesicht mit bestimmter Zeichnung wie eine feste Maske hingebannt' (183). This is Loskine, daughter of the Gypsy leader, and a 'Gebilde der eigensten Schönheit' (184). Under her erotic and aesthetic spell, he remains with the band. Her beauty is above all a new aesthetic. He mocks what a scholastically inclined German Professor of Fine Arts might say to this. But his artistic vocation consists in the 'Entdeckung originaler Formen' (184). By observing these 'wilde [. . .] Leute' (184), he discovers an inexhaustible resource of material with surprising features and images of mankind 'in seiner gesundesten physischen Entwicklung' (184). All this will sharpen his perception of Nature (184). More significant, Loskine, apart from her fund of Gypsy poetry and extensive knowledge of healing medicines (186), is another personification of living beauty, an enticing mixture of irreconcilable naivety and cleverness, earnest and transgressive merriment, unusual even among the Gypsies (185), but to Friedrich's aesthetic eye the necessary order of a higher harmony (185). Like many such Gypsy girls, she reminds us of Goethe's fascinatingly contradictory naive personification of poetry in *Wilhelm Meister*, Mignon. The erotic bond between the artist and his new ideal however leads to intercultural catastrophe. A confrontation with Loskine's possessive but not freely chosen Romany lover[44] causes Friedrich to leave, but Loskine — exercising the heightened agency typical of the fictional Gypsy woman — has deceived Marwin, and joins Friedrich in the *gadjo* world. That act of resistance performed, Loskine leaves only two traces of her presence in the *gadjo* world. Friedrich, so we hear from his philistine brother, marries her against the wishes of his anti-Gypsy family. But she dies giving birth to the (as the brother calls her) 'Bastard' (192), that is, hybrid, Gypsy-*gadjo* Elisabeth (191). The brother reports that homesickness has made her ill, and suggests that the Gypsy need to wander will have caused marital tension (191), but this information is framed by his strongly foregrounded, crassly anti-Gypsyist tendency. Otherwise, all that is left of Loskine is Friedrich's one-sided testament to the intercultural encounter, his transgressive portrait of her astonishing, as the narrator calls it, 'demonic' beauty (192), which — save for the eyes (Elisabeth's are black, 172; Loskine's brown, 192) — demonstrates the uncanny resemblance of mother and daughter. The fearful brother conceals this powerful Orientalist image in his attic (192).

Of course it is this arch-Romantic motif of the demonic portrait — most prominent, for example, in E. T. A. Hoffmann's *Die Elixiere des Teufels* — which also motivates the Theobald Nolten plot. Theobald has inherited his uncle's talent and follows a typologically parallel path, studying at the academy and then in Rome and Florence. But even these glorious examples of the Classical tradition cannot erase a more fundamental aesthetic imprinted upon his mind as a child (195): the experience of Loskine's image in his father's attic. The child's fascination with this image becomes the determining factor of the man's vocation when he, now sixteen years old, actually encounters Elisabeth on a rural ride. Elisabeth already possesses the charisma of the Romantic Gypsy woman. Irresistibly drawn to her siren song — the narrator compares it with an Aeolian harp, instrument of nature's spontaneous poetry (171) — Theobald and his sister Adelheid find in her presence 'ein auffallendes Gepräge von Schönheit und Kraft, alles war geeignet, Ehrfurcht, ja selbst Vertrauen einzuflößen' (172).[45] But it is the striking resemblance to Loskine's portrait, as if a Pygmalionic ideal were miraculously made flesh (179), which shocks Theobald into a swoon from which only Elisabeth's Gypsy healing arts can save him. This literally ecstatic experience of something transcending his received categories of interpretation indelibly marks Theobald's aesthetic. In an exchange to which no-one is privy and on which even the narrator can only speculate, Theobald and Elisabeth swear 'ein gegenseitiges Gelübde der geistigen Liebe' (195), and his austere artistic vocation is decided (compare 202). Henceforth all of his revolutionary, bizarre, and fantastic (8) aesthetic productions are in some way images of Elisabeth (164).

But these are also deeply problematic, disharmonious images, very different from that of Friedrich. In the most characteristic sketch Elisabeth features as a musical spirit, pondering her imminent return to the grave, with death pumping the bellows of her organ as others dance by moonlight (10–12). This aesthetic, then, stands in that long, morbid Germanic tradition which sees the experience of beauty as ultimately opposed to life; and the novella is in part a comment on that. The tension of Theobald's artist's career, such as it is, thus lies in his failure to reconcile his primal, seemingly pre-destined commitment to this kind of art with the demands of a bourgeois existence. The failed affairs with naive Agnes and knowing Constanze, both compromised by Theobald's hesitancy, both traduced by the insistent, seemingly fatal interventions of Elisabeth, symbolize this. In the course of the action Elisabeth's aura of power gradually modulates into one of fatal threat, as she appears with apparently supernatural foreknowledge at critical junctures to maintain what she regards as her justified sole claim on Theobald (in Constanze's life, 230–33; in Agnes's life, 46–47, 61, 288, 343–45), and so destroys these incipient relationships. Thus the novella's conclusion — seen only in the exalted imagination of a blind boy and beautifully echoing the description of the organist sketch at its opening — finds Theobald dragged unwillingly to the realm of the dead by the organ-playing Elisabeth, consumed literally by his aesthetic and so seemingly fulfilling his doom as a Romantic artist (379–80). Only at certain points, when the machinations of his friend Larkens to reunite him with Agnes seem close to success, does Theobald move towards a free, non-autobiographical, non-narcissistic style, which might have set him on another path (217).

But if Mörike, all along self-consciously citing the discourse of higher *Zigeunerromantik*, picks up (in the shape of Elisabeth) Arnim's image of the hybrid, Gypsy–*gadjo* aesthetic utopia, he also surrounds this image with a field of largely negative associations. Mörike does, we saw, ironize Elisabeth's denunciation as 'Bastard', and he takes care to present the Gypsies with whom she lives ('einer übrigens öffentlich geduldeten Zigeunerhorde', 175), in a caring and positive light, as indeed he does Loskine. Nevertheless Mörike also reactivates the most ancient *gadjo* prejudice against the Gypsies, child-theft, and so seems to revalorize the underlying taboo of cultural and physiological hybridism behind that. For Elisabeth, who after the death of her mother in childbed had spent seven years with her father Friedrich, is stolen by her Gypsy band (191–92) as an act of revenge and reappropriation and brought up with them. She however, unlike Loskine, is presented not only as an aesthetic ideal, but also *thanks to this divided inheritance* as a fundamentally divided psychopathological case. She is not at home in the Gypsy world. Loskine is willing to renounce that realm, but Elisabeth is torn between it and what she still regards as her *gadjo* home. Her first appearance to Theobald is motivated by her need to see the *Heimat* again (175, 179). Given Friedrich's apparent death and the assimilation of his home to the ducal estates (176, 193) this need can also never be satisfied. A return to Gypsydom seems equally impossible: the Gypsy song of her grandmother Faggatin — 'wild wie ein flatternd schwarzes Tuch' (174) — can treat the symptom of her 'Leid' (176), but not cure it. Indeed Elisabeth, perhaps because of this mixed provenance, seems in some constitutional sense weaker than her mother, requiring unlike her and despite her apparent aura of majesty a man's assistance to leave the Gypsy world (179). Elisabeth's realization, then, of an ultimate beauty which will cross the cultural divide, is bought at the price of a life-threatening pathology which she moreover transmits to every *gadjo* with whom she becomes close, and which motivates an opulent harvest of death at the novella's end. Most tellingly: Theobald and Elisabeth, unlike Friedrich and Loskine, produce no children, and Elisabeth perishes abjectly if unpitiably by the roadside. Theobald's spiritual death is thus both the last trace of her presence and Mörike's tragic comment on higher *Zigeunerromantik*.

In Karl Immermann's remarkable, much more politically accentuated, and even more culturally pessimistic contribution to the literary discourse on the Gypsy, *Die Epigonen* (1836),[46] Germans once more meet Romanies at key junctures when their identity is at stake. In this novel the Romany identity, initially foregrounded in the shape of the Mignon-like Flämmchen and her mother, a mysterious old Gypsy woman, is in fact finally dissolved. However so too is every other received identity in the novel. For here Immermann shows Germany itself to be undergoing the identity crisis of an emergent nation state in the throes of belated industrial revolution. In this upheaval none of the old structures — political, economic, legal, social, aesthetic — any longer serves its intended purpose for the generation which inherits them. These Romanies who are not quite Romanies thus stand *as such* for the process of unclosed social and cultural transition which Immermann argues to be the paradoxical character of his epoch.

The main vehicle of this argument on the German side is Hermann. This poetic and patriotic young man is emblematically named, after the legendary Cheruscan chief who in some sense founded the German nation by uniting divided tribes and routing the Roman invaders in the Teutoburg Forest in AD 9. Kleist's *Hermannsschlacht* (1808) memorializes him. But Immermann's Hermann is by comparison a sadly reduced figure, in this the symptom of the generational identity crisis. Only at the conclusion does he find out who he is — or at least what he must become — and so understand something of what it means to be a German in the nineteenth century. From the start he feels himself to be an epigone, a man, not of a decadent generation, but born too late to feel at one with a great culture now overtaken by history. A disjointed sense of irrelevant and impotent wisdom dominates his mentality: '"Wir Frühgereiften!"', he says of his generation, '"[. . .] mit dem Schnee auf dem Haupte werden wir schon geboren"' (Immermann III, 19).[47] Hermann's despairing and self-consciously aimless (III, 17) search for an alternative identity is thus Immermann's frame to accommodate an ambitious social panorama[48] of his complex, constitutionally divided age (III, 36).

Chief of these divisions is the conflict of the aristocracy and the bourgeoisie, representatives respectively of old and new orders. Both are in fact concerned to respond to the new challenges. The nobility is attacked as a 'Ruine' (III, 158). But some, whilst remaining on the land, do seek to modernize. The Duke at whose castle Hermann lodges for a time has eagerly informed himself about (then advanced) English agriculture (III, 154). At the same time they — supported in part by moderate *Bürger* like Hermann and the Duke's lawyer and doctor (III, 282; 109–11; 242–43) — also follow the strategy of restorative Hallerian legitimism.[49] Hence we find an attempt by the same Duke to reinforce the nobility's diminished status with (farcical) public masquerades of belated feudal ceremony modelled on Scott's then-fashionable *Ivanhoe* (III, 245–46, 275–86, 309–22). Conversely Hermann's uncle, representative of the new, middle-class industrialists, sees himself as the liberal and meritocratic enemy of the aristocracy (III, 297). This uncle has not only planted a factory in an idyllic valley (IV, 7–24), but also set about social engineering: transforming the class of otherwise disinherited small farmers into factory technicians on (another variety of) the English industrial model (IV, 21). Worse, he has designs on both the social role and property of the Duke's family. He has acquired the nearby castle of the Duke's brother, Count Julius, in lieu of debt, and ruthlessly converted it too into industrial plant (IV, 7–8). Nor is this the limit of his ambition to appropriate the feudal inheritance of a nation in flux. He has exploited his hold over Julius to have himself recognized in place of the Count as the heir of the Duke's property should the main family line fail. Indeed, he is currently pursuing an action to have the Duke disinherited altogether, on the basis that an ancient document purporting to confirm the ennoblement of one of the Duke's commoner ancestors — and so authenticating his legitimacy as aristocrat and estate owner — cannot be produced.

Perched on these quaking foundations, Hermann's identity — and by extension his legitimacy as inheritor of the past and manager of the future — is also anything but secure. He thinks of himself as a bourgeois, the son of a Senator and affluent Bremen Hanseatic merchant. As the Uncle's nephew, Hermann would, on the death of his appointed heir Ferdinand[50] and after the forfeit of the Duke's estate to the Uncle, have been the legitimate heir of both the industrial settlement *and* the aristocratic estate (IV, 223), rightful master of the contradictions in German society and symbol of the middle-class triumph. But this cannot be. For Hermann's true father turns out to be none other than the Duke. He has had an illicit affair, impregnated Babette, and persuaded his Bremen friend to adopt the child through marriage (IV, 244–60). Thus Hermann is in truth of aristocratic blood. Worse, the ancestral letter of ennoblement seems when finally uncovered to be counterfeit (IV, 162–65). Poor Hermann therefore emerges in the last analysis as both a bourgeois who is not *and* an aristocrat who is not (IV, 262) — as an altogether new, as yet undefined kind of German. The novel's closure is thus as ambiguous as its opening. Hermann *does* inherit a home, the property of the past generation, whether affiliated to the old order or the new. But he inherits with no legitimacy, by pragmatic expediency alone, and at the price of a lie — concealing his true parentage (IV, 262). In this new age without truth (III, 416–17) Hermann must therefore remake his identity and earn his legitimacy under some new, self-made order; a task he unpromisingly begins by attempting to escape the process of industrialization (265–66).

Here the Gypsy figures fit in. *Die Epigonen*, whilst it may not feature any true Gypsies, begins with two resonant citations of German–Gypsy discourse. First, the very start of the novel cites the primal scene of German–Gypsy encounter. Through the forest a sweating and panting group of Biedermeier policeman is pursuing without success an old Gypsy woman and a child, Flämmchen (III, 15–16), the former of whom is suspected of stealing the latter. The Gypsy woman is at once identified as such: '"Ich habe es oft dem Landrat gesagt"', says a policeman, '"er solle das Luder von hier fortweisen zu den Zigeunern nach Friedrichslohra"' (15). Friedrichslohra was the small but well-known community founded in 1775 by Frederick the Great of Prussia near Nordhausen in Thuringia, which was intended to enourage the acculturation — discipline, settlement, steady labour, assimilatory education, and missionary evangelization — of the Romanies, and regularly maintained by state and charitable agencies until around 1838.[51] The police clearly see Friedrichslohra and its oppressive assimilation techniques as the best solution to this particular manifestation of the Gypsy problem. Yet this constellation of identities, scarcely established, is at once called into question. Another policeman claims to have known the alleged Gypsy during the War of Coalition against Napoleon, where she earned her living as a subaltern and Courasche-like camp follower, and who has now turned her hand to the better-rewarded Gypsy trade (15). It is unclear at this point whether the alternative attribution disproves her Gypsy identity, for the narrator continues here and throughout to refer to her as 'die Zigeunerin' (16), and in any case we know that *Zigeuner* connotes the vagrant lifestyle as well as the race. But the foregrounding of the Gypsy problem and the Friedrichslohra motif have already served their purpose. The homeless and illegitimate Gypsy pair whose parental relationship is at issue and who may or may not be subject to assimilation mirror the novel's main cognitive interest: integration of heterogeneous phenomena into new collective structures in an age of transition.

The second citation, another primal scene, underscores the link of German and Gypsy. As the policemen end their search in the nearest tavern we now encounter the bearer of the great Cheruscan's name, like his predecessor, deep in the trackless Westphalian forest. But this citation is a travesty. For this Hermann, having been abandoned in the forest by his philhellenic companion, is feeling not like the leader and father of the nation but 'wie ein ausgesetzter Findling' (III, 19), disorientated and unprotected and, moreover, cursed by the loss of the wallet which contains his proof of identity. It on this note that Flämmchen embraces him from behind, the 'Gypsies' are introduced into his world, and the emblem of today's orphaned Germany, in a further inverted allusion to the traditional Gypsy–German foundling encounter, is adopted by Flämmchen (20) as her lover. Henceforth these vagrants' lives, in their eccentric pursuit of home, legitimacy, and identity, shadow Hermann's paradoxical fate as outsider in his own culture.

Both Flämmchen and the old Gypsy woman thus incorporate the familiar qualities of the literary Gypsy as tragic utopian outsider. Flämmchen, like Mignon and other 'little Gypsy girls' to whom she is related,[52] is androgynously beautiful (III, 267). Emerging like a Dryad from a tree to meet Hermann (III, 20), she is from the outset identified with pre-cultural nature. Wholly constituted by fantasy (III, 124, 266) and uneducated, she practises a kind of fetishistic religion, characteristic, says the doctor, of those nations, '"die sich noch auf der Stufe der Kindheit befinden"' (125). The identification with nature turns her into a living work of art (267), another instantiation of *Naturpoesie*. Hypersensitive to natural energies, she at last develops a compulsive need to dance, delivering ecstatic, improvised performances which are accompanied by the old woman's chanting in an uncomprehensible tongue and — for their duration at least — reconcile her wounded psyche with the terror of existence (III, 267; IV, 70–71). This closeness to nature bestows on Flämmchen a certain divinatory talent. '"Vorbei! Vorbei! Vorbei! [. . .] Aufs neu! Aufs neu! Aufs neu!"' (20), she comments when listening to Hermann's heart, recognizing in its rhythm the essence of an identity poised between the no longer and the not yet. This quality too causes her to reject the theatre. Brought up by a jobbing actor, she has been cast in a performance of Adolph Müllner's popular — if anti-Gypsyist — fate tragedy *Die Schuld* (1815)[53] as Otto, Spanish grandson of the Gypsy-cursed Laura (Müllner, 114). However theatre is from her perspective a lie, and she reduces the performance to chaos by wearing ape make-up and leaping into the stalls (Immermann, 68–69). She is fixated on Hermann, whom she, guided by her mother, believes to be her fated fairy prince (III, 20, 168–69), and he does, for a time, take her under his wing. For her part the old woman, racial Gypsy or no, shares Flämmchen's heightened sensual perception, and practises the standard Gypsy arts of fortune-telling (IV, 59; III, 168–69) and healing (III, 166; IV, 89).

Now these Gypsies, associated as they are with a sympathetic figuration of German identity, are as in Arnim and Brentano favourably contrasted with a deceiving Jew. This Jew, in the shape of a vagrant, blond-haired and blue-eyed, seemingly patriotic revolutionary, befriends Hermann on his journey to Berlin, only to steal his horse before being apprehended and unmasked as a bewigged simulator (III, 351–55). But despite this the main role of Immermann's Gypsies is as tragic foil to Hermann to symbolize a failure to resolve the generational problem. Hermann, despite his constitutional lack of identity, finds an inheritance, a home, and a marriage with the promise of new life and a future. Flämmchen had, for a time, established a kind of German home, or asylum, an alternative, carnivalesque, Bohemian colony in the deceased prelate's Berlin villa, which resembles nothing so much as Callot's Gypsy camp cartoons (IV, 67–68) and contrasts sharply with the grim discipline of Friedrichslohra. However, this novel of the new Germany has no home for the two women. Even as a widow, Flämmchen's rights to the villa are dependent on her possessing a child. Hence even though she claims to be pregnant (IV, 242) and to that end actually sleeps incognito with Hermann (IV, 101–02; 242–43), her inheritance, unlike Hermann's, is finally confiscated by law.

The Gypsy women thus finally come under the domain of death. Flämmchen and the old Gypsy woman — both with flowing brown-black hair despite the latter's age (III, 20; 267) — are associated by Hermann with the erotic, yet mortifying gaze of Medusa (III, 65; IV, 97).[54] The old woman purports at one stage to know the secrets of the grave, claiming to have died, but to have made a pact with the devil which has brought her back a living corpse from the beyond (IV, 97). Flämmchen dances that tale (97). When she sleeps with Hermann, she generates the near-fatal illusion in his mind that he has slept with his sister Johanna. In the end death fetches them. Evicted, the two women are eventually found again only in Book IX, where Flämmchen is delivered of Hermann's stillborn son in the wild, pre-cultural and law-free countryside which is now their home (IV, 189–90); but he dies in childbirth. Of course the old Gypsy woman — having survived still another *Scheintod* after Flämmchen's demise (IV, 236–37, 241) — finally reveals herself to be a Spanish nun, raped by a handsome Polish invader on the altar of the Virgin as the nunnery burns around her during the Coalition Wars in Spain (IV, 98).[55] Her virtuoso faith broken by the failure of the Virgin to respond to her prayers in her hour of need, she has moved to the opposite extreme and espoused the religion of nature. Flämmchen, the pure child of nature, abandoned to the actor in Westphalia when the Polish father is killed in the wars, is the result. Now the old Gypsy woman, come to herself again, is at her own request at last put into a home ('Spital', IV, 241). But all trace of the younger family members is effaced. The grave of Flämmchen's little boy is beautified by nature but also concealed under a stone in a heathen cemetery (IV, 239), and Flämmchen's own deep grave in the meadow is soon grown over (IV, 236–37). Only her death — as she returns Hermann's deceitfully obtained betrothal ring — removes his sense of incestuous guilt, rescues his decentred self-consciousness (IV, 234–45), and makes the future possible. Thus this prototypical Gypsy figure, like Mörike's Elisabeth, at last also symbolizes the irreconcilability of this culture of the Other with Germanic culture.[56] Immermann shares Mörike's shift to intercultural pessimism, and indeed extends it to incorporate the future of the German nation itself.

Thus at last three trends emerge from our overview. It is clear that the literary representation of the Gypsy in Germanophone culture around 1800 covers a wide spectrum of cultural possibilities. First, as predicted, the literary writers both affirm and subvert the disadvantaging, pseudo-scientific discourse of official Gypsy anthropology. Secondly, the literary discourse on the Gypsy is constantly orientated around the notion of the Gypsy as exotic, Orientalist other, and this focus is consistently used to problematize not only Gypsy but also *German* identity, be it national, political, or sexual. Most striking under this head is the sense in which the literary Gypsy is used both as negative foil for an affirmation of a sense of healthy Germanness but also as its logical opposite, as the utopian image of what healthy Germanness should be, but is not. Both of these latent potentials are contained within a prior dual structure of utopian alterity, typically instantiated in the literature as the opposition of Gypsy and Jewish nations. Almost as striking, there are not one, but two kinds of *Zigeunerromantik*, one trivial and anti-Gypsy, the other anything but. Only in the tradition of high literary Romanticism, despite its fundamental idealism and proverbial (alleged) escapism, is there in fact a genuine openness to the Gypsy other, both in terms of the miscegenation taboo and in terms of cultural hybridity — at least in so far as that is possible for an unlettered culture. Finally, precisely that openness, as Mörike and Immermann demonstrate, is slowly superseded with the end of Romanticism by a cultural pessimism which in Immermann even engulfs the German sense of self. The next chapters will investigate the realist response to the Romantic failure.

Notes to Chapter 2

1. See on this Nicholas Saul, 'Leiche und Humor: Clemens Brentanos Schauspielfragment *Zigeunerin* und der Patriotismus um 1813', *Jahrbuch des Freien Deutschen Hochstifts* (1998), pp. 111–37, and 'Clemens Brentano: *Zigeunerin*', ed. by Nicholas Saul, *Jahrbuch des Freien Deutschen Hochstifts* (1998), pp. 138–66; also, on *Die mehreren Wehmüller*, Saul and Tebbutt, 'Gypsies, Utopias and Counter-Cultures in Modern German Culture'.
2. The pioneers are Wilhelm Ebhardt, *Die Zigeuner in der hochdeutschen Literatur bis zu Goethes 'Götz von Berlichingen'* (Erlangen: Buchdruckerei des Werraboten Otto Fischer, 1928) and Fernand Baldensperger, 'L'entrée pathétique des tziganes dans les lettres occidentales', *Revue de littérature comparée*, 18 (1938), 587–603.
3. See Heidi Berger, 'Das Zigeunerbild in der deutschen Literatur des 19. Jahrhunderts' (PhD dissertation, University of Waterloo, Waterloo, Ontario, 1972); Claudia Breger, *Ortlosigkeit des Fremden: 'Zigeunerinnen' und 'Zigeuner' in der deutschsprachigen Literatur um 1800* (Cologne, Weimar, and Vienna: Böhlau, 1998); and, most recently, Stefani Kugler, *Kunst-Zigeuner: Konstruktion des 'Zigeuners' in der deutschen Literatur der ersten Hälfte des 19. Jahrhunderts* (Trier: Wissenschaftlicher Verlag, 2004). Breger, beginning with Goethe, offers a broad analysis of the utopian moment in a very wide range of Romantic authors from Arnim to Kleist, Eichendorff, Hoffmann, and Mörike. Kugler concentrates once more on *Zigeunerromantik* in Arnim and Brentano. Despite her title she too only reaches Mörike (1832) (Kugler, pp. 252–318). Berger's splendid, if now dated, survey contains a vast but even so admittedly incomplete list of literary Gypsies before (and after) 1830 (Berger, pp. 199–214). I have drawn with gratitude on these studies.
4. See Said, *Orientalism*.
5. Notably in Foucault's discourse theory. See Michel Foucault, *L'ordre du discours* (Paris: Gallimard, 1971). Instructive on this: Jürgen Fohrmann, Harro Müller, 'Einleitung: Diskurstheorien und Literaturwissenschaft', in *Diskurstheorien und Literaturwissenschaft*, ed. by Jürgen Fohrmann and Harro Müller (Frankfurt a.M.: Suhrkamp, 1988), pp. 9–22. See also Foucault, 'What is an Author?', in *Modern Criticism and Theory*, ed. by David Lodge and Nigel Wood, 2nd edn (London: Longman, 2000; 1st edn., 1988), pp. 174–87; On this see Simon During, *Foucault and Literature: Towards a Genealogy of Writing* (London and New York: Routledge, 1992), esp. pp. 120–25. Hartmut Böhme and Gernot Böhme, *Das Andere der Vernunft: Zur Entdeckung von Rationalitätsstrukturen am Beispiel Kants* (Frankfurt a.M.: Suhrkamp 1985), esp. pp. 105–06 apply the notion to Kant. See finally Paul Ricœur, *The Rule of Metaphor: Multi-disciplinary Studies of the Creation of Meaning in Language* (Toronto and Buffalo: University of Toronto Press, 1977), esp. pp. 216–313.
6. Edward Said, *Culture and Imperialism* (London: Vintage, 1993), esp. pp. xi–xxx, 14–16, 230–32. For another critique of Said see John M. MacKenzie, *Orientalism, History, Theory and the Arts* (Manchester: Manchester University Press, 1995), esp. pp. xv, 20–35; for an interesting, if still dualistically orientated development into 'Occidentalism' see Suzanne Zantop, *Colonial Fantasies: Conquest, Family and Nation in Precolonial Germany, 1770–1870* (Durham, NC and London: Duke University Press, 1997), pp. 1–16; for a critique of the idealism and cultural uniformitarianism implicit in conventional Orientalism see Russell Berman, *Enlightenment or Empire: Colonial Discourse in German Literature* (Lincoln, NB and London: University of Nebraska Press, 1998), pp. 1–18; for a highly differentiated view of the methods for describing cultural difference and transculturation see Ritchie Robertson, *The 'Jewish Question' in German Literature 1749–1939:*

Emancipation and its Discontents (Oxford: Oxford University Press, 1999), esp. pp. 1–8, 428–65. For an overview and defence of literature against Cultural Studies as place of otherness see Todd Kontje, *German Orientalisms* (Ann Arbor: University of Michigan Press, 2004), esp. pp. 1–14, 237–44.

7. Homi Bhabha, *The Location of Culture* (London and New York: Routledge, 1994). As Bhabha reveals, hybridity was inspired in part by Goethe's notion of *Weltliteratur* as intercultural dialogue (pp. 11–12). The best overview of the many post-Saidian theoretical positions is still *The Post-Colonial Studies Reader*, ed. by Bill Ashcroft, Gareth Griffiths, and Helen Tiffin (London and New York: Routledge, 1995).
8. In another parlance Mary Louise Pratt coined the term 'contact zone' as a functionally analogous space of productive cultural overlap and exchange between the seemingly unmediated worlds of the imperialist and the subject nation. See Mary Louise Pratt, *Imperial Eyes: Travel Writing and Transculturation* (London and New York: Routledge, 1992), pp. 1–11, esp. pp. 6–7.
9. For strategic applications of this trend see Elizabeth Boa, '*Hermann und Dorothea*: An Early Example of *Heimatliteratur*?', *Publications of the English Goethe Society*, 69 (2000) 20–36; *'Denn du tanzt auf einem Seil': Positionen deutschsprachiger MigrantInnenliteratur*, ed. by Sabine Fischer and Moray McGowan (Tübingen: Stauffenburg, 1997); Herbert Uerlings, *Poetiken der Interkulturalität: Haiti bei Kleist, Seghers, Müller, Buch und Fichte* (Tübingen: Niemeyer, 1997); also Paul Cooke, *Representing East Germany since Unification: From Colonization to Nostalgia* (Oxford and New York: Berg, 2005).
10. See Clemens Brentano, *Die mehreren Wehmüller und ungarischen Nationalgesichter*, in Clemens Brentano, *Sämtliche Erzähllungen*, ed. Gerhard Schaub (Munich: Goldmann, 1991), pp. 142–88 (p. 181).
11. The words, as Gerhard Schaub notes, are Brentano's (Brentano, p. 234).
12. On contemporary modes of assertive Romany artistic production see Tebbutt, *Sinti and Roma*, pp. 129–44; Saul and Tebbutt, 'Gypsies, Utopias and Counter-Cultures', and Breger, pp. 366–79.
13. *The Little Gypsy Girl* (*La gitanilla*), in Miguel Cervantes de Saavedra, *Exemplary Stories*, trans. by C. A. Jones (Harmondsworth: Penguin, 1972), pp. 19–84.
14. Pius Alexander Wolff, *Preciosa: Schauspiel in vier Aufzügen* (Leipzig: Reclam, n.d.).
15. See Friedrich Hebbel, *Sämtliche Werke: Historisch-kritische Ausgabe*, ed. by Richard Maria Werner, 16 vols (Berlin: Behr, 1904–07), IX, p. 389.
16. See entry no. 2180 in Hebbel's *Tagebuch*, in Friedrich Hebbel, *Tagebücher*, ed. by Karl Pörnbacher, 3 vols (Munich: dtv, 1984), I, p. 410.
17. See Theodor Fontane, *Effi Briest*, in Theodor Fontane, *Gesammelte Werke*, ed. by Peter Bramböck, 5 vols (Munich: Nymphenburger Verlagsbuchhandlung, 1979), III, pp. 65, 283. See on the novel, Effi, and Romanticism Russell Berman, '*Effi Briest* and the End of Realism', in *A Companion to German Realism*, ed. by Todd Kontje (Rochester, NY: Camden House, 2002), pp. 339–64.
18. Kogalnitchan, p. 26. Compare Tetzner, pp. 106–09. The Preciosa image is at last attacked in Pott, I, p. x; Reinbeck, pp. 23–24; and Liebich, *Die Zigeuner*, p. 38.
19. Eduard Devrient, *Die Zigeuner.* Romantische Oper in vier Akten (1832), in Edward Devrient, *Dramatische und dramaturgische Schriften*, 10 vols (Leipzig: Weber, 1846–69), III, 337–443.
20. See Saul, 'Leiche und Humor'.
21. Devrient exploits the possibilities of the camp fire scene (III, 341–44), and also uses the *Zigeunerlied* (III, 401–02).
22. Citations are from Caroline von Wolzogen, *Die Zigeuner*, in *Taschenbuch für Damen* (Stuttgart: Cotta, 1802), pp. 84–152. On the story see Claudia Breger, *Ortlosigkeit des Fremden*, pp. 212–26; and Stefani Kugler and Dagmar Heinze, 'Von der Unmöglichkeit, den Anderen zu lieben: Caroline von Wolzogens *Die Zigeuner* und Caroline Auguste Fischers *William der Neger*', in *Das Subjekt und die Anderen: Interkulturalität und Geschlechterdifferenz vom 18. Jahrhundert bis zur Gegenwart*, ed. by Herbert Uerlings (Berlin: Erich Schmidt, 2001), pp. 135–54.
23. The original proponent of this view was of course Sigrid Weigel. See Sigrid Weigel, 'Der schielende Blick: Thesen zur Geschichte weiblicher Schreibpraxis', in *Die verborgene Frau: Sechs Beiträge zu einer feministischen Literaturwissenschaft*, ed. by Inge Stephan and Sigrid Weigel, 3rd edn (Hamburg: Argument, 1988; 1st edn, 1976), pp. 82–137 (pp. 86–87).

24. See Breger, pp. 223–24.
25. Günter Oesterle and Ingrid Oesterle, 'Die Affinität des Romantischen zum Zigeunerischen oder die verfolgten Zigeuner als Metapher für die gefährdete romantische Poesie', in *Hermenautik — Hermeneutik: Literarische und geisteswissenschaftliche Beiträge zu Ehren von Horst Peter Neumann*, ed. Holger Helbig et al. (Würzburg: Königshausen & Neumann, 1996), pp. 95–118.
26. See on this Hermann Kurzke, *Romantik und Konservatismus: Das 'politische' Werk Friedrich von Hardenbergs (Novalis) im Horizont seiner Wirkungsgeschichte* (Munich: Fink, 1983).
27. See notably the competing monographs of Breger and Kugler.
28. Citations are from Achim von Arnim, *Isabella von Ägypten, Kaiser Karls des Fünften erste Jugendliebe: Eine Erzählung*, in Achim von Arnim, *Erzählungen*, ed. Gisela Henckmann (Stuttgart: Reclam, 1991), pp. 34–154. See on this story especially Christoph Wingertszahn, *Ambiguität und Ambivalenz im erzählerischen Werk Achim von Arnims* (St Ingbert: Röhrig, 1990), pp. 96–120; Sara Ann Friedrichsmeyer, 'Romantic Nationalism. Achim von Arnim's Gypsy Princess Isabella', in *Germanness: Cultural Productions of Nation*, ed. by Patricia Herminghouse and Magda Mueller (Providence, RI and Oxford: Berghahn, 1997), pp. 51–65; Breger, *Ortlosigkeit*, pp. 265–301; Kugler, *Kunst-Zigeuner*, pp. 117–66.
29. See Grellmann, pp. 3–4.
30. Achim von Arnim, 'Von Volksliedern', in *Des Knaben Wunderhorn*, 3 vols (Munich: dtv, 1966), pp. 233–57, esp. pp. 242–43.
31. Who is mentioned in the Bärnhäuter section (p. 63).
32. Also mentioned (p. 147).
33. Indeed the Jews are also implicated in the original Gypsy sin, when Arnim suggests that the Gypsies turned the Holy Family away because they mistook them for Jews (p. 36).
34. Bella is half-Belgian (p. 40), and so has already transcended the fictional miscegenation taboo.
35. See on this Gerhard Kluge's commentary, in *Clemens Brentano, Sämtliche Werke und Briefe, historisch-kritische Ausgabe*, ed. by Jürgen Behrens, Wolfgang Frühwald, and Detlev Lüders, 36 vols (Frankfurt a.M.: Suhrkamp/Stuttgart, Berlin, Cologne, and Mainz: Kohlhammer, 1975–), XIX, pp. 658–96; *Clemens Brentano: Erzählungen*, ed by Gerhard Schaub, pp. 434–58; Gerhard Schaub, 'Mitidika und ihre Schwestern: Zur Kontinuität eines Frauentyps in Brentanos Werken', in *Zwischen den Wissenschaften: Beiträge zur deutschen Literaturgeschichte. Bernhard Gajek zum 65. Geburtstag*, ed. by Gerhard Hahn, Ernst Weber, et al. (Regensberg: Pustet, 1994), pp. 304–17; Hans-Jürgen Schrader, 'Brentanos *Die mehreren Wehmüller*: Potenzieren und Logarithmisieren als Endspiel', *Aurora*, 54 (1994), 119–44; Michael Böhler, 'Clemens Brentanos *Die mehreren Wehmüller und ungarischen Nationalgesichter*. Kunst. Kommerz und Liebe im Modernisierungsprozeß', *Aurora*, 54 (1994), 145–66; Oesterle, '"Zigeunerbilder"'; Saul and Tebbutt, 'Gypsies, Utopias and Counter-Cultures'; and Kugler, *Kunst-Zigeuner*, pp. 167–219.
36. Although it is still there, in the figure of the apparently Jewish 'Susanna' (Brentano, p. 167). See on the dual structure of the Romantic utopia Saul, 'Leiche und Humor', pp. 137–38.
37. The Vizegespan notes chillingly in passing their status as 'vogelfreies Gesindel' (p. 181).
38. See Grellmann, pp. 103, and 153–54, n. 66; also Schaub, p. 435, passim.
39. See *Heinrich von Ofterdingen*, in *Novalis. Schriften, Historisch-kritische Ausgabe*, ed. by Paul Kluckhohn, Richard Samuel, Hans-Joachim Mähl, and Gerhard Schulz, 6 vols (Stuttgart, Berlin, Cologne, and Mainz: Kohlhammer, 1960) I, 224–25. On this theme see Ulrich Stadler, *'Die theuren Dinge': Studien zu Bunyan, Jung-Stilling und Novalis* (Bern and Munich: Francke, 1980).
40. In Theodor Körner, *Sämtliche Werke*, 2 vols (Berlin: Bibliographische Anstalt/A. Warschauer, n.d.), I, 1–32.
41. Compare Kugler on this (*Kunst-Zigeuner*, pp. 208–15).
42. Citations are from Eduard Mörike, *Sämtliche Werke*, ed. by Jost Perfahl, 2 vols (Munich: Winkler, 1976), I, 5–383.
43. See on this Heidi Berger, pp. 112–30; Breger, pp. 175–80; Kugler, pp. 252–318.
44. Kugler (Kugler, p. 271) suggests that Gypsy society really only mirrors *gadjo* society, in particular through mechanisms of patriarchy, so that Mörike undermines both the received notion of Gypsies as pre-cultural and the corresponding, received female role. But Grellmann, for example, also notes the crude possession of Gypsy women by patriarchal men in his portrait

of the Gypsies as *Naturvolk* (Grellmann, pp. 119–20). Moreover as we saw, Friedrich, despite his relative freedom from prejudice, has no doubt that the Gypsies are 'wild' (Mörike, p. 184). Similarly, the association of Elisabeth's song with the Aeolian harp (p. 171) again suggests her category to to be the traditional one of *Naturpoesie*.

45. Compare pp. 47, 173, 220, 344.
46. Karl Immermann, *Die Epigonen: Familienroman in neun Büchern*, in *Immermanns Werke*, ed. by Harry Maync, 4 vols (Leipzig and Vienna: Bibliographisches Institut, n.d.), III, IV, 5–268. See on this Peter Hasubek, 'Karl Immermann: *Die Epigonen*', in *Romane und Erzählungen zwischen Romantik und Realismusk*, ed. Paul Michael Lützeler (Stuttgart: Reclam, 1983), pp. 202–30; Michael Minden, 'Problems of Realism in Immermann's *Die Epigonen*', *Oxford German Studies*, 16 (1985), 66–80; Ulrike Landfester, '"Da, wo ich duldend mich unterwerfen sollte, da werde ich mich rächen" — Mignon auf dem Weg zur Revolte', *Internationales Jahrbuch der Bettina von Arnim-Gesellschaft*, 4 (1990), 71–97; Gustav Frank, *Krise und Experiment: Komplexe Erzähltexte im literarischen Umbruch des 19. Jahrhunderts* (Wiesbaden: Deutscher Universitätsverlag, 1998), pp. 17–105; Marcus Hahn, *Geschichte und Epigonen. '19. Jahrhundert'/'Postmoderne', Stifter/Bernhard* (Freiburg im Breisgau: Rombach, 2003), pp. 176–232.
47. Compare III, 55, III, 136.
48. See on the novel's synthesis of social and temporal genres Dirk Göttsche, *Zeit im Roman: Literarische Zeitreflexion und die Geschichte des Zeitromans im späten 18. und im 19. Jahrhundert* (Munich: Fink, 2001), pp. 484–504.
49. The reference is to Karl Ludwig von Haller (1768–1854), whose *Restauration der Staatswissenschaft* (1816) laid the ideological foundations of the restorative Biedermeier age.
50. In fact also the offspring of an illicit aristocratic–bourgeois liaison between his wife and Count Julius (IV, 217).
51. It later failed. See, for a full account of the conditions Barbara Danckwortt, 'Franz Mettbach: Die Konsequenzen der preußischen "Zigeunerpolitik" für die Sinti von Friedrichslohra', in *Historische Rassismusforschung. Ideologen — Täter — Opfer*, ed. by Barbara Danckwortt, Thorsten Querg, and Claudia Schöningh (Hamburg: Argument, 1995), pp. 273–95.
52. Breger (p. 132, n. 17) comments aptly on the contamination of the Mignon and Gypsy girl traditions involved here and the relative significance of the Gypsy substrate.
53. Adolph Müllner, *Die Schuld: Trauerpiel in vier Akten*, 4th edn (Tübingen: Cotta, 1821; 1st edn, 1815), pp. 1–204.
54. Contrast this with Hermann's voyeuristic gaze. His look, as Flämmchen undresses in her forest grotto, strangely echoes both the exploitative, scientistic gaze of Brentano's Alberto and Mörike's Friedrich in like situations (III, 21–22). As the action progresses Hermann becomes strangely indifferent to Flämmchen, allowing her to be taken from his care — by the doctor, by the renegade prelate — with little discernible emotion, still less nostalgia.
55. A citation of the rape scene in Kleist's *Die Marquise von O.*
56. Compare the educator's critique of A. W. Schlegel's Orientalism (III, 213–16).

CHAPTER 3

❖

Secularized *Zigeunerromantik*: Literary Gypsies and Realism in Storm and Stifter

German literary realism is traditionally viewed as extending over two phases. The first, featuring the immediately post-Hegelian, post-Goethean generation, extends from one failed revolution around 1830 to another in 1848. The second, featuring both the veterans of that epoch and the tyros of the new, reaches from 1848 or so until around 1900. The first phase, exemplified by an author like the much-imprisoned and much-censored Karl Gutzkow — part journalist, part ideologue, part writer of fiction — is generally characterized by literature of political agitation, be it progressive or reactionary. The second, exemplified by an author like Gustav Freytag — in equal measure journalist, ideologue, and fiction writer — is of a fundamentally more pragmatic and accommodating bent. The difference of mentality is clear. But whether members of Gutzkow's politically activist or Freytag's conservative and pragmatic post-1848 cohort, German realists were united in thinking little of German Romanticism and even less of *Zigeunerromantik*. They did so, of course, because they thought of Romanticism, with Heine, as having lost contact with the firm foundation of reality, and considered their own aesthetic as remedying precisely that defect. Now this did not mean that they censored Gypsies from their literary production. Far from it. But inevitably, as we shall see, they inclined in their versions of the Romany presence to emphasize the earthbound dimensions of Gypsy life at the expense of the transfiguring energies which adorn the portrait of Gypsy life in the Romantic productions of, say, Arnim and Brentano. Yet oddly, even under realism's antagonistic régime, *Zigeunerromantik* — surely the transfiguring quintessence of the Romantic project — did not so much die as live on in another guise, as an ambiguous discourse of the other still available for citation under the new rules. In both strands of realist writing gender, art, and nation are thus, perhaps to our surprise, again the dominant semantic potentials released from this source. One line of realists, in a strand of writing extending throughout the century but here exemplified by an early work of Theodor Storm and later work of Adalbert Stifter, exploits a very restricted range of the spectrum of association afforded by *Zigeunerromantik*, its semantic potential either as code of the mythical *femme fatale* or as a symbol of aesthetic beauty — as a resource for reflection on gender and art. Another line of realists, from Gottfried Keller to Wilhelm Raabe, Victor von Strauss, Gustav Freytag, and Karl May, takes a far more complex stance. These authors engage critically with *Zigeunerromantik* as a representative strategy and channel the resource into extremely ambitious explorations of Germanic identity after the cultural and political earthquake of 1848. The present chapter considers Storm and Stifter.

'Heute, nur heute / Bin ich so schön': Storm's *Immensee*

Storm's classically beautiful early artist novella *Immensee* (1849),[1] a bittersweet elegy of unfulfilled love, is a model of the early realist reponse to the Romantic image of the Gypsy. An objective and distancing narrative frame, couched in the imperfect tense but referenced to the present of the aged writer Reinhardt Werner, contains the epiphanic memory of a youthful love that was both authentic and false, both predestined and yet never to be, both past and yet demanding to be resolved through the act of literary remembrance.[2] The wider social reality of mid-nineteenth-century Germany barely surfaces in this text. It is there perhaps in the form of the new 'Spritfabrik' (Storm, p. 316) on the Immensee estate, the gender sterotype of the women, and Storm's glimpse of the Gypsies at the margin of economic life. In this frame, however, a Romantic Gypsy encounter plays the central role in the narrator's belated act of self-understanding. Yet even in its unblinking inward gaze on the protagonists' fragile subjectivity, even in its self-conscious deployment of Romantic leitmotifs such as symbolic flowers, folksongs, and mysterious Gypsies, the novella maintains a bleak, psychologistic, and transcendence-free argument undeniably of a later time.

Reinhardt's memories are of Elisabeth. Even as a child she had been his muse, object of his yearnings, keeper of his writings, promised — if hesitant — companion on future travels to exotic and dangerous India (297–98). Yet his studies in a distant city draw them apart, and in his absence his place in her life is slowly usurped by the artist Erich, who at last marries her and settles on the prosperous Immensee estate. Outwardly content, this — childless — marriage is a mistake. When years later, to Elisabeth's surprise, the naive and unsubtle Erich invites Reinhardt to stay, she realizes what might or should have been. The fault, such as it is, lies in her. She has weakly allowed herself to be swayed in her affections by her mother, whom she has always permitted to dominate, who for undeclared reasons prefers Erich, and who even now shares her daughter's house. But fault lies also on Reinhardt's side. For Reinhardt has remained strangely silent during his periods of residence in the city (308). When the time came to declare his affections he unaccountably found himself unable to do so, instead mumbling of some secret (313) and pleading for loyalty. In a sense this secret is never unveiled, remaining, so as far the surface of the text is concerned, opaque to Reinhardt's self-consciousness. The dark bottomless lake, with its beautiful lily surmounting a deadly entanglement of clinging roots (323), symbolizes this, as do the folksongs he collects and studies, which have no author, but which uncannily reveal our innermost doings (320). But the secret is of course the beautiful, licentious yet pure, zither-playing Gypsy girl whom Reinhardt had encountered with her fiddler companion in the city *Ratskeller* (305–06). As if answering his yearning for exotic and dangerous India, she refuses to play save for him alone. He toasts her beautiful and sinful eyes (305). For that moment alone, so it would seem, she is his (305). Reinhardt, according to the surface of the tale at least, does not return to the *Ratskeller*. But he gives away half of the Christmas cake Elisabeth had sent him, and spends the night compulsively writing to her, wearing the new cuffs she has sent him like manacles (309). Only at Immensee, as it dawns on Reinhardt and Elisabeth that their love was both authentic and doomed, do the daemonic Gypsies resurface. Now outwardly de-poeticized — the fiddler a knife-grinder, the beautiful girl a beggar (325–26) — they may or may not be the *Ratskeller* Gypsies. But recognition is clear in all parties. Elisabeth, sensing defeat, gives all her money and flees; as does the stunned Gypsy girl. But the same song as in the *Ratskeller* lingers in the air as she leaves, and Reinhardt vainly calls a name — not shared with the reader — after her (326). It is this repressed and guilty, censored memory, the revelation that his muse is both a blond German *and* a dark Gypsy, which seals the end of the affair, and the unremittingly tragic vision of the white lily on the black lake is the last object before his inner eye. From fiddler to knife-grinder: the role of the Gypsy as less ethnic representative[3] than symbolic requisite of fate — making a melody, then cutting a thread — is clear enough. Storm has plainly also activated the myth of the Gypsy girl as sexualized *femme fatale*, instantiation of innocent eroticism. This eroticism is only of the moment. Even so, as vehicle of a too-brief fulfilment, it inexorably also undermines the lifelong love of Elisabeth. *Immensee*, then, and its Gypsies, are the vehicle of a post-Romantic artist's tragedy in the tradition of *Maler Nolten*.[4] But if the symbolism is Romantic, the harsh materiality of the conclusion, with the lonely old man bent over his books, symbols of his dead youth, bespeaks the mentality of a harder time. What we find in Theodor Storm, then, is a *Zigeunerromantik* which has been secularized.

'. . . die schönste Menschengestalt': The Nature, Culture and Ethnography of Stifter's Gypsies

The artist novella centring on the tragic charisma of the exotic Gypsy girl is also the vehicle of Adalbert Stifter's long goodbye to Romanticism. Gypsies are perhaps not the central theme of his writing. Nonetheless they exercise on Stifter by contrast to Storm[5] a marked and continuing fascination as the channel of esoterically coded self-confession, in particular of his restorative — and decidedly un-realistic — aestheticism. Like Storm, Stifter seems not independently to have studied Romany cultural anthropology, and hence on the one hand to follow the received official tradition of Grellmann, and on the other rather to exploit the received discourse of literary *Zigeunerromantik*.[6] In this Stifter, despite his familiar anti-Romanticism, in fact represents a more complex, paradoxical continuation *and* rupture of the Romantic tradition. Three stories — *Die Narrenburg* (1842/44), *Katzensilber* (1853), and *Der Waldbrunnen* (1866)[7] — exemplify the point.

Die Narrenburg[8] is the only early work where a Gypsy, or at any rate someone called (by Erasmus, the Wirt *Zur grünen Fichtenau*) 'eine [. . .] wunderschöne [. . .] Zigeunerin' (*GW* I, 333), features prominently in the text.[9] Otherwise, the Romanies tend in this phase to appear like the Gypsy girl Apollonia in Edgar Reitz's first *Heimat* series, fleetingly and tantalizingly at the margin of other concerns. There are for example the fascinating Gypsies who emerge from the forest when the grandfather dies at the end of the first version of *Die Mappe meines Urgroßvaters* (*GW* I, 673), and those itinerant Gypsy musicians at the well before Stephan Murai's great house in *Brigitta* (*GW* II, 205), who also disappear as soon as they are introduced. But Chelion, even if she is of marginal provenance, is of anything but marginal significance in *Die Narrenburg*. This is one of the earlier tales Stifter used slowly to free himself from the Romantic tradition, which adapts obviously Romantic devices to make decidedly un-Romantic arguments. Thus we have a family dynasty, the Scharnasts (in whom some see features of Stifter himself: A. St.-ast), which suffers a kind of congenital madness — an obviously Faustian or Romantic, subjectivist striving for the realization of a highly individual vision. Typical of this is Jodok's overweening desire personally to experience a kind of universal harmony: 'Ich habe die Erde und die Sterne verlangt, die Liebe aller Menschen, auch der vergangenen und der künftigen, die Liebe Gottes und aller Engel — ich war der Schlußstein des millionenjährig bisher Geschehenen, und der Mittelpunkt des All' (*GW* I, 414). Every Scharnast seems to seek, but not to find, a balancing point at which this subjective desire achieves an objective poise, in which the destabilizing urges of human subjectivity are counterbalanced by objective or natural correlates in the great tradition of *Bildung*. Examples of this would be the renewal of the family stock[10] by intermarriage of the aristocratic male Scharnasts with women of lower estates (Heinrich and Anna, Julius with the 'Bauerndirne'; 335, 402). Another example is the symbolic topography, which opposes the Narrenburg itself, as monument of the sentimental striving for second nature which is culture, to nature in the strict sense of the beautiful Fichtenau vale (object of Heinrich's studies). Thus the Narrenburg, divided from the Fichtenau by a high wall with no visible entrance for ordinary mortals, is literally filled, behind its sphinxes (like the 'Saal der Vergangenheit' in *Wilhelm Meisters Lehrjahre*), with the monuments to the striving for cultural harmony of successive heads of the Scharnast dynasty, from (most notably) the Gothic tower (369) and Aeolian harp (399) of the astrologer Prokop (in search of the music of the spheres), to the Parthenon pastiche (369, 399) of Jodok (symbol of his pursuit of humanistic universality). The Narrenburg, as has been said, is thus a microcosm of German cultural history — and a series of experiments all gone tragically wrong.[11] The ultimate symbol of this endless cycle of cultural striving and natural failure is the writing therapy, imposed as the condition of their stewardship of the Narrenburg (321) on all his heirs by the first Count, Hans. Each successive head of the dynasty is obliged not only to write his autobiography, which is archived in the Rothenstein at the heart of the Narrenburg, but also to read those of all his predecessors. Thus self-knowledge and its sharing by the 'schauderhaft durcheinanderredende Gesellschaft' (415) of the Scharnasts should at last, or at least tendentially, in an endlessly approximative asymptotic progression, overcome the foolishness of the dynasty; but never has yet.

All this is the context for the introduction of the miraculously beautiful Gypsy Chelion into the tale. She, we learn from his autobiography, is Jodok's deed in answer to the urging of his daemon (413). She is, first and foremost, physically beautiful. Typically of Jodok, who is sceptical of the denotative power of language (414), and of course typically of the committed realist and painter Adalbert Stifter, no words can describe her beauty: 'aber schön war sie, schön über jeden Ausdruck, den eine Sprache ersinnen mag' (416). Indeed, she is also beyond pictorial representation (416). But inexpressible physical beauty is not her sole major quality. She also, just as importantly, represents from the tale's internal perspective positively valued Oriental otherness. Jodok, in pursuit of humanist universality, having at this stage uncritically internalized the seemingly valid lessons of the other autobiographies, rejects the entirety of occidental culture as folly. Thus he turns to the Oriental other in terms of a highly sentimentalized, originary nature: 'Da fiel mir ein [. . .], ich wolle nach dem Himalaja gehen. Ich wollte die riesenhaften und unschuldigen Pflanzen Gottes sehen, und eher noch wollte ich das große, einfache Meer versuchen' (416). Of this idealized nature the beautiful, gazelle-eyed Gypsy vegetarian Chelion is the ultimate expression. But tragedy ensues. At one level it is a tragedy of intercultural naivety. Jodok realizes too late that this simple Pariah woman is incapable of adjusting to occidental life — despite the existence of the alternative Oriental environment he has constructed for her in the form of hothouses, walled gardens, special diet, etc. It is he who should have made the cultural adjustment: 'aber mein hartes Herz war in seinem Europa befangen, und ahnete nicht, daß es anders sein sollte, daß ich, der Stärkere, hätte opfern sollen und können, was sie, die Schwächere, wirklich opferte, aber nicht konnte. Ich hörte die Stimme nicht, bis es zu spät war' (419). At another level, Chelion in her naivety and moral weakness betrays Jodok with his brother Sixtus, and eventually — in part because the murderous look in Jodok's eyes undermines her sense of belonging — pines away. Chelion, then, the beautiful, Eastern, feminized ideal of authentic nature, fount of renewal for all occidentals since the Romantic age, fails to live up to the role Jodok has scripted for her. He consigns the edifice of his life, the Parthenon, to the flames, allows the Indian garden to decay, and fills the time until his death by making other absurd monuments in place of lost love: the blue-veiled portrait of Chelion in the Grüner Saal (384, 390), where her Indian skin turns so oddly pale as marble; the non-representative cuboid monument to 'Jodokus und Chelion' (399) in the ruined garden; and finally his autobiography. As the painting suggests — 'Die kleine, weiße Hand lag auf Marmor und spiegelte sich drinnen' (389) — Chelion is not only slowly turning white under the relatively sunless European sky, she is turning from a veiled Isis into a statue, symbol of a Galatea in reverse, the mortified Pygmalion fantasy of her Romantic husband, who now realizes that European happiness is not co-extensive with Indian (418).[12] With its emphatic, intertextual reference not only to the beautiful Gypsy Mitidika in the anthropological tradition of Grellmann and the literary tradition of Brentano, but also to Novalis's famous symbolic language from *Die Lehrlinge zu Sais* (in which of course a young scholar's subjective yearning to discover the truth of nature leads him to a fantasy union with the eastern goddess Isis), Stifter's tale is thus nothing less than his personal, formalized farewell to Romanticism.[13] Jodok's Romantic consciousness of the East is exposed as an Orientalist construct, the imposition of a sentimentalist vision of ideal natural authenticity on something exotic which is in truth merely a disguised wish-fulfilment, so that 'das Naive' (as Peter Szondi showed) is once more revealed to have been a projection of 'das Sentimentale'[14] all along; and the opposition of nature and culture (if not of German and Gypsy) becomes slippery indeed.[15] As Jodok later sardonically notes: 'dort sah ich das Bramanenleben, ein anderes als unseres, das heißt anders töricht' (416). The Gypsies, then, in this phase of Stifter's career, are self-consciously presented through the lens of Romantic Orientalism, a perspective which is finally rejected as subjectivist fantasy and replaced, as locus of utopian hope, by Heinrich Scharnast's quite differently orientated study of the book of nature.

Chelion, the reader has noted, is called Pariah and Indian as well as Gypsy. Is she really a Gypsy? It is only Erasmus who calls her thus. Elsewhere she is identified as a Pariah. Stifter has also been inspired here by Goethe's ballad 'Paria' (1822–24),[16] and Chelion's hybrid behaviour, of sublimely loyal ethereal love and naively licentious betrayal, mirrors precisely the behaviour of Goethe's hybrid goddess, with her divine Brahmin head on her sinful Pariah body. Indeed, it might be noted in parenthesis, Chelion (together with her descendant Pia) is at a deeper, structural level a relative of the Italian Mignon.[17] But she is nonetheless *still* a Gypsy. Gypsy ethnographers of Stifter's age from Grellmann on, we know, are united in the view that the Gypsies are none other than emigrated Pariahs.[18]

Katzensilber[19] and *Der Waldbrunnen* belong together. The latter is in one sense an interpretation of the former. But there are also clear parallels to *Die Narrenburg*. In *Katzensilber* there features again what is almost the Stifterian primal scene, the situation of a mysterious, brown-skinned, charismatic child of nature interacting with representatives of middle European high culture, whose pedagogical task it becomes to educate and acculturate the outsider. Is the nut-brown girl a Gypsy? The racial attribute, as with Chelion, cannot quite be said to be definitively singular. There are several key discursive inputs into the composite figure that is the 'braunes Mädchen' (and her mother and grandfather). One, inevitably, is Mignon, others are the folktales of wild people still living in the remote forests of Europe. Another is however definitively Romany, for which claim we have Stifter's own authority: as he wrote to Luise von Eichendorff on 31 March 1853 in reply to her complimentary remarks: 'Sie sprechen auf die schönste Weise von dem armen Zigeunermädchen das aus, was ich bei der Arbeit fühlte. Ich hielt das *Katzensilber* für das beste und zarteste Stük'.[20] The nut-brown girl is certainly equipped with the traditional attributes of Romany physical beauty: the brown skin, the black hair, the flashing white teeth (257), the magnetic black eyes (257, 264), the always bare arms (257, 285), the athleticism, evidenced as she rescues brown-haired Sigismund, her best friend, from the fire (304–05). Nor can we forget the sexuality. A child at the start of the tale, she naturally grows taller and slimmer. As the tell-tale signal of the onset of sexual maturity, her hair — initially worn short — becomes ever longer and more opulent (285): 'in noch größerer Fülle', says the narrator of her hair at the mid-point (296); by the end she possesses 'dichte [. . .], dunkle [. . .] schöne [. . .]

Locken' (315). Perhaps a further esoteric hint of her ethnic grouping is the special attachment which the narrator shows as obtaining between Sigismund and the nut-brown girl. Sigismund has the valedictory last scene of the tale all to himself, as he, from his appropriately sovereign, panoramic viewpoint, still mourns her parting (316). The reader's attention is deliberately drawn to Sigismund's name (314). It was of course his namesake, the King, later Emperor, Sigismund, who granted the Gypsies his letter of protection in 1423.[21] Grellmann reproduces it (Grellmann, 343–44). But a further factor here, as so often with Stifter's Gypsies, is the ghost of Romantic Gypsy discourse. For, looking at the girl and her relatives, the 'schwarzer Mann' (253) who appears mysteriously from the forest to reveal to the shepherd the existence of the 'Karfunkel' in the watery grotto — her grandfather, presumably — plainly signals Stifter's intention again to link his Romany words with a Romantic provenance (Novalis's imagery from *Heinrich von Ofterdingen*). And of course the nut-brown girl's magnetic intuition of the imminent hailstorm, perhaps even her ability to defy the fire in the house,[22] might also be seen as attributes of the Romantic Gypsy — both, of course, seeming to flow from her quasi-animalistic closeness to nature.

However, if the carbuncle is a treasure of nature which eventually passes into the realm of culture to adorn a crown, the same cannot be said of the nut-brown girl. As with *Die Narrenburg*, the experiment in intercultural education is at last a failure. Two factors seem to condition this. Sexuality, as in *Die Narrenburg*, is one. As the nut-brown girl stands on the threshold of cultural ingress, she is also, we saw, crossing that of puberty. The shift from androgynous shorts to modest women's dress underlines the point (313). She nonetheless seems unable to participate in the social events which signal the entrance of the bourgeois city girls onto the sexual marketplace, preferring solitude in the garden. This could be read in accordance with the Gypsy custom, recorded in Grellmann (Grellmann, 119–20), never to marry outside the ethnic group (*Katzensilber*, 313–15). The other factor would be the death of her mother Sture Mure, with its implication of responsibility and the assumption of a role elsewhere. The girl's educative encounter with the cultivated bourgeois family is far more sophisticated than that of the maid Sture Mure with the farmer Hagenbucher. It can be seen as a kind of cultural potentialization of that. Nevertheless on the occasion of the parent's death (246–47) she follows the behaviour of her mother with typological exactitude. The pull of natural ties elsewhere, only hinted at in the text (the girl's life, as the bourgeois father finds to his cost, has no discoverable origin or end), is stronger than all other culturally conditioned links. *Katzensilber*, then, is another version of Stifter's long goodbye to Romanticism and the Romantic Gypsy discourse, another demonstration of intercultural — or internatural — failure. The carbuncle may well adorn a crown, but the nut-brown girl will never marry Sigismund. Read concretely, such a stance would place Stifter as an educationalist in total opposition to the Josephinist policy of ruthless Gypsy acculturation.

Put thus, *Der Waldbrunnen*,[23] set in the same topography of Stifter's beloved Sesselberg in the Bayerischer Wald, can only be read as an intertextual commentary on *Katzensilber*, a commentary which, moreover, culminates in an apparent retraction of Stifter's anti-Romanticism. Here again there features an intercultural variant of the pedagogic *Urszene*. Again Stifter seems to thematize an intrinsic link between a reflection on aesthetic beauty and cultural (or natural) exchange. In this framework tale at least one, and perhaps two, Gypsy girls, or women, play central roles. But as scholars have always noted, it is an odd frame. In a recently published letter to the editor of the journal in which *Der Waldbrunnen* first appeared, Stifter comments that he found the framework 'verdächtig' — 'da mir der Eingang der Erzählung selber verdächtig vorkam'.[24] The frame is certainly odd in the sense that it is a double frame, yet only one frame, the inside one, so to speak, is actually closed. The inner frame, the story of the beautiful Juliana figure at the summit of the Rigi, who may well be of Romany provenance, is closed at the end of the text, so that an identification of her with the inset tale figure Jana may be made and a degree of closure achieved in her story. The other frame, an extraordinary description of a nameless Gypsy girl in a street, is not. It stands irritatingly, like an erratic in a rocky landscape, at the gateway of the tale. If the inner frame might be related in some way to both the central character's experience and that of the narrator, the portrait of the Gypsy girl can only relate to the person of the narrator, to his perspective on the tale as a whole. It will therefore be treated first.

The most striking attribute of this seventeen-year-old Romany is that she, like Chelion, at least for the young lawyer who narrates the tale, is (inevitably) beautiful. We can recognize the familiar features of the Romany pulchritude topos in his description, stretching back all too recognizably to Grellmann's originary discourse. Even if scantily dressed in exotic and motley rags, this Gypsy girl possesses elegant and simple facial features, a straight nose and full lips, bodily proportions of perfect regularity, a bronzed skin with bare arms and feet, large eyes blacker than the blackest coal, and long hair, equally black, which winds its way fantastically entwined down her neck and back (639). She transcends the beauty of any natural realm: mineral, plant, animal (639). Like Chelion, this Gypsy girl is quite beyond representation by painter or sculptor. She transcends Raphael's Sistine Madonna and the entire canon of Greek plastic art. But, as this remarkably hypertrophic series of comparisons indicates, this girl is even more than another Chelion, she is her ultimate potentialization. Were she by some miracle transformed into art every nation on earth would kneel before her in veneration (639). In short, she instantiates absolute transcendent living beauty, a beauty which transfixes the young man in Platonic astonishment, so that he can merely gaze at her, just as she herself merely gazes in eerie silence (640). As all this suggests, the Romany girl, even if she is not capable of being translated into art, is nevertheless *herself* pure aesthetic spectacle, pure exteriority for the young lawyer (640). This he readily admits: 'ich habe nur die Gestalt angeschaut und um ihr Wesen mich nicht bekümmert' (644). And it is clear that the description of the Gypsy girl is more like the *ekphrasis* of some classical statue than it is of a real person. The girl is posed, still, poised like Risach's aesthetic ideal in the Nausikaa gesture, midway between rest and movement beside a doorway,[25] neither entering nor leaving. She is in the throng yet not of it. For maximum aesthetic effect she is set against the chaotic and noisy activity of a typical imagined genre scene by painters such as Carl Löffler or Peter Johann Nepomuk

Geiger[26] in the main street of Neukirchen, of Gypsies arriving (or leaving) in three covered wagons drawn by bony nags with masses of baroque Gypsy gear. These Gypsies, unlike her, are both male and female as black as the Moorish magus in traditional illustrations of the Three Kings (638). But this young woman is totally unconcerned with the sublunary activity all around; she stands 'als ginge sie das alles nichts an' (638). It is this characteristic Kantian note of disinterest which gives her Oriental appearance the seal of classical beauty, and her claim to Kantian aesthetic universality of taste contrasts with the travesty of universality associated with the mannered appearance of the other Gypsies, dressed as they are in the tattered 'Trachten verschiedener Zeiten und Länder' (638).

But that is not all. The sheen of disinterested classical beauty also veils one particular, not quite so selfless interest of the lawyer, who in this mimics the questionable stance of Baciochi in Brentano's *Die mehreren Wehmüller*. For his gaze too is plainly also an erotic, voyeuristic one. As aesthetic discourse Stifter's Gypsy *ekphrasis* recalls not only Kant, but also his mentor Herder's haptic (touch-orientated) classical aesthetics, the *Plastik* (1778), which of course emphatically placed sculpture at the apex of the pantheon of the arts as a Pygmalionic revelation of the highest truth in human form. In particular here the erotic gaze of the lawyer is fascinated by the role of the material drapery of the girl's clothing, which as it modestly conceals only erotically reveals the contours of the body beneath:

> Der Oberkörper war in ein rötlich braunes, ausgebleichtes Zeug gehüllt, das so dünn war, daß man alle Gestaltungen durch dasselbe verfolgen konnte [. . .]. Von den Hüften war ein Rock mit gelben und roten Streifen bis über die Kniee hinunter, der aber die Schwingungen der Gestalt vollkommen erkennen ließ. (639)

Herder, whose *Plastik* frankly recognized the erotic dimension, had speculated that the draperies of classical Greek statuary were carved as wet to perform this function.[27] And Grellmann, again without my wishing to be positivistic, also emphasizes how little the dress of Gypsy women leaves to the male imagination (Grellmann, 67). Thus it may well have been this aspect which Stifter found 'verdächtig', when his framing introduction was suggested to be rather too long. This Gypsy girl, then, reveals perhaps rather more about the narrator than he initially suspected, a fundamental dualism of the erotic and the ethereal in his attitude to beauty. Stifter was plainly conscious of this, since to criticize this undercurrent of his aesthetic obsession explicitly — on the reader's behalf, perhaps — is clearly the role of the narrator's wife. She of course, in a sort of Biedermeier feminine waspishness, deconstructs the erotic undertones of his roving eye by noting how he finds beauty only in women whose skin resembles the metal used for casting bells, if only when no longer quite pristine, and he hastily has to assure her that he values her Viennese looks and her beauty of soul (644). The function of this unclosed frame, then, is to condition our understanding of the narrative voice, and to read what follows in that light. Concretely, moving away from the lawyer's perspective, it is a meditation by the late Stifter not quite, I think, as Ursula Naumann argued,[28] on beauty as lying beyond good and evil, so much as on beauty as an *adiaphoron*, a morally indifferent and so pervertible thing. It uses the resources of the Gypsy discourse to do so.

The inset Jana–Juliana tale is thus significant in two major respects. First, it is significant in respect of the erotic dimension of feminine beauty and its integration into the fabric of cultivated occidental society. The narrator cannot decide which of these two women should head his personal hit parade of feminine beauty. But there is a great difference between the two. The Romany girl offers at best an unresolved dualism of aesthetic beauty. By contrast Juliana, considered at least from the outside, is unambiguously the purified and acculturated version of the Gypsy girl. Her provenance, it is true, is clouded in ambiguity, obviously designed by Stifter, as with the nut-brown girl, to be irresolvable. The narrator's wife suggests (understandably perhaps) Malayan origins (644). As Jana, her parents are said only to be '[h]ergelaufene Menschen' (653). But when we see her as Juliana on the Rigi, she bears the familiar attributes of Romany beauty, the black eyes, black hair, dazzling white teeth, tastefully dark skin, tall stature, regular proportions, and so forth; and she too recalls the ideal of ancient classical sculpture (641). That said, the striking difference from the nameless Gypsy girl is her dress, which is of chaste black silk, closed at the throat, with a white ruff at the neck and a white fan (641). She of course resembles, in this almost priestly clothing, the painting of Chelion (*GW* I, 367), which itself is the etherealized version of that Gypsy woman. Juliana, then, represents acceptably restrained, domesticated erotic beauty. Jana, who like the nut-brown girl passes through puberty in the tale, can, unlike the nut-brown girl, overcome the natural ties of her family circumstances and integrate herself both socially and sexually into the Heilkun family — redeeming them in a sense as they redeem her. Unlike the nut-brown girl, Juliana *does* marry a brown-haired man. There seems no sense of undialectical loss, even if the question of her erotic temptation for the male is never quite answered. As the narrator carefully notes at the conclusion, on his next visit to the Rigi he is accompanied by his wife (*GW* III, 681). In this sense the first frame of the tale might also be said to be closed.

The other great change here in the series of Stifter's Gypsy figures, now considering Juliana in other contexts, is the superposition of aesthetic talent on this one. Juliana, uniquely, is an artist-figure. It is this expressive authority that qualifies her at last — like Sigismund — to own the panoramic gaze from the mountain-tops, be it the giant rock beside the mountain spring, the vision from the Drei Sessel, or the summit of the Rigi. In a tale suffused with autobiographical-confessional content, from the loaning of the name of Stifter's deceased stepdaughter, to the attribution of Stifter's own professional career path to Stephan Heilkun and the setting in a fictionalization of his own Lackerhäuser in the Bayerischer Wald, this tale is one of Stifter's most obviously self-revelatory. On Jana–Juliana he has also conferred his own aesthetic talent. As critics from Gustav Wilhelm to Gerhard Neumann have noted, her first incoherent written nominalistic stammerings are co-extensive with those Stifter recorded contemporaneously in his unpublished autobiography as his own: 'Burgen, Nagelein, Schwarzbach' (656).[29] Juliana's fate, the control of the erotic-aesthetic impulse within, in some sense — a utopian sense — bespeaks Stifter's. Like him, she projects her subjective impulses from the mountain-top onto the objective landscape below — even if *Der Waldbrunnen* refuses to share that sovereign achievement with the narrator or reader.

That said, Stifter's portrayal of Gypsies, measured even against the dismal ethnographic achievement of official Gypsy cultural anthropology, is narrow and one-dimensionally harnessed to the service of his art's cognitive interest, which as a rule in these texts consists in a meta-aesthetic reflection. Of the social reality of Gypsy life little is shown, except in so far as some small glimpse might represent another aesthetic potential, an interestingly mannered contrast to the classical aesthetic ideal. Stifter's Gypsy is thus always, indeed obsessively, the received image of *Zigeunerromantik*, the anachronistic and decontextualized paradigm of *Naturpoesie*, adapted, as in Storm, to his own post-Romantic ends. In *Die Narrenburg* there lurks, perhaps, a trace of the border-crossing utopian cosmopolitanism and interculturality which inspires Michaly and Mitidika in Brentano's hymn to the interculturality of the Habsburg state, *Die mehreren Wehmüller*. But that of course is turned on its head as an expression of terminal cultural pessimism. That apart, the middle and later Stifter of *Katzensilber* and *Der Waldbrunnen* capitalizes on the received Romantic stereotype of Gypsy beauty, with its wider associations of sensuality and artistry, as the vehicle of veiled autobiographical aesthetic confession. More often than not the veiled confession has a critical and/or tragic function: it intimates just how problematic the reconciliation of subjective and objective, culture and nature is, and even in *Der Waldbrunnen* the achieved reconciliation is translated by the narrative frame into the status of a precarious, self-conscious utopia.

Thus Stifter's Gypsies are ultimately the chosen symbol of his particular and highly complex relation to modernity. If it can be said with Glaser that a dominant element in Stifter's *œuvre* is the unrealistic 'Restauration des Schönen',[30] the deployment of an older, classical discourse of beauty by an artist deeply critical of the modern age and seeking to recuperate what has been lost, then the Gypsies, given their association in his mind with absolute beauty, are prime examples of that utopian project. As with every generation after Goethe, Hegel, and the Romantics — after the 'Kunstperiode' — Stifter shares the consciousness of modernity as characterized by rupture and division, by loss of what was once (allegedly) whole and immediate and meaningful, especially the bond of subject and object — witness his repeated critique of modernity in every aspect, from economic life to railways, cities, women's fashions, furniture, jewellery, and art.[31] His stance is of course itself nothing more than the archetypal expression *of* modern consciousness. This is the sense in which Stifter's curiously anachronistic, obsessive montage of the post-Romantic Gypsy in his characteristically stiff realist discourse should be understood. For realists, says Gerhard Plumpe,[32] are writers who do not wholly reject the modern. Rather, they *are* modern, part of a modernity *de longue durée* which extends from early Romanticism to classical modernism. Modern art so understood is both constituted by modern, deficient social reality and protests aesthetically against it. Thus it protests against the deficits of modernity from *within* the modernist project. In the case of the realists, and Stifter, the protest consists in the attempt to restore the link of the bewildering complexity of the new age of iron and steam and city and mass to traditional values for the sake of orientating their anxious bourgeois readership. Stifter's montage of *Zigeunerromantik*, such as it is, drained of ethnographic significance, is the inscription of that fragile aesthetic restoration, symbol of the healing powers of aesthetic discourse, and protest too against the absolute end of art signalled by his own despairing artist novella *Nachkommenschaften*.

Notes to Chapter 3

1. Citations are from Theodor Storm, *Sämtliche Werke*, ed. by Karl Ernst Laage and Dieter Lohmeier, 4 vols (Frankfurt a.M.: Deutscher Klassiker Verlag, 1987–88), I, 295–328. The citation is from p. 305.
2. On subjectivity and memory in Storm see the (still current) Clifford A. Bernd, *Theodor Storm's Craft of Fiction: The Torment of a Narrator* (Chapel Hill: University of North Carolina Press, 1963). On *Immensee* see especially M. A. McHaffie and J. M. Ritchie, 'Bee's Lake or the Curse of Silence: A Study of Theodor Storm's *Immensee*', *German Life and Letters*, 15 (1962), 36–48; Fritz Rüdiger Sammern-Frankenegg, *Perspektivische Strukturen einer Erinnerungsdichtung: Studien zur Deutung von Storms 'Immensee'* (Stuttgart: Heinz, 1976); Eckhart Pastor, *Die Sprache der Erinnerung: Zu den Novellen von Theodor Storm* (Frankfurt a.M.: Athenäum, 1988), pp. 48–69; also Clifford Albrecht Bernd, *Poetic Realism in Scandinavia and Central Europe 1820–1895* (Columbia, SC: Camden House, 1995), pp. 148–50; and David A. Jackson, *Theodor Storm: Dichter und demokratischer Humanist* (Berlin: Erich Schmidt, 2000), pp. 80–86.
3. See Storm's letter to Helen Clark, the tale's first translator, cited from the literary estate in *Sämtliche Werke*, I, 1030.
4. Compare Pastor, pp. 61–63.
5. Storm makes further use of the Gypsy motif only in *Der Schimmelreiter* (1889), but here again the Gypsy is a fatal requisite, as the agent for selling Hauke Haien his dappled horse.
6. See on Stifter's reading Erwin Streitfeld, 'Aus Adalbert Stifters Bibliothek: Nach den Bücher- und Handschriftenverzeichnissen in den Verlassenschaftsakten von Adalbert und Amelie Stifter', *Raabe-Jahrbuch* (1977), pp. 103–48. This inventory, whilst obviously very incomplete, contains however no hint of intensive specialized scholarship.
7. Quotations (save where indicated) are from Adalbert Stifter, *Gesammelte Werke*, ed. by Max Stefl, 6 vols (Wiesbaden: Insel, 1959) [=*GW*].
8. *GW* I, pp. 319–440; second version.
9. Recent scholarship includes Christian Begemann, *Die Welt der Zeichen: Stifter-Lektüren* (Stuttgart: Metzler, 1995), pp. 210–41; also Adalbert Stifter, *Die Narrenburg*, ed. by Christian Begemann (Vienna: Residenz, 1996), pp. 121–43; and Marcus Hahn, *Geschichte und Epigonen: '19. Jahrhundert'/'Postmoderne', Stifter/Bernhard* (Freiburg im Breisgau: Rombach, 2003), pp. 293–310.
10. Stifter, as Streitfeld reveals (p. 136), possessed a copy of the first — untowardly critical and distorting — German translation of *The Origin of Species* (1859), *Über die Entstehung der Arten im Thier- und Pflanzenreich durch natürliche Züchtung oder Erhaltung der vervollkommneten Rassen im Kampfe um's Dasein* (1860); but does not seem to have been influenced by it.
11. See Begemann, *Welt der Zeichen*, p. 224.
12. See Gerhard Neumann, 'Der Körper des Menschen und die belebte Statue: Zu einer Grundformel in Gottfried Kellers *Sinngedicht*', in *Pygmalion: Geschichte des Mythos in der abendländischen Kultur*, ed. by Mathias Meyer and Gerhard Neumann (Freiburg im Breisgau: Rombach, 1997), pp. 555–91.
13. See Nicholas Saul, '"*Poëtisirung* d[es] Körpers": Der Poesiebegriff Friedrich von Hardenbergs (Novalis) und die anthropologische Tradition', in *Novalis — Poesie und Poetik*, ed. by Herbert Uerlings (Tübingen: Niemeyer, 2004), pp. 151–69.
14. The reference is of course to Peter Szondi's classic essay 'Das Naive ist das Sentimentale: Zur Begriffsdialektik in Schillers Abhandlung' (1972), in Peter Szondi, *Lektüren und Lektionen: Versuche über Literatur, Literaturtheorie und Literatursoziologie* (Frankfurt a.M.: Suhrkamp, 1972), pp. 47–99.
15. On this see Christian Begemann, 'Natur und Kultur: Überlegungen zu einem durchkreuzten Gegensatz im Werk Adalbert Stifters', in *Adalbert Stifters schrecklich schöne Welt: Beiträge des*

Internationalen Kolloquiums zur Adalbert-Stifter-Ausstellung (Universität Antwerpen 1993), Acta Austriaca-Belgica, 1 (1996), pp. 41–52.

16. In Goethe, *Werke*, ed. by Erich Trunz, 14 vols (Hamburg: Beck, 1948–60), I, 361–68.
17. See G. H. Hertling, 'Mignons Schwestern im Erzählwerk Adalbert Stifters: *Katzensilber, Der Waldbrunnen, Die Narrenburg*', in *Goethes Mignon und ihre Schwestern: Interpretation und Rezeption*, ed. by Gerhard Hoffmeister (New York: Peter Lang, 1993), pp. 165–97. Hertling's argumentative basis is too narrow for so eclectic and mythical a figure as Mignon, and still less for Chelion. One could argue the other way around, that the dominant discursive formation of Mignon (as of Chelion) is the Gypsy tradition, not vice versa.
18. See Grellmann: 'Ich komme nun zum Ziele meiner Abhandlung, zu dem Satze, daß die Zigeuner aus der niedrigsten Classe der Indier, nähmlich Pareier, oder wie sie in Hindostan heißen, Suders sind' (Grellmann, pp. 327–42, here p. 327). Compare further (restricting the range of reference to Stifter's contemporaries) Tetzner, pp. 138–40; Heister, p. 3; Reinbeck, pp. 3, 7; and Liebich, *Die Zigeuner*, p. 15; also Borrow, p. 17; and Liszt, pp. 53–60.
19. *GW* III, 241–316.
20. See Adalbert Stifter, *Sämtliche Werke*, ed. by August Sauer, 25 vols (Prague/Reichenberg, 1904–), XVIII, 159.
21. Perhaps it was this resonance which persuaded Hofmannsthal to introduce Gypsies into the fifth act of his tragedy of the (of course *Polish*) Sigismund *Der Turm* (first version, 1924). Martin Ruch, *Zur Wissenschaftsgeschichte der deutschsprachigen 'Zigeunerforschung' von den Anfängen bis 1900* (Diss., Freiburg im Breisgau, 1986), pp. 35–47, points out that Sigismund was not the only German ruler to protect the Gypsies; but this of course hardly diminishes the historical aura Sigismund *de facto* possessed.
22. A traditional feature of Gypsy magic. Compare Achim von Arnim's 'Das Feuerbesprechen' in *Des Knaben Wunderhorn*.
23. *GW* III, 638–82. On this in addition to previously cited works see Ursula Naumann, *Adalbert Stifter* (Stuttgart: Metzler,1979), pp. 67–68; Christine Oertel Sjøgren, 'The Frame of "Der Waldbrunnen" Reconsidered: A Note on Adalbert Stifter's Aesthetics', *Modern Austrian Literature*, 19.1 (1986), 9–25; Rosemarie Hunter-Lougheed, *Adalbert Stifter: Der Waldbrunnen. Interpretation und Ursprungshypothese* (Linz: Adalbert-Stifter-Institut des Landes Ober-Österreich, 1988); Eva Geulen, *Worthörig wider Willen: Darstellungsproblematik und Sprachreflexion in der Prosa Adalbert Stifters* (Munich: Iudicium, 1992), pp. 143–50; Gerhard Neumann, '"Zuversicht": Adalbert Stifters Schicksalskonzept zwischen Novellistik und Autobiographie', in *Stifter-Studien: Ein Festgeschenk für Wolfgang Frühwald zum 65. Geburtstag*, ed. by Walter Hettche (Tübingen: Niemeyer, 2000), pp. 162–87.
24. See Peter Greipl, 'Drei bisher ungedruckte Stifter-Briefe', in *Stifter-Studien*, pp. 255–59 (p. 257); Stifter to Breidenbach, 5 March 1865.
25. See *Der Nachsommer* (*GW* IV, 12, 378).
26. Löffler (1823–1905) and Geiger (1805–80) were established genre painters and friends of Stifter. Geiger was a professor at the Vienna Academy and also turned out Oriental scenes.
27. See Herder, *Werke*, IV, 243–326 (pp. 263–64).
28. See Naumann, p. 68.
29. Compare Stifter, *Mein Leben* (*SW* 25; p. 180); Wilhelm (*SW* 13, 1; p. lxxi) and Neumann ('"Zuversicht"', p. 186, n. 107).
30. See Horst Albert Glaser, *Die Restauration des Schönen: Stifters 'Der Nachsommer'* (Stuttgart: Metzler, 1965).
31. See for a representative selection of Stifter's critiques: on modern art and the modern mentality *Der Nachsommer* (*GW* IV, 459–60, 586, 636); on mass society, modern culture, and railways *Wien und die Wiener* (*GW* VI, 50–52); on the city *Der Nachsommer* and *Der Waldbrunnen* (*GW* IV, 730; III, 650); on restoration and furniture *Der Nachsommer* (*GW* IV, 93–96, 297–301); on modern women's dress *Der Nachsommer* (pp. 504–05, 518, 566, 846) and *Der Waldbrunnen* (III, 641).
32. Gerhard Plumpe, 'Einleitung', in *Bürgerlicher Realismus und Gründerzeit 1848–1890*, ed. by Edward McInnes and Gerhard Plumpe (Munich: Hanser, 1996), pp. 17–83 (pp. 82–83).

CHAPTER 4

❖

Gypsies, German Identity, and *Heimat* in Hebbel, Raabe, Keller, and Strauss

Despite their professed anti-Romanticism, despite the realistic aspirations fulfilled elsewhere in their *œuvre*, indeed despite the more or less secure ethnic identity of their Gypsy figures, one looked in vain for an authentic encounter with Romany culture in Storm and Stifter. Some of the features foregrounded in the contemporary anthropological report and literary image are of course authentic. Gypsies without doubt did, as Storm and Stifter fleetingly hint, and as Mörike's Friedrich Nolten and Franz Liszt in person observed, travel at their own pleasure, nomadically, in large bands, through forest and plain, on foot and in horse-drawn covered wagons, plying their marginal trades by day in the *gadjo* contact zone, hunting lower varieties of game, and congregating of an evening around the camp fire, where they would smoke their beloved tobacco, drink spirits, tell their ancient tales, play their stirring improvised music, and perform their traditional dances. That said, significant dimensions of the reality of Gypsy life form no part of the cognitive interest of writers in this strand of the literary tradition. What, then, was life *really* like for a Gypsy in mid-nineteenth-century Germany?

The main feature of everyday life for Gypsies in mid-nineteenth-century Germany was police control. If anti-Gypsyist social antagonism was (and is) the great constant of Gypsy life in Germany across the centuries, that dominant attitude took different forms from epoch to epoch. The tenor of German–Gypsy relations from around the end of the eighteenth century to the late 1830s was determined by the various attempts at forced cultural assimilation and settlement of the exotic strangers. Thereafter, in a change of emphasis from the 1840s on, German states in the epoch of the North German Confederation (founded in 1866) and the Empire (founded in 1871) used the law and the police strategically to minimize the vagrant Gypsy presence in German lands.[1] 'Der Roman soll das deutsche Volk da suchen, wo es in seiner Tüchtigkeit zu finden ist, nämlich bei seiner Arbeit', was the slogan of the critic and literary theoretician Julian Schmidt, which Gustav Freytag placed at the head of *Soll und Haben* (1855), his foundational novel of the new German nation after 1848.[2] As the new German nation-state crystallized and emergent German self-consciousness was cast in this mould, the correlated notions of work and *Heimat* came to determine the legitimacy of the Gypsy presence among hard-working Germans.[3] The *Heimatrecht* or *Heimatprinzip* was the key to the new policy,[4] which rested ultimately on identifying the authority responsible for supporting those — such as Gypsies and other itinerants — seemingly unable to support themselves save by begging or criminal means. That authority, from 1842 in Prussian lands, was the *Heimatgemeinde*,[5] a place of ascribed provenance which even those of the wandering lifestyle were obliged to possess. Only by fulfilling the requirement of uninterrupted residence over a number of years could a *Heimatschein* be obtained. Only then could a *Wandergewerbeschein* be obtained which permitted the holder to engage in trade from place to place and settle from time to time on public land. The consequence was that Gypsies became subject to rigorous police control on arrival at any new destination. If satisfactory documentation was not produced, they were moved on. It is immediately clear that such a system of controls could be and was applied to ensure that a *Heimatschein*, while necessary for obtaining the means of life, could rarely or never be legitimately acquired, so that those lacking it were forced into a marginal existence at the edge of formal legality and physical control. The system of control was intensified after 1871, by which time all Gypsies possessed German citzenship — though not the power to exercise the rights of labour and mobility that citizenship conferred on them.[6] All non-German Gypsies were henceforth summarily refused admittance to the Empire and — thanks to a binding inter-state agreement[7] — transported back whence they came. German Gypsies for their part were permitted the *Wandergewerbeschein* only if they could produce evidence of settled residence, evidence that their means of economic existence was secure (so that they would not beg), and evidence that their children would and could attend school.[8] If any of these conditions went unfulfilled — and few schools for example would accept Gypsy children — again the Gypsies would be moved on. As the nineteenth century merged into the twentieth, these harsh conditions were ever more inventively enriched, and the presumption of criminality, police registration, and circulation of information on the Gypsies, by telegraph and railway, became ever more elaborated.[9] Criminalrath Richard Liebich, perhaps the most acute, if not most sympathetic, observer of Romany circumstances around the middle of the nineteenth century, provides a telling account of the typical reception awaiting a Gypsy group — the 'Landplage' as he terms them[10] — on entering a new place.[11] The Gypsies, he says, will tend to send one or two representatives ahead, so that they do not frighten their hosts through sheer force of numbers. Only later, once accommodation is secured, will the remainder arrive. Passports should then be rigorously controlled by the police, and suspect Gypsies to this end interrogated separately. The officer should take care to avoid being deceived by simulations of illness or digressive garrulity. He might usefully apply chloroform or a certain physical violence. Once the genuine *Heimat* (so to speak) of the suspect Gypsy has been ascertained in this way, he is then summarily to be directed 'auf den Schub daheim' (Liebich, 110). Mere removal across the border is insufficient. He must be securely transported all the way back to his original provenance. Otherwise, says Liebich on the basis of his thirty years' experience (Liebich, vii), he will merely return at once. Only thus is the land to be cleansed of the tramp and vagabond riff-raff ('vom Stromer- und Vagabundengesindel rein zu halten', 110).

'. . . eine ganze Zigeunerbande [. . .] vor dem Tribunal': Hebbel's Gypsies

If this is something of the reality elided by the quite other cognitive interest and perspective on Romany life of Storm and Stifter, then Wilhelm Raabe and Gottfried Keller — and, for a start, Friedrich Hebbel — offer a very different analysis of the Romany situation. Hebbel, given his conventional affiliation to the classical aesthetics of Hegelian idealism, does not as a rule feature in accounts of realism, still less in treatments of the literary encounter with cultural otherness.[12] This is unfortunate, given his densely observed early novellas[13] and marvellously perspicuous travel writing.[14] For Hebbel had a lifelong, if frankly unsympathetic, interest in Romanies, and not least as a consequence of that his travel writing, highly sensitive to the spirit of the age, pre-emptively captures the realistic turn of Gypsy representation. Thus Hebbel's Gypsies constantly feature in contact with the organs of public discipline, the army and police.

A *feuilleton* of 1850 is the first example. When in that year his wife Christine played Judith (the star part in his early tragedy *Judith*) in Agram (capital of Croatia, now Zagreb), Hebbel, as was his wont, recorded his impressions of this undeveloped nation on Germany's eastern borders for the *Bildungsbürger* of Vienna in the columns of *Der Wanderer.*[15] Prefaced with a half-hearted profession of cosmopolitanism and Germanic cultural modesty, Hebbel's *feuilleton* in fact offers a grim delineation of eastern cultural inferiority by contrast with the Germans, beginning with the Croatians and ending with the Gypsies. All nations together, Hebbel protests, make up the human race. As with the colours of the rainbow, each race makes its own, uniquely valuable contribution to the fullest unfolding of human potential (*Agram*, 844). That said, if a city is a silhouette of a nation, then Agram itself is like a half-dressed person, a city which should be one of the most beautiful in Europe, but is in truth half-decayed (843). Alas, the Croats themselves are too feeble as a nation to remedy this. They have foolishly declined German help, for (as Hebbel scoffs) they fear Germanicization (844–45). In fact, so Hebbel rather threateningly concludes, fertile but empty Croatia is an obvious destination for the wave of emigration which would heal the economic misery of post-1848 occidental Europe (847). Thus a sudden tumult beneath his hotel window offers Hebbel the perfect speaking image — of racial and cultural hierarchy — with which to close his argument:

> Was erblickte ich? Eine Zigeunerfuhre! Natürlich eilte ich sogleich auf die Straße und besah mir die ägyptischen Gäste. Weibergesichter, die man kaum noch unter die menschlichen rechnen konnte; schwarze, zottige Haare, die noch nie gekämmt worden waren; Augen, deren Blicke förmlich stachen. An gelben Brüsten säugten sie schmutzige Kinder, zugleich aber zankten sie in ihrer unverständlichen Mundart aufs heftigste mit den Soldaten, die ihren Wagen abluden, weil sie gestohlen hatten [. . .] Zwei Kroaten niedrigster Bildungsstufe, wie wir sie zuweilen in Wien mit ihren rauhen Jacken durch die Gassen ziehen sehen, schlossen das Bild; sie schauten mit Verachtung auf die wilden Barbaren des Waldes herab. Es wäre etwas für den Historienmaler gewesen; ich dachte an unseren Freund D. [Dittenberger, Johann Gustav] in Wien. (847–48)

Barely human, these forest-dwelling Gypsies are stationed on the lowest rung of the racial and cultural scale. Unkempt, half-naked, uninhibited yet naive, the aggressively piercing scavengers' eyes of the (sarcastically so termed) Egyptian guests have led them into trouble with the militia for thieving. Even the coarse Croatians despise them. At best they are the subject for an interesting genre painting[16] — or a *feuilleton*, one might add — under the German gaze. In Agram itself, as we know from Liebich, there still persisted Gypsy slavery at this epoch.[17]

By 1862 Hebbel's negative fascination with the Gypsies had only intensified. A still more ferocious literary genre painting from the *Wiener Briefe* of that year presents the Romanies in the full bloom of Orientalist realization as naive, kleptomaniac and irrational savages, vengefully incapable, when it fails to serve their interest, of comprehending the distinction between right and wrong:

> In einer Völkerpolyglotte, wie Oesterreich, bieten auch die Gerichtssäle manche Seltenheit dar. So stand kürzlich eine ganze Zigeunerbande, Männer, Weiber und Kinder, vor dem Tribunal. Sie wurde des Diebstahls angeklagt und zwar des Diebstahls an baarem Gelde, nicht, wie gewöhnlich, an Victualien, Wäsche und ähnlichen Dingen, die der 'Aegypter' sonst mitgehen zu heißen pflegt. Alle waren natürlich im Läugnen stark und suchten die sie am meisten gravirende Anwesenheit in dem Dorfe, wo die That begangen war, dadurch zu motivieren, daß sie erklärten, sie hätten sich von da nach einem benachbarten Wallfahrtsort begeben und dort — beichten und ihre Andacht verrichten wollen. Das half ihnen nichts, denn sie waren bei der Arretierung auf einem dem Wallfahrtsort ganz entgegengesetzten Wege betroffen worden, und sie wurden also verurtheilt. Nun aber ergab sich eine Szene, die auf erschütternde Weise zeigte, daß diese Menschen der Natur wirklich noch unendlich viel näher stehen, wie der kalte Abendländer. Die Männer heulten und tobten durch einander, wie Wellen und Winde, einige Weiber stürzten, nachdem sie den in ungarischer Sprache verkündeten Spruch gehört hatten, in schwerer Ohnmacht, wie todt, zu Boden, andere zerrauften sich die Haare und zerstießen sich den Kopf an der Wand, ein Paar andere hielten dem Gerichtshof ihre Kinder entgegen, eine Alte aber rief einem Zeugen mit der Poesie der Verzweiflung in dämonischer Erhabenheit mit wild flatternden Locken hinzu: 'Der Wind soll Dir nachbrausen und jedes Deiner Gebeine in eine andere Hölle tragen, Du sollst mit Blindheit und Wahnsinn geschlagen sein, Du und Deine Kindeskinder, damit Du sie anders siehst und hörst, als sie sind, weil Du heute anders gesprochen, als gehört und gesehen hast.'[18]

It is notable that in each of these pleasingly horrible genre scenes Hebbel not only foregrounds the alleged Egyptian provenance of the Romanies, but also, despite his brutal realism, concludes with the role of the Romanies in art of some description: in the former case with a hint that they present a suitable motif for Dittenberger, in the latter by emphasizing both the Romanies' helpless (traditionally pseudo-Christian) lie to the court and the amusingly sublime, visionary curse of the aged Gypsy matriarch. As we note from the presence of quotation marks around the attribute of Egyptian origin, Hebbel well knows this to be a fiction. However, he has good reason for maintaining that fiction, for Egypt has a special place in Hebbel's personal aesthetic mythology. If all good art for Hebbel as a nineteenth-century thinker serves the end of 'life',[19] then Egyptian art, with its constant focus on the cult of death, and which had become so fashionable in the cultural discourse of the mid-nineteenth century,[20] is for Hebbel the anti-type of good art. His early travelogue of Munich for Cotta's *Morgenblatt* documents with a shiver the contrast in Klenze's new *Glyptothek* between the life-serving classical art of antiquity, Thorwaldsen, and Canova, and the death-serving stones of ancient Egypt.[21] The Gypsy matriarch's death curse exemplifies disturbingly the 'Egyptian' tendency of Romany poesy.

It is thus no surprise that Hebbel's final utterance on the Gypsies, also from 1862, issues an anathema on Gypsy art which is centred on its mythical emblem, the violin, and possibly occasioned by the recent publication of Liszt's *Die Zigeuner und ihre Musik in Ungarn*. Hebbel's laconically titled poem 'Aus dem Wiener Prater'[22] — this time acknowledging the Indian origin of the Gypsies — consists in five quatrains savagely denouncing Gypsy music as daemonic and death-dealing. The writer hears 'die geigenden Zigeuner' on the Prater. Their wild and ever-quickening music, unchanged since it was first played by the Ganges a thousand years since, drives Hungarian Hussars and German girls alike into a frenzied, subject-threatening Bacchanalian dance. But soon, the writer warns, a string will break and a heart burst: 'Denn der Tod ist im Geleite | Einer so dämonschen Lust'. In fact both 'Instrument und Musikanten | Sind dem Untergang geweiht' and nothing will remain of the entire group, musicians and dancers, save the 'dunkle Zauber-Weise' which has driven them into the abyss. As the association of Gypsy music with the siren song suggests, this drastic tirade is both a verdict on the (non-existent) future of the race, a symbolic denunciation of the *Zigeunerromantik* aesthetic which consigns the fiddle to the depths of hell, and perhaps too the index of latent anti-Gypsyism in a substratum of Hebbel's realism. Tellingly, we recall how Hebbel was amused by the 'Leben' embodied in the fake Gypsies in the performances of Wolff's *Preciosa* at Munich in 1838 and Hamburg in 1840.[23]

'. . . eine Art Heimatsberechtigung': Raabe's *Die Kinder von Finkenrode*

In his third novel, *Die Kinder von Finkenrode* (1859),[24] which of course features a band of Gypsies, Wilhelm Raabe (1831–1910) too — although with markedly different intent — consigns a Gypsy violin to the grave. To say that Raabe too is neglected is to voice a commonplace.[25] Yet he published some sixty-nine novels and stories, and, if he experienced periods of neglect during his lifetime, he was also, particularly at the outset, one of the most successful writers of the realist epoch.[26] Two works reveal Raabe's chief, constantly recurring themes: sharply realistic observation of his age in the service of an equally sharp critique of the complacent German bourgeois mentality. His first and most commercially successful novel, *Die Chronik der Sperlingsgasse* (1857), combines late-Romantic, humoristic narration (by an aged observer from a high garret window) with pioneering observation from this vantage-point of proletarian life in big-city Berlin. Its analysis of new formations of metropolitan life as indicators of socio-economic change may have a sentimentalist structure, but the *Chronik* is also, precisely on that account, a realistic novel of its time, a *Zeitroman*, of the same kind (if not necessarily of the same stature) as work by Dickens or Balzac.[27] Raabe's next best-known work is the novel *Stopfkuchen* (1890) from the penultimate phase of his career. This records the attempt of a German colonist from south-west Africa to make narrative sense of the various kinds of shocking, ethically decentring disillusionment which he has just experienced at the hands of his eponymous former schoolfriend Stopfkuchen on a brief visit home. This unsparing critique of the smugly materialist, philistine German bourgeois mentality exposes the values of the German *Heimat*, pillar of its narrator's self-understanding, not only to the temporal contrast of then and now but also to the cultural contrast of colonial life.[28] In this *Stopfkuchen* reveals Raabe's long-standing interest in problems of interculturality — something most notably exemplified in perhaps his next most significant achievement, *Abu Telfan* (1869), another *Heimkehrerroman*[29] which savagely deconstructs the then fashionable exotic novel by discovering the exotic and the barbaric not in West Africans but in nineteenth-century Germans.[30] *Abu Telfan* no less than the later *Stopfkuchen* shows how the self-consciously subjective, humoristic narration, appropriated by Raabe from his favourite authors Sterne, Hoffmann, Jean Paul, and Thackeray, is placed at the service of a realist cognitive interest right at the start of Germany's colonial expansion.

Die Kinder von Finkenrode contains elements which both remind us of the *Chronik* and point forward to the intercultural critique of *Abu Telfan* and *Stopfkuchen*. Another *Heimkehrerroman*, it tells the first-person tale of two months in the life of 29-year-old Max Bösenberg (*Kinder*, 7), as he returns from his post in metropolitan Berlin in 1857–58 to his roots in the provincial town of Finkenrode, in order to claim an unexpected inheritance. In Finkenrode Bösenberg too, like his fellow *Heimkehrer* Hagebucher (from *Abu Telfan*) and Eduard (from *Stopfkuchen*),[31] encounters an exotic culture, in this case the Gypsies. But first some exposition of the domestic context in which Raabe sets this intercultural encounter.

In a sense this *Heimkehrerroman* could also be described as a *Künstlerroman*, since Bösenberg is a writer, a sentimental novelist slightly known for his novel 'Heiratsgedanken' and his collection of 'fromme Liebeslieder' (*Kinder*, 19). But although the novel has something to say about literature of various kinds, it is focused less on Bösenberg's literary development than on the changes in his self-understanding produced by the encounter, after a gap of twenty years (25, 79–80) in the big city, with the small country town that moulded his personality. Bösenberg in fact is less a literary artist than a 'Vertreter der deutschen Journalistik' (26), a staff writer on a Berlin journal of the progressive tendency rejoicing in the name *Das Chamäleon* (7). Of course the name of the journal reveals something significant about the mentality of its employee. As the chameleon takes on the colour of its changing environment and leaves doubt as to its original hue, so too does Bösenberg's consciousness. Time is the key to this. We meet Bösenberg at his grubby desk, registering nothing but the passing of time, on the day after his birthday, noting gloomily for the *Chamäleon* that the number of deaths in the past week's official statistics outweighs the births and, like his editor Weitenweber, dwelling on thoughts of his own demise (7–8), as under the ceaseless rain of wintry Berlin the 'ununterbrochene Strom der Bevölkerung' (8; compare 11, 33–34) passes anonymously by his grimy window (211). Bösenberg, then, is the servant rather the master of time, caught up at the end of his youth in the modern mode of experience: registering time's constant flow of change through the pages of the fashionable journal, rather than firmly rooted in something other than transience, an intransitive observer of mass metropolitan life, as unrealized as the people whose statistical coming and going he writes about — all like him defined by the battle for survival (a recurrent, here probably more anti-capitalist than Darwinian undertone) (15). His yearning to escape from this is of course hinted at in the titles of his slightly known literary works, and escape from this is precisely what Finkenrode seems to offer when (as so often in fiction) a letter, revealing that he is the new owner of his uncle's house in his home town, trips the mainspring of the action. As he himself says on the long journey from Berlin to Finkenrode: 'Zu Hause! Wo ist mein Haus? Wo ist meine Heimat? . . . Mein Blick verlor sich in dem dichter gewordenen Nebel draußen' (14–15). Thus it is clear that *Die Kinder von Finkenrode* establishes the scheme later followed with variations in *Stopfkuchen*. The chronotope of the novel, *Heimat*, that mythical place which is the locus of the German psyche, is explored by being measured against that which it is not, in this case the metropolis, locus of nineteenth-century progress — but also, as we shall see, the exotic other of the Gypsies.

In his home town Bösenberg endures a process of disillusionment. As he settles into his inheritance Bösenberg's mood is at first tinged by a smooth metropolitan disdain for provinciality, which he associates with 'Backwoodsmen' (22). But above all Finkenrode is less a reality than the screen onto which he unconsciously projects hope for the establishment of fixity in his oceanic existence. It is a hope born of genuinely idyllic childhood memories, especially of Sidonie Fasterling (34, 44) and Cäcilie Willbrand (51, 71, 79–81, 93, 124–25). But it is also, as the titles 'Heiratsgedanken' and 'fromme Liebeslieder' suggest, a hope which springs from the epigonal Romanticism of his consciousness. It is no coincidence that Bösenberg, alluding of course to Eichendorff, sees himself as a 'Taugenichts von Literaten' (32); nor that, as he passes from the endless flat north German plain to the beautiful, heavily wooded mountain landscape of Finkenrode (which is based on Raabe's home town Holzminden, west of the Harz), as Bösenberg observes, 'von Viertelstunde zu Viertelstunde wurde die Landschaft romantischer' (24); nor that, as he sits dreamily in his railway compartment during the night journey, his attention is seized by a 'Jungfrau mir gegenüber', who 'hatte den grünen Schleier über ihr schönes Gesicht fallen lassen und das Haupt gesenkt wie eine schlafende Blume — um ein fadenscheiniges Gleichnis wieder hervorzusuchen' (14) — an obvious allusion to the mythology which associates predestined love with rediscovered origin in Novalis's *Lehrlinge zu Sais* and *Heinrich von Ofterdingen*, and which even Bösenberg finds hackneyed. She nonetheless later comes into his mind (146),[32] when, slowly ceasing to feel an 'Eindringling' (63), he finds himself against his expectation increasingly at home (82, 140) in Finkenrode, and decides that he has fallen in love with Cäcilie (144). The muse-like Cäcilie thus provokes a crisis in his life:

> Ach, ich brachte doch aus meinem früheren Leben gar wenig mit, was mir jetzt als Gegengewicht gegen meine jetzige Seelenstimmung hätte dienen können. Was konnte ich ihr bieten für ihre reine, fleckenlose Seele? Ich — bedeckt

> mit dem Staub und Schweiß des Kampfes, mit aller Welt Jämmerlichkeit und Erbärmlichkeit?
>
> Was hatte ich getan im Leben, um ihrer würdig zu sein? War nicht alles Tand und Torheit, was ich geschafft hatte? War nicht alles hohle Lüge, alles Phrase? Wo hatte ich je männlich der Wahrheit ins Auge geschaut? Ich, geleitet von der Meinung des Tages; ich, scheu vor jeder höchsten Konsequenz seitwärts schleichend. (143–44)

As a result, he hopes for some unspecified process of maturation. 'Unaufhaltsam', he feels as a new year approaches, 'ging meine moralische Häutung vor sich' (153); he feels wrapped in a chrysalis from which, when he declares his love to Cäcilie, something new will emerge (153). Alas, before the chance comes Bösenberg of course discovers that her heart is already promised to another childhood friend of his, Arnold Rohwold, now Pastor in nearby Rulingen (211–12): 'O süßes, seliges Heimatsgefühl', he sighs, 'was kann dem, welcher dich verloren hat, Ersatz dafür geben?' (208). Wiser only by the measure of his disillusion, Bösenberg returns after two weeks in bed to his desk at the *Chamäleon* in Berlin, where it is still raining, the competition of the rival (unenlightened) journal *Der Halbmond* is still as fierce as ever, and only the incomprehensible cries of the throng outside his blind office windows can be discerned (218–19): 'Mir war wirklich weh, sehr weh ums Herz . . . mir war sehr übel zumute! — ' (219).

Now this novel clearly inhabits a late-Romantic narrative mode. Quite apart from the mannered, digressive movement of the plot, which explores the narrator's subjectivity just as much as the objective world of Finkenrode, Raabe's second novel features a number of self-reflexive devices unmistakably in the Romantic tradition. The first edition of *Die Kinder von Finkenrode* purported according to its title-page to have been written by 'Jacob Corvinus' (Latin: *corvinus* — Rabe), and this same Corvinus turns up at the end of the novel in the offices of the *Chamäleon*, giving broad hints (211, 218–19) that he will be conveying Bösenberg's tragicomic story to the public. Back in the *Heimat*, Bösenberg is moreover surprised to discover that in addition to the house and a housekeeper Renate, he has inherited a tame raven, inevitably also called 'Jakob' (64) — 'mehr als eine bloße Tierseele leuchtete aus seinen schwarzen Augen' (143) — given to issuing Delphic advice in three languages. All of this, sometimes slightly leaden, reflexivity indicates, if we think of similar devices in Brentano, Hoffmann, and Jean Paul, just how much of the young Wilhelm Raabe is contained in Max Bösenberg. But of course one chief point of the novel is anti-Romantic. If Bösenberg learns anything from his experience, it is that his callow Romanticism blinds him as much as the opaque windows of his Berlin newspaper office to the reality of the *Heimat*. One last reflexive device seals this view: the hyper-Romantic Günter Wallinger, a fiddler and *Stadmusikant*, who went out into the world to do great things in music, returned a failure to Finkenrode (60), fell hopelessly in love, and became deranged when the object of his yearning proved unreachable. Wallinger's fate — he dies at the end of the novel — of course prefigures one possible outcome for Bösenberg.

That apart, what Bösenberg actually experiences in his *Heimat* is remarkable. If Berlin is all motion and change, Finkenrode is all philistine, changeless continuity. This rural community of 7,000–8,000 souls has, we are told, existed harmlessly, embedded in the ancient German forest by the Weser, at least since the age of the Cheruscans (27–28), and the descendants of the chieftains Werimar and Mangingeld, of the Thuringians and Saxons who once disputed the terrain, live there to this day as the tailor Bremer and the blacksmith Manegold (29). (A Käthchen Manegold is one of the chief bit players in the Finkenrode plot.) Some of those who live there once achieved things in the world outside. Hauptmann Fasterling, Sidonie's father, for example, is an old *Franzosenfresser* (41–42), who however lives permanently entrenched in the glorious past. A kindly Philistine who first appears in the signature nightgown (40), he, like every other *Bürger* of Finkenrode (49–50, 70), reads the benighted *Halbmond* and opposes the democratic tendencies of Bösenberg's 'gottlose[r] Satansbande' (41) of journalists. All that Max really does during his stay in Finkenrode apart from exploring his ramshackle house is to make his dutiful round of visits to old friends and relatives, the Fasterlings and the Willbrands, the Wachtels, and finally, in a scene which contrasts with the synchronous funeral of the mad Romantic *Stadtmusikus* Wallinger, to Käthchen Manegold, now married and living in a house called 'Im Himmelreich' (83) in the forest hamlet of Rulingen, for the christening of her newborn child. Apart, then, from social rituals and the archetypal events of love, birth and death, virtually nothing happens in Finkenrode. Max reflects: 'Zwanzig Jahre mit ihren Revolutionen und Schlachten waren über die Welt dahingezogen; Städte waren zerstört, Länder verwüstet; in diesem kleinen, engen Raum war alles geblieben, wie es war; nur mehr und mehr hatten sich die Bewohner auf diesem vergessenen Erdenfleck eingenistet' (79–80). This lovingly portrayed nullity of Finkenrode and all that lives in it is the reason for one of the novel's sardonic and teasing mottos, from Propertius: 'Maxima de nihilo nascitur historia'.

The chief content, then, of Max Bösenberg's journey back home and back into himself, is the transition from the modern world of progress to the old world of tradition, from one characteristic mode of temporal experience to another, dynamism and stasis, both in their own way (for him at least) empty. It is a primal scene of the German nineteenth century. This is symbolized most powerfully by the means of transport Bösenberg uses on his circular journey from Berlin to Finkenrode and back again, in particular that signature feature of the nineteenth-century novels, the railway.[33] It is not chance that Finkenrode, even in 1857, remains unconnected to the German railway system. The industrial revolution may have come later in Germany than Britain or France, but when it came, and with it the industrialization of travel through the railway, it came with a vengeance. The first train in Germany of course ran between Nuremberg and Fürth only in 1835, but by 1871 there were 18,600 km of track in the network, by 1875 27,800 km, and by 1914 no less than 60,000 km.[34] With its overwhelming technologization, the ensuing denaturalization, dehumanization, and commodification of the experience of travel, with its characteristic annihilation of the received modes of experience of time and space, the railway of course rapidly came to symbolize the nineteenth century as an age of unstoppably disorientating progress.[35] In *Die Kinder von Finkenrode* Raabe carefully stylizes the shift in texture of experience from the big city to the home town through the shift in means of travel as Bösenberg experiences them, in order to position the hero's mentality in precisely this context. He begins needless to say in the train by emphasizing in an apt kaleidoscopic metaphor the characteristic subjective disorientation of perception,[36] the inability to focus on what is near, caused by the great speed of the travelling machine and the framing of the landscape through the window:

> Die schwarzen Föhrenwälder, bald näher heranziehend, bald in der Ferne zurücktretend, die weit in die Ebene hineinfunkelnden Wasserflächen der großen Havelseen, die Lichter in den vorbeifliegenden einsamen Häusern, Dörfern und größern Ortschaften glitten vorüber wie in einer Zauberlaterne, und alles paßte gänzlich zu der Stimmung, in welche ich seit Dunkelwerden hineingeraten war. (13)

Only when the train has magically dissolved the distance between the big city and the Harz does Bösenberg, descending at midnight in Sauingen (probably Kreiensen, still today a railway junction), encounter the reality of the province. Finkenrode itself, he discovers to his horror, is still not connected to the railway and lies four hours hence by horse-drawn coach — 'ein vierräderiger, etwas räudiger Kasten' (23) — which only departs in the morning (17). If the train journey occupied three pages of subjective narration (13–16), the next stage, shorter as it is, occupies eight (23–31). At least the landscape can be enjoyed in the pre-industrialized mode, and of course Raabe takes this opportunity to set the idyllic scene of Finkenrode and environs. But the 'räudiger Kasten' is not the last travelling variation. There is an accident, the coach tips over, and Bösenberg makes the rest of the journey as nature intended: on foot. From the top of the mountain he can at last, naturalistically, observe his home town, by contrast to the opaque window of his Berlin office, the kaleidoscopic train window, or the blind window of the capsized coach: 'Ein Blick überflog meine ganze Kindheitsgegend' (27).

But if all this indicates that Max Bösenberg, modern German in search of a fixed identity, must recognize that the *Heimat* is not for him, and must return to the big city (even if that is not necessarily for him either), he does take something back with him from his encounter with the otherness of home. Bösenberg, it should be recalled, had always thought of himself as a 'Taugenichts von Literaten' (32; compare Fasterling, 40), and like the Taugenichts foregrounded the notion of wandering in his self-understanding. When he pitches up in Sauingen, he is the 'vagabundu[s] litterariu[s] Max Bösenberg' (22), and when he encounters another returning child of Finkenrode, Alexander Mietze (who has designs on Sidonie), the ex-actor Mietze characterizes the pair as '[z]wei Vagabunden, zwei Seefahrer, ans Land gestiegen aus den Wogen der süßen Liederlichkeit' (36). The Finkenrode Philistines may well be a strange encounter for Bösenberg. But the most powerful cultural encounter he has in Finkenrode stands under this sign of vagabondage, and relates not only to the paradoxical strangeness of the German heartland he has returned to, but also to strangers *in* this German heartland: the Gypsies. When he is to meet the local band of Gypsies through Mietze and their protectress Sidonie we hear: 'wahrhaftig, ich fühle mich ganz kollegialisch zu den Vagabunden hingezogen' (104). Indeed, he had played with them in his youth (107). The Gypsies, then, have a role to play in Bösenberg's exploration of his identity as a German in the nineteenth century. As part of his *Heimat* they define him in the system of cultural co-ordinates through their difference — and affinity.

So let us now look at how Raabe presents the Gypsies of Finkenrode. He presents them in a strategic variety of modes. One is of course the Romantic tradition. The Gypsies of the family Nadra are associated first, if not foremost, with the mad Romantic fiddler Wallinger. Wallinger, it should be recalled, is one of the chief mirrorings of Bösenberg's personality in Finkenrode. Cäcilie (unsurprisingly, given her name, after the patron saint of music) is Wallinger's special friend, indeed the only one who understands him (60, 80–81). Clearly a highly talented musician (indeed, as one would expect in Finkenrode, the descendant of a dynasty of musicians, 59–60, 130), Wallinger's life story reads as if Hoffmann had invented him. His Romantic striving for ideal beauty has resulted in an excess of Romantic fantasy over reality. He has fallen in love with a Melusine-like fantasy muse during a moonlit expedition into the Finkenrode forest (132–33) and, tragically, abandoned his flesh-and-blood beloved Anna Ludewig. This representative and victim of Romanticism thus leaves Finkenrode for the wide world (130) in search of his muse (170), only to return decades later a failure, his blond hair whitened and his senses dulled, like Tannhäuser from the 'Zauberberg' (134). This, then, is the Wallinger who now ekes out a living with music lessons and village dances. Significantly for our interest, he lodges with the Gypsy family Nadra, and presents his father's best violin (130, 132) on his deathbed to Martin Nadra (197), the *paterfamilias* of the small Gypsy tribe. Thus the Gypsies are presented as appointed keepers of the Romantic inheritance. They share Max Bösenberg's mentality, already associated with Wallinger, to this extent. With this carefully positioned link between Gypsies, the emblematic violin, and Romanticism Raabe thus at one level, with his habitual, faintly rogueish literary self-consciousness, cites the familiar discourse of *Zigeunerromantik*, the established mode of presence of the Gypsies in the German literary mind.

Another prime example of Raabe's cited *Zigeunerromantik* is Marianne Nadra, Martin's daughter. We meet her during one of the miniature adventures which pass for history in Finkenrode, when Sidonie and Cäcilie are caught by a sudden downpour in the Romantic forest (114). Looking 'sehr hübsch, wild und romantisch' (115–16) with her glistening black hair and clinging wet clothes, it is she who discovers the young women in their rudimentary shelter, and helps to guide them home.[37] But perhaps the best instance of the Gypsy stereotype is the aged matriarch, grandmother Janna Nadra. Janna's domain is Gypsy magic. On this same forest adventure it is Janna, at the head of the tribe's womenfolk, who speaks a Gypsy 'Wettersegen' (117) against the rainstorm, a piece of intercultural *Volkspoesie* which Sidonie — in Raabe's gesture to the received topos of *Die mehreren Wehmüller* and *Immensee* — has carefully written down. It is reproduced in full. Janna is full of folklore and oral history, knows charms against animal and human illnesses, and possesses a black hen which intuits changes in the weather (117). She knows both of the 'Wassersegen' (119) against the flooded local river the Hurlebach and a charm that would ease Wallinger's passing (157). Janna is clearly in the tradition of mystically awesome Gypsy matriarchs as portrayed first by Scott in *Guy Mannering*

(1815) in the shape of Meg Merrilies.[38] Finally under this head, the depiction of the Gypsy household also belongs somewhat in the Romantic tradition, rather in the style of a mannered *Genrebild* after Jacques Callot (or perhaps Dittenberger). The Nadras are a 'wunderbare[s] Volk' (87), who possess a bear, two monkeys, two donkeys, three goats, and countless children (87), members of a household described as 'wimmelnd [. . .], kreischend [. . .], quieckend [. . .], brummend [. . .]' (87): 'die tollste Vagabunden-Wirtschaft', says Bösenberg later, 'die ich jemals gesehen habe. Ein Gewimmel von Menschen und Tieren erfüllte die unteren Räume mit einem verworrenen Getöse. Ein Säugling schrie hinter einer Tür, und eine Mädchenstimme sang ein halbwildes Wiegenlied' (156).

That said, there is more to Raabe's image of the Gypsies than this elaborately foregrounded montage of *Zigeunerromantik*. For Raabe, despite presenting the Nadras in the conventional manner as nomads — 'eine [. . .] diese[r] wandernden Familien' (87) — also notably foregrounds the Gypsies' *settled* domestic arrangements. His Gypsies, despite their undoubted ethnic authenticity, do not in fact wander. They live in a *fixed* domicile, the chaotic hovel we have just read of, which is situated at the opposite end of the little town to the well-off Fasterlings, 'wo sich die ärmlichsten Häuser und Hütten dicht neben dem jetzt verschneieten Kirchhof gesammelt hatten' (156). Raabe's Gypsies, then, are in a sense not only exotic outsiders, but also *of* Finkenrode — albeit domiciled next to the place of death. But they do not live thus by choice. They do so because, as Raabe carefully notes, they have been compelled, 'durch unsere jetzigen polizierteren Verhältnisse [. . .], irgendwo eine Art Heimatsberechtigung zu erlangen' (87) — forced to settle, in short, by the police measures of the *state* (Braunschweig, presumably) with which we are familiar, and to obtain something which is not quite as official or unquestionable as that which Bösenberg — the aboriginal descended down the generations from the Cheruscans, Thuringians, and Saxons — automatically possesses, merely '*eine Art* [my emphasis] Heimatsberechtigung'. Thus Raabe, positioning his Gypsies uncomfortably between compulsory settlement and forced acculturation on the one hand and compulsory eviction on the other, presents a very different version of the reality of Gypsy life in mid-nineteenth-century Germany from that in Storm, Stifter, and their ilk. This realism, so far as I can tell, is a first and indeed unique in German nineteenth-century literature. Its major significance is of course as the indicator of a fundamental subversion of the cited Romantic discourse.

The truth is that Raabe's compulsorily settled Gypsies, despite possessing 'eine Art Heimatsberechtigung', and despite Bösenberg's affinity with them, are anything but at home in Finkenrode. They are in permanent conflict over petty disputes with their neighbours and the law (87). Of course the law always takes against them, for example when their dog Rollo allegedly steals a chicken, loses his tail, and ends up dead himself (107–08). After father Martin and mother Lena have taken justice into their own hands over the Rollo incident (104–06), Bösenberg is delegated by Sidonie to negotiate their release from the town dungeon — as we know from Liebich, the Gypsy's worst nightmare.[39] But this act of solidarity merely exposes the urbanized Gypsies' abjection in their adopted home. When as their 'erklärte Beschützerin' (87) Sidonie categorizes the Nadras as incapable of taking care of themselves, she is merely following the received anthropological tradition:

> 'Ach, was für Not mir das gelbe Volk macht!' rief Sidonie altklug. 'Wie Kinder sind sie! Wie Kinder lachen sie, weinen sie, sind sie boshaft, zänkisch, diebisch — artig und unartig. Das sind seltsame Menschen. Hätten sie uns nicht, den Papa, die Cäcilie und mich, es ginge ihnen gewiß sehr übel.' (111)

The Finkenrode Romanies repay this protection with absolute loyalty, promising to pass through fire and water for Sidonie (108) — a promise confirmed by the tale of the forest rainstorm and the raging Hurlebach (111–15).

But in the age of progress things are changing even for the abject *Naturvolk*. Unlike that of Meg Merrilies, grandmother Janna Nadra's Gypsy magic, her weather, water, and death charms, either do not work or have been irretrievably lost, because the only person who knew them — her husband Friedel — has been hanged many years since under the old legal dispensation (119, 157), which disappeared with the Holy Roman Empire. The old order, then, when there still existed Romanticism, magic, and judicial murder, has passed. Raabe's Gypsies live in the disenchanted world of the modern state. Their subjection to the state, enforced settlement, and compulsory labour have, as this exchange between Sidonie and Janna in the forest suggests, resulted in a bybrid mode of existence which grimly travesties their former way of life:

> 'Wo sind denn eure Männer?' fragte ich, und die Frau Nadra wies nach Westen. — 'Sie graben an der Eisenbahn, der Landrat hat sie hingeschickt. Wir mit den Tieren liegen im Dorf Rulingen und helfen den Bauern im Feld, und die Kinder müssen da in die Schule gehen, sonst nimmt man sie uns weg.' — ''s ist nicht mehr wie in alter Zeit' — sagte die Großmutter kopfschüttelnd: 'O je, die Männer graben, die Weiber sitzen und spinnen, die Kinder lernen die schwarzen Zeichen! Seit das römisch' Reich all geworden ist, ist's aus mit der freien Herrlichkeit des fahrenden Volkes.' (118)

The travelling people of yore live as enforced settlers, but work where? — building the railway that will soon, inevitably, link Finkenrode to Sauingen, Berlin, and the nineteenth century. They are assimilated, then, in a telling reversal, into the same symbolic order of modernized, industrialized, temporalized — and disorientated — experience as that of their fellow contemporary vagabond Max Bösenberg.

But if Raabe's Gypsies of the industrial age achieve a kind of hybrid form of labour, partly in the new, partly in the old style, the result at the level of cultural integration — as the forced assimilation of the children into the lettered culture indicates — leaves much to be desired. They do, as Janna's carefully recorded 'Wettersegen' reveals, attempt to construct a kind of hybrid compromise which enunciates a negotiation between Gypsy and *gadjo* culture:

> Jesus Christus, ich bitte dich! Jesus Christus, Sohn Gottes, laß uns nicht vergehen!
> Buro, Baro, Kiru, Ofel, Jop! — Mausa, Coma, Broit, Zorobam —
> Haltet den Wind! Haltet den Wind!
> Jungfrau Maria, sei uns gnädig! Sei uns gnädig!
> Halt den Blitz! Halt den Blitz!
> Jesus, Maria, Lukas, Markus, Matthäus und Johannes, legt Ketten an den

> Donner! Kaspar, Melchior, Balthasar —
> Schützet uns! Schützet uns! (117)

'Welch ein tolles Gemisch von Heidentum und Christentum!' (117), comments Bösenberg aptly on what is in fact a fake (even the attempt at *Romanes* in the second line).[40] But its theological eclecticism, in intention an irenic aggregate of Christian and Romany divinities,[41] typifies their chameleon-like effort to take on something of the colour of their cultural environment in the cause of acceptance. One might also mention here that the father, Martin,[42] actually bears the name of the patron saint of Finkenrode (31). Less decorously, at the level of animal miscegenation, it turns out that Rollo is, or was, the father of the Fasterlings' *gadjo* dog Waddel, whom he conceived with the pet dog of his later nemesis, Pastor Wachtel (108).[43]

However, Raabe sets this well-intentioned if limp, modernized, and industrialized hybridity in a sharply critical context which uncannily anticipates today's post-colonial discourse. For when we first meet the Gypsies, it is not the entire spectacular family we encounter, but only the sixteen-year-old son of Martin and Lena, Anton Nadra, who is working as Alexander Mietze's servant. He does not however feature as 'Anton'. '"Caliban! Caliban!"' (87; compare 94, 120) is Mietze's preferred, only semi-humorous appellation for his servant, and poor Anton is indeed presented just like the servant of Prospero from Shakespeare's *Tempest*, as a grotesque figure, 'halb Mensch, halb Gnom' (87), scurrying to do his master's every bidding.[44] Thus Raabe sets his portrayal of Gypsies in the German *Heimat* self-consciously in a colonialist or, better, anti-colonialist perspective. For *The Tempest*[45] is not only the story of the banishment of the Duke of Milan, it is also the story of the colonial expropriation of their island by the magician Prospero from its original owners, the witch Sycorax and her monstrous son Caliban.[46] Caliban is not only monstrous, and in this the epitome of repellently un-Western physical otherness, he is also the epitome of impotent aboriginal resentment of the colonizer's injustice. Compelled to learn the language of the colonizer, he embaces its cognitive superiority, but can only impotently curse his master in it, as Prospero exploits the island's natural resources through the magic which conquered that of Sycorax and resides in his printed books (*Tempest*, 18–19). Relegated to his cave because of an attempt on Miranda's virtue (19), the '[s]ervant-monster' (47) Caliban can only intrigue pathetically to serve still more colonizers (Trinculo and Stephano) so as to regain something of his natural inheritance. But above all, this Eurocentric play presents Caliban as an irredeemable creature of nature. To Prospero, master of technology and creator of the 'brave new world' (72), he is '[a] devil, a born devil, on whose nature | Nurture can never stick: on whom my pains | Humanely taken, all, all lost, quite lost' (63). Raabe, it is clear, critically appropriates this colonial perspective for his account of the Gypsy 'Heimatsberechtigung'. Of course here the *Gypsies* are at one level the intruders in the *German* homeland. But as we see in Anton's servile relationship to his Prospero, in the abject servility of the Gypsies towards Sidonie, and in Martin Nadra's brisk 'zu Diensten der ganzen Welt!' (*Kinder*, 106), the resultant abjection of the infantilized Oriental other is at another level clearly the result of an *internal* colonization. The Saxons and Thuringians who have coexisted peacefully for two thousand years in the homeland they in truth expropriated from the original settlers, the Cheruscans

(27–29), will not accord the Gypsies — *themselves* true children of Finkenrode — an equal status. Sidonie and Alexander Mietze, German children of Finkenrode, are innocently complicit in this abjection — as too, despite his childhood friendship with the Gypsies, is Max Bösenberg.[47] In this systematic undermining of apparently inherited rights to place and identity, and in its subversive reference back to the 'original' age of Hermann, Raabe's novel is intensely reminiscent of Immermann's pessimistic, or sceptical, *Epigonen*. If we consider for a moment one of our main cognitive interests, the Gypsy presence in German nineteenth-century literature in the context of the Romany Holocaust, it is also clear that Raabe's presentation of the Romanies in *Die Kinder von Finkenrode* in the horizon of Shakespeare's troubled colonialism belongs in a hospitable, deeply liberal, anti-nationalist, and anti-racist tradition.

Raabe's novel does not, however, offer endings (still less happy or satisfactory ones) to all the discourses intertwined in this complex set, for to leave tensions unresolved is the signature of this sardonic writer. Vulgar Romanticism, as exemplified by the *Zigeunerromantik* and Max's naive utopianism, certainly dies the death. As we heard, the novel ends on an appropriately mixed note of birth and death, the birth and christening of Käthchen's child, the death and funeral of Wallinger. Wallinger achieves an epiphanic moment of redemption when, in a scene of great ironic pathos, he mistakes Cäcilie for his lost muse and attains a kind of lucidity (193–97). But at the funeral Weitenweber, Max's hard-boiled editor, ensures at the last moment that the violin is *not* in fact passed on to its appointed inheritor, Martin. The symbolically charged instrument is instead consigned to the grave (218) in the churchyard next to the Gypsies' hovel, unambiguous indicator of Raabe's verdict on *Zigeunerromantik*. Max, however, experiences no closure after his encounter with the strangeness of home.[48] His last words — 'mir war sehr übel zumute!' (219) — reveal division unhealed even after the process of writing, and this failure surely makes him a pristine example of the transcendentally homeless nineteenth-century hero, a German who is also, in a higher sense, a Gypsy. Twice he tries to recognize himself in the mirror of Finkenrode's children, once with the German natives, once with the transient Romany settlers. But both attempts at self-identification are dissolved in the acid of Raabe's anti-Romanticism and anti-colonialism. The settled Philistines do not measure up to Max's Romantic projection of them. The transient Gypsies, forced to settle, reveal both the hard, proto-colonial character of the real German *Heimat* and, most disappointingly, the illusory nature of the vagrant idyll under modern conditions. There is no visible alternative on his horizon, no sign of that utopian community which Jeffrey Sammons has argued to be the constant focus of Raabe's fiction.[49] It comes as no surprise, then, twenty years after the end of *Die Kinder von Finkenrode*, to find Max *still*, characteristically, sitting in the train between Berlin and Finkenrode, in Raabe's novel *Alte Nester* (1878)[50] — Raabe tended to think of all his works as forming one great macro-text. He may be part of another story, but he is still poised between the same polarities. Resigned, he now lives in his house in Finkenrode, has put on a lot of weight, and become a *Stadtrat* and a Philistine.[51] He may now both have a house and live in it. But he is still homeless. A bachelor even after all these years, he still has a picture of a woman and child on his wall, and still oscillates between the province and the metropolis on the railway which now reaches Finkenrode, built by the Gypsies and inscribed with their symbolic potential, as the last trace of the alternative in modern Germany.

'. . . ich habe keinen Taufschein und keinen Heimatschein': Keller's *Romeo und Julia auf dem Dorfe*[52]

In his near-contemporary novella *Romeo und Julia auf dem Dorfe* (1856), one of ten in the masterly cycle *Die Leute von Seldwyla*, Gottfried Keller offers the Swiss pendant to *Die Kinder von Finkenrode*. Where Raabe deploys the Gypsy and his emblematic violin to deconstitute the concept of *Heimatrecht* in the German provincial heartland, Keller too uses such a figure — the black fiddler — to expose the hollow conceptual foundations of Swiss-German provincial identity. His deceptively simple tale is quickly summarized. The young lovers Sali and Vrenchen, children of respectable peasant farmers Manz and Marti, become tragic victims of an unremitting enmity which develops between the fathers after a dispute over ownership of an apparently abandoned strip of land between their plots. Marti finally purchases it. Yet in previous years each of them, Marti and Manz, has by tacit consensus illegally ploughed away and so appropriated a strip of land from the middle acre. Manz demands this triangular portion back from Marti, who refuses. The ensuing spiral of conflict ends in a legal dispute ruinous for both and, worse, a violent confrontation between Sali and Marti. Their love impossible, Sali and Vrenchen celebrate an unofficial and paradisal wedding, before committing suicide in the deep river. The desire for *Heimat*, potentialized *ad absurdum*, has led to the destruction of its would-be owners.

As its declarative title at once signals, the densely intertextual *Romeo und Julia auf dem Dorfe* foregrounds Shakespeare[53] even more prominently than *Die Kinder von Finkenrode*. Now Keller's realism — once, in the tradition of Fontane,[54] dismissed as an epistemologically naive recourse to the fairytale tradition — is today recognized to possess a thoroughly self-conscious literary constitution, in which (as with Raabe) the reference to literature complements and enriches the reference to reality. Thus not only does Shakespeare play a role in *Romeo und Julia*, it is now recognized that (for example) Homer's *Odyssey* too is a basic reference point for many of Keller's narratives. Odysseus' eccentric journey back home to wife (and/or sister or mother) frequently recurs as the deep structure of texts from Keller's *Bildungsroman*, *Der grüne Heinrich*, to his novella of Seldwyla, *Pankraz der Schmoller*.[55] Keller's *Sinngedicht*, we know, is modelled both on an epigram by Friedrich von Logau about Pygmalion and Galatea[56] and Goethe's *Faust*, and his *Sieben Legenden* spring from devotional texts by the Rügen poet Kosegarten.[57] In fact *Romeo und Julia* too declares (at least) a double intertextual referentiality, both to the Shakespeare play and to the niche poetic realist genre of the *Dorfgeschichte*, a Biedermeier novella variant, popularized by writers like Berthold Auerbach and Jeremias Gotthelf, which focuses exclusively on the everyday life in the *Heimat* of a simple peasant farmer community. Obviously, Keller derives his village setting from that.[58] Of this more later. As for the Shakespeare, Keller's use of intertextuality is not restricted to claiming by implication the status of world literature for a novella of the Swiss provinces. Unlike Shakespeare himself,[59] Keller makes a positive virtue of his debt to the literary tradition[60] by emphasizing in his introduction that the popularity and infinite variability of the motif in fact, like some deep-structural rule of Chomskyian grammar, reveals a fundamental insight into human nature which — properly applied — can be articulated again and again into individually meaningful utterances (*SW* IV, 69). He further capitalizes on this by building into his tale a perspectivism which demands that the reader decide for himself on the relative validity of the viewpoint taken by the narrator at the outset and, for example, the contrasting version of the *sujet* offered by still another rendition of the primal motif, the dismissive and moralizing fictive newspaper report of the lovers' death at the end (*SW* IV, 144).[61] That said, Keller's main manipulations of this intertextual 'source' — and he was of course a keen student of drama in his long Berlin years — are designed primarily to simplify the plot and so maximize tragic affect. Rosaline, Juliet's competitor for Romeo's affection, is omitted. The love of Sali and Vrenchen is motivated more powerfully than in the Shakespeare by making them childhood friends, and setting the motif in the isolated rural, *Dorfgeschichte* location, so that the hatred of the families is sparked only after a period of firm friendship (and complicity in crime) between the fathers. Equally, the tragic motivation for suicide is improved (which is not to comment on Shakespeare's supreme love-poetry). In the Shakespeare, neither Romeo nor Juliet really *wants* to commit suicide. There is for Shakespeare's lovers no pact of a joint love-death, no climactic night of fulfilled love as anticipatory compensation for life unlived, and they kill themselves only in reaction to misapprehension and accident. The love-death of Sali and Vrenchen is by contrast superlatively motivated in the materialistic and possessive mentality of the fathers and the village society, which they share to a mild extent, but which still destroys them.

However, still another, as yet unacknowledged dimension of intertextuality leads us past Shakespeare and the tragedy to the Gypsy motif and the main cognitive interest of the tale. For Keller not only decreases the dramatis personae by comparison with Shakespeare, he also *increases* it in one important respect: there is no 'schwarzer Geiger' in *Romeo and Juliet*. This, surely the most prominently contoured figure in the novella, is Keller's main vehicle for comment on the nineteenth-century model of Swiss-German *Heimat*, centred as it is on the rights to the disputed strip of land. The uncanny figure of the black fiddler appears directly or indirectly only in three scenes. But it is he who focuses the contemporary social thematics most sharply, for in this novella of *Heimat* he is the outsider who, through his otherness, through the negation of his identity by the villagers, as a foil, stabilizes the identity of the otherwise shapeless provincial community. He is first and foremost dispossessed, vagrant. It becomes clear in an early exchange between Manz and Marti that he is probably the true owner of the disputed acre. The evidence for this is written in his remarkable face (*SW*, 72–73), with its huge, strangely formed nose and disproportionately tiny, round, puffing, and whistling mouth (103). It is a face made for a trumpet player, one might think, and he does indeed bear a great resemblance to the last known recorded owner, the village trumpeter (another *Dorfmusikant*, then), who long since disappeared to join the local group of vagrants with whom the fiddler has always lived. Unfortunately his face alone is not evidence enough to prove his right to the land. Unchristened, he possesses no certificate of baptism which would prove his identity. (Tellingly, the narrator never names him or his father.) Like a Gypsy, therefore, he also has no 'Heimatsrecht' (72), no right of abode in the village community; still less does he as a legal non-person have a right to the land.[62] All this opens the way for the initial crime of his father's neighbours and the ultimate dispossession of both families. Now Simon Schama[63] has written eloquently of the extent to which human modification of land into landscape inscribes into the very stuff of the land the story of our relationship with it, and his study *Landscape and Memory* is an attempt to recover that lost or buried writing. Keller's peasants exemplify this very process. The furrows they plough symbolically overwrite the existence of the border between their land and his, and so obliterate the last material trace of the black fiddler's provenance. When the peasants refuse to witness the fiddler's unmistakable family resemblance to the previous owner (72–73), they merely fulfil the final condition of possibility for the compulsory purchase of the land, which legalizes the initial crime. Their later refusal to accept the oral testimony of other vagrants who were present at the fiddler's birth even makes it impossible for the fiddler to receive the money paid to the municipality, which would have permitted a new life elsewhere (103) — if only at the price of uncovering (yet accepting) the original crime. Thus the great pyramid of stones left on Manz's disputed strip (81) is the last monument to the otherwise effaced original crime and touchstone of the fiddler's identity. It is appropriately here, then, that the fiddler appears in person for the first time. Perched atop the great pile like an oracle of higher truth from beyond the contingent domain of culture, he reveals to Sali and Vrenchen the guilt of their parents, rejoices in their families' downfall, and predicts the two lovers' early demise. If until now it is clear that the fiddler has been reduced to a pre-cultural state of nature, his later appearance capitalizes on his strangeness to turn him into the modern, objective correlate of the lovers' Nemesis. Once their fate is sealed, they cannot but encounter him at every turn. But he is not a vengeful figure. Unbaptized and unordained, he nevertheless performs under his own, self-appointed authority an alternative marriage ceremony over the lovers (139). His wild, Dionysian music merely provides the appropriate accompaniment to the lovers on the final stage of their journey to self-dissolution, as they wander to the symbolical 'Paradiesgärtlein' (132) tavern and perform their dance of death. As his extemporized fiddle music echoes into nothingness, so the two lovers leave the furrowed path of their fathers (102) they have till now followed for the trackless waters beyond language and memory.

The non-Shakespearean figure of the black fiddler thus offers as focalizer of this perspectivist tale the proper standpoint to pass judgement on the Shakespearean lovers. Sali and Vrenchen understand his significance very well. In this highly self-conscious novella, they of course reflect unceasingly on their predicament. They know that their situation represents not only an existential crisis but also a crisis in their relation to the *Heimat*. A mark of that is the pathetic gesture of self-interpretation they make, of purchasing a gingerbread house at the harvest festival fair (129), for this metonym of *Heimat* is all the home that they will have (130). They also understand that the black fiddler is the harbinger of the homelessness that awaits them, and what it means when the gingerbread house is crushed during the last dance (133). When, therefore, they reject the black fiddler's offer — he makes it seemingly knowing that they will die before him (103) — to join his vagrant band and live in (a kind of) freedom beyond the domain of the written law (137–38), they understand that it means not only death, but also a rejection of the alternative values of the unsettled folk, or, better, a continued, paradoxical, and ultimately tragic affirmation of the value system which has driven them to this point. Keller's defence of their suicide[64] is thus ambivalent to this extent — which is hardly to diminish the heightened *Humanität* he so memorably confers on them.

But if there is no conformability of world-view between the lovers and the black fiddler, that cannot be said of the narrator's — and possibly Keller's — relationship to him. It is no coincidence that the black fiddler is an artist figure. He is of course at the meta-level of the text a symbol of the true artist, an expatriated voice resident in a realm transcending the borders of materialistic nineteenth-century culture. He may be powerless to effect change (and indeed incapable of writing), yet he discloses the truth despite all attempts to efface it. But only thanks to the narrator. It is the latter's novella, even more than the stone pyramid or the fiddler's speech (and music) which stands as a permanent, commemorative monument to the fiddler and the truth. *Romeo und Julia auf dem Dorfe* is in this sense, for all its gritty realism, a celebration of art in art. But the black fiddler is not only an isolated artist figure. He, like so many other features in this text, also has literary antecedents. We might, for example, see in him yet another variation on Keller's favourite Odysseus figure, who this time cannot find his way home. But perhaps the inspiration lies closer to home than classical antiquity. As a Gypsy-like outsider figure,[65] he is also, more fundamentally, an indicator of Keller's rarely acknowledged debt to the Romantic tradition.[66] The black fiddler's vagrancy, his homely homelessness, his fiddling, his abstract freedom, his closeness to nature, the sexual licence characteristic of his domain, his tinkering, his un-Germanic black colour, all these mark him out as the literary descendant of *Zigeunerromantik*, the relative, in some sense, of Clemens Brentano's Michaly.

But if this fiddler *is* a descendant of the Romantic literary tradition, then we should also take account of Keller's drastic rewriting of the figure. That means for one thing the fact that the fiddler, in striking contrast to his Romantic forebears, is real, and ugly. Moreover this fiddler, whilst he may dwell in a country beyond human borders, in fact wishes nothing more than to reinscribe those effaced borders. Worse: unlike Brentano's Michaly, he provokes not harmonious resolution but final discord. And if he is the vehicle of truth, it is only as the instrument of Nemesis and bringer of death. Thus Keller's black fiddler in truth inverts, indeed deconstructs the Romantic personification of poesy, and Keller's self-consciously poetic realism is in this light more an *un*poetic realism or a realistic unpoesy. Of course, account must be taken of the fact that this Gypsy-like figure, despite the obvious appeal to the literary model, is explicitly *not* a true Gypsy. However to emphasize this would be to miss Keller's point utterly. For this black fiddler, whilst he may be a *gadjo*, is not the fake Gypsy *redivivus* so familiar from Cervantes to Devrient (and beyond). This outsider is indeed the outcast logically required to promote the internal coherence of a closed, non-pluralist society or culture. But he comes, or came, from *inside*. His parents are from the village: 'seine Eltern [haben sich] einmal unter die Heimatlosen begeben' (72). Exotic as he may be, he is in truth *one of them*. In all members of the community, Keller seems to be saying, is an *inner Gypsy*, in all those secure in their unreflected homely identity lies hidden the outcast exotic other.[67] And *this*, the fact that the production of *Heimat* also *eo ipso* creates homelessness, is the grim inner structure Keller discerns of Swiss-German identity formation.

Thus, like Hebbel and Raabe, Keller self-consciously weaves the discourse of *Zigeunerromantik*, in the shape of the dark fiddler, into the very texture of his realism. As with Hebbel and Raabe, his Gypsy fiddler both symbolizes an art in the service of death and serves as a metatextual signal which consigns the discourse of *Zigeunerromantik* to a dead end of literary history — in his case by the deconstruction of its aesthetic claims. At another level, however, Keller and Raabe transcend Hebbel's horizon. Hebbel uses his Gypsy as the negative foil to bolster the self-consciousness of the emergent German nation. Like Raabe, Keller takes the opposite course. Raabe uses his Gypsies, themselves children of Finkenrode, to demonstrate that even the German children of Finkenrode are immigrants, that their German *Heimatrecht* merely extends a little further back in history, and then only to the conflict with the 'original' Cheruscan settlers (so that even this right is seen to derive from the historical wrong of colonization). Keller too deploys a Gypsy (or Gypsy-like) person in the heart of the *Heimat* as his instrument to attack the premises of (Swiss) German identity. He shows that a native (Swiss) German can be turned into a figure indistinguishable from a Gypsy outcast by the very process which makes the rest of the community into (Swiss) Germans. In each case the generous liberalism and fierce critical intellect of these writers exposes the hollowness of the artifice which distinguishes insider from outsider. Thus even in these pungent negations of received *Zigeunerromantik* a magnetic correlation persists: these German realist writers, like their deplored Romantic forebears, still deploy the literary Gypsy as the means to disclose whatever true Germanic identity might be; even if they do not find it.

'. . . als wäre die Feder der Geigenbogen': *Zigeunerromantik*, Interculturality, and Communication in Victor von Strauss und Torney's *Tuvia Panti aus Ungarn*

But even the savage literary dismantlings by Hebbel, Raabe and Keller failed to destroy so potent a resource of symbolic capital as the discourse of *Zigeunerrromantik*. Victor von Strauss und Torney (1809–90)[68] is not written large in the annals of German literary history. He is today perhaps best known for being the grandfather of Lulu von Strauss und Torney, who married the prominent publisher Eugen Diederichs, and became a successful minor literary figure around 1900. Strauss was however in his own right a many-sided man, sometime acquaintance of Tieck and Goethe, scholar of religious history, archivist, politician, member for Schaumburg-Lippe of the *Bundesversammlung* 1853–66, and not least a prolific writer. His *Zeitroman, Altenburg* (1865), and his pioneering translation of Lao Tse's *Taò-te-King* (1870) made their mark. Strauss also wrote a noteworthy contribution to the corpus of German-Gypsy literature, the tragicomic novella *Mitteilungen aus den Akten betreffend den Zigeuner Tuvia Panti aus Ungarn* (1871).[69] Set in large part in a Gypsy's prison cell, *Tuvia Panti* uniquely combines both unblinking realistic depiction of the Romany in conflict with German law with secularized *Zigeunerromantik* reborn, in one further attempt to secure the contact zone of Gypsy–*gadjo* cultural integration. In this contact zone too the emblematic violin plays a central role.

Hence Strauss returns to the older, pre-realistic paradigm. In her 1912 introduction to *Tuvia Panti* Lulu von Strauss und Torney records (Strauss, 15) that her grandfather found the material for his story on a tour of Slavonia (eastern Croatia). That, given the considerable quantity (and quality) of authentic ethnographic detail embedded in the tale, is not to be doubted. It is however also arguable that this tale of an orphaned Gypsy boy, who is purchased by a wealthy German couple, educated as their adoptive son in the city of B., develops a virtuoso violin technique, but after eight or nine years of failed assimilation flees back to his Romany tribe, is also in some measure inspired by Franz Liszt. In his *Die Zigeuner und ihre Musik in Ungarn* Liszt, it will be recalled,[70] told the true story of Jozsy, a Gypsy orphan around twelve years old who was given into his care by Graf Sander Teleky in Paris. This Jozsy, like Tuvia Panti, was an emergent violin virtuoso, and Liszt attempted by way of experiment to assimilate him into occidental culture. But he too, as Liszt puts it, could not renounce his Romany nature. He becomes a dandy and philanderer. Moves to different environments — Strasbourg, the Black Forest — convince Liszt that acculturation is impossible, and Joszy is finally released into the keeping of his original Gypsy family. *Die Zigeuner und ihre Musik* preserves Liszt's later correspondence with the regretful but unrepentant Jozsy.[71]

As the parallels suggest, Strauss's contribution to the Gypsy–*gadjo* integration debate, despite its undoubted originality, is best approached as a literary commentary on Liszt's culturally pessimistic anecdote and the Gypsy anthropology project which it exemplifies. Liszt's key argument, we recall, is that intercultural expression of the authentic Romany voice has been stifled by the uniformitarian presentation of Grellmann's rationalistic anthropology. Authentic expression of Romany identity was to be found not in *gadjo* words, but in Rom music. That music Liszt himself, as self-appointed redemptive national poet, counting on his elective affinity with the Romany race, would restore to its original pristine expressivity in the would-be national epic of the *Hungarian Rhapsodies*. Thus he would restore the abject Gypsy race to its well-merited place of fully realized humanity in the aesthetic utopia of intercultural *Weltmusik*. *Tuvia Panti* explores both the possibilities and the limits of Liszt's project by setting the musical utopia in the real world of German police control.

To achieve the Lisztian unsilencing of the Gypsy voice in the literary sphere Strauss uses by contrast to Liszt an accomplished montage technique uncannily resembling that used in 1974 by Heinrich Böll in his documentary novella *Die verlorene Ehre der Katharina Blum*. Its most prominent feature, as with that much later work, but also in the authentic spirit of Liszt's project, is the *omission of a master narrative voice*. As the title indicates, Strauss's text purports to consist solely in an unmanipulated montage of authentic documents from the court archives in the city of L. These display a wide variety of text-types, from the would-be objective (internal memoranda of the local judiciary, records of Panti's and Dr Philippi's police interrogations, Chief Magistrate Bevern's judicial verdict on Panti's case, and his *Steckbrief* or descriptive arrest warrant) to the wholly subjective (private letters, journal entries, and two frankly confessional, complementary autobiographies). Apart from their being set in chronological order over thirty-nine years (22 April 1801–19 May 1840), there is no attempt by an external narrator to merge the fragments into a continuous narrative, still less to submit them to the single perspective of an authoritative value judgement. It is thus the reader's task, beyond any pre-conceived framework of cultural value, to recognize immanent contrasts or contradictions in the often divergent accounts contained by the documents, and impose his own, unprejudiced interpretation on the data set out.

That said, there is little doubt that Strauss here intends to break a lance for the abject Gypsy. The emblematic violin stands as so often at the centre of the cultural and judicial conflict. Tuvia Panti, we learn at the outset in Assessor Wildung's protocol of the interrogation, is accused of having stolen Dr Philippi's Stradivarius. Panti's account (Strauss, 20–27) provides a highly innovative justification for the well-worn accusation of Gypsy thieving: he has performed an act of liberation on the oppressed and abused instrument. This wandering Hungarian Romany has one evening in search of new melodies chanced upon a beautiful instrument being fearfully misused by its owner. Unable to contain his indignation at this affront to music, he is compelled to steal the instrument — but merely in order to demonstrate how it should be played. He has been arrested in the garden of his victim's house as he fumbles with the lock of the violin case. Equally implausibly, he insists that he could have paid for the valuable instrument many times over. Physician Dr Philippi, in his counter-deposition, grudgingly concedes in the face of the physical evidence that the Gypsy may well not have wished permanently to steal the violin. But he vehemently disputes his aesthetic judgement. He has, after all, at the age of forty-three, played first violin in the city's amateur orchestra for twenty years. Following an equally vehement and inconclusive oral disputation *de gustibus*, the Gypsy is summarily condemned to three months' imprisonment. Thus Gypsy and *gadjo* aesthetic judgement stand against Gypsy and *gadjo* legal judgement, and the Romany is condemned on each count. Wildung's unsolicited protest at the harshness of the verdict is dismissed. As Magistrate Bevern insists, the homeless Panti remains obstinately silent about both his person and the acquisition of his astonishingly fluent German (and Latin); he is perhaps the agent or spy of a foreign power (39).

This apparently definitive and factual opening of course merely prompts the analytical exposition of the Gypsy's true motivation and, finally, validation of his otherwise unvalidated and silenced testimony. After a mere ten days of insufferable incarceration Panti, for whom the violin and freedom are his only treasures (28), escapes. In his haste however he leaves behind a further document, something rare to the point of being unknown in Romany cultural history: his written autobiography. In his state of unfreedom, deprived of violin and even tobacco pipe, Panti has out of sheer boredom asked for paper and ink — the tools of the unfree, city-dwelling *gadje* (44) — and resorted to the *gadjo* art of writing. But his autobiography — fully reproduced (43–72) as the centrepiece of the documentation — is not intended as evidence for the *gadjo* court, to which he has already refused to reveal more than is absolutely necessary about his identity (20, 27). It is — for the moment mysteriously — to be delivered at his death to another, unnamed individual (44). With the forced removal of his natural instrument and medium of self-expression, then, this member of the otherwise proudly unlettered race crosses the cultural divide, and substitutes in his time of need the medium of *gadjo* self-expression for his own preferred, but confiscated instrument: 'als wäre die Feder der Geigenbogen und meine Erinnerung die klingende Saite' (55). As in Liszt's theory then, we find here the fictionalized writing-back of the Gypsy in the language of the master. Only chance, through the agency of the well-meaning Wildung, has brought it to the attention of the *gadje*.

Concrete details apart, Panti's prison-born account largely mirrors the basic structure of Liszt's Jozsy anecdote, with however the major addition of an intercultural love affair which perhaps also dimly postfigures Romeo and Juliet. His father shot like a wild animal, his mother having pined away (54), Panti has been raised in the oak forest of Hungary by the tribe's Mahamadri or wise woman until around the age of ten. Then, as the tribe is summarily evicted from its long-standing forest camp by soldiers (53), he is sold to the elderly white couple Kronau, on the understanding that he will slip away and return as soon as possible. Disorientated, however, he loses his opportunity to escape, and so remains with the Kronaus until around his twenty-first year (64), when at last his Gypsy blood drives him to return to the tribe (67–69). This accidental experiment in acculturation is thus the occasion of Panti's otherwise undesired acquisition of *gadjo* cultural skills. His name changed by the Kronaus to the more German-sounding Tobias Panting (75, 80), Panti adapts thanks to his proverbial Romany quick-wittedness easily to *gadjo* culture (59), and passes out as best pupil of his school (63; compare 61). Yet he is forbidden by Kronau and his teacher Professor Wolfart (named perhaps after the ideal bourgeois-German hero of Freytag's patriotic *Soll und Haben*) to follow the career best suited to his talents — music — and compelled (again like Freytag's Wolfart) to take up his adoptive father's merchant profession. On Kronau's death, Panti/Panting is to inherit everything. Unrequited love for his adoptive sister Lodoiska Kronau — she seems to disdain the Gypsy and prefer a blond German doctor — however combines with his inner failure to acculturate, and he disappears with only his violin, to return after many adventures to his tribe. He henceforth earns his living as a wandering Gypsy violinist. Lodoiska, with whom despite his permanent absence he has kept faith over the last eight or nine years, not only inherits house and fortune, but is of course also the addressee of this intimate confession.

More significantly, this intentionally unpublic account of Panti's innermost self contains a fierce critique of *gadjo* culture and a correspondingly powerful apology of the Romany standpoint. Blond Professor Wolfart, for example, is always friendly and kind, but 'doch ein Tyrann' (58); in fact all Germans are 'doch Tyrannen' (58). The German language to which his disaccustomed hand must in prison willy-nilly readjust (44) and which at last paradoxically contains the intimate confession of his identity, is itself the language of compulsion: 'Mit welchen Worten erlernt ich zuerst Euere Sprache? Du mußt, du sollst, du sollst nicht, du darfst nicht, damit umwebten sie mich, wie mit Netzen, damit beschmiedeten sie mich, wie mit Ketten' (58). The object of all this learning, what Germans call knowledge, is for Panti a frozen deposit of short-sighted commonplaces: 'Ein Wissen war es, den Eiszapfen gleich, und wo es endete, wußten sie nichts mehr' (61). With especial bitterness he recalls learning of the Romany exclusion from *gadjo* cultural history by this system of knowledge: 'Eure alten Geschichten, die nichts wissen vom Sindevolke' (61). The acculturation efforts of his parents and teachers are in short an unwanted rebirth, the attempt to efface and overwrite his innate Gypsy identity: 'Wie umgeboren war ich in eine Welt des Zwanges, der Dienstbarkeit und Unfreiheit' (58–59). Panti has adapted not to integrate but only strategically, as a tactic to protect his threatened inner core of cultural identity until the chance arose to escape: 'Ich tat's wie auf Kauf, um es abzuschütteln' (59).

Only with great trouble can Panti reacquire the Romany language of his youth — 'entartet' as a Gypsy (68), he calls himself in an innocently ironic metaphor. But the centre of his repressed cultural identity, so his paradoxical confession in *gadjo* language reveals, is not the Romany language. Rather, music, and in particular the violin, is the core of everything Panti seeks to protect:

> und wie hätt' ich ertragen im wallenden Herzen die kalte Helle und die Last des Herzens, den Zwang und die Bande beim ewigen Wälzen leerer Gefäße, all den gläsernen Wust, wäre sie nicht gekommen, die Zauberin Musik, der verborgenen Wunder ahnungsvolle Zunge, hätte sie nicht die Geige in die Hand mir gelegt, um hinauszutönen aus den Tiefen der Brust was keiner wußte, was keiner aussprach? (62)

When he first plays the violin among the *gadje*, he discovers that he can express something untaught and unnotated, something that he can otherwise only dimly recall, originating from beyond the light-filled realm of his German hosts: the mystical, emotion-saturated life of his Romany childhood in the bosom of nature, Gypsy truth mediated by a spontaneous creativity transcending the fixed knowledge and printed notes of his host culture: 'Wo lerntest Du das?' his amazed teacher asks: ' — Das Beste, dacht' ich, ist nicht zu lernen!' (63); 'Wie hätt' ich es in Noten fassen können? Es kam und es tönte, und war dahin' (63). The analogy to Liszt's theory of Gypsy music as inspired and improvised transmedial, non-archivable response to linguistic and cultural marginalization is especially clear at this point. This music is at the heart of the idyllic Gypsy life he describes in the first part of his autobiography. In direct contrast to Hebbel's portrayal and in anticipation of Carl Hauptmann,[72] the Gypsy culture is shown to use music as the ritual means which transports them around the symbolic fire through the ecstasy of the communal Orphic dance from the narrow constraints of the everyday into a communion with the stars (50; compare 70), locus of their religion and/or knowledge, a domain beyond the *gadjo* ken. Hence his passion for the Stradivarius, and the higher legality of his act of theft. Otherwise, this black fiddler has no desire for his *gadjo* patrimony.

With this hypostatized valorization of the Romany standpoint from behind the prison walls Strauss couples an alternative myth of Romany origin. When the young Panti asks: 'woher sind wir?' (51), the wise old Mahamadri of the tribe tells him a meta-Christian tale (51–53) of the Gypsy origin in power and sin but without redemptive potential. The man beyond the stars — the Manichean-dualistic 'Sternenmann' (51) — has magically created the earth to belong to the white race. But their unfreedom displeases him, for he wants people in his image, brave, and free. Thus he has split apart a great Eastern mountain as high as the sky. From its earth have come the brown nation of the Sinde. These were indeed in his image: brave and free, powerful and sovereign, conquerors of the whites. But only so long as they lived free and wandered the earth. Foolishly, however, and against the warning of their wise women, they conceived the desire to take the great city of the whites. They conquered them in battle, occupied the city, mixed Sinde blood with that of the white women. Henceforth they were in punishment doomed by the starman to lose all bravery and lust for life, and to wander the world ever and anon, shy and outcast (51–53). Only Gypsy music and dance release them from their bondage, then, freely to participate in the starry vision. And this, Panti reveals to Lodoiska, was his life until his unjust imprisonment. With this full-blown (if ventriloquized) Gypsy self-confession Strauss tellingly contrasts the curt and reifying description of the man and musician Panti — an anticipation of the language of Dillmann's *Zigeunerbuch* (1905)[73] — in the chief magistrate's *Steckbrief* circulated on Panti's escape (72–74). Just as Keller's narrator recuperates the evanescent text of the black fiddler and symbolically enacts the redemptive function of art in a materialistic age, so too Strauss's rescue of Panti's hybrid autobiography from the prison of the archives suggests the utopian emancipatory potential of aesthetic discourse.

Against this background the tale concludes as an intercultural tragedy. Lodoiska, in fact tragically faithful to Panti, never receives his text, which remains locked in the archive. But she does hear of the case in the local paper of B. and writes to Wildung, who communicates what he can recall of the document. Her own confessional letter (79–89) confirms Panti's story, so far as it co-extends with her own biography, in every detail. Panting is indeed, to this day, the legitimate possessor of the Kronau house and fortune. But despite a higher court's grudging willingness to reconsider the case on Panti's rearrest, nothing more is heard. Only in May 1822, twenty years after the initial encounters, does Dr Philippi report to Wildung — now a chief magistrate despite the career-threatening pro-Gypsy activity of his youth — that a recent occurrence has jogged his memory. Both last year and this a mysterious Gypsy has appeared and offered large sums for his Stradivarius, which he has refused. Only now does Philippi link these repeated occurrences with the events of 1801. Informed of the development by Wildung, Lodoiska tells of a fruitless search in Hungary. Her health broken, a convert to the Pietism become newly popular after the Wars of Coalition, she has — in evident compensation — allowed Jesus to take a place in her heart beside Panti. But this does not prevent her moving to L., where she on his death in 1835 purchases Philippi's house and contents (including the Stradivarius), and lives in constant hope of Panti's return. Alas, only after a further eighteen years have passed since his last visit, in May 1840, is a half-frozen vagrant — Tuvia Panti, now aged around seventy — found with his violin under a hedge in L. The humane Wildung reunites him at last with both the stolen Stradivarius and Lodoiska. Blind, he nonetheless at once recognizes the instrument and renews his offer to buy. As Lodoiska mutters his — Germanicized — name, he recognizes her too. But they do not speak. Instead — 'So höre, so höre!' (106) — he plays Gypsy music, in Wildung's inadequate words: 'so weich, so süß, so überirdisch, wenn auch noch immer seltsam, daß ich kaum zu atmen wagte. Nie habe ich etwas Ähnliches gehört. Die Töne schienen aus einer anderen Welt zu kommen' (108). With a tremendous disharmony the violin falls to earth and Panti dies, to be followed a week later by Lodoiska.

Thus at one level we find Strauss, like Liszt, inviting the thinking reader through the hypostatized fiction of writing back both to affirm the dignity of the Gypsy culture and to defend the race's reputation against traditional *gadjo* calumnies. In substance Strauss's Romanies are also the literary realization of Liszt's theory. Doubtless a *Naturvolk*, they can nevertheless be redeemed in their full humanity through our understanding of their compensatory focus on music as the adequate form of their cultural self-expression. Indeed their musical gift promotes them in a sense to a position of cultural superiority, at least by comparison with the philistines of L.; and Panti is certainly also presented as the equal in creative genius to the established masters of occidental written music (63). It is this total commitment to musical self-expression which is seen to motivate and, in a sense, justify Panti's apparent crime, and this in turn exposes the latent anti-Gypsyism of the social and legal community in L. Gypsies otherwise, a little harmless fortune-telling apart, are seen to be unjustly persecuted by their *gadjo* hosts. Even the attempted embezzlement of money from the Kronaus through the apparent selling of Tuvia in fact affirms Romany family values and must be set in the context of his father's murder and the tribe's arbitrary eviction from their camp. That said, it is clear that Strauss's Romanies, despite the undoubted ethnographic authenticity of their presentation in this text, the power of Strauss's skilful ventriloquism, and the humoristically cloaked urgency of his attack on legalized anti-Gypsyism, are in the last analysis, as the Stradivarius signals, another literary resurrection of higher *Zigeunerromantik*, exemplars of the Romantic thesis that music is the universal language.

At another level however we find unrealized love in the *post*-Romantic tradition as intercultural tragedy. Neither Tuvia Panti nor Lodoiska Kronau can quite grasp why their love across the cultural divide has failed to be realized. Yet the reader recognizes it as a deeper failure to cross a communicative threshold. Panti, trapped in the prison house of the German language, cannot find words to express his love. He *has* played his violin to her (then uncomprehending) ears; but she has fled (65–66). He thus assumes that she, despite her proto-Gypsy brown colouring, somehow felt 'daß der braune Sinde nicht zu Euch gehörte' (66). She for her part has a sense that the Kronaus had intended her — as dark-haired and brown-skinned (if wholly German) — to be Panti's wife (83; compare Panti, 65), has sensed their growing intimacy, and is fascinated by his music (83). Yet she is also confused by his insecure brittleness, his apparent expectation that the first word must come from her (84). Her willingness to dismiss the blond doctor comes too late (84). Thus whilst he cannot speak the necessary words, she will not, and when he does confess his love in his natural language, music, she cannot understand. A deeper cultural alienation is betrayed by the fact that Lodoiska always, even after his final return (106), refers to him by his German name of Panting. And Panti too is perhaps influenced by the Mahamadri's myth of Gypsy origin, which implicitly condemns intermarriage between the free Gypsy and unfree *gadjo*. Thus only on his deathbed, forty years after his autobiographical confession, can Panti finally communicate his love in his intended medium, the music of the violin, to Lodoiska, and their union — if union it be — is consummated only in the grave.

As the intercultural marriage utopia evaporates like Gypsy music into the ether or is buried like Panti's autobiography in the legal archives, Strauss seems at last to share Raabe's and Keller's bleak, realistic view of the Gypsy condition under police control in mid-nineteenth-century Germany. He may not undermine the structures of cultural identity formation as radically as Raabe or Keller, but his Gypsies are as constitutionally homeless and abject as any of theirs, and his analysis of the conditions of possibility of intercultural exchange is equally pessimistic. In *Tuvia Panti* even the Gypsies are unwilling to cross the communicative border, let alone the majority of philistine Germans, and Strauss's Gypsies seem (still) to observe the miscegenation taboo. That said, Strauss, alone in this peer group of writers, is finally unwilling to accept the loss of a utopian perspective. For in the final words of his story we learn that the emblematic Stradivarius — in the right hands the perfect instrument for mediating between legalized prejudice and the aesthetic Gypsy — has been bequeathed by Lodoiska to the children of Romany-friendly new Chief Magistrate Wildung, and the symbolic capital of *Zigeunerromantik* is given another chance. *Tuvia Panti* in this presents a remarkable, and curious, synthesis of these opposing energies, *Zigeunerromantik* and legalized anti-Gypsyism, and points forward to Carl Hauptmann.

Notes to Chapter 4

1. See on this Hehemann, esp. pp. 64–87; also Lucassen, pp. 77–116, 117–73.
2. See Gustav Freytag, *Soll und Haben: Roman in sechs Büchern*, 86th edn (Leipzig: S. Hirzel, 1916), title page.
3. Compare Hehemann, pp. 89–90
4. Compare Hehemann, pp. 64–87, 243–60, 277–85; Lucassen, pp. 108–10.
5. See for what follows Hehemann, pp. 84–86.
6. Hehemann, pp. 87, 215–16.
7. Lucassen, p. 111.
8. Hehemann, pp. 249–52.
9. See Hehemann, pp. 265–66, 297–98, 405–07; Lucassen, pp. 118–68.
10. Liebich, *Die Zigeuner*, p. 3.
11. Liebich, *Die Zigeuner*, pp. 103–13.

12. The exception is Karl S. Guthke, 'Hebbels "Blick in's Weite": Eurozentrik und Exotik', in *Resonanzen: Festschrift für Hans Joachim Kreutzer zum 65. Geburtstag*, ed. by Sabine Doering, Waltraud Maierhofer, and Peter Philipp Riedl (Würzburg: Königshausen & Neuman, 2000), pp. 363–73.
13. For the traditional relation of the novellas to Hebbel's work in other genres see Ingrid Kreuzer, 'Hebbel als Novellist', in *Hebbel in neuer Sicht*, ed. by Helmut Kreuzer (Stuttgart, Berlin, Cologne, and Mainz: Kohlhammer, 1969; 1st edn, 1963), pp. 150–63; more differentiated is Andrea Rudolph, *Genreentscheidung und Symbolgehalt im Werk Friedrich Hebbels* (Frankfurt a.M.: Peter Lang, 2000).
14. On the travel writing see Ingrid Oesterle, 'Peripherie und Zentrum — Kunst und Publizistik — Wahrnehmungsgrenzfall "große Stadt": Die Aufzeichnungen Friedrich Hebbels in Paris', in Barkhoff and others, pp. 187–206; on the link of novellas and travelogue prose see Nicholas Saul, 'Zum Zusammenhang von Hebbels früher Erzähl- und Reiseprosa: Kunst, Leben und Tod im Übergang zur Moderne', *Hebbel-Jahrbuch* (2004), pp. 72–89.
15. See *Agram*, in Friedrich Hebbel, *Werke*, ed. by Gerhard Fricke, Werner Keller, and Karl Pörnbacher, 5 vols (Munich: Hanser, 1965), III, 843–48.
16. Hans Gustav Dittenberger von Dittenberg (1794–1879) was a pupil of Peter Cornelius, acquaintance of Hebbel, and specialist in landscape and genre.
17. See Liebich, *Die Zigeuner*, pp. 16–17, on conditions in Agram in 1845; also Reinbeck, pp. 68–70, 74–75.
18. See *Wiener Briefe* (1861–62), no. 9: *Wien, im Februar* (1862), in Friedrich Hebbel, *Sämtliche Werke*, ed. by Richard Maria Werner, 1. Abteilung: *Werke*, 12 vols (Berlin: Behr, 1911–13), X, 217–350 (pp. 275–76).
19. Art's role is 'das *Leben* in allen seinen verschiedenartigen Gestaltungen ergreifen und darstellen' (*Sämtliche Werke*, IX, 34).
20. See Hebbel on Napoleon's obelisk in Paris, capital of world, in *Erinnerungen an Paris* [1843–48], *Werke*, III, 796–803 (pp. 797–98).
21. Compare: 'In den *egyptischen* Saal, mit seinen starren, finstern Götterbildern, in denen Nichts lebt, als die in schauerlicher Einförmigkeit ewig wiederholte Idee des Todes, und die des Künstlers furchtsame Hand nicht einmal loszulösen wagte von dem fesselnden Stein, wird man zuerst gewiesen' (*Sämtliche Werke*, IX, 371).
22. *Werke*, III, 162.
23. See Chapter 2.
24. All citations are from Wilhelm Raabe, *Die Kinder von Finkenrode*, in *Sämtliche Werke*, ed. by Karl Hoppe, 20 vols + 5 suppl. vols (Göttingen: Vandenhoeck & Ruprecht, 1951–) [=Braunschweiger Ausgabe, BA], II, 5–219. Here, p. 87.
25. Raabe is notable for his omission from the otherwise enlightened *Cambridge History of German Literature* (Cambridge: Cambridge University Press, 1997). The most effective apologia of Raabe is Jeffrey Sammons, *Wilhelm Raabe: The Fiction of the Alternative Community* (Princeton: Princeton University Press, 1987).
26. See on the life and reception history Hans Oppermann, *Wilhelm Raabe* (Hamburg: Rowohlt, 1970); Horst Denkler, *Wilhelm Raabe: Legende — Leben — Literatur* (Tübingen: Niemeyer, 1989); Jeffrey L. Sammons, *The Shifting Fortunes of Wilhelm Raabe: A History of Criticism as Cautionary Tale* (Columbia, SC: Camden House, 1992).
27. See on the theme of temporality in Raabe's novels especially Dirk Göttsche, *Zeitreflexion und Zeitkritik im Werk Wilhelm* Raabes (Würzburg. Königshausen & Neumann, 2000); also Dirk Göttsche, *Zeit im Roman. Literarische Zeitreflexion und die Geschichte des Zeitromans im 19. Jahrhundert* (Munich. Fink, 2001), pp. 739–52.
28. See on this theme Philip Brewster, 'Onkel Ketschwayo in Neuteutoburg: Zeitgeschichtliche Anspielungen in Raabes *Stopfkuchen*', *Raabe-Jahrbuch* (1983), 96–118.
29. See Regine Schmidt-Stolz, *Von Finkenrode nach Altershausen: Das Motiv der Heimkehr im Werk Wilhelm Raabes als Ausdruck einer sich wandelnden Lebenseinstellung, dargestellt an fünf Romanen aus fünf Lebensabschnitten* (Bern: Peter Lang, 1984).
30. See on this novel Peter J. Brenner, 'Die Einheit der Welt: Zur Entzauberung der Fremde und Verfremdung der Heimat in Raabes *Abu Telfan*', *Raabe-Jahrbuch* (1989), 45–62; also John Pizer,

'Wilhelm Raabe and the German Colonial Experience', in *A Companion to German Realism 1848–1900*, ed. by Todd Kontje (Rochester, NY: Camden House, 2002), pp. 159–82.

31. In Raabe's choice of name it is possible to see a characteristically subtle swipe at Adalbert Stifter's position on intercultural exchange as set out in *Katzensilber.* In Stifter the peasant farmer for whom Sture Mure, mother of the nut-brown girl, works, is of course the 'Hagenbucher' (Stifter, *GW,* III, 246). The interculturally challenged chief protagonist of *Abu Telfan* is, we know, Leonhard Hagebucher (*Abu Telfan*, BA VII [*Werke*, II, 9)], and Eduard, the undermined narrator of *Stopfkuchen*, writes the text of the novel as he returns to Africa on the ironically christened good ship 'Hagebucher' (*Stopfkuchen*, BA XVIII, 8).
32. Note too the prefigurative dream of Cäcilie's death in a stream (of ink, in this case, 169) which pastiches that of Mathilde's in *Heinrich von Ofterdingen.*
33. See Stanley Radcliffe, 'Raabe and the Railway', *New German Studies*, 2 (1974), 133–44. This (far from comprehensive) overview does not extend to *Die Kinder von Finkenrode.* Dirk Göttsche (*Zeitreflexion*, p. 75) touches, but does not explore, the theme of the railway in *Die Kinder von Finkenrode.*
34. Compare Johannes Mahr, '"Tausend Eisenbahnen hasten . . . Um mich. Ich bin nur die Mitte!" Eisenbahngedichte aus der Zeit des deutschen Kaiserreichs', in *Technik in der Literatur: Ein Forschungsüberblick und zwölf Aufsätze*, ed. by Harro Segeberg (Frankfurt a.M.: Suhrkamp, 1987), pp. 132–73 (p. 133).
35. See above all Wolfgang Schivelbusch, *Geschichte der Eisenbahnreise: Zur Industrialisierung von Raum und Zeit im 19. Jahrhundert* (Frankfurt a.M.: Fischer, 2000; 1st edn, 1977); also Manfred Riedel, 'Vom Biedermeier zum Maschinenzeitalter: Zur Kulturgeschichte der ersten Eisenbahnen in Deutschland' (1961), reprinted in *Technik in der Literatur: Ein Forschungsüberblick und zwölf Aufsätze*, ed. by Harro Segeberg (Frankfurt a.M.: Suhrkamp, 1987), pp. 102–31; and Mahr, '"Tausend Eisenbahnen"'.
36. See on this Schivelbusch, *Geschichte der Eisenbahnreise*, pp. 19–20.
37. This mock-heroic adventure might again be said to parody Stifter's *Katzensilber*, in particular the nut-brown girl's rescue of the bourgeois family from the sudden violent hailstorm.
38. Compare Sir Walter Scott, *Guy Mannering, or the Astrologer*, ed. by P. D. Garside (Edinburgh: Edinburgh University Press, 1999), esp. pp. 145–46.
39. See Liebich, *Die Zigeuner*, p. 81.
40. Thanks to Ian Hancock and Ken Lee for confirming this.
41. Compare Homi Bhabha, 'Signs taken for Wonders', in *The Post-Colonial Studies Reader*, ed. by Bill Ashcroft, Gareth Griffiths, and Helen Tiffin (London: Routledge, 1995), pp. 29–35.
42. He is first introduced as Michel (87) — an even more emblematically German name — which however swiftly changes to the localized Martin. Raabe retained this error, if it be such, in the second edition, and the editors of the historical-critical edition have also left the text thus.
43. Given Effi Briest's marked inclination to Romantic-Gypsy culture (and indeed to railway travel), it might be speculated that the Romany associations of 'Rollo' here persuaded Fontane to call her beloved pet by this name. (Thanks to Rüdiger Görner for the reminder.)
44. A dramatic contrast to the beautiful Romantic appearance of his full sister Marianne.
45. Citations are from William Shakespeare, *The Tempest*, ed. by Sir Arthur Quiller-Couch and John Dover Wilson, in *The Works of Shakespeare*, ed. by John Dover Wilson et al. (Cambridge: Cambridge University Press, 1977; 1st edn, 1921), pp. 1–78.
46. See on this Bill Ashcroft, 'Caliban's Language', in Bill Ashcroft, *On Post-Colonial Futures: Transformations of Colonial Culture* (London and New York: Continuum, 2001), pp. 81–102; also Octavio Mannoni, *Prospero and Caliban: The Psychology of Colonization* (Ann Arbor: University of Michigan Press, 1950).
47. It is therefore no coincidence that he once lightheartedly compares himself with a 'Conquistador, der mit dem Schwert in der Hand an das Gestade des neuentdeckten Amerika sprang' (122).
48. Nor does the search of the Germans for identity find definitive closure. As Wallinger enjoys last moments of lucidity on waking from his Tannhäuser's dream, it again falls to Weitenweber to tell him the bitter truth about how little has changed in Germany over the last decades: 'Wie steht es im deutschen Land?' 'Es ist, wie es war! Auf derselben Stelle halten wir Schule für die Völker, die da kommen und gehen. Fühlende, denkende — zweifelnde Männer quälen sich auf

derselben Stelle, gleich unfähig zum Glauben, zur Liebe wie zum Haß, unfähig deshalb, *Ein* großes Volk zu sein.' (196)

49. See Sammons, *Fiction of the Alternative Community*.
50. See BA XIV, 148–58.
51. There is just a hint, even, that something similar may have happened to the Gypsies. After they have rescued the young women from their forest adventure, they receive a reward from Hauptmann Fasterling. In a gesture deliberately modelled on that of the innkeeper in *Hermann und Dorothea* towards the dispossessed *émigrés*, it is an old Turkish nightgown (*Kinder*, p. 120; compare *Hermann und Dorothea*, Canto I, ll. 29–37) — the uniform of the bourgeois philistine. See however for a counter-image also Raabe's bleak Gypsy/vagabond lyric 'Auf der Landstraß im Grabe, da bin ich gefunden' (BA XX, 328).
52. All references are to Gottfried Keller, *Romeo und Julia auf dem Dorfe*, in Gottfried Keller, *Sämtliche Werke*, ed. by Thomas Böning, Gerhard Kaiser, and Dominik Müller, 7 vols (Frankfurt a.M.: Deutscher Klassiker Verlag, 1985–96), IV (1989), 69–144. Here, p. 103. This edition is hereafter cited as *SW*. Letters are quoted from *Sämtliche Werke und ausgewählte Briefe*, ed. by Clemens Heselhaus, 3 vols (Munich: Hanser, 1958) as *SWAB*. There is a vast secondary literature on this tale. I have found most useful Martin Swales, 'Gottfried Keller's *Romeo und Julia auf den Dorfe*', in *Zu Gottfried Keller*, ed. by Hartmut Steinecke (Stuttgart: Klett, 1984), pp. 56–67; Robert C. Holub, *Reflections of Realism: Paradox, Norm and Ideology in Nineteenth-Century German Prose* (Detroit: Wayne State University Press, 1991), pp. 101–31; Erika Swales, *The Poetics of Scepticism: Gottfried Keller and 'Die Leute von Seldwyla'* (Oxford and New York: Berg, 1994), pp. 80–97.
53. See on the general theme of Shakespeare in the German novella Roger C. Paulin, *The Brief Compass: The Nineteenth-Century German Novelle* (Oxford: Clarendon Press, 1985).
54. See *SW* IV, 644; also J. P. Stern, *Idylls and Realities: Studies in Nineteenth-Century German Literature* (London: Methuen, 1971), p. 138.
55. See Hans Wysling, 'Und immer wieder kehrt Odysseus heim: Das "Fabelhafte" bei Gottfried Keller', in *Gottfried Keller: Elf Essays zu seinem Werk*, ed. by Hans Wysling (Munich: Fink, 1990), pp. 151–62. The pioneering work on Keller's self-conscious literariness is Klaus Jeziorkowski, *Literarität und Historismus: Beobachtungen zu ihrer Erscheinungsfrom im 19. Jahrhundert am Beispiel Gottfried Kellers* (Heidelberg: Winter, 1979).
56. See Neumann, 'Der Körper des Menschen und die belebte Statue'.
57. *SW* VI, 836–38; *SWAB* III, 1180 (Keller to Freiligrath, 22 April 1860).
58. See *Gottfried Keller: Romeo und Julia auf dem Dorfe. Erläuterungen und Dokumente*, ed. by Jürgen Hein (Stuttgart: Reclam, 1977), pp. 27–29; also Jürgen Hein, *Dorfgeschichte* (Stuttgart: Metzler, 1976).
59. I have used the edition of the *Most Excellent and Lamentable Tragedie, of Romeo and Juliet* (*c.* 1595) in *The Works of Shakespeare*, ed. by John Dover Wilson et al. (Cambridge: Cambridge University Press, 1977; 1st edn, 1955), pp. 1–111.
60. See Hein, *Romeo und Julia*, pp. 23–25.
61. Two further realizations of the *sujet* complement Keller's version: the original 'source', a story from the *Zürcher Zeitung*, 3 September 1847; *SW* IV, 690; and Johannes R. Becher's 'Romeo und Julia auf dem Dorfe. Nach der gleichnamigen Erzählung von Gottfried Keller', in Johannes R. Becher, *Romane in Versen* (Berlin: Aufbau, 1946), pp. 7–20.
62. On the problem of 'Heimatsrecht' and vagrancy see a writer Keller valued, Theodor Mügge, *Die Schweiz und ihre Zustände* (Hanover, 1847), cited in Hein, ed., *Erläuterungen*, pp. 77–78. See too *SWAB* III, 1106.
63. Simon Schama, *Landscape and Memory* (London: HarperCollins, 1995), p. 7.
64. Keller possessed a highly differentiated view of the moral problem of suicide (*SWAB* III, 1265–66).
65. Such figures are of course identified by Friedrich Theodor Vischer as offering the epic writer in the modern prosaic world a 'green place' for recuperating the poetic and the truly humane. See the extracts from Vischer's *Ästhetik oder Wissenschaft des Schönen* (1846–57) in the anthology by *Theorien des bürgerlichen Realismus: Eine Textsammlung*, ed. by Gerhard Plumpe (Stuttgart: Reclam, 1997), pp. 240–47.
66. For Keller on Romanticism, see his equally differentiated comments in 'Die Romantik und

die Gegenwart' (1849) (*SW* VII, 689–91). See also Karl S. Guthke, 'Gottfried Keller und die Romantik: Eine motivvergleichende Studie', *Der Deutschunterricht*, 11.1 (1959), 14–30.

67. Compare the parallel location of the exotic in the domestic in Keller by Helmut Pfotenhauer, 'Die Wiederkehr der Einbildungen: Kellers *Pankraz, der Schmoller*', in Helmut Pfotenhauer, *Sprachbilder: Untersuchungen zur Literatur seit dem achtzehnten Jahrundert* (Würzburg: Königshausen & Neumann, 2000), pp. 175–86, here p. 179.
68. See for bibographical information the article in the *Deutsches Literatur-Lexikon*, XX (2000), cols. 600–03; also *Literaturlexikon*, XI (1991), cols. 252–53.
69. Citations are from *Mitteilungen aus den Akten betreffend den Zigeuner Tuvia Panti aus Ungarn und Anderes von Victor Strauss*, ed. by Lulu von Strauss und Torney (Berlin, Vienna: Meyer & Jessen, 1912), pp. 17–107. In her introduction (pp. 3–15) Lulu von Strauss und Torney records that the novella first appeared in the journal *Daheim* in the 1860s (pp. 12–13).
70. Franz Liszt, *Die Zigeuner und ihre Musik in Ungarn* (Pesth: Heckenast, 1861), pp. 93–100.
71. Liszt, pp. 99–101 (Note).
72. See Chapter 7.
73. See Chapter 7.

CHAPTER 5

German Knowledge, German Nation, and German Paths to Selfhood in Freytag and May

That curious close bond of German and Gypsy, so prominent in both Romantic and immediately post-Romantic epochs, is if anything strengthened in the increasingly nationalist writers of high realism. But the scepticism and cultural pessimism of Keller and Raabe are now forgotten. Differing as they do in many respects, both Gustav Freytag's *Die verlorene Handschrift* (1864) and Karl May's *Scepter und Hammer* (1879–80) nonetheless portray the Romany at a crucial juncture in German history as playing a positive, indeed central, part in an historical process which, as they see it, will bring the German nation into full possession of its birthright. In both cases it is a political birthright. In Freytag's case it is an intellectual one as well.

Die verlorene Handschrift[1] develops themes already established in the work which made his name, the hybrid social *Bildungsroman*, *Soll und Haben* (1855). The chosen form of the later work is the *Professorenroman*, a variant of the mainstream genre which focalizes the familiar social and educative interests through the figure of the professional scholar, and so has something specific to say about this class and the fate of the nation. In *Soll und Haben* Freytag (1816–95) had sought to produce the national liberal founding myth of the new German state after 1848. His emblematically named hero Anton Wohlfart, representative of the hard-working bourgeois estate and graduate in ethical as well as economic ideology of T. O. Schröter's Hanseatic trading house, eventually makes his fortune and comes into his own. Surviving economic and cultural conflicts in a German colony on the Polish border, he at last — after that decadent dynasty has nearly succumbed to the speculative intrigue of the Jew Veitel Itzig — restores the finances of the aristocratic Rothsattel family. He had wished to marry Freiherr von Rothsattel's daughter Leonora, but is rejected by reason of his bourgeois origin. Thus, in fulfilment of Freytag's programme of German renewal, he recognizes his mission and marries Schröter's daughter. That missionary programme — the rise to power of the bourgeoisie in a modified, constitutional German state — validates Wohlfart's capitalistic expertise and work ethic through pungent contrasts: a class contrast with the decadence of the Rothsattels, and a racial contrast with Itzig's parasitic manipulations and the slovenly mentality of the Polish neighbours. The novel thus also celebrates and legitimizes German colonies across the border, and stands at the beginning of what became a dubious tradition.[2] Nine years on, *Die verlorene Handschrift* too links a reflection on the German national destiny with an Oriental encounter. This time, however, it is neither the Jews nor the (equally 'Oriental') Slavs who play foil to the ideal German hero, but the Gypsies, and the cognitive interest shifts from the function of labour and free trade in the German body politic to the nature of the German system of knowledge[3] and its function to establish cultural well-being in that same body.

Let us treat the basic plot and sense of the text first. The motif of the lost manuscript links the reflection on knowledge with that of political culture. On the one hand, this manuscript represents the chief research motivation of the ideal hero, a young but already distinguished professor of classics at a large university, Felix Werner. He discovers a clue that the lost complete manuscript of Tacitus's (only partially preserved) *Histories* may have been concealed in the mid-seventeenth century in a house somewhere near the Rossau monastery, shortly before it was sacked by the invading Swedes. This is important not only in itself, but also because of the national interest. It will shed new light both on the Roman emperors and the earliest history of the 'Germanen' (Freytag, I, 13). The search for the manuscript eventually brings Felix and his colleague Fritz Hahn (a private scholar specializing in Indo-Germanic philology and myth) into contact with their ruler, and Freytag develops the hint of a Germanic dimension implicit in the pursuit of knowledge to link with the second, political thematic complex. For this novel is set, not in contemporary Germany, but (as Freytag's narrator informs us) in a politically presented 'schwachen kränklichen Zeitraum unserer Entwickelung' (II, 154). In this bad phase of German history Felix's once idealistic Prince has allied himself with 'ein fremder Eroberer' (154) — evidently Napoleon — only to abandon that alliance in good time to retain his crown. He is now the distant and self-indulgent ruler of a weakened, highly taxed, clearly Biedermeier nation with no public opinion and governed by a formidable bureaucracy (155). The principles of the *Vormärz* and 1848, the 'neue Zeit, welche sich auch in seinem Lande regte' (155), have yet to establish themselves. It is here that another dimension of Tacitus's *œuvre* becomes relevant. For Tacitus, as Felix fearlessly expounds him to the Prince, is also a didactic author, who teaches the dangers of 'Cäsarenwahnsinn' (II, 279), the 'dämonische Krankheit der Könige' (I, 15). This disease is not limited to Roman emperors. It breaks out when a ruler forgets the self-discipline necessary to his function in the system. He then considers himself above the law, inculcates a slavish mentality in his subjects, confuses the national interest with self-interest, and so starts a vicious cycle of political and cultural decline (II, 275–81) in which the failings of the ruler are reinforced by those of the nation; and so on. These two themes are finally integrated through a love-intrigue. In the shape of vigorous Amazonian blond Ilse, symbol of ideal German womanhood from time immemorial (I, 81, 96, 180), daughter of the farmer in whose house near Rossau the search begins, Felix has met his appropriate partner. But Ilse has also captivated the lascivious Prince, who has long since succumbed to 'Cäsarenwahnsinn'. Feigning an interest in the lost manuscript, the Prince summons newly wedded Felix and Ilse to the *Residenz* and intrigues to separate them. His seductive daughter lures Felix away to her isolated castle in pursuit of another clue, and there (II, 337 ff.), in an ancient attic full of emblematically decaying relics, Felix must choose between a glamorous future in the service of a dying system — the court[4] — and the more austere service of the new (II, 204–05), embodied by marriage with Ilse and middle-class values. At last the Prince, who has by now identified with Tiberius (II, 387 f.), is forced by more democratically minded courtiers to abdicate — but not before, in a dramatic finale, he has pursued Ilse recklessly across country to her ancestral farm and almost drowned in a flood. With that, the timeless critique embodied in Tacitus has been implemented in nineteenth-century Germany, and the new era dawns.

It thus matters little that the lost manuscript is never found.[5] It serves merely as a device which allows the protagonists to demonstrate their academic virtues and vices. For what is at stake here is something like a doctrine of the role of 'Wissenschaft' in the inculcation of Freytag's ideal national culture. Felix is the Wohlfart of the university. Books, he tells us, are '"die großen Schätzehüter des Menschengeschlechts. Das Beste, was je gedacht und erfunden wurde, bewahren sie aus einem Jahrhundert in das andere, sie verkünden, was nur einst auf Erden lebendig war"' (I, 247). The scholar's bookish world is a utopian community of remembrance and creative intellect transcending spatio-temporal contingency:

> 'So bildet der Inhalt aller Bücher ein großes Geisterreich auf Erden, von den vergangenen Seelen leben und nähren sich Alle, welche jetzt schaffen. In diesem Sinne ist der Geist des Menschengeschlechts eine unermeßliche Einheit, der jeder Einzelne angehört, der einst lebte und schuf, und jetzt athmet und Neues wirkt'. (249)

As a '"bescheidene[r] Arbeiter in diesem irdischen Geisterreich"' (249), Felix's role is to establish a positive bond between this world and the consciousness of the 'Volk'. Thus when his prospective father-in-law questions the relevance of his current project for the life of the common people: '"Wenn Sie von Ihrer Wissenschaft etwas erzählen wollten, meine Knechte würden vor Ihnen stehen wie Neger"' (I, 69), Felix launches an eloquent defence. In every age '"ernste wissenschaftliche Forschung"' may well, he concedes, seem esoteric. It nonetheless has always controlled '"ganz unsichtbar und in der Stille Seele und Leben des gesammten Volkes"' (69). Theory eventually informs practice, cultivated language eventually informs manners, the sense of right and law, the standard of living (69 f.). To settle questions of truth and untruth, beauty and ugliness, good and bad, these (decidedly Kantian) activities also make millions of people both free and better (70). In a later dispute with the village preacher, Felix adds a Hegelian note of harmony between struggle and unity, reason and faith. If life is conflict and destruction in one dimension, then we also sense an underlying unity, and it is the scholar's mission to uncover '"den innern Zusammenhang dieser Lebensgewalten"' (118). To make explicit that intellectual form ('"ewige Vernunft in Allem"', 118) which faith can only sense bonds faith and reason. The study of history, he teaches Ilse in equally Hegelian style, demonstrates that the nation ('"Volkskraft"', 347) recuperates what is lost in the individual. From this standpoint history is not ruin and death, but — thanks to the scholars — life, the triumphant progress of culture in nations (347). So it is that Felix can recognize as a mistake the Princess's beguiling offer of a post at court intended to revitalize its bond with the nation (II, 346), for he realizes that the court's decadence is too far gone (II, 397). Hope — he is thinking of the idyllic world of magisterial Ilse — lies elsewhere: '"Solange die Nation sich selbst verjüngt, vermag sie auch ihre Fürsten und die Leiter ihrer Geschäfte mit neuem Leben zu erfüllen. Denn wir sind nicht Römer, sondern warmherzige und dauerhafte Germanen"' (401). So, finally, Felix can take this notion of the sovereignty and sacred duty of the scholar in the process of cultural history as the basis for denunciation and secular excommunication of his nefarious colleague Magister Knips. For it is Knips who, in the service of his Prince and in emulation of that Prince's false consciousness (II, 242 f.), has faked a fragment of the lost manuscript and placed it in the attic of the Princess's country seat, there to play its part in the attempted seductions of both royal personages:

> Kein Purpur ist edler und keine Herrschaft ist machtvoller als die unsere, wir führen die Seelen unseres Volkes aus einem Jahrhundert in das andere, unser ist die Pflicht über seinem Lernen zu wachen und über seinen Gedanken. Wir sind seine Vorkämpfer gegen die Lüge und gegen die Gespenster aus vergangener Zeit, welche noch unter uns wandeln mit dem Schein des Lebens bekleidet. Was wir zum Leben weihen, das lebt, und was wir verdammen, das vergeht. Von uns werden jetzt die alten Tugenden der Apostel gefordert, gering zu achten, was vergänglich ist, und die Wahrheit zu verkünden. Sie waren in diesem Sinn geweiht wie Jeder von uns, Ihr Leben verpflichtet Ihrem Gott. Auf Ihnen lag, wie auf uns allen, Verantwortung für die Seelen unserer Nation. Sie haben sich dieses Amtes unwerth gemacht, und ich traure, ich traure armer Mann, daß ich Sie davon scheiden muß. (II, 423–24)

Some have argued that Knips is Jewish.[6] If that were so, his activity as faker would fit well with the traditional stereotype of the Jewish nation, and reinforce in a further respect his role in the novel's symbolic economy as contrastive foil to Felix.

But if in this utopian novel German 'Wissenschaft' is the cultural therapy for the disease diagnosed by Tacitus, what, then, is the role of the Gypsies? In one dimension the Gypsies are a vehicle for mild satire on Freytag's utopia of 'Wissenschaft' when misapplied. Frau Oberamtmännin Rollmaus, wife of the village's highest dignitary and a close relative of Mrs Malaprop, represents (by contrast to the learned wives of the university professors on the one hand and Ilse on the other) petty bourgeois, provincial pretence. On learning of Fritz Hahn's specialism (ancient Indian languages), this would-be learned woman helpfully observes that he is wrong to search for Indians in these parts. In that line of things they have only Gypsies. She has recently noted the presence of a small band of these thieves, and they of course, as she knows from her 'Conversationslexikon' (I, 112–13) originate in India.[7] But as the farmer's children scurry to check this information in their own, later edition of the lexicon, the subject is dropped. Something much more significant for Frau Rollmaus's credulous mentality has emerged: Professor Felix Werner *himself* is the subject of an article in the last volume (114). Henceforth his authority is never challenged.

In this way, however, the Gypsies are also skilfully introduced as actors and linked with the theme of knowledge and nation, at least as objects of knowledge.

Ilse and Felix soon after encounter the band in question, which is for the most part presented in wholly conventional terms as the familiar pre-cultural stereotype and polar opposite of the Germans (and indeed differs in no material respect from the image in the *Conversationslexikon*). The band of six or eight persons is realized in typically exotic colours, interestingly dressed and with a variety of animals in tow (166–67). For Ilse they are '"ihr Wilden"' (167). They surround her like savages, staring greedily, shamelessly plucking at her person, and begging (166–67). Once a 'Landplage' (168), they are now rarely seen in these parts and considered only a minor nuisance. Ilse can quell them with her own, natural matriarchal authority and a telling reference to their need for (non-existent) passports (167). She forbids the (in any case illegal) begging, insists that money is given only in exchange for work, and assigns them a place to stay for one night only. But although security measures are intensified, the Gypsies still attempt to steal two children, and Felix is injured in repelling the attack (171–72). The band melts away in the night, never to be seen again.

But that is not the last of the Gypsy motif in the novel. The meeting in the wood also serves to introduce a key figure in the political intrigue. It will come as no surprise to the attentive reader of these pages that the band of Gypsies is led by a charismatic, once beautiful (I, 167) matriarch. During her first encounter with Ilse she delivers in strangely cultivated German and in contravention of Ilse's reprimand another kind of knowledge, a prophecy which is true or not true, depending on the referentiality selected for its metaphors:

> 'Der Herr da neben Ihnen sucht einen Schatz, aber er soll sich hüten, daß er ihn nicht verliert; und Sie, stolzes Fräulein, werden einem Manne lieb sein, der eine Krone trägt, und Sie werden die Wahl haben, ob Sie eine Königin werden wollen, die Wahl und die Qual'. (I, 170)

Felix's treasure is of course Ilse herself, not the lost manuscript. Ilse's 'king' could be taken literally to connote her erotic fascination for the Prince, and the dilemma in which she is (theoretically) placed by his intrigue; or, as she herself notes, it could refer to Felix's rise to the office of rector (II, 5), 'monarch' of the university. This quasi-mystical note of the validated fatal prophecy contrasts curiously with the mockery to which Frau Rollmaus's belief in Gypsy clairvoyance is subjected (I, 113; II, 322), and certainly leavens the novel's otherwise unrelieved Hegelian scientism. With this strangely prominent epistemological counter-discourse is linked her agency in the intrigue. As her educated accent in German betrays, this nameless Gypsy woman — none of the Gypsies is named in *Die verlorene Handschrift* — has participated in *gadjo* life in an earlier period. She is in fact, as the first, dramatic confrontation of the two majestic women, the ideal German Ilse and the charismatic Gypsy leader, suggests, a double or mirror of Ilse herself. Driven by conscience, driven to the extent that she forces her tribe into imprisonment and death in the hostile German environment, so that she is its last free survivor (II, 321), it is she who much later accosts Ilse at the *Residenz* and reveals the truth about the fate — as his mistress — which the Prince has prepared for her. For she too, in her beautiful youth, has played that part: '"Geben Sie junge Frau, einer Kranken von der Landstraße, die einst denselben Weg gegangen ist, den Sie jetzt schreiten"' (321; compare II, 462). The charismatic Gypsy woman, it turns out, was once also commandeered from the road into the princely household. Worse, when removed by his mother from the Prince's environment, she is forced to act as the companion of his next mistress, who is driven insane by her fate (462–63). She has thus returned to warn Ilse, and it is of course this intervention, motivated in meta-rational intuition, which works. It is the sight of her, standing at the flooded river bank, which causes the impassioned and maddened Prince to lose his mind and collapse into the purging waters (467). She is last seen, however, cradling his head in her arms (467).

Thus in addition to their wholly conventional representation as abject and amoral outsiders, Freytag discloses a further dimension of the Gypsies in Germany and a further, very unexpected dimension of his theory of knowledge. The charismatic and heroic Gypsy woman is not only Ilse's opposite, but also her equal and counterpart. She is on the one hand conscience and solidarity embodied, and on the other the return of the Prince's repressed. Something oddly analogous is true at the epistemological level of her clairvoyance. For despite the novel's overweening scientistic ideology, her action on the authority of an alien, 'Oriental' paradigm of knowledge ensures the establishment of a utopian German constitution. This valorization of an alternative, unofficial, 'Oriental' concept of knowledge in the symbolic order of the novel links curiously with the figure of Felix's colleague Fritz Hahn, specialist in comparative Sanskrit and German mythology. Fritz is attacked by the established Felix, 'Kind der Sonne' and child of Enlightenment (I, 5), for his '"Suchen im indischen Götterglauben und deutscher Mythologie"'. His youthful energies should not be expended in a field of (suspect) '"unklaren Anschauungen und Bildern unter wesenlosen Schatten"'; he should take up an official position at the university (18). His book indeed seems to suggest deep-lying affinities of the ancient Indians with pre-modern, pre-Faustian, pre-Enlightenment Germans:

> handelte [. . .] von den alten Indern, wie von den alten Deutschen, es besprach das Leben unserer Vorfahren, vor der Zeit, in welcher diese den verständigen Entschluß faßten, auf dem Blocksberg artige Brockensträuße zu binden und im Vater Rhein ihre Trinkhörner auszuspülen. [. . .] es enthüllte [. . .] viele geheime Tiefen der Urzeit"'. (295)

The book is a great success, but it does not persuade Fritz into the academy. Thus Freytag's novel seems to conceal an esoteric counter-discourse, defending 'Oriental' modalities of insight, implying an atavistic Gypsy-Indian affinity with the Teutonic, and defending an unofficial, frankly Romantic science outside of the university, which is deeply at odds with its Hegelian progressiveness. Given that this alternative episteme provides a further contrast with the 'Jewish' Knips's fakery, it can be seen that Freytag also reinscribes the familiar Romantic notion of the dual alterity, Jew and Gypsy. Even so the chief representative of Gypsy knowledge receives no historical reward for her pains. Like Ilse the leader of a family, the Gypsy heroine leads her family not into a utopian political future but into the imprisonment and death which even the utopian German state will not change; and Freytag's novel shows no sign of mitigating that unrelieved tragedy.

Karl May's Gypsy writings are pitched at a lower level of intellectual ambition than those of Freytag but evince numerous thematic and ideological parallels. May (1842–1912),[8] prolific and phenomenally successful author of exotic adventure tales, inventor of the legendary Winnetou, Old Shatterhand, and Kara Ben Nemsi, produced two Gypsy novels: *Scepter und Hammer* (1879–80) and *Die Juweleninsel* (1880–82).[9] His cultural knowledge base is traditionally suspect. He only travelled to the 'Orient' in 1899 and America in 1908, so that any ethnographic authenticity in texts predating those journeys derives from his study of travel literature and other sources, including fiction.[10] On this account it is also generally held that the referential meaning of his exotic narratives focuses in true Orientalist style less on the target culture than recursively on his native Germany.[11] *Scepter und Hammer* being by far the more elaborate and successful of May's two major Gypsy-related novels,[12] it will serve as prime example of his Gypsy image.[13] May's Gypsies, it will be argued, are deeply ambiguous. On the one hand, unlike those of Freytag and regressively in terms of the tradition, they belong in the *Preciosa* tradition of the fake Gypsy and embody the visceral anti-Gypsyism which that connotes. On the other they also deploy elements of the higher *Zigeunerromantik* tradition, in that they use Gypsy actors to make a statement about Germany's political constitution — and this in the age when the incipient nationalism of Freytag's day is at its apogee and beginning to develop colonial ambition.

It seems likely, to begin with the *Preciosa* tradition, that Eduard Devrient's opera libretto *Die Zigeuner* (1832)[14] influenced the basic situation of *Scepter und Hammer*. In that text, the reader recalls, we encounter the Gypsies in an illegal encampment on the estate of Graf Hohenegk, where they have lost their *Wayda* (leader), and turn for advice to the wise woman Beda. The man who takes that role, Polgar, is not a Gypsy but, following the fake Gypsy tradition, the lost son of Graf Hohenegk. This man, enraged by the (false) suspicion of his wife's infidelity, had abandoned wife and son many years ago in the forest. The Gypsies have rescued the boy and brought him up as one of their own. In the happy *dénouement* Polgar casts off any superficial acculturation, re-internalizes his original identity, returns (as Beda cries) like a young eagle to the nest (Devrient, 407), takes on his true role as redeemer and continuer of the decadent Hohenegk line in troubled political times, and magnanimously permits the Gypsies permanent residence in the forests which are now his.

The situation, symbolism, and political interest of May's *Scepter und Hammer* reveal several basic parallels to this. Here too we find an illegal, if tolerated encampment of Gypsies, this time under the leadership of the *Vajdzina* Geza (212), on the estate of the Herzog von Raumburg.[15] There lives Katombo, a young man who proudly identifies with the Romany nation (218), but whose appearance — tanned, yet visibly dyed fair skin, glossy black, but visibly dyed blond hair, the 'unbedingt nordisches Gepräge' (214) of his face, his blue-grey eyes and distinctive, self-assured body-language — instantly signals his true *gadjo* racial origin. Raumburg, like Devrient's (and Freytag's) villains, is tolerating the Romanies in order to pursue a predatory sexual interest in the beautiful Gypsy girl Zarba, who however happens to be Katombo's lover. In this Raumburg is only repeating a family behaviour pattern from one generation to the next. His father had been fascinated by none other than *Vajdzina* Geza in her youth, who had left the tribe for him, but returned when abandoned. In revenge Geza has stolen the boy-child of his new German wife (244–45). As the faded and distorted eagle tattoo on his arm reveals (213–14, 240, 244, 253), that stolen son is none other than Katombo. Thus Katombo at last assumes the title, office, and name of his true father Raumburg (672 f.) and so enters into his Germanic cultural and institutional inheritance, whilst also, like Polgar, retaining his friendship and proto-kinship with the Gypsies.

However, May's articulation of this slender Gypsy-German plot paradigm is a good deal more inflated in its political pretensions than Devrient's watery critique of the Biedermeier aristocracy, and even more ambitious than Freytag's. The political dispute in which these Gypsies are involved concerns not some remote provincial patrimony but an entire nation, or, better, the fate of two great constituent German states, which figure in *Scepter und Hammer* as the rival kingdoms of Norland and Süderland. These states, both with absolutist constitutions (79), are locked in mutual distrust (79) and engaged for the duration of the action in a customs dispute in their mountainous border region (61, 78, 576). They finally fight a war with constitutional consequences for both. Norland and Süderland, it is plain, are thinly disguised fictionalizations of the major North- and South-German political entities from 1848 to 1862 and, more significantly, after.[16] At that time of course the 39-state *Deutscher Bund*, following the reaction against the 1848 Revolution, consisted in an uneasy union of the more or less constitutional Prussian monarchy and the restorative-reactionary, neo-absolutist monarchy[17] of Franz Josef's Austria-Hungary. Yet this union was constantly threatened by the inner border separating the southern partner from the *Zollverein*[18] of the northern states under the dominance of an ambitious, expansionist Prussia. Following the Prusso-Austrian campaign against Denmark over the Schleswig-Holstein question in 1864 and the subsequent Prusso-Austrian war of 1866, the *Deutscher Bund* was of course dissolved in favour of the *Norddeutscher Bund* under Prussian — Bismarckian — hegemony and the Austro-Hungarian monarchy. Both were soon to undergo further constitutional reform, and the Second German Empire would come in only five years. Into this transparently allegorized version of the major German political conflict of the age, no less, May plunges his Gypsies.

In this context, of power and empowerment, May's Romanies have a curiously duplicitous aspect. As we saw with Katombo/Raumburg, May is on the one hand concerned from the outset to present one of the two major Gypsy figures and most significant actors in the narrative as a non-Romany. Katombo is never confused by his Romany companions with a true Romany, but remains loyal to his adopted nation, and always feels he must prove '"daß ich trotz meiner weißen Haut ein ächter Brinjaare bin!"' (218). Even so, he remains in them rather than of them. Apart from his eloquently Germanic appearance, he possesses intellectual, linguistic, and aesthetic powers acknowledged to be superior in every respect (save that of prophecy) to those of the Romanies (214–16) — as for example when Zarba begs him, as recognized poet of the tribe, to versify her vision of the Gypsy nature goddess Bhowannie in her dualistic positive and negative aspects (215–17). Forced after the conflict with Raumburg over Zarba to build a new life in Egypt — this perhaps seen as a homecoming[19] — Katombo, by now described as 'der frühere Zigeuner' (323), displays the thoroughly un-Romany-like quality of autodidactic book-learning (347–48, 394), and this transforms him — in this surely a meta-fictional portrait of May himself[20] — into the even less Romany-like person of brilliant naval architect and sea-captain. A Christian rather than a devotee of Bhowannie (although that is not explained, 483), he there chooses a Christian wife, Ayescha (349, 445) who is as deeply opposed to the Islamic doctrine of Kismet as he (347–48), and structures his life in conscious opposition to 'Oriental' practice (348, 445) on the basis of free will: without servants or harem, according to his — presumably innate — 'abendländische[. . .] Anschauungen' (454). In a sense, Katombo/Raumburg also brilliantly exploits his hybrid upbringing (if not ancestry) to mediate between Occident and Orient. He designs or modifies two ships, the *Selim*, a Nile barge which, thanks to his innovative sailing tackle (352) and sharply contoured keel (158–59), is also capable of voyaging the high seas, and indeed rescues his family from an Egyptian conflict thanks to this very quality (352, 394). He also comes into possession of the *Tiger* (479), which over the course of time is modified to contain the very best synthesis of cutting-edge western technology (a petroleum-powered steam engine, 167, a jet-system in place of a propeller, 661)[21] and eastern tradition. This remarkable vessel, which thanks to its ingenious folding masts (151) and smoke-consuming boiler (661) is also capable of numerous camouflaging changes in appearance (150–51), is the match of any steam-powered gunboat a conventional western navy can produce and the tool of Katombo's later, all-conquering sea campaigns. The *Tiger*'s metamorphic ability is matched only by that of its architect, as Katombo, prior to assuming the identity of a Raumburg at the conclusion, changes into Nurwan Pascha, High Admiral of the Turkish Navy (429, 431). None of this prominently foregrounded occidental Christianity, rationalistic mastery of technology, or protean culturality, however, prevents Katombo also finding his main motivation for existence in the (allegedly) Romany principle of revenge — on Raumburg for the ruination of his proposed union with Zarba (218).

As for the 'true' Gypsies, they are presented with a mix of deeply contradictory ethnographic conventionality, slovenliness, and invention. Much is conventionally apologetic. May's Gypsies naturally live in cultural primitivity and social denigration. They do not belong to 'jenen nomadisierenden Horden [. . .], die Raub und Diebstahl als ihr eigentliches und einträglichstes Gewerbe betreiben' (211). Their comfortable forest settlement is however merely tolerated (225–26) on sufferance of the feudal lord thanks to his erotic incontinence. Thereafter they are forced into nomadism (674) and the usual marginal, illegal trades of begging and smuggling (14–15). Yet this lawlessness is also seen as explicable by anti-Gypsyism: '"Der Gitano ist ein gehetzter Hund, der sich nur wehren kann, wenn er nicht nach dem Gesetze fragt"' (89), says Zarba's brother Karavey. Zarba at one stage has to be rescued from drowning as an alleged witch (116). Inevitably, Zarba is presented first as an erotically beautiful Gypsy girl and then, after a mere twenty years have elapsed and before the age of fifty, as prematurely aged Gypsy crone (212–13, 14). Despite their low status, Gypsies are however in truth honourable, loyal and trustworthy to those who defend them (116–17). Zarba, despite the example of Katombo, offers a fierce and well-founded critique of occidental Christianity's perversely bloody history and apology of heathen creeds (116).

May otherwise presents his Gypsies with entertainingly minimalized concern for consistency or ethnographic scruple. They are referred to by the narrator and other *gadjo* figures in the narrative indiscriminately as 'Zigeuner/Zigeunerin' (82, 252), 'Lampardaaren'/'Lambardaaren' (17, 385) or 'Brinjaaren' (17, 114, 218), 'Zingaaren'/'Zingaritto'/'Zingaritta' (16, 114, 223, 247, 253) and 'Gitani'/'Gitana' (214, 223, 599), and even adopt this helplessly mixed terminology in their own talk (214, 218).[22] Culturally speaking, their most striking feature is the *Carmen*-like love of tobacco, which Zarba constantly enjoys in her pipe (28, 114), and which is especially imported, it transpires, from the home mountains of the Brinjaaren, where it is harvested by virgins under the light of the moon on the slopes of Mount Pandjköra (114). Only princes can afford its price (114); no Gypsy will touch *gadjo* tobacco (114). Men and women smoke different kinds (212). This tobacco, indeed, catalyses the other chief feature of Gypsy culture in May's imagination, the women's power of prophecy. The virgins enjoy its leaves before seeing the future in their temple (114). Zarba possesses the power in greater measure than any other of her tribe (115) and demonstrates it (17, 118, 673–74) with unerring accuracy, so that her observations project fatal compulsion over the chaotically unfolding action. As for their home, May's Gypsy nation is presented more or less definitively as originating in India, but commanded — for no given reason — by the goddess Bhowannie to wander strange lands, 'und hat weder Ruhe noch Rast, bis der Wunderbaum gefunden ist, an welchem es sich versammelt, um die Erde zu beherrschen' (17). Bhowannie at least has a home, on the island of Madagascar, called by the Brinjaaren 'Nossindambo' (214). As for Bhowannie's people, May never explains what or where their utopian 'Wunderbaum' might be.[23] But perhaps the almost inaccessible 'Tannenschlucht' (88), placed in the most sublime location on the mountainous border of Norland and Süderland, site of the customs conflict and the smuggling trade, gives a hint. Here, guarded by the aged 'Lowenji' Tirban in his 'Lowenja' (hut), situated '"stets an der Grenze zweier Länder"' (89), is a continually maintained place of '"Zuflucht und Hilfe"' (89) for the troubled Romanies. There, as the action of the novel matures, resides (so far as she resides anywhere) Zarba. She indeed turns out like Isabella, Mitidika, and Freytag's charismatic Gypsy woman to be both abject vagrant and Gypsy princess in one, and, like Esmeralda in Hugo's *Notre-Dame de Paris*, to stand at the head of a secret, yet powerful Gypsy state-within-a-state. But as with Katombo, and as ever with May, the execution of justice (individual rather than official) is the chief motivation of all action,[24] and the real mainspring of Zarba's tragic life is revenge (668). Just as Geza stole Katombo in revenge for her betrayal by Raumburg senior, so Zarba seeks revenge on Raumburg junior, for his destruction of her love-affair with his full brother Katombo. '"Des Gitano höchstes Gut"', says Geza, '"ist die Rache"' (246), and Zarba's simulated love for Raumburg (116) is '"das Werkzeug der Rache"' (247). Poor Raumburg junior is thus the target of a pincer movement in revenge by both Katombo, the fake Gypsy, and the real Gypsy Zarba.

Their common desire for personal sexual revenge mediates the Gypsies' entry into the high political intrigue. As in Freytag's Germany, so in Norland and Süderland discontent is brewing beyond the horizon of the Gypsy world. Apart from the customs war, Wilhelm II of Norland is failing to govern his people. He *is* a man of the people. Sceptre-bearer though he be, he is often found hammering the anvil of court blacksmith Albert Brandauer (59–60). He even asks Brandauer's view of the customs war (61), and is godfather to his son (13). Yet his indecisiveness divides the various estates of his country (80). Apparently childless, he is thus the unwitting target of a plot led by none other than Raumburg, now first minister in his brother's, the King's, government (80) and complicit with Max Joseph, King of Süderland. This king, by contrast to Wilhelm (but like the Austrian Emperor Franz Josef), personifies the neo-absolutist dynastic tradition of '"l'état c'est moi"' (79) and follows a brutally nationalist and isolationist policy. Raumburg's goal is thus to destabilize Norland internally (to which end he is even conspiring with international Jesuit-anarchist forces, 36, 41), to assume power with Süderlandish support after Wilhelm's overthrow, to marry his son (the third generation of dissolute Raumburgs) to Princess Asta of Süderland (16, 94–95), and so ensure dynastic survival. Thus both realms will at last be fused in personal union into a new 'großdeutsche Lösung', a second, pan-German empire.

The stage is thus set for the Romany interventions. Katambo, who grows ever less significant in the plot, makes his contribution in the guise of Admiral Nurwan Pascha. For Norland, like Bismarck's Germany,[25] has developed a 'Kolonialkompagnie' (151), and Katombo is raiding their ships (151, 481–82) on the high seas. At home it is Zarba, the full-blooded Gypsy, who foils the uprising. She, it turns out, has consummated her affair with Raumburg (30), indeed married him in due legal form (672), so that his own son by a *gadjo* mother — destined for Asta — is illegitimate. Equally, she has monitored the progress of Raumburg's conspiracy from afar (135–36), and knows his most important secret: '"Prinzenraub"' (30). Wilhelm *has*, after all, sired a son and heir. However Raumburg has bribed the midwife to exchange him with a girl. Knowing that the Herzog would soon threaten the heir's life even at his foster parents', Zarba's revenge has therefore taken the traditional Gypsy form of still another child-theft. She has swapped the legitimate heir with *another* baby boy, the son of court blacksmith Albert Brandauer, man of the people, intimate and informal counsellor of the King (670–71). Thus it emerges that not only is Katombo, the fake Gypsy, the legitimate son of the Herzog von Raumburg, but the smith's son Dr Max Brandauer, seemingly a bourgeois, is the legitimate son of the King and heir to the throne of Norland. Gypsy child-theft is valorized by May as an instrument which produces revenge and justice in equal measure.

It is therefore only appropriate that as Katombo fades Max Brandauer should join Zarba to combat the Jesuitical-anarchist-absolutist-greater German conspiracy. Max solves the Jesuits' secret code (28, 51–52, 537) and has them and Raumburg arrested. Wilhelm, prompted by criticism from Max's bourgeois perspective (508–09), gives his people a constitution drafted by Max (573). Hearing this, members of all estates in the *Volk* (647–48) rush to defend their country as Süderland invades at the border pass. The brave and apparently patriotic Norlandish Gypsies join with Norlandish forces to stop them (573, 644–45). Raumburg dies in a ravine attempting to escape across the border (673). Right-thinking Süderlanders (including Asta) bring down the Süderlandish régime from within, and Süderland too receives a constitution (666). Last but not least, the border tolls are to be dropped (576). Just as Zarba — in this mimicking Freytag's Gypsy leader — had prophesied (17), the bourgeois son of a blacksmith sits on the throne of Norland, and 'Scepter und Hammer' (674), the union of ruler and *Volk*, becomes the motto of the new, rejuvenated régime.

What might this exotic confection mean? In political terms May, it is clear, has delivered a National Liberal political sermon in novel form, more or less sanctioning Prussian policy under Bismarck and legitimating in retrospect the 'kleindeutsch' status quo of 1871. The 'großdeutsch' conspirators are thwarted. The anarchistic, revolutionary socialists and their Catholic fellow-travellers (or the Jesuits anyway) are condemned. A moderate, constitutional, Prussian-style monarchy is propounded as the alternative, symbolized by the accession to the throne of a man imbued with bourgeois political beliefs. A bourgeois writes the constitution, but he was the King's son all along. Max Brandauer's proudly independent bourgeois stand against legitimist feudal privilege is lauded (16). The unmodernized nobility is attacked in the style of Immermann and Freytag. France is the ideological enemy. Free trade, in the form of the abolition of all customs duties, is advocated. Technological progress is extolled. The colonial expansion, about which Bismarck was for decades undecided, is clearly advocated.[26]

But the Gypsies' role in all this is still wholly ambiguous. True, May makes them into the major agent of reform and reconstituting the German body politic. The Gypsies' battle at the pass is compared with the Spartans' defence of (more or less) democratic Athens at Thermopylae (640), no less, and the secret nation of right-minded patriotic Norlandish Gypsies is scrupulously contrasted with the *Kulturkampf* symbol of the secret internationalist neo-Jesuit society. Zarba is acknowledged as his royal equal by Wilhelm II when they conduct their first summit meeting (668). Zarba is a mastermind, strategic child-thief, and mythical agent of freedom and justice. May's Gypsies as a whole are noble mediators, exotics with a mystic gift, but possessed of courageous National Liberal, indeed sound proto-Prussian instincts.

That said, May's closures tell another tale. True, the *gadjo* sailor Balduin Schubert and Karavey attest to the possibility of friendships across the cultural divide (80 ff.), catalysed by the shared love of tobacco. Some intercultural and -racial marriages are sanctioned. Arthur von Sternburg marries Katombo's half-Egyptian daughter Almah (577–78, 660). The hybrid child of Zarba's revenge union with Raumburg, Hauptmann von Wallroth (76), is finally acknowledged as heir to Katombo's bloodline. But there are powerful counter-indicators. Only Prussians — the brilliantly protean Katombo-Raumburg and the master decoder Max Brandauer, both Norlanders privileged by an encounter with otherness of culture or class — seem capable of intercultural competence. The interracial unions (as we shall see later in Jensen) which are sanctioned always consist in marriage *into* the German bloodline and cultural sphere. Most tellingly, Zarba herself stands under the sign of homelessness and death. She rejects Wilhelm's offer of a place in the family as Katombo's wife, preferring to wander until her soul returns to Bhowannie (673). When in *Die Juweleninsel* she finally dies, murdered by Raumburg's son, it is as 'die letzte Königin der Zingaren' (*Juweleninsel*, 573). Her death merely mirrors that of her entire nation: '"Ich versinke und verschwinde wie unser Volk, ohne Heimath, im Windesrauschen"' (573).[27] The Gypsies, then, for Karl May, may serve the end of realizing a constitutional, colonial, Protestant German nation-state. But they themselves, as the counter-indicators betray, are doomed by a sentimental racism — closely similar to that of Fenimore Cooper — to the fate of the last Mohicans, and the only good Gypsy for May turns out to be either a Prussian at heart or dead.

Together, Freytag and May represent the extraordinary continued vitality of the Germans' identification with their Orientalist equal and opposite nation in this paradoxical century. As if Keller and Raabe had never written their gloomy deconstructions of Germanic self-constitution strategies, Freytag and May revive the Romantic paradigm, and present the encounter with the Gypsy as something like the *conditio sine qua non* of Germanic national self-becoming. In each case the Gypsies seem to play the role of saviour. But in each case, and despite Freytag's fleeting affirmation of the Gypsy way of knowing, that act of salvation also seems to involve the saviour's tragic self-sacrifice.

Notes to Chapter 5

1. Citations are from Gustav Freytag, *Die verlorene Handschrift: Roman in fünf Büchern*, 38th edn, 2 vols (Leipzig: S. Hirzel, 1904).
2. See on this Kontje, *German Orientalisms*, pp. 196–209.
3. See for an excellent study of this aspect Volker C. Dürr, 'Idealistische Wissenschaft: Der (bürgerliche) Realismus und Gustav Freytag's Roman "Die verlorene Handschrift"', *Zeitschrift für deutsche Philologie*, 120 (2001), 3–33.
4. He has never dedicated a book to any member of the ruling estate (II, 176).
5. The sole remnant, its ornate front board, is found buried in the soil in the grotto where Felix and Ilse first declared their love.
6. See Martin Gubser, *Literarischer Antisemitismus: Untersuchungen zu Gustav Freytag und anderen bürgerlichen Schriftstellern des 19. Jahrhunderts* (Göttingen: Vandenhoeck & Ruprecht, 1998), esp. pp. 187–238, 239–47. Compare on *Soll und Haben* Robert C. Holub, *Reflections of Realism: Paradox, Norm and Ideology in Nineteenth-Century German Prose* (Detroit: Wayne State University Press, 1991), pp. 176–86.
7. Compare for example the similarly denunciatory terms of the article 'Zigeuner' in the *Kleines Brockhaus'sches Lexikon für den Handgebrauch*, 4 vols (Leipzig: Brockhaus, 1856), IV/3, 801. Thanks to Frank Möbus for obtaining this article.
8. See for a representative view of trends in recent Karl May scholarship Nina Berman, 'The Appeal of Karl May in the Wilhelmine Empire: Emigration, Modernization, and the Need for Heroes', in *Companion to German Realism*, ed. by Todd Kontje, pp. 283–305; also, for a sceptical assessment of May's status, Jeffrey L. Sammons, *Ideology, Mimesis, Fantasy: Charles Sealsfield, Friedrich Gerstäcker, Karl May, and Other German Novelists of America* (Chapel Hill and London: University of North Carolina Press, 1998), pp. 229–56. For interesting comments on sedimented techniques of avant-garde narrative structure in May's work see Gustav Frank, *Krise und Experiment: Komplexe Erzähltexte im literarischen Umbruch des 19. Jahrhunderts* (Wiesbaden: Deutscher Universitätsverlag, 1998), pp. 544–67. The *Sonderband Karl May* of *Text + Kritik* (1987) offers a good overview of earlier scholarship and a select bibliography by Jürgen Wehnert (pp. 279–96).

9. References are to Karl May, *Scepter und Hammer* and *Die Juweleninsel*, in *Karl Mays Werke: Historisch-kritische Ausgabe für die Karl May-Stiftung*, ed. by Hermann Wiedenroth (Bargfeld: Bücherhaus, 1993–), Abt. 2, Bd. 1 and 2 (1998; first edn, 1987). The editions *Zepter und Hammer* (Vienna and Heidelberg: Karl May Taschenbücher im Verlag Carl Ueberreuter, 1952) and *Die Juweleninsel* (Vienna, Heidelberg: Karl May Taschenbücher im Verlag Carl Ueberreuter, 1952) are spectacularly corrupt. May also published *Der Gitano: Ein Abenteuer unter den Carlisten*, in *Der Beobachter an der Elbe*, 2 (1874–75), no. 52.
10. See on this Berman, 'Appeal of Karl May', pp. 285–86, and Sammons, *Ideology, Mimesis, Fantasy*, pp. 243–45.
11. See for example Volker Klotz, 'Machart und Weltanschauung eines Kolportagereißers: Karl Mays *Das Waldröschen*', in *Text + Kritik. Sonderband Karl May* (1987), pp. 60–89, esp. pp. 60–66. See on May's Orientalism Nina Berman, *Orientalismus, Kolonialismus und Moderne: Zum Bild des Orients in der deutschsprachigen Literatur um 1900* (Stuttgart: Metzler, 1997), pp. 41–164; also Kontje, *German Orientalisms*, p. 233.
12. *Die Juweleninsel* is the sequel to *Scepter und Hammer*, but features only a few — Zarba, Katombo/ Raumburg, and Karavey — of the Gypsy cast so prominent in the earlier novel, and then only in background roles.
13. So far as I can tell, May's Romany texts, chief among them *Scepter und Hammer* and *Die Juweleninsel*, have with one exception only been cursorily treated by previous scholars, and scarcely at all in respect of Romany culture. The exception is Eckehard Koch, '"Der Gitano ist ein gehetzter Hund": Karl May und die Zigeuner', in *Jahrbuch der Karl-May-Gesellschaft* (1989), pp. 178–229. This meritorious study of the motif of the Romany in Karl May's *œuvre* treats *Scepter und Hammer*, pp. 211–17. However, its cognitive interest is largely exhausted by speculative, positivistic investigation of May's possible sources and an enthusiastic defence of May's Gypsy image. There is no interest in assessing the role of the Gypsies *as* Gypsies in the generation of (for example) the novel's meaning. See on other aspects of *Die Juweleninsel* Volker Klotz, '*Die Juweleninsel* — und was daraus werden könnte. Lese-Notizen zu den Erstlingsromanen nebst einigen Fragen zur Karl-May-Forschung', *Jahrbuch der Karl-May-Gesellschaft* (1979), 262–75; also, on the Gypsies as fatal requisite and exoticized outsiders in *Das Waldröschen* (1880–82), Klotz, 'Machart und Weltanschauung', pp. 71–72, 86–87; also, for a good survey, Christoph F. Lorenz, '*Scepter und Hammer*' and '*Die Juweleninsel*', in *Karl-May-Handbuch*, ed. by Gerd Ueding and Klaus Rettner, 2nd edn (Würzburg: Königshausen & Neumann, 2001), pp. 305–12. In the tradition of specialist Romany scholarship May is scarcely represented. See Hehemann, pp. 147–48, and Michail Krausnick, 'Images of Sinti and Roma in German Children's and Teenage Literature', in *Sinti and Roma*, ed. by Susan Tebbutt, pp. 107–28 (pp. 115–16).
14. See Chapter 2.
15. It is interesting to note that the popular edition of *Scepter und Hammer* (Karl May, *Zepter und Hammer: Ungekürzte Ausgabe* (Vienna-Heidelberg. Karl May Taschenbücher im Verlag Carl Ueberreuter, 1952), 318 pp.), uses the name 'Hohenegg' for the Raumburg family. That said, this extraordinary edition merits a scholarly study of its own. Not only is the text (despite the claim) drastically cut, it is also narratologically and ideologically manipulated. The original flashback narrative structure is clumsily transformed into linear chronological order. Germany's nineteenth-century colonial activities are valorized and promoted, an insistent anti-Britishness (Britain as bitter and faithless colonial rival of Germany) quite opposed to the anglophile tenor of the original is introduced, the anti-Catholic and anti-clerical Jesuit motif is elided, the rival kings are relegated to mere dukes, and the hybrid Gypsy-German Major von Wallroth is — for racial reasons? — killed off.
16. Compare Christoph F. Lorenz, 'Karl Mays kleines Welttheater', *Mitteilungen der Karl-May-Gesellschaft*, 42 (1979), 31–33, and Christoph F. Lorenz, 'Von der *Messingstadt* zur *Stadt der Toten*: Bildlichkeit und literarische Tradition von *Ardistan und Dschinnistan*', in *Text + Kritik. Sonderband Karl May* (1987), pp. 222–43 (p. 22). Also Blackbourn, pp. 236–59.
17. See Blackbourn, p. 226.
18. See Blackbourn, pp. 243–59.
19. May presents the Gypsies as of 'indische oder ägyptische Abstammung' (214), and Zarba possesses an 'ideale Stirn, etwas egyptisch vorstehend' (212).

20. Such was May's sly habit. Another such partial self-portrait is doubtless the characterization of Arthur von Sternburg's lyrical (Orientalizing) description of Egyptian womanhood as '"ethnographischen Essay"' (pp. 142–44, esp. p. 144).
21. Compare however p. 167 for an inconsistency.
22. Compare Balduin Schubert: '"Gitano, Zingaritto oder Zigeuner, mir Alles gleich"' (p. 83).
23. Eckehard Koch has made strenuous conjectures on May's ethnographic researches concerning the elaborate superstructure of Gypsy religion and the Gypsy relation to Madagascar (Koch, '"Der Zigeuner ist ein gehetzter Hund"', pp. 207–09). Grellmann and other Gypsy ethnographic authorities record no such divinity in the world of Gypsy devotion. In fact May's source seems much more likely to have been A. E. Brachvogel, *Friedemann Bach*, 2nd edn, 3 vols (Berlin: Otto Janke, 1859; 1st edn, 1858), II, 252–53. In that novel Brachmann has Bach undergo a spiritual crisis, from which he emerges healed by an encounter with Gypsies in the Bohemian forests. The chief agent of this transformation is a Gypsy woman, who teaches him the cult of 'Bhowané, die ewige Mutter der Liebe und des Hasses"' (*Friedemann Bach*, III, 14). This cult features for example the myth of a 'Wunderbaum' (16) — doubtless related to the tree of knowledge in the first book of Genesis — under which the Romany race is born. Bhowané, '"Urmutter Bhowané"' (p. 13), '"Mutter der Armen, die Nacht"' (p. 26), is the constant protectress of the Gypsy nation after it has been cursed by the highest divinity, 'der Anfanglose' (p. 14), and expelled into the world. Despite her dualistic régime of love and hate, the Gypsy cult here centres on something like the doctrine of karma and a principle of love, rather than the revenge which May emphasizes. Nonetheless her eventual redemption of the Gypsies does also entail revenge: '"wir sind ihr geweiht im Tode, sie wird uns wandeln in ein neues Kleid und zu neuer Liebe und unsere Thränen rächen an der verdammten Menschheit!"' (p. 14). Brachvogel's source — perhaps some work of Indian ethnography or cultural history detailing the cult of the goddess Bhavani, 'giver of life', and a manifestation of the Hindu goddess Shakti — remains to be found. Madagascar does not feature in Brachvogel.
24. See Klotz, '*Die Juweleninsel*', esp. pp. 271–72.
25. See on Prussia's reluctant colonial project Hans-Ulrich Wehler, *Bismarck und der Imperialismus* (Cologne and Berlin: Kiepenheuer & Witsch, 1969), esp. pp. 13–38, 112–93, 412–502. One of the chief contemporary proponents of colonial expansion was Friedrich Fabri, *Bedarf Deutschland der Colonien? Eine politisch-ökonomische Betrachtung* (Gotha: Perthes, 1879).
26. It should be noted in this context that Katombo, despite his upbringing in Oriental abjection and loyalty to the Turkish throne, and in ignorance of his high German birth, attacks the Germanic ships not for their colonialist exploitation, but solely for personal revenge; other vessels of colonial exploitation he explicitly and unconcernedly exempts (499).
27. In respect of Koch's claim for the authenticity of May's presentation of Gypsy culture, it should be noted here that Zarba wants to be buried in a coffin, and that Karawey will erect a stone cairn in her memory (*Juweleninsel*, p. 575). Neither of these features is founded in the authentic burial practice of wandering Romanies such as Zarba. See for example Block, pp. 140–41.

CHAPTER 6

Gypsies, Race, Culture, and Hybridity in Wilhelm Jensen

In his day Wilhelm Jensen (1837–1911) was an enormously popular writer and editor in the style of Gustav Freytag, the author of works which fill 140 volumes, and the respected friend and colleague of both Wilhelm Raabe[1] and Theodor Storm. Now he is nearly forgotten. Despite occasional pleas for scholarly reassessment in terms of his professional status[2] or as a writer of exotic novels,[3] he is, thanks to Sigmund Freud, remembered only as the author of *Gradiva — Ein pompejanisches Phantasiestück* (1903).[4] Even so committed a defender of lost causes as Jeffrey Sammons[5] can manage only a double negative on Jensen's behalf: 'not an untalented writer'; and even this is rapidly qualified by a withering comparison with Raabe: 'one of them was an artist and the other was not'.

And yet Jensen, even if we might not wish to plead for a grand revival, has a telling part to play in our story. He is the writer who first connects reflection on the Gypsies with the authentically scientific discourse of nineteenth-century racial theory. Before becoming a writer, Jensen concluded his studies with a doctoral dissertation in German literary history (the *Nibelungenlied*). But even if he never practised, he was also a trained medical practitioner. He studied Medicine for ten semesters at Kiel, Würzburg, and Breslau from 1857 to 1860. A letter of 21 April 1860[6] records the tension Jensen experienced between the literary and the scientific vocation. The 'Studium der Physiologie' was nothing less than 'die erste Wissenschaft der Welt', to have seen this a turning-point ('Wendepunct') in his life. Yet as this language suggests, the young Jensen in fact regarded physiological exploration of 'die geheimsten Tiefen des Lebens' in a more edifying than scientific light. He had developed, so he claimed, a religion of nature opposed to the materialism then dominating German science. Thought, according to the materialist line, was merely 'eine electrische Wirkung zweier an einander gerückter Nervenmolecüle'. Repelled by this, wedded to the notion of thought as 'freies Selbstbewußtsein', Jensen concluded that his true inclination was less the systematic dissection of nature than love of it, and it was this which had turned him into a student of the human heart in the literary sense. That said, the physiological and scientific perspective was permanently imprinted onto Jensen's literary world-view. Darwin's *Origin of Species* (1859) appeared in its first German translation in the last year of his medical studies.[7] His correspondence with Raabe is peppered with references to Darwinian evolutionary theory, usually in the form of humorous allusions to humanity's place in the fossil record which Darwin's source Lyell so emphasized.[8] Jensen corresponded for years with the most famous popularizer of Darwinian evolutionary theory in Germany, Ernst Haeckel,[9] and both Jensen and his wife Marie were close enough friends to attend Haeckel's 60th birthday feast at Jena on 16 February 1894.[10] Both Jensen and his wife proclaimed their allegiance to Eduard von Hartmann's monistic synthesis of Darwin and Schopenhauer in the philosophy of the unconscious.[11] Wilhelm in particular sympathized with the replacement of traditional Christianity by the combination of Darwin and literature which David Friedrich Strauss — in this the mouthpiece of an entire age — proposed in *Der alte und der neue Glaube*.[12] Indeed, Jensen was also well-connected with the racial and cultural theorist Max Nordau, who stayed at his Kiel house in April 1874, and in 1893 sent him copies of later works, including the notorious, and highly influential, essay on 'degenerate' culture, *Entartung*.[13]

Against this biographical background[14] we can reconstruct Jensen's approach to the Gypsy problem from two early works which contrast usefully with Raabe's liberal, heterophilic line in *Die Kinder von Finkenrode* and *Abu Telfan*. *Die braune Erica*, a novella of 1868, and *Unter heißerer Sonne*, a long novella of 1869, treat the problems of miscegenation and adaptation: Germanic and Gypsy in one case; Black, American Indian, Hispanic Creole, and Germanic in the other.

As a literary thought experiment in racial and cultural theory, the exotic *Unter heißerer Sonne*[15] will be treated first. Contrast — of North and South, self and other, culture and nature, white and black, intellect and sensuality — is the structural principle. A thirty-year-old doctor of botany,[16] Friedrich Woldmann of Bremen, travels to Venezuela in search of exotic specimens for a German museum, but also in fulfilment of an indeterminate lifelong yearning (28). At his expedition base, a town perched between the banks of the Orinoco and the jungle, he however suddenly falls in love with the Creole Juana, wife of his host, Don Amedeo Miguel di Velasquez. Twenty years before Amedeo, on a visit to Bremen, had inspired his yearning for the exotic South (22, 27). Woldmann's love is reciprocated. His European sensibility is thus shocked at his own uncontrolled affront to orthodox morality (98–99). But he is even more shocked to discover with what indifference Don Amedeo in particular reacts. For Amedeo, despite his wife's charismatic beauty, has been conducting an affair with the luscious Margarita (122–24). Under the burning tropical sun sensual passion, he declares, is inflamed even in the European soul of the Creoles — only all the sooner to subside — so that frequent changes of partner are normal (265–66); even the otherwise rigoristic Roman Catholic Church accommodates such behaviour (299). Accordingly, when Woldmann becomes lost in the jungle and Juana follows in search of him, Amedeo seizes his chance to declare Juana dead and introduce Margarita as his new wife (264–65). The potential for conflict is greater in Woldmann's case, for it is compounded not only by his Protestant conscience but also by the racial and cultural divide. Yet it is defused almost as easily. On his rescue from the jungle by the Chinos (South American Indians) in Juana's service he and Juana flee to Germany. Five years on, as Woldmann leafs through the divorce papers thoughtfully forwarded by Amedeo, the novella concludes with a charming tableau of the German–Creole pairing and their two children in snow-covered Bremen. The scientific project has been quietly forgotten. Only Juana has been brought back from the tropics.

From the implicit author's perspective the main interest of *Unter heißerer Sonne* is, however, less the smoothly resolved emotional conflict than what lies behind it: Jensen's exposition of racial difference, in particular of Darwinian-evolutionary adaptations to environment, which Jensen portrays as being starkly evident in the tropical environment. On deck at midday (4–5) the 'Tropenfremdling' (11), despite his studies, is wholly unready for the shock of first contact. The title alone characterizes Venezuela as an environment conditioned by the ferocious power of the sun. Under its searing heat the jungle appears as a sublime temple of nature, its canopy supported by the cathedral-like pillars (4–5) of giant trees, beneath which there teems an infinitely complex, interdependent network of opulent and beautiful life forms. Yet the jungle is as threatening as it is beautiful, as indifferently destructive of life as it is creative. These forms compete (with obvious Darwinian resonances) ruthessly for survival, revealing 'ein grausames Geheimnis der Natur, ein unversöhnlicher Kampf um Raum, um Licht und Leben' (5). The kaleidoscopic spectacle (6) overwhelms not only Woldmann's European senses but also his arsenal of scholarly weapons for managing the existential shock: 'Er sprach manchmal halblaut, unwillkürlich einen lateinischen Pflanzen- oder Thiernamen vor sich hin, aber sein Geist vermochte nicht ordnend, auffassend zu verfahren, nicht die fessellose Natur in Klassen der Wissenschaft zu bannen' (6). And yet in these 'Gestalten der heißen Zone, zauberisch-glühend und grausam erbarmungslos' Woldmann recognizes '"die Leidenschaft der Natur, die der Norden nicht kennt und nicht begreift, und die doch die Wahrheit und den Kern des Lebens enthält"' (9).

On this Darwinian basis, an explicitly racial — and thereby also cultural — hierarchy of the Venezuelan population is elaborated. At the bottom are the Blacks. They are presented in frankly racial physiological and physiognomic terms, and their role in human society — basic physical labour — is always suggested to be conformable to their innate physical and intellectual qualities. Thus as Woldmann's ship docks, there launches itself onto the deck a mass of 'glänzend schwarzer, athletischer Gestalten mit [. . .] dicken, aufgeworfenen Lippen' (12–13). Their task is to load 'unbegreifliche Gewichte auf ihr dickes, krauslockiges Haar' (13). The sweat-glistening black bodies swarming chaotically yet purposefully over the quay are pointedly compared to 'eine aufgestörte Ameisenschar' (13). Only the Blacks, of all the racial groupings, go out in the midday sun. For a white man, so the narrator assures us, even the shortest walk would produce 'Sonnenstich, lähmende Erschöpfung, unfehlbarer Tod' (15). Even the native Indians avoid it (13). It is the Blacks' work to carry Woldmann through the midday heat in a sedan chair to his destination. Elsewhere they form the lowest servant class, and again animal metaphors dominate their presentation. In Juana's household the scantily dressed 'Negerweib' (17) Rafaele runs the kitchen. Her many naked children are compared to 'ein Rudel junger Hunde' (19), a simile also used by Juana's Creole companion Mariquita, when she complains of the 'unerträgliche Nachlässigkeit, Faulheit und Liederlichkeit dieser schwarzen Rasse, von der das sinnlose Gesetz verlangte, daß man sie als Menschen und nicht, wie es ihr zukomme, als Hunde behandeln solle' (53–54). The limits of the Blacks' intellectual capacity and manual dexterity are shown by their failure to master proper rules of waiting even after twenty years of instruction (31) and, when Juana adopts a more philanthropic, teaching role, to master more elaborate skills of cooking or sewing (129, 140–42). Rafaele's 'senegambische[s] Blut' (141) is too strong.

The next rung in the racial ladder is occupied by the Chinos, the 'Urbewohner des Landes' (13). Of these there exist two varieties: those who dwell in the hybrid realm of the town, and those still in their natural habitat, the jungle. The latter are creatures of the sun and its jungle law. Small as their number is, related as all the tribes are, immeasurably vast as their forest domain is, they still follow the Darwinian law of struggle: 'Sie haben Raum wie kein anderes Geschlecht auf Erden, aber die Losung des Urwaldes ist ihnen als Erbteil geworden: unerbittlicher, rastloser Kampf auf Tod und Leben' (107). As with the Blacks, Jensen describes their physical presence in racially emphatic, aesthetically grounded detail. Woldmann's jungle guide is typical, with his 'kupferbraune Gesichtsfarbe, gegen die das bläuliche Weiß des Augapfels weniger grotesk als in den Zügen der Neger, aber fast unheimlicher absticht' (168–69). Yet here is more intelligence of a certain kind: 'Es liegt etwas Verschlagen-Listiges, etwas Lauerndes in der alten Indianerphysiognomie' (169). As deposed masters of the land the Indians hate all interlopers, black or white. They hate the Whites as masters more intensely. Yet in the domain of the Whites the Chino is subservient, obsequious, cowardly, pursuing his hidden aim through dissimulation — something he has learnt from 'Kultur' (107). In this domain he is nevertheless the supervisor of the Blacks (13, 169). The Blacks may be slaves no longer, but the observant Chino can still execute the law of the jungle, exert the power of life and death over the black worker through manipulation of the white master (169). In the jungle, where he still rules, the Chino reverts to type,[17] competing only with the jaguar for fearsomeness, and deploying animal instinct and sharpened senses in a pitiless war of destruction against Blacks, Whites, and his own kind (170). So it is that Mateo, a servant in Amedeo's household, ruthlessly abandons Woldmann to his fate in the jungle, from which no amount of white man's science can save him. But civilization has also removed Mateo from his roots; for only Macusi, his still-native brother, is capable of tracking the lost Woldmann.[18] Only between women (as the sex close to nature) is there a kind of solidarity, as Juana is afforded hospitality and care by Macusi's (nameless) wife, for the duration of the search (203, 224–27). The Indian wife can also, by contrast to the Blacks, learn — Spanish — with astonishing rapidity (227, 236).

At the top of the racial ladder are the Creoles, the naturalized, now indigenous Hispanic conquerors. A tiny minority, the Creoles consider themselves as the only true humans in the state: 'd[ie] allein berechtigte [. . .] und einzig menschliche [. . .] Rasse der "Criollos"' (29). They are Venezuela's master race. As Amedeo's parenthetic '"uns Weiße"' (63) reveals, they regard themselves as equal to the race of 'der junge Germane' (33). That said, however, Jensen deploys perspectivist technique to expose the drastic differences climate and adaptation have produced over the centuries between these apparently equal races. For their part, the Creoles consider the Caucasian (31) Woldmann and other northern races (including the French) frankly, if not without narrative irony, as cultural Barbarians (37, 277–79). The blond, blue-eyed, bearded, white linen-clad, industrious Woldmann is an '"Eismensch"' (57), who cannot follow his sensual desires spontaneously, reads books (56), pursues a pointless scientific discipline (10–11), cannot safely drink neat town water (31),[19] go out unprotected in the midday sun (15), or explore the jungle without a guide (63). Woldmann, on the other hand, is appalled from his Germanic standpoint by the habit of the siesta (11) and the universal indolence. Amedeo does no obviously productive labour beyond smoking endless *cigarillos* in endless social *tertulias*, and receiving trade and plantation income (68). Similarly Woldmann, whilst wholly unconcerned by the racial structure of the social hierarchy, is repelled by the primitive living conditions, which contrast so unfavourably 'mit der Behaglichkeit und Sauberkeit eines deutschen Hauswesens' (35), and is puzzled by the Creoles' positive distaste for reading (66, 115). He is prudishly shocked that the free circulation of sexuality seems the major focus of social activity (124, 267–68, 272–78). In fact the narrative perspective frankly legitimates Woldmann's eurocentric view. In the mixed environment of the town, he notes, the same jungle law of struggle obtains amongst all the races (77). Thus, as the acquired ability of the Creoles to orientate themselves like natives in the trackless jungle (63) suggests, the white immigrants have themselves over the centuries undergone a process of adaptation to the conditions of their new habitat. The 'fremden, blaßgesichtigen Eindringlinge' once conquered, we read, '[m]it kluger Berechnung, gewinndurstend und mutig' (108). Yet despite their victory over the Chinos, the law of the sun now governs them too, through its instrument 'glühende Sinnlichkeit' (109). Acquisition of a tell-tale swarthy complexion (109, 262)[20] is only the first sign of an adaptive change which a suitably botanic metaphor of transplantation makes clear:

> Einer Pflanze des Nordens gleicht es [das Geschlecht der Europäer], die unscheinbare Blüte trug, aber im Herbst mit reicher, nährender Frucht bedeckt war. Da verwehte der Wind ihren Samen weit hinüber in den heißen Süden und verwandelte ihre Natur, denn sie trug keine Früchte mehr, und alle Säfte ihrer Wurzeln schossen in üppige, brennende, betäubende Blüten hervor. (109)

Like a northern plant imported into the tropics, the Creoles channel their vital energies under changed conditions into the production of newly luxuriant, glowing, and intoxicating displays of sexuality (the flowers). But they do so at the price of their fertility. This not only connotes the paralysis of intellect (110), which, as already signalled, has stunted the culture of reading and entailed the characteristic ahistoricity of life in the tropics. It also suggests an explanation for the striking lack of children in any of the Creole pairings[21] (which contrasts sharply with Juana's fertility in Germany). The power of this environment to change Whites brooks no exception. Woldmann's capitulation to sexual passion and his failure to keep his daily journal (43, 103, 258–59) suggest that he too, like the Creoles, is beginning to regress.[22]

Thus the reader too is prepared for Jensen's chief cognitive interest: to explore how far racial and cultural differences can be mediated. Here Amedeo, the only other male character in the text to cross an ocean, is the negative foil to Woldmann. He has, we know, visited Bremen, but he can barely recall the language (22). Despite his extravagant praise of Germany and emphatic self-deprecation, he plainly prefers retrenchment in his own environment to the synthesis of cultures. The most evident indicator of this is his own abandonment to uncensored sexuality. He has neglected Juana for the past two years (123) in favour of Margarita, the 'Perle Venezuelas' (274), Venezuela's greatest beauty, as the narrator confirms. This very fact reveals the most telling aspect of Amedeo's adultery. For the most beautiful woman in Venezuela is not of pure race, but a brown *mestize*, a cross between Creole and Chino. It is precisely from this crossing that her overpowering beauty and erotic charisma derive.[23] '"Ich aber sage Euch"', confides Amedeo during a man-to-man talk with Woldmann, '"es gibt keine Frau von reinem spanischem Geblüt, die sich mit dem Reize, den eine Kreuzung mit dem verachteten Geschlechte der Chinos zu erschaffen vermag, messen kann"' (117). Amedeo's affair is thus a betrayal of his race, a dilution of its stock with a woman generally condemned (even) in Creole society not for her morals, but for her mixed race (262).

Woldmann and Juana offer by contrast a model of racial intermingling in which harmonious and reciprocal cultural exchange replaces one-sided and regressive transfer. Woldmann, the story's focalizer, is treated in the greater detail and (as one might expect from the author who so fascinated Freud) through the mode of confessional dreams as indicator of inner change. His tale is of managing exploding sexuality. As the jungle disorientated his intellectual map, so the encounter with Venezuelan eroticism subverts his emotional discipline (99). Thus Woldmann must choose between two versions of sexual love. He has on the one hand been captivated by an erotic, yet chaste vision of an etherealized, marmoreal Juana in her bath (79–80). Yet on the other the sexually aggressive Catalina is also flirting shamelessly. An erotic encounter with a veiled woman — he takes her to be Catalina — in the aptly subterranean realm of a crypt leaves Woldmann in dualistic turmoil (99–100). Rhapsodic dreams portray him as an Odysseus torn between strangely masked women, a Juana who looks like Aphrodite or Nausikaa and a Catalina who waits at home like Penelope (113–14). Only the vision of Juana and a lock of her hair keep Woldmann going during his jungle ordeal (234). But her loyal pursuit of him confirms his commitment to her. His resistence to a last determined attack on his virtue by Margarita (on the night before her wedding; 272–76) marks the adaptive synthesis he has achieved between German ethics and Creole sensuality. Thus he can at last transport his 'Rose der Tropen' (268) back to her European origin.

Juana for her part is subjected to progressive Europeanization.[24] At the outset she is the typical Creole, who despises the cold German and yet finds him sexually attractive. It was in fact she who met Woldmann in the crypt. But Woldmann is at last able to stir her dormant European spirit — through the medium of the letter. Tortured by the tedium of a sleepless night it was she who suddenly, to Mariquita's horror, felt the need to read (56). First it is a leftover Spanish version of *The Cid*. Ultimately, however, it is Woldmann's initially disdained gift of a Spanish *Odyssey* — his canonical '"Buch der Bücher"' (115), the master narrative of classical European culture — which radically changes her self-understanding. Once she has read this volume Juana, as her dress indicates (125), changes to match the Nausikaa of Woldmann's fantasies. This is why she develops egalitarian-philanthropic tendencies, begins (to their astonishment, 127) to attempt to educate the Blacks in her kitchen and emulate a German housewife (120, 130). All this makes Woldmann feel increasingly at home (130). When at last the two read the Spanish *Odyssey* together, when Woldmann recites the original Greek and then the German version — so much closer in spirit to the original than the Spanish (146–47) — we find Juana herself speaking halting German as the mark of her adaptation. German pearls, as Woldmann notes, are hidden in her soul (151). The *Odyssey* is the only artefact Juana takes back with her to Europe (234). Thus she, not the scientific expedition, is the fulfilment of the childhood yearning implanted in the German explorer at the time of Amedeo's visit (131). Little Juanita (blonde with dark eyes) and Fritz (dark with clear blue eyes) symbolize the successful hybridity of the union. Fritz, notably, is encouraged with an eye to the future to go out and steel his body in the German snow (300).

Now Jensen's presentation of race and environment is highly conformable to the Darwinistic orthodoxy of German science in his day. Gobineau, the fashionable pre-Darwinian godfather of racial theory, had set a cultural hierarchy of races at the centre of his theory of cultural development which was widely accepted even after Darwin. Of the three major races Gobineau identifies — white, black, and yellow (*Versuch*, I, 195), he makes it plain that only the white (285), and the Germanic in particular (122), is capable of creating civilization. No civilization can survive without white support (285). If the white race tops the scale, the black occupies the bottom. Whilst always maintaining the character of the human (95), the black race bears most resemblance to the animal. It is incapable of intellectual progress or civilization (96, 278). In the middle comes the essentially mediocre yellow race. This dominates the field of practical activity, but desires nothing so much as ease, and is destined for the mass or the petty bourgeoisie (280). The white race, by contrast, is the energetic race, the only one capable of higher values and intellectual leadership (281), if notably deficient in sensuality ('Sinnlichkeit', 281). Following this lead, Carl Vogt, professor at Geneva and a prominent figure in mid-nineteenth-century German evolutionary research,[25] insisted in his popular *Vorlesungen über den Menschen* (1863)[26] rather more radically that the races of man were as distinct from one another as man from the higher apes (*Vorlesungen*, 285). Thus he denied the unitary descent of the species of black and white men (I, 224, 241, 248–49; 284–85)[27] and used this differentiation to support wide-ranging claims about the rank of black and white in the evolutionary scale. '*Germane*' and '*Neger*', he says, stand at opposite ends of the spectrum of human forms (216). Black and white children develop intellectually in parallel, but only until puberty. Then, however, the black child's development halts in the individual and the race. The regressive changes in the structure of the skull and jaw in the black race which entail this stoppage uniquely parallel those in higher apes (240–41) and so demonstrate their closer relation to the higher apes (244). As for adaptivity, Vogt claims that only the Jewish race is capable of unlimited acclimatization; 'alle übrige bis jetzt untersuchten europäischen Rassen', he notes gloomily, 'die man aus gemäßigten in wärmere Climate versetzt, [müssen] nothwendig im Laufe der Zeit zugrunde gehen' (II, 226). All races will change their appearance markedly under different conditions (he mentions the Irish transplanted to Connacht under oppressive British rule), only to revert to type as soon as those conditions are removed (230–32). Clearly, the salient features of racial imaging in *Unter heißerer Sonne* — the racial and cultural hierarchy of white, yellow, and black in the presentation of *Schwarze*, *Chinos*, and *Weiße*, Mariquita's judgement of the Blacks' humanity, the presentation of their ability to learn, the vulnerability of the otherwise superior white man to the climate, the cultural regression of the Creoles in the tropics, the natural regression of the Chinos in the town, and the cultural renaissance of Juana in Europe — all demonstrate that Jensen is here propagating mid-nineteenth-century racial orthodoxy. The same applies to his depiction of racial mixing. Miscegenation, the hybridization of white and Chino, is seen negatively, as capitulation to a charismatic but culturally dangerous, un-Germanic sensuality; but the marriage of German and Creole produces an unexceptionable synthesis of what are of course at bottom two European races.[28]

In this context Jensen's Gypsy novella *Die braune Erica*[29] makes interesting reading. Here we find the same fundamental situation mildly varied: an unmarried German natural scientist of a certain age is translated by a restless, still unconscious, and misunderstood longing into a zone of exotic otherness. There he discovers what he thinks he wants. But he also discovers more than he had bargained for, as his occidental-scientistic mindset is dislocated, and the first object of his desire, a rare plant, is revealed to be the mere symbol of his true object of desire: an exotic and beautiful woman of different race. She changes him before he can win her. Nevertheless this prize too he carries back in triumph to the civilized world, there to live life in a *Heimat* transformed.

Here too polar contrasts and cultural exchange are twin foci of attention. Thus we meet Raimund in a Faustian 'enges Studirzimmer' (3)[30] on a beautiful May day with the blinds half-drawn and surrounded by an abstract version of the great wide exotic world — maps of foreign places, pictures of giant trees with huge fruits, glass cases of stuffed or preserved animals and insects, indeed everything but humans. Through green-tinted glasses he is poring over a dust-covered folio (3–4). Only one thing is missing from his attempt to capture the world in his scientific microcosm: '"Erica janthina"', a rare and beautiful heather found only on the moors (3). The rays of the morning sun — not quite so warm, perhaps, as in Venezuela, but with similar effects — stir him. His maid, the aged Margret, finally triggers the escape by throwing the windows wide, scolding him for living in a coffin, deploring his unmarried state, launching a tidal wave of spring cleaning, and reconnecting him with the search for meaning by reminding him that it is the first day of Pentecost. As in *Unter heißerer Sonne*, it is modern technology which mediates the occidental scientist's experience of the exotic and primal: not a steamship, but the railway, which transports him from his north German university city to the moor at Timaspe two and a half hours distant, where a long-lost sister of Margret, Rike, apparently also lives, as an eccentric dropout (7–8). On the journey, which is realized using the well-worn *topoi* of the kaleidoscopic disorientation of the senses (12)[31] and railway sleep,[32] the Professor, who has begun the journey imposing the positivistic constructions of natural science on his experience of the world — using his map (11) and applying Latin terminology to natural phenomena (9–10) — gradually begins to respond to nature with a less reflexive, more instinctual, corporeal language. The song of a lark outside his window distracts him from calculating equations for the swooping caustic curves described by the telegraph wires and inscribes 'wie ein unsichtbarer Telegraphenbeamter des Frühlings ein Lächeln um seinen Mund' (13). Later on the moor, as he rediscovers the athletic suppleness of his body, nature writes a different complexion on his face: 'fröhliches Roth kam wie die ursprüngliche Palimpsesthandschrift der Natur auf den Wangen wieder hervor' (24). More significant than this incipient *memoria* of the primal language of nature are the dreams which, prompted by a casual conversation of young artisans he has overheard (13–18), well up in Raimund's consciousness as he sleeps. The lads are returning from Whitsun celebrations in the city to Timaspe, and their conversation focuses by chance on Margret's sister Rike and her family. Stoffel is jealous of '"die braune Rike"' (14). This witch (14) of a girl — the daughter, not Margret's sister — has fascinated Lisbeth, the object of his affections. An outsider, she lives on the moor as a child of nature in a kind of burrow, called by the village lads the '"Maulwurfshaufen"' (17), with a sallow-complexioned, blue-black-haired father (15) who mysteriously appeared in the area thirty years ago. These scraps of information inspire Raimund's inner poet to compose a predictive-confessional dream, in which he repeatedly returns to a kind of primal scene, searching for yet never finding his desired *Erica janthina* on the heath, yet also meeting insects with human smiles on their faces — a preemptive image of nature humanized which reminds the lads of Rike's talk (18–19).

Of course Raimund, despite his map and scientific equipment, becomes as lost on the moor as Woldmann was in the jungle. He too must spend a night in the open, only to be rescued by the woman he will later marry — in this case brown Erica, who (as will become clear) hardly needs the assistance of the local *Naturvolk* to trace him. This Gypsy girl is presented in terms of the familiar discursive tradition, from Grellmann to Brentano's Mitidika, Immermann's Flammetta, Raabe's Marianne, and Stifter's Juliana. She is young, lithe, androgynous yet erotically beautiful,[33] brown-skinned with glistening long blue-black hair, skimpily dressed in the colours of the heath, and in her expressive body language she seems to possess qualities of all the creatures of the moor (29–30). In the otherworldiness of the night, as the dreaming Professor murmurs her name (in scientific language) and she hears her name (in natural language), they kiss. He is taken the following morning to the 'Maulwurfshaufen', where he encounters Rike's parents. Of course the Professor and Rike fall in love across the racial and cultural boundary. But this is not without potentially fatal risk. It is agreed that Rike will guide him to the place where the rare heather is to be found, and thence to the nearest railway station (Krummbeck, 60). But as Rike impatiently races to the spot and they uproot the plant, she is bitten by an adder. Recognizing the symptoms yet powerless to treat her, the Professor carries her to an inn where Whitsun celebrations are taking place. Resigned to the impossibility of union with Raimund, Erica has accepted death (68, 76). Yet when Raimund (for the second time, 66) asserts his love and wish to take her with him to the city (76) she decides to live. To his astonishment, she heals *herself*— by applying the exact opposite of orthodox modern scientific therapy. Where he insists that she remain still, in order to hinder the circulation of the poison, she begins a wild, unending, ecstatic dance to the point of exhaustion (78–80). Astonishingly, she is cured. The Professor leaves behind an explanatory letter for her father, and Erica returns with him in city clothes, the very image of a successful hybrid union.

The parallels to *Unter heißerer Sonne* are clear. Indeed the conclusion, with its harmonious vision of racial and cultural hybridity, seems even more optimistic, in that Erica is a child of nature rather than a member of a 'civilized' race. This optimism is owed perhaps to Jensen's uncritical deployment of the Romantic models so sharply criticized by Keller and Raabe. The story of a northern man, who is inspired by a stranger's visits to yearn and searches in a southern realm for the object of that yearning, reminds us in *Unter heißerer Sonne* and *Die braune Erica* inevitably of *Heinrich von Ofterdingen.* Both Juana and Erica are symbolized by flowers (*Unter heißerer Sonne*, 268; *Erica*, 87). But *Die braune Erica* recalls Novalis still more powerfully, in particular Novalis's novel of science, *Die Lehrlinge zu Sais.* Hyacinth, in that novel's embedded fairytale, is a natural scientist disturbed by an unsatisfied yearning, who is sent by a wise old woman on a journey to search for someone embodying something more than the banal nature of his abstract world-view. At last the petrified statue of the Oriental nature-goddess Isis is transformed Galatea-like[34] into into the real flesh and blood of German Rosenblüthchen, abstract science is redeemed by authentic human emotion, existential distance from nature is bridged by love, and dream becomes reality. Nearly seventy years on, the shadowy outline of this hypotext is surely discernible only just below the surface of *Die braune Erica.*

This affinity of Jensen's text with the abhorred Romantic tradition no doubt also accounts for the Romantic aura of his poetic-realist Gypsies. Erica, we know, is transcendently beautiful, leaving the Professor, like Stifter's narrator before the Gypsy girl of *Der Waldbrunnen*, speechless:

> So konnte er sie nur stumm betrachten, wie sie schweigend daherging. Er sagte sich, daß er sie bisher mit naturwissenschaftlichen Augen mustere, und daß sie das Vollendetste sei, was er gesehen. Ihre Glieder boten ein wunderbares Ebenmaß; in dem braunen Röckchen ging sie elastischer und mit größerer Anmuth, als die elegantesten Frauen, die er kannte. (63)

She by contrast expresses herself not only in prose but also in spontaneous free verse reminiscent of Goethe's 'Mahomets Gesang'.[35] Rike's father signals just as clearly the discursive tradition of the Gypsy as *Naturpoesie.* Despite his advanced age he too possesses 'gracil-muskulösen Gliederbau', 'rüstige Kraft', and 'katzenartige Gewandtheit' (51). His clothing displays 'instinctiver, malerischer Geschmack' (51). Like all Romantic Gypsies he sets nature and freedom as his highest values (53).

The Romantic influence doubtless also explains why Jensen's Gypsies are presented as possessing a special kind of knowledge of nature beyond the Professor's. This does not mean chiromancy or any other crass form of traditional Gypsy magic.[36] The Gypsy world is, rather, the realm of a symbolic nature which exists beyond the Professor's intellectual horizon and language. Into its secrets he is initiated over the forty-eight hours of his stay, exemplified again through the technique of contrasting perspectives. The fairytale quality of Erica's perspective is initially dismissed. She charmingly sees the railway train thundering through the night across the heath as the 'Heidefrau', a witch in possession of the evil eye, who steals the souls of anyone Erica does not protect with a kiss (35). Even in his dream the Professor realizes what is behind this personification of the machine (37). Yet beyond the naivety is of course the privileged, intuitive insight which permits Erica to know life on the moors like no one else, indeed to speak the language of its creatures. It is this which makes the village youths demonize her in their turn, to the point of threatened violence and rape (70–71). Conversely the limits of Erica's horizon are well-drawn by her notion of the distant, barely visible city as a forest (37–38) whence the white people come, and by her childlike obedience to the Professor's authority in this strange habitat (88).

The Romantic tradition, if we think of Cervantes's Preciosa, Wolzogen's Aloisia, Brentano's Mitidika, or Borrow's Zincali,[37] also provides the motif of the dance. To it, however, Jensen gives a new twist, as Erica's means of self-healing. This wild tarantella[38] of course transcends the Professor's received medical knowledge: '"Die Ruhe wäre der Tod, so klug du bist, unser Blut weiß es besser als das Eure"' (78). But Erica's beautiful whirling barefoot dance also transforms the Professor through the language of the body: 'wie electrisch strömte es allmälig aus ihren Gliedern in die seinen und ergriff ihn mit ungestümer Leidenschaft, wie sie selbst. Wie auf Flügeln trug es ihn hinauf, hinab' (78–79). '"Seltsame Heilquelle der Natur [. . .] keine Operation hätte so schnell und so glücklich geholfen. Unsere Wissenschaft vermöchte noch gar Manches aus dem schlichten Instinkt des Volkes zu erlernen"' (81), Raimund must admit. As the browning of his skin under the (as it were) exotic sun of Timaspe moor indicates (89), the Professor has by the end acquired something of the Gypsy, something of the hybrid, during his adventure. Indeed, as his espousal of the *Märchen* (81) as the key to the riddle of life suggests, he has also become something of a Romantic.

But if all this suggests the unqualified triumph of a (very) late Romantic critique of positivistic natural science, foregrounding a remembered, primal language of corporeality as the kernel of an argument for harmoniously mediating the cultural and racial divide, then Jensen has a surprise in store. At one level, this lies in the fact that Erica is in truth not a full-blooded Gypsy. She is *already* a hybrid, in that her mother (as we know) is Margret's long-lost sister, the (elder) Rike. Thus Raimund is not only marrying into a Gypsy family, but also into that of his German maidservant. Erica's return to the city in Jensen's terms merely activates something of the *gadjo* which was already there, rather than marking the authentic learning of a new culture. Erica's father confirms the suspicion that all is not quite so simple as it might have seemed. In him the scholarly gaze of the Professor instantly detects 'die osteologische Racenverschiedenheit der Zigeuner' (54). With his bronze complexion, falcon-like hooked nose, and bold yet dreamy gaze (50), he is the only full-blooded Gypsy in the tale. We never learn his Gypsy name, only that the villagers call him 'Bienenfritz' (51) for the way he earns his living as a beekeeper. He is the mouthpiece of the Romantic-Gypsy philosophy of nature: '"Ich habe gefunden, daß jedes Geschöpf am besten geräth, wenn man es seiner Natur gemäß gewähren läßt"' (53), and this is the secret of both his upbringing of Erica (59) and his successful honey-producing enterprise (54–55). Yet behind the Gypsy physiognomy, as Raimund swiftly discovers (54), is concealed a very different mentality. He may possess the deep Romantic-Gypsy knowledge of nature. But he has also, from his time as an assistant gardener in Spain (57), acquired the Latin terminology of plants (56–57). He has, moreover, chosen to live in isolation not only from the suspicious and aggressive *gadjos*, but also from his own kind, and prefers the sedentary life in the 'Maulwurfshaufen' to traditional travel. Equally, he has chosen a *gadjo* wife. To this extent, then, the 'Bienenfritz', despite his authentic Gypsy provenance, in fact synthesizes the two cultures of Gypsy and German. More significant is his sense of Gypsy identity. Whilst he makes no attempt to integrate with the hostile culture of the village (59–60) and indeed hopes that his daughter, despite her freedom, will not move to the city (59), nevertheless his sense of identity is suffused by a pessimistic conviction of imminent racial extinction: '"Unser Stamm paßt nicht mehr für die Welt, weder für's Land, noch für die Stadt, es ist am besten, wenn er ausstirbt"' (59). The 'Bienenfritz' is thus preparing to be the last of his race.[39] There is no return home. Thanks to their travels through history and culture, the Gypsies, as he himself exemplifies, have acquired hybrid characteristics; they have *become* hybrids or maladapted species variants. As such they are a diaspora paradoxically without a homeland, adapted neither to their alienation (the Occident) nor their origin (the Orient). They therefore cannot transmit their inheritance:

> 'wenn wir uns weiter vererben sollen, müssen wir in das Land zurück, woher unsere Väter gekommen, und dort würden wir es mit dem, was hier an uns hängen geblieben, auch nicht ertragen. Wir sind Amphibien und leben nirgends in unserem Elemente mehr. Es thut mir Leid um das Kind'. (59–60)[40]

There are no original Gypsies left. This, no doubt, is the reason for his choice of the settled lifestyle and interracial marriage with Rike on the margin of the settled Germans' territory. Erica's move to further intermarriage and city domicile is in this light nothing more than the logical extension of this process of survival via willed dissolution, or transformation, of the self into the dominant type of the Germanic race.

Darwin of course, fearful of religious controversy, had scrupulously avoided applying the theory of evolution to the human race in the *Origin of Species*. In Germany, however, this extrapolation was rapidly made (if not quite as Darwin was later to do in the *Descent of Man*). Ludwig Büchner, in what is generally taken to be the first German response to Darwin,[41] notes that the full import of the theory is unfolded only when applied to humanity. For in humanity, as the most intellectually and physically sophisticated animal equipped with the highest drive toward perfection (95), the struggle for existence is at its most vehement, merciless, and successful (95). Humanity struggles with other species, but mainly with other races of its own species: 'unter den jetzt lebenden Menschenrassen wird ein gegenseitiger Kampf geführt, wie kaum irgendwo unter Naturwesen, ein Kampf, bei dem die jüngsten und demnach vollkommensten oder wenigstens am besten angepaßten Rassen auch die meiste Aussicht auf Erfolg haben' (95). Before the onward march of the white races the oldest races — he cites Polynesians and 'Rothäute' (95) — are currently disappearing with incredible rapidity. Gradually, the youngest and most vital races will dominate (95) — even if they in turn will inevitably be supplanted by other, still better adapted races. It seems that the 'Bienenfritz', with his sense of the maladaptation of the 'amphibious' Gypsies to either their original or their western environments, has internalized precisely this interpretation of Darwinian evolutionary theory, and acquiesced in it. The Gypsies are to be assimilated into the German bloodstream, and that is just how — according to this interpretation of the Darwinian law — it should be. In Jensen, then, friend of Haeckel, the pioneer of Darwinism, preacher of Social Darwinism, and founder member of the Society for Racial Hygiene, we have one of the first Social Darwinist interpretations of the place of the Gypsy in Germany, one which, despite all its friendly Romanticism, is nonetheless also fatally accepting of the notion that it is right for the Gypsies to die out; and it even puts that sentiment into the mouth of a Gypsy.[42]

Notes to Chapter 6

1. See *Wilhelm Raabe: Briefwechsel Raabe-Jensen* (BA Suppl. vol. 3); Wilhelm Fehse, *Raabe und Jensen: Denkmal einer Freundschaft* (Berlin: Grote, 1940); Denkler, *Wilhelm Raabe*, pp. 100–10; Sammons, *Wilhelm Raabe*, pp. 22–27.
2. See Uwe-K. Ketelsen, 'Wilhelm Jensen — oder der Typus des Berufsschriftstellers in der zweiten Hälfte des 19. Jahrhunderts',*Raabe-Jahrbuch* (1996), 28–42; Walter Hettche, 'Nach alter Melodie: Die Gedichte von Julius Rodenberg, Wilhelm Jensen und Paul Heyse zum 70. Geburtstag Wilhelm Raabes',*Raabe-Jahrbuch* (1999), 144–56; also the bio-bibliographies by Adalbert Elsenbroich (*Neue Deutsche Biographie*, X, 404–06) and Eckhardt Meyer-Krentler (*Literatur-Lexikon*, VI, 96–97).
3. See Wolfgang Struck, 'See- und Mordgeschichten: Zur Konstruktion exotischer Räume in realistischen Erzähltexten', *Raabe-Jahrbuch* (1999), 60–70.
4. Wilhelm Jensen, *Gradiva — Ein pompejanisches Phantasiestück* (Dresden, Leipzig: Reißner, 1903). See on this Freud, 'Der Wahn und die Träume in W. Jensens *Gradiva*' (1907), in Sigmund Freud, *Studienausgabe*, ed. by Alexander Mitscherlich and others, 14 vols (Frankfurt a.M.: Fischer, 1982), X, 9–85.
5. 'Wilhelm Raabe's and Wilhelm Jensen's Scandinavian Fiction: A Contrast in Nationalisms', in *Studies in German and Scandinavian Literature after 1500: A Festschrift for George C. Schoolfield*, ed. by James A. Parente and Richard Erich Schade (Columbia, SC: Camden House, 1993), pp. 116–28 (pp. 124, 125).
6. Jensen-Heyck papers, Landesbibliothek Schleswig-Holstein (Kiel), shelfmark Cb 28.
7. *Über die Entstehung der Arten im Thier- und Pflanzen-Reich durch natürliche Züchtung oder Erhaltung der vervollkommneten Rassen im Kampfe ums Dasein*. Nach der 2. Auflage mit einer geschichtlichen Vorrede und andern Zusätzen des Verfassers für diese deutsche Ausgabe aus dem Englischen übersetzt und mit Anmerkungen versehen von H. G. Bronn (Stuttgart: Schweizerbart, 1860). A second, improved version became the standard: *Über die Entstehung der Arten durch natürliche Zuchtwahl oder die Erhaltung der begünstigten Rassen im Kampfe um's Dasein*. Nach der 4. engl. Ausgabe übers. von J. V. Carus (Stuttgart: Schweizerbart, 1867).
8. See for example the *Briefwechsel Raabe-Jensen*, p. 37 (27 January 1869), p. 444 (2 November 1889). For Darwin on the fossil record (with constant allusions to Lyell), see *The Origin of Species by Means of Natural Selection* (London: Murray, 1901) (based on the 6th edn, 1872; 1st edn, 1859), pp. 272–96. On Raabe's relation to Darwinian evolutionary theory see Eberhard Rohse, '"Transzendentale Menschenkunde" im Zeichen des Affen: Raabes literarische Antworten auf die Darwinismusdebatte des 19. Jahrhunderts', *Raabe-Jahrbuch* (1988), 168–210. For his friend Storm's more limited reception of Darwinism see Regina Fasold, 'Theodor Storms Verständnis

von "Vererbung" im Kontext des Darwinismus-Diskurses seiner Zeit', in *Storm-Lektüren: Festschrift für Karl Ernst Laage zum 80. Geburtstag*, ed. by Gerd Eversberg, David A. Jackson, and Eckhart Pastor (Würzburg: Königshausen & Neumann, 2000), pp. 47–58.

9. The Jensen–Heyck papers in the Landesbibliothek at Kiel contain letters and cards from Haeckel to Jensen from 1882 to 1894 (Cb 28). On Haeckel see Alfred Kelly, *The Descent of Darwin: The Popularization of Darwinism in German 1860–1914* (Chapel Hill: University of North Carolina Press, 1981), pp. 22–28; also Paul Weindling, *Health, Race and German Politics between National Unification and Nazism, 1870–1945* (Cambridge: Cambridge University Press, 1989), pp. 40–47.
10. The dishes, in a remarkable echo of Jensen's own, earlier culinary jokes to Raabe (cf. 'gebratene Ammoniten mit Sauriersoße', *Briefwechsel*, pp. 36–37) all derive from passages in Haeckel's works (e.g., on Jensen's copy of the printed menu: 'Archeaopterix mit Sauerkraut vgl. Natürl. Schöpfungsgeschichte 8 Aufl. 1889. P. 641'; Jensen-Heyck papers, Cb 28).
11. See 18 February 1870, 16 October, and 9 November 1871 (*Briefwechsel Raabe-Jensen*, pp. 95, 146, 151); also Eduard von Hartmann, *Philosophie des Unbewussten*, 6th edn (Berlin 1874; 1st edn 1869), esp. pp. 37, 248–49, 582–611.
12. See the letters of 27 November 1872 and 21 December 1873 (*Briefwechsel Raabe-Jensen*, pp. 182, 209); also *Der alte und der neue Glaube: Ein Bekenntniß*, 6th edn (Bonn: Emil Strauss, 1873; 1st edn 1872). For Strauss's verdict on Darwin, pp. 176–229.
13. See Nordau's letter of 5 September 1885 and card of 7 June 1893 in the Jensen–Heyck papers at the Landesbibliothek in Kiel (Cb 28); also Max Nordau, *Entartung*, 2 vols, 3rd edn (Berlin: Carl Duncker, 1896; 1st edn 1892–93).
14. Marie Jensen, an acute critic of her husband's work, noted the autobiographical character of *Die braune Erica* and *Unter heißerer Sonne*. Both, she says aptly, feature sentimental-poetic professors who show too much love and too little character interest (to Raabe, 19 February 1869; *Briefwechsel Raabe–Jensen*, p. 47).
15. References are to Wilhelm Jensen, *Unter heißerer Sonne* (Berlin, Vienna: Ullstein, n.d.). Here pp. 20–21.
16. Jensen's adoptive maternal grandfather, Jacob Paul Moldenhauer (1766–1827), was Professor of Botany at the University of Kiel.
17. Jensen sees the South American Indians as 'Stammesverwandte' (p. 170) of the North American Indians, so that we unfortunately find his Chinos swinging tomahawks (pp. 170, 202), living in wigwams (p. 216), and describing themselves as 'Rothaut' (p. 216).
18. Conversely Mateo must lead Macusi through ther plantation (p. 205).
19. Although he can drink water from the jungle source, which saves his life and gives him hope (pp. 216–17).
20. By 1871 in the *Descent of Man*, Darwin himself dismissed climate as a factor influencing racial characteristics such as skin colour. See *The Descent of Man and Natural Selection in Relation to Sex*, based on the 2nd edn of 1874 (London: Murray, 1901), pp. 298–99.
21. There may be an intended link here to Darwin's early notion of the occasional sterility of unadaptive colonist species in a new habitat: 'Many cultivated plants display the utmost vigour, and yet rarely or never seed!' (*Origin of Species* (1901), p. 7). Nonetheless later, in *The Descent of Man*, Darwin argued that only uncivilized races became infertile under changed climatic conditions (293–93). Kelly, however, notes the general lack of influence in Germany of *The Descent of Man* by comparison with *The Origin of Species* (Kelly, *Descent of Darwin*, p. 32).
22. Of course Darwin himself (*Descent of Man*, pp. 925, 943) saw sexual selection as the major factor determining the evolution of racial difference.
23. In this Jensen is taking up an argument first made by Gobineau, the founder of racial theory in the nineteenth century. In his *Essai sur l'inégalité des races humaines* Gobineau noted that whilst racial aggression is the motor of cultural history and racial mixing is generally regarded with repulsion by conquering races, nevertheless an equal and opposite attraction also occurs; and only from successful crossing (miscegenation) does constant progress derive. See Arthur Graf Gobineau, *Versuch über die Ungleichheit der Menschenrassen*, trans. by Ludwig Schemann, 4 vols (Stuttgart: Frommann, 1939–49), I, 37–42. This certainly confirms Robert J. C. Young's contention that the theory of race in the nineteenth century is not only a theory of culture but

also a theory of sexual desire. See Young, *Colonial Desire: Hybridity in Theory, Culture and Race* (London and New York: Routledge, 1995), pp. 16, 96–98, 99–109.

24. Compare Amedeo: '"Eure Anwesenheit unter meinem Dach, Caballero, scheint bereits einen europäisierenden Einfluß auf meine Frau geübt zu haben"' (120).
25. Darwin esteemed him (*Descent of Man*, pp. 1–2).
26. Carl Vogt, *Vorlesungen über den Menschen[,] seine Stellung in der Schöpfung und in der Geschichte der Erde*, 2 vols (Giessen: Rieker, 1863).
27. Darwin disagreed (*Descent of Man*, pp. 272–78).
28. Compare this again with Darwin's liberal generosity of view (*Descent of Man*, pp. 264–68).
29. References are to Wilhelm Jensen, *Die braune Erica: Novelle*, 2nd edn (Berlin: Paetel, 1873; 1st edn 1868). The novella was then a smash hit, running through six editions by 1875 and serving as a textbook for anglophone students of German in the early twentieth century.
30. Gottfried Keller's Reinhard, of *Das Sinngedicht* (1881), is placed in a remarkably similar Faustian situation.
31. Compare Raabe, *Kinder von Finkenrode*, p. 13; also Schivelbusch, pp. 51–66.
32. Schivelbusch, pp. 106–16.
33. Compare among the contemporary Gypsy anthropologists for example Reinbeck, *Die Zigeuner*, p. 53.
34. See Saul, '"*Poëtisirung* d[es] Körpers."', pp. 151–69.
35. *Die braune Erica*, p. 36.
36. An amulet does feature (p. 39).
37. Borrow's *Zincali* was widely read in mid-nineteenth-century Germany, and would be a likely immediate inspiration for Jensen's focus on the Gypsy dance. See George Borrow, *The Zincali: An Account of the Gypsies in Spain* (London: Dent, n.d.; 1st edn, London, 1841), pp. 56, 77–78. The dance as Schillerian meta-language of linguistically marginalized Gypsy women also features in Caroline von Wolzogen, 'Die Zigeuner', *Taschenbuch für Damen* (Stuttgart: Cotta, 1802), pp. 84–152, esp. pp. 141–43.
38. The tarantella also features in *Heinrich von Ofterdingen*, albeit in a more negative context, in 'Klingsohrs Märchen', as the poetic justice visited upon the *Schreiber* and the fates for their attempt to destroy poesy. They are bitten by tarantulas and must dance forever. See *Novalis: Schriften*, I, 307–09. Arnim (see Chapter 2) takes this up in 'Von Volksliedern' (FBA VI, 437).
39. See Fiona J. Stafford, *The Last of the Race: The Growth of a Myth from Milton to Darwin* (Oxford: Oxford University Press, 1994), esp. pp. 232–60, 289–306.
40. Erica too seems to have a passing acquaintance with inheritance theory, as when she assures Raimund of her ability to heal herself: '"Uns hilft Niemand, wir müssen uns selbst helfen, und die Väter vererben es auf die Kinder"' (77).
41. Dr. Louis Büchner, 'Das Schlachtfeld der Natur oder der Kampf um's Dasein', *Die Gartenlaube: Illustriertes Familienblatt*, 6 (1861), 93–95. Compare Darwin, *Descent of Man*, pp. 7, 196–97, 241–42.
42. In this he continues in post-Darwinian manner the pre-Darwinian tradition of sentimental anthropology. See Chapter 1.

CHAPTER 7

Carl Hauptmann's Gypsies between Racial Hygiene and *Bohème*

Carl Hauptmann (1858–1921) today shares Wilhelm Jensen's fate. As his modern editor noted, Hauptmann too is now virtually forgotten.[1] This is in his case perhaps even less deserved. As Gerhart Hauptmann's elder brother and a late starter in the poetic profession, Carl Hauptmann often felt overshadowed by Gerhart and underestimated (or indeed misrecognized) by critics on that account.[2] Yet he wrote a large number of successful plays in styles ranging from naturalism to impressionism and expressionism, which were performed throughout his career at major theatres all over Germany. Of these, perhaps the Silesian dialect drama *Ephraims Breite* (1900) is the most distinguished and the visionary expressionist trilogy *Die goldnen Straßen* (1918), part of which Max Reinhardt directed with huge success at the *Deutsches Theater* in Berlin,[3] the most ambitious. An anthology of lyrics and aphorisms, *Aus meinem Tagebuch*, went through three editions between 1900 and 1929. He published fine early impressionistic stories and *Novellen* in major contemporary journals such as the *Freie Bühne* (1891, 1893) and *Morgen* (1907). Of his three novels the second, *Einhart der Lächler* (1907), was published by Marquardt in a first impression of over 3,000 (*Chronik*, 173), with a further three by Curt Wolff from 1915 to 1917 (379). By 1922 35,000 copies had been sold,[4] and a fifth, popular edition by the Horen Verlag appeared in 1928. Hauptmann had distinguished artistic connections too: friendships with the Worpswede circle of painters,[5] particularly Otto Modersohn, Paula Modersohn-Becker, Heinrich Vogeler, and Otto Mueller; with Rainer Maria Rilke and Lou Andreas-Salomé; also with the prominent writers and publicists of the *fin de siècle* Bruno Wille, Franz Blei, Wilhelm Bölsche, Peter Hille, John Henry Mackay, and Frank Wedekind.

But if all this might suffice to justify the modest Hauptmann revival currently underway in today's scholarship, he merits his place in our story thanks to two other, major, and still largely neglected features of his *œuvre*: the frequency and importance with which Gypsies are treated in his literary writings; and the fact that like Jensen Hauptmann was not merely a writer but also a trained natural scientist, albeit in biology and zoology rather than medicine. As with Jensen, we shall find that these two preoccupations of Hauptmann are intrinsically linked in his works. Gypsies are written large throughout Hauptmann's poetic career. They are the subject of two early stories, 'Fahrendes Volk' (1896) from the first collection of tales *Sonnenwanderer* (1897),[6] and 'Der Landstreicher' (1905) from the collection *Miniaturen* (1905).[7] They feature centrally also in dramas: *Ephraims Breite* (1900)[8] and *Musik* (1918)[9] from the trilogy *Die goldnen Straßen*. Last but not least, the heroes of Hauptmann's most successful novel *Einhart der Lächler*[10] and two early versions of it, both called *Habakuk* (1905),[11] are Gypsies. As for the rest, Hauptmann's first love was natural science. Darwinistic evolutionary theory of course did not yet feature on the school syllabuses.[12] Yet with his close friend Alfred Ploetz, Hauptmann was reading Ludwig Büchner by 1875 (*Chronik*, 14) and studying Darwin, Ernst Haeckel, and Büchner's *Kraft und Stoff* by 1879 (16). In 1880 Hauptmann was studying zoology with Haeckel at the University of Jena and was an enthusiastic contributor to the activities of the *Naturwissenschaftlicher Verein Studierender* (18–19). He finally wrote a doctoral dissertation *cum laude* for Haeckel in 1883[13] on a key unresolved problem of heredity theory, remained linked with his Professor for many years, and indeed just missed meeting Wilhelm Jensen at the opulent celebrations of Haeckel's sixtieth birthday — attending only the day after the palaeological banquet (17 February 1894) for the unveiling of Haeckel's bust in the Jena *Zoologisches Institut* (60). He began medical studies in 1885 with August Forel and others at Zurich (*Chronik*, 40). But his interest was finally captivated by the Zurich philosopher of natural science Richard Avenarius, and Hauptmann concluded his studies with a very favourably reviewed philosophical *Habilitation* from the monistic standpoint on the apparent duality of mind and body.[14]

However, perhaps the most significant aspect of Hauptmann's scientific formation is the long-standing close friendship with Alfred Ploetz (1860–1940). For Ploetz — himself a qualified medical doctor — of course invented the term 'Rassenhygiene' and was the chief animator of the racial hygiene movement both in Germany and internationally (with Francis Galton).[15] He founded a *Bund zur Ertüchtigung der Rasse* at Breslau in 1879 (with the aim of a utopian regeneration of the race), and the Racial Hygiene Society at Berlin in 1905, both of which Carl (and Gerhart) Hauptmann joined. Now the notorious Robert Ritter, who with his assistant Eva Justin was responsible for the Nationalist Socialist racial persecution of Gypsies, dedicated his pseudo-scientific and denunciatory but influential study of Gypsy genealogy *Ein Menschenschlag: Erbärztliche und erbgeschichtliche Untersuchungen* (1937)[16] to 'Alfred Ploetz[,] dem Altmeister der Rassenhygiene[,] in dankbarer Verehrung'. Yet it would be an error simply to equate Ploetz's early racial hygiene ideas with National Socialist racist ideology of the kind undoubtedly represented by Ritter. Ploetz was in truth originally motivated by utopian socialist ideals. He was for a time close to August Bebel,[17] as was Carl Hauptmann.[18] The young Hauptmann records him in his journal in April 1881 (*Chronik*, 22) as declaring: 'sein Ziel sei, *das Elend der niederen Volksklassen zu mildern*'. He visited the *Ikarier*, a utopian socialist colony in the United States, in 1884 (*Chronik*, 35–36) and another at Meriden (Connecticut) in 1893 (64), only to be disillusioned by the possibilities of realizing socialist ideals under capitalism. A version of evolutionary theory came to be his alternative panacea. Ploetz's mentality was, furthermore, formed in an epoch when, against the background of the rise of Darwinian evolutionary theory, an expert class of medical scientists assumed unprecedented institutional and ideological authority and became a dominant contributor to public political discourse on social ills, particularly those generated by rapid industrialization and the uncontrolled formation of mass urban centres.[19] Darwinian evolutionary theory, in its initial dissemination in the 1860s through the charismatic figure of Haeckel, Büchner, and many others, had tended to take the form of a naturalistic, liberal ideology, a materialistic, progressive, and atheistic opponent of official doctrine. But as liberalism slowly crumbled in the last thirty years of the century, collectivist and scientistic solutions to social problems such as mass alcoholism, over-population, and rising criminality seemed more convincing than the essentially divisive and conflicting proposals of strictly political ideologies, especially those of egalitarian social democracy. Cesare Lombroso, for example, adapting Bénédict-Augustin Morel's pre-Darwinian theory of degeneration,[20] had argued in his *Der Verbrecher in anthropologischer, ärztlicher und juristischer Beziehung* (1876; German 1887)[21] — highly influential in Germany — that morally deviant and criminal behaviour was at bottom not socially but biologically determined, by inheritance rather than environmental factors. Criminal behaviour, like insanity, resulted from the individual's atavistic regression (*Verbrechen*, I, 96, 249) to a lower evolutionary phase, thanks to poor inherited qualities. Criminals were stigmatized semiotically by cranial and facial distortion (asymmetry, protruding jaws, and suchlike), and resembled both the 'lower' human races and each other more than they did the 'higher' race whence they originally derived (175, 236). Education, therapy, and punishment were powerless against the constitutional amoral deformation of personality (135, 536). Against this background — the seemingly unchallengeable authority of Darwinistic explanatory models and the widespread fear of collective degeneration in modern, mass industrial society — racial hygiene, with its suggestion that the laws of inheritance were adequately understood and could be manipulated as a form of preventive medicine against the ills of the body politic, seemed to offer a plausible solution.

Thus we find Ploetz, in his seminal study *Die Tüchtigkeit unsrer Rasse und der Schutz der Schwachen* (1895),[22] struggling from a rigorously Darwinian evolutionist standpoint to reconcile these convictions with the egalitarian counter-arguments of socialism, with which he also sympathizes (*Tüchtigkeit*, v–vii).[23] The time has come, he argues with a glance at the alleged degeneration of the French nation (1, 65–69),[24] to ensure the fitness of the race. Darwinian principles involving the struggle for existence and the survival of the fittest must be applied in society. Yet this involves selection — of the fittest for survival, and of the unfit for extinction. There is thus a fundamental conflict between the great humanitarian tradition, which on principle protects and treats the weak and the ill. For this 'individual hygiene' *counter-selects*, militates against the ultimate authority of evolutionary selection. If the weak and the sick pass on their inheritance, the race on this logic must inevitably degenerate (4). Thus the time of conflict at the intersection of politics and science has come (9–10). As the collective imperative to transmit fit life across the generations takes precedence over mere individual rights, so racial hygiene must become the dominant principle of the state (13). Variation should be encouraged as the means of perfecting adaptation (20–21, 98–100). Society should institutionalize the struggle for survival by controlling sexual partnership and maximizing the number of births (45–47). Contraception is attacked (63, 73–74), as is of course counter-selection through protection of the less fit (115).[25] On the positive side, Ploetz pleads for the empowerment of women as arbiters of sexual partnership and for improved methods of artificial selection (218–19).[26] He doggedly foregrounds how dubious the ethics of racial hygiene must appear from the traditional standpoints. His deliberately shocking and one-sided racial hygiene utopia (143–48) involves for example an ideal couple's unquestioning acceptance of their firstborn's testing for fitness, condemnation, and subsequent killing. But he also counters this with an equally dystopian image of the dangers posed by today's practice (148–51). Just as Ploetz's views are significantly remote from National Socialism,[27] so too he cannot be termed a conventional racist. He accepts the received, Gobineauesque racial hierarchy, the adaptive superiority of White over Black (91), and the opposition of 'Culturmensch' and 'Wilde' (19). He shares Lombroso's neo-physiognomic prejudices (108–10). He identifies cultural progress exclusively with so-called Aryan races (5), in particular the West Aryans (European, predominantly Germanic, races, 131),[28] who dominate most of the globe. And he sees the Germanic races in particular (Scandinavian, German, Anglo-Saxon) as thriving. But he also admires the equally thriving Jewish nation as fully equal in cultural dignity and achievement (137), and dismisses anti-semitism with contempt (141–42). Indeed, he argues that most races are today *de facto* irredeemably mixed (130), the Jews included (141).[29] Later this position, whilst always qualified and relativized, tends to harden. Ploetz's racial hygiene pamphlet of 1911, *Ziele und Aufgaben der Rassenhygiene*, concludes with hymnic praise of the Nordic race as 'die hellhäutige, blonde, blauäugige, hochgewachsene, steilgesichtige [. . .], die edelste Ausprägung der weißen Rasse in körperlicher und geistiger Beziehung' (*Ziele*, 27).[30] In 1904 Ploetz founded an *Archiv für Rassen- und Gesellschaftsbiologie* to pursue his ends.

Given our knowledge of the Romany Holocaust 1938–45, Ploetz and his racial hygiene circles would hardly seem to be a promising environment for the production of writings on Gypsies. Carl Hauptmann, as we saw, certainly made common cause with Ploetz. Ploetz's *Tüchtigkeit unsrer Rasse* contains several passages of extravagant praise for Hauptmann's *Metaphysik in der modernen Physiologie*.[31] This in turn, whilst not a work of racial hygiene, is metaphysical only in the sense that Kant's analysis of the categories in the *Kritik der reinen Vernunft* contains a metaphysic of experience, and in fact attempts to ground the primal monist contention that mind is consubstantial with matter. The mechanical law of the conservation of energy alone, Hauptmann argues here at one point, positively compels us to assume that the animal organism is a closed system of corporeal processes and so not in need of any subjective principle of action, by which we may take him to mean an autonomous mind (*Metaphysik*, 265). At another level, what seem to be actions commanded by a conscious will turn out merely to be effects motivated by pre-emptive, subliminal responses of satisfaction or dissatisfaction (281–82) to contingent arising situations. At still another level, the objective world itself — and here Hauptmann clearly draws on Ernst Mach — is less a collection of static, irreducibly final, atom-like elements than a constantly shifting, constantly active web of merely functional elements (292), never-ending chains of basic processes. Psychical forms are merely more complex structures in this continuum than their physical counterparts (293), and there is no distinction of principle between inner and outer experience. The question of adaptive behaviour raises another dimension of the problem. How is such behaviour guided, if not by a rational mind? To this Hauptmann gives an answer motivated by Zarathustra's contention that there is more reason in the body than our best philosophy.[32] If we consider that matter organizes and orientates itself in the physical world as if guided by a rational mind, then the subjective psyche itself can unproblematically be considered as a dependent subsystem ('*die subjective Abhängige*', 305) of the organism itself. Consciousness is thus formed by laws analogous to those by which the physiological organism orientates itself (305). All forms of life represent Darwinian variations resulting from adaptive interactions of the elementary processes, formed in different ways to achieve the dynamic balance of productive and destructive forces which is survival (330–45). Psychology and physiology are intimately linked in the developmental process (369), even if it is as yet unknown exactly how adaptive energies are communicated to the 'Keimplasma' or human generative substance (380–85) and passed on. *Ueber Rassenvervollkommnung: Ideen zur Entwicklung des Menschengeschlechts*, an unfinished and tantalizingly unpublished essay begun on 12 December 1895 (*Chronik*, 73),[33] perhaps in response to Ploetz's monograph, demonstrates Hauptmann's continued commitment to the racial hygiene cause.

But these were Hauptmann's last scientific writings. He had been discreetly collecting his occasional literary productions since 1885 (*Chronik*, 38). As he wrote in autobiographical retrospect to Günther Schmid on 14 November 1916, he had during his time as natural scientist become

> ganz Künstler und Schauender unterdessen [. . .] An die Stelle des analytischen oder scientifischen Wissens ist das mythische Annähern und Umfassen von Menschen und Welt getreten. Eine andere Art Rätselstellung und Rätsellösung ist heute in mir lebendig. Wenn es sich auch immer um ein und dieselbe, mehr oder weniger weite Wahrheit handelt.[34]

An earlier aphorism from *Aus meinem Tagebuch* suggests that Hauptmann increasingly felt in the Romantic tradition[35] that only literature could transcend the cognitive limits imposed on abstract scientific and philosophical discourse in the attempt to grasp life:

> Der Sinn des Lebens kann nicht gedacht, er kann nur mit dem ganzen Wesen erlebt sein. — Aber wer kann es ganz ausdrücken — dieses Geheimnis?! — Wenn wer — dann nur der Künstler. — Die Kunst hat kein anderes Ziel. Sie ist die Darstellerin des Wesens an sich, ohne alle Ration.[36]

In what follows we shall look at Hauptmann's Gypsy writings against the background of both his philosophical monism and the racial hygiene movement. We shall look both at his treatment of the Gypsies in his earliest stories, 'Fahrendes Volk' and 'Der Landstreicher', and at the dramatic treatments of the Gypsy theme in *Ephraims Breite* and *Musik*, but concentrate on the more ambitious narrative treatment of Gypsies in the *Habakuk* variants and *Einhart der Lächler*. We shall see that despite his commitment to a mythical discourse, Hauptmann is well versed in the naturalistic *milieu*, the social reality, of Gypsy life. Authentically experienced details of Gypsy life are however also skilfully interwoven with elements from the tradition of *Zigeunerromantik*, especially (and inevitably) the identification of the Gypsy with the true, Bohemian artist. Ultimately, however, Hauptmann transcends both the realist and the Romantic tradition by constructing his Gypsy characters in the context of racial theory, and linking their creativity with their racial inheritance.

'Fahrendes Volk' and 'Der Landstreicher' are typical early lyrical, mythifying performances. Both extrapolate the *Zigeunerromantik* tradition. 'Fahrendes Volk' (*SW* I/1, 74–85) is a diptych, each panel of which portrays a contrasting kind of Gypsy. A sharply contoured, experiencing, and narrating consciousness integrates these elements. The narrator has had a singular encounter with a fascinating individual, a vagabond who calls himself the Graf di Santa Rocca (74). However, in order to come to terms with what has evidently been a cathartic experience he must first tell the tale of a whole, extraordinary summer's day. Thus he also recalls a first encounter that day, in the clear blue light of an idyllic Mecklenburg country morning, as he rides out on his bicycle. Only one thing other than him is moving in the midday sun: a convoy of green Gypsy wagons. He is captivated, 'es war etwas Seltsames an ihnen' (74). Scarcely has he gathered his wits than he realizes that the caravan has stopped, and he is surrounded by ragged youths and women.[37] The situation rapidly gets out of control. The men feign indifference. Two younger, beautiful Gypsy girls approach to beg with humble gestures. But before he can respond the older, ugly, wild-haired and wild-eyed, keening and chattering women roughly grab his hand. He is mobbed as he tries to move pre-emptively, shrugging the witches (75) aside and taking out his purse to give to the younger women. Pocketing the money, the girls draw back. But the older women thrust them brutally forward again, this time as an unwilling, crassly sexual offering. Before he has time to react the mother rips away the girl's chemise, so that 'diese mit nacktem Oberkörper wie eine schimmernde Bronze dastand, packte und riß sie, zugleich zu mir gewandt, geil anpreisend und feilschend, roh und schamlos die zarte Brust des Mädchens' (76). As the exposed girl staggers, the narrator gallantly supports her and makes as if to strike the other, only to arouse the older woman's fury. She and the other older women perform an insulting, savage, and obscene dance, bending and exposing their buttocks, while the young ones look on with contempt. At last all withdraw to their wagon. But any thought of relief is misplaced. Voices are raised in the wagon, and the older woman, whom he now recognizes to be pregnant, attempts to force the girl on him once again. This last episode of the encounter has something of the fetid, visceral, embarrassing quality of sexual challenge in comparable contemporary texts such as Musil's *Törleß* or Hofmannsthal's *Reitergeschichte*. The narrator is repelled: 'Ihre Inbrunst hatte etwas unglaublich Widerliches' (77). On his rejecting the offer elemental forces are again loosed: 'Aber ebenso plötzlich kochte auch schon ein grausiger, tierisch-erotischer Zorn in ihr auf' (77); and he is punished with what is surely one of the most original insults in German literature — not the words '"Du Hurer"' (78), which she idiotically hurls at him, but something in the language of the body, as she, repeating on herself the gesture she formerly visited on her daughter, tears open her blouse and presses 'die krampfende Hand in ihre volle Brust, daß ein Strahl Milch weit über die Straße sprützte' (78). With a coarse laugh she and the Gypsy column are gone. The narrator rides on, reflecting still on the magnetic presence of this Gypsy chorus, the witches' cries resonating impressionistically in his nervous ears, the after-image of the beautiful girls still in his mind's eye (78).

Underlying similarity and shocking contrast are the keys to this encounter. Of course both the narrator and the Gypsies are travellers. Both idle aimlessly through the landscape as others — 'was sonst Kraft in den Armen hatte, das war im Felde' (74) — labour. Yet despite that hidden relationality this is an encounter of travellers from polar opposite provenances, the writer from the world of German culture on his (technologically advanced!) bicycle, the Gypsies of course, as he notes in his lyrical language, on their wagons 'aus Indiens Gärten' (78), the one in search of a sentimentalized nature, the others *themselves* nature, a *Naturvolk* in search of the means of survival. The shock of course emanates from the clash of values. For the Gypsies, linked as they are with the animalistic world, the narrator is clearly their prey. They want only to coerce him into accepting whatever they offer — the beggar's thanks, the chiromancy, the sex — in exchange for money. All else, humane value of any kind, is subordinated to that end. Refusal is met with the unveiling of the 'savage's' true contempt for the 'civilized' man, expressed in the primal language of the body, as the woman's expressed breast milk enacts a shockingly direct parody of phallic sexuality — and a waste of the stuff of life. For the narrator, by contrast, the Gypsies are at the outset clearly the received fantasy construct of *Zigeunerromantik*. Thus we have on the one hand the genre painting in words of abject, ragged, and mischievous Gypsies — the 'Gewimmel von Weibern, Lumpen und Kindern' (75). On the other we have the familiar dualistic anthropological cliché of the charismatically beautiful, erotic (and virtuous) young Gypsy girls, like classical bronzes come alive,[38] but also the no less charismatically ugly, prematurely aged (and vicious) generation of the Gypsy mother.[39] The fascination the Gypsies exert over him suggests that his sentimental travelling consciousness is searching for some as yet undisclosed commonality. Yet when the mischief turns nasty, and the Gypsies' sexuality, ugliness, amoral physicality, and tactical violence — their sheer otherness — are openly displayed, the narrator's sentimental consciousness is simply overwhelmed. Stunned, he can only reflect inconclusively, in barely coherent syntax, on the received terms of his dualistic construct, the reason for his fascination still hidden from him:

> Obschon — wie ich jetzt wußte — so ein Chor Zigeunerweiber — flatterköpfige, runzelige, feueräugige Hexen mit großen Zähnen, wenn sie einen gierig umringen — und dahinter scheu und flehend, wie Frühlingsschatten die Jüngeren, schwül und duftend und finster, Nachtblumen aus Indiens Gärten — eine eigene Macht ausüben, wenn man, wie ich, mutterseelenallein in der Sommerlandschaft steht. (78)

All this brings him to the Graf di Santa Rocca,[40] who is a Gypsy of another kind. As the day wears on the narrator finally makes his way to the 'Kirchdorf'

(74) glimpsed earlier on a steep hill in the distance. By the light of the setting sun his talk in a tavern garden wakes a tramp, shamelessly sleeping in the dust at the roadside, who then introduces himself, with ludicrous disproportion of title and person, as the Graf. The disproportion is intended. On one level, this man is presented as unromantically as the wanderers in Hans Ostwald's bleak tramping novel *Vagabonden* (1900).[41] His clothes are indistinguishable from the dust in which he wallows, his hair short and frazzled, his skin burnt brown (79). Indeed, this exposes the latent prejudice we have already discovered in the narrator's mentality. Like all the central characters in *Sonnenwanderer*, he is pursuing self-renewal in nature, symbolized by the mythical sun. Yet although (as we now learn) he has days ago left behind 'alles, was Kultur und Gesellschaft heißt', although 'meine Seele nur dem reifenden Sonnenglück und der Sonne aufgethan [war]' (79), he forgets the primal, ontological sameness of people, old Adam stirs within, and he mocks the tramp. And yet there is more to this tramp. His eyes are 'etwas blöde' (79). But his face has 'etwas Nobles', 'einen Strich ins Kühn-Männliche' (79). Indeed he is very different from another tramp the narrator encountered a few days before. *This* man conformed to type. Just released from prison after sixteen years, his first thought is — to the Ploetz circle of course anathema — drink. The narrator finds him in drunken sleep in a forest, his face so thoroughly smeared with blueberry juice that he resembles a black devil. This degenerate figure — Hauptmann knew and valued Lombroso[42] — has lost his will to *live* (in the transitive, Darwinian sense), 'das Leben unter seine Füße getreten' (80), the life principle symbolized by 'das goldene Licht [. . .] in Augen und Seele' (80) is snuffed out by his hate, he can talk only of death, and dies in a week. But the Graf is different. Again, something in him fascinates the narrator (80, 82). In him, despite his vagrancy, there is 'eine unverbitterte, kräftige Seele' (81). As his ability to laugh — to distance himself humoristically from negation — and his harmonica suggest (81), he is of course an artist figure, the first of many such in Hauptmann's *œuvre* and a precursor of Einhart. Even as an artist he is dualistic. Like one of Lombroso's geniuses on the edge of folly,[43] his consciousness shifts seamlessly between phases of visionary lucidity and blank idiocy. Thus he earns his living by playing and singing coarsely suggestive songs for the farmers at dances and in taverns, and gives a sample. But both he and the narrator primly disdain such pragmatic concessions of aesthetic gift to the survival instinct, so closely analogous to the Gypsies' prostitution. As if prompted by this spark of communication, this recuperation into something higher of the crass physicality which had distressed the writer in the earlier encounter, the Graf launches an extraordinary, semi-coherent confession of visionary faith. His world is simply divided, into 'Knechtschaft' and freedom. One kind of life, the conventionally socialized life of those who labour for money, the life of the farm labourers, for example (83), is null. They are he says, drawing on Darwinism's dominant trope, like apes: '"Ich kenne doch die Affen, die auf zwei Beinen 'rumlaufen! — Das ist doch überall das aller Lächerlichste in der Welt!"' (83). What counts in life is only '"das Herrlichste"' (82), a highest value which participates in many names — '"Menschenliebe und Gottesliebe"' (82), but also the sun, the moon, the stars — in sum: '"es ist doch immer nur das Licht!"' (82). Who lives

thus lives truly, freely, like Luther — and dies an authentic, redemptive death (83). Only art, in the form of the church organ's sublime tones (not the preacher's voice) can raise consciousness to this level of insight, disclose order in the world, destroy the '"große Knechtschaft"' (84). With that the Graf sinks once more into his idiot's blank-eyed torpor. But the brief explosion of incoherent lucidity has been enough. The two have become brothers. '"Bruderherz"' (84), stammers the Graf. The narrator's parting gesture contrasts sharply with his farewell to the Gypsies: 'Und nun standen zwei Menschen gegen einander — zwei fahrende Leute, die einander die Hand reichten — beim Vorübergehen — weil sie sich verstanden"' (84). The final image is of night, as the narrator rides on (not home), from the popular tavern where the Graf is about to play. But the narrator has been converted to the Graf's visionary creed of faith in the 'Urmacht' (85), and his bicycle lamp comfortingly recreates the transfiguring points of light, indicators of the veiled 'Ordnung', in the night sky (85).

The Gypsies, then, whilst highly defined in this tale, ultimately signify existential error. The artist figure of the narrator can ultimately reaffirm his chosen anti-bourgeois travelling identity, evidently modelled on the Gypsy tradition. But just as his aestheticized perspective on the Gypsy 'chorus' in the great tragedy of life turns out to be inadequate, so he must grasp that the Gypsy mode itself — undiluted Darwinian nature — is regression. Only a recuperation of the Gypsy qualities into a *third* realm — the sublimated *Bohème* which is darkly adumbrated in the semi-degenerate figure of the Graf — will do. Of course this tale is a thinly veiled autobiographical account of Hauptmann's own developing artistic mission.

Hauptmann later tended to dismiss the *Sonnenwanderer* as youthful bagatelles,[44] but 'Der Landstreicher' of 1905 is no less serious in its contamination of racial and philosophico-aesthetic issues. This intense 'miniature' embeds the tale of another exotic, contrastive encounter in a frame of sublime lyric reflections on nature by an equally passionate if less existentially involved narrator. In its imagery of night as source and mother of creation the preface (as so often in Hauptmann in this phase) echoes Novalis's Romanticism, especially the *Hymnen an die Nacht* and the prelude to *Die Lehrlinge zu Sais*. The observing eye, we hear, constantly seems to recognize anthropomorphic, animate forms in natural phenomena such as clouds, which quickly vanish, and rocks, which last for millennia. But on nature's immense timescale even the strange traces of form in rock are ephemeral. Creative nature, the night, is older than all this; its streams run like a great wave through all phenomenalized form. Yet this is a monist nature, not Novalis's realm of sleeping spirit. Night-nature-mother creates, but is also 'das große Grab' (284). This is the true dark wisdom in the faces we see, the 'Launenzüge [. . .] aus der Welle in's Blut geschrieben' (284), the sense of the inner continuity of life and death, the understanding of inevitable return to the 'Urgrund' which lights up in the eyes of a kid even as it sucks its mother's milk (284). This weighty engine of interpretation is then focused on the appearance of a Gypsy tramp on a sunny Sunday in an idyllic German mountain village. Hauptmann rather strenuously exposes the inbred smugness of the prosperous local farmers, as they put on their Sunday best and strut ostentatiously to the church: 'Er strahlte jetzt Würde und Sicherheit, sah sich um und dachte kaum an werktägliche Dinge. Er hatte es im Blute, wie sein weißes Hemd, und machte ein ganz feierliches Gesicht' (284); 'die ganze Würde des Dorfes war in jedes Blut gehoben' (285). Into this smug community of believers, as the toll of the bells fades and the preacher begins his sermon on the rich man and poor Lazarus (Luke 16, 19–31), irrupts the figure of another charismatic Gypsy tramp. Like the Graf he enacts before the stunned congregation exactly what authentic faith and worship are. Like the Graf he is the colour of the earth whence he sprang, 'ein grauer, staubiger Mann' (286). Unlike the Graf, he is almost certainly a true Gypsy, his brown skin marking his provenance 'aus einem südlichen Vaterlande' (286) and his forehead streaked with the trademark lock of floppy black hair which characterizes all of Hauptmann's Gypsy figures (286–87).[45] All, including the 'established' local beggar, shrink back, as they recognize 'ein richtiger Vagabond' (287). But his charisma — signalled by the 'heimlicher Strahl' (286) which has followed him through the door — exerts a fascination on the congregation and a *metanoia* in them equal to those of the Graf on the narrator of 'Fahrendes Volk'. The Pastor's sermon, carefully focused by Hauptmann on an appropriate text, has been a perfectly adequate homily on Christ's living out the gospel in deeds rather than words, irrespective of outward appearance. But as all eyes are drawn to the tramp, so the inner barrenness and unwitting pride in humility (287) of the Pastor's words becomes evident: 'Sein Mund sprach weiter, aber auch ihm verhallten seine Worte, weil sich der fremde Landstreicher in seine Kirche drängte und in seine Seele' (286). The tramp for his part utterly ignores everyone present. He has been drawn to this place by the outward sign of the (obviously symbolic) tower, place of inner concentration, and the inner need for devotional sustenance, 'diesen Durstigen nach der Quelle' (287). His devotion is simple. Moving directly to the altar steps he crosses himself, prostrates himself 'tief demütig' (287) before the image of the dying Christ, mutters a few 'heimliche [. . .] Worte' (287), crosses himself again, and leaves as hastily and shyly as he had come, to continue his wandering. The only sign of his inner journey are the streams of sweat which, like the great wave of creation, flow down his Gypsy brow (286–87) throughout. But as another ray of sunlight enters the church on his exit, so all have been changed by this spectacle, all have drunk from the source now revealed: 'Die Worte des Pastors klangen nun fast freudig. Die Seelen in den Bänken hatten die Quelle gespürt. Der Pastor hatte die Quelle gespürt. Der graue Landstreicher hatte die Quelle angerührt und getrunken' (288). Despite the effect, despite the Pastor's thinking him Catholic or Orthodox (287), this is — again in the Romantic religious tradition — not only a Christian experience. As the narrator remarks: 'Die Quelle rann auch irgendwo unter ihnen' (288). It is of course the older, primal, at bottom monistic religion[46] of the preface, into which the life-in-death of the suffering Christ is seamlessly inserted by Hauptmann. The narrator thus closes the frame with images which recuperate the Gypsy tramp into the neo-Romantic cosmogeny of the preface: dressed in dust, his face of grey stone, majestic in his abjection, the tramp will wander on through the millennia, mediating between the human and the natural, always and everywhere finding the source that stops his thirst and ready for the death that is identical with life (288).

Thus again we find a kind of existential privileging of the Gypsy figure in Hauptmann. The closeness to (cosmic) nature is emphasized. But this abject figure of dust is far from *Zigeunerromantik*. His charisma emerges, like the sweat from his pores, from his sheer ontic physicality; there is something of the messiah, something of the highest truth, in the Gypsy race.

Ephraims Breite, Hauptmann's highly successful naturalistic drama of 1900, casts the now-familiar motif of the Gypsy outsider in a very different mood in the mould of a gender and race tragedy. Ephraim, a struggling peasant farmer, is at the age of sixty (*Ephraims Breite*, 45) at the point where he must organize his inheritance. Here the tragic conflict arises. His son Ernst is a good-for-nothing continually at odds with his father (14–15). His handsome daughter Breite (Brigitte) is made of the right stuff (45–46) — hence the title. But the man to whom she is sexually drawn, bronzed, dark-haired, dark-eyed Joseph, is a 'zigeunerischer, finsterer Mensch' (15), connected to a nomadic band of 'Böhmscha' (27) on the margins of the village who (of course) live by playing music at fairs and weddings. The conflict has two dimensions. In Breite's mind it arises from Joseph's outsider social status. He is proud but hard-working, far more useful than Ernst (with whom he fights, 16, 47–48). Yet Breite's family and most of the village folk are fundamentally prejudiced against his race (18–19, 78–85). Both Ephraim and his wife Beate are thus reluctant to allow the union (51) and the passing of their inheritance into Joseph's possession (58). Ephraim increasingly turns to drink (73). Worse, Breite is pregnant (52), a fact she conceals until it emerges scandalously (87). Joseph for his part is also concerned at the racial prejudice against him (18–19). He speaks *Hochdeutsch* rather than dialect (16–17), but he cannot find words to ask for Breite's hand when alone with her father (63–64). Yet when Ernst is driven from the house — ironically to begin a vagabond's life (56, 65) — and the marriage finally, despite the scandal, takes place, Joseph discovers that he in truth wants, or needs, more than Breite and the freedom to dispose of the farm. He has always angrily complained, like the Graf, of the 'Knechtschaft' (38) he endured under Ephraim, always insisted that despite his ancestry he is 'nicht weniger ein Mensch geworden, wie Dein Suhn und Deine Tochter' (85). And yet when it comes to this point he discovers that, whilst Ephraim, Beate, Breite, and indeed all the servants acquiesce in his new position of power (101), he himself is paradoxically incapable of living the role he had envisaged. Breite had on occasion challenged Joseph about his association with Franzel, 'das Harfamadel' (18), a beautiful, erotically fascinating Gypsy girl musician. In the last act, set a year after the scandalous marriage, it emerges that Joseph has been sleeping with Franzel all along, and we have already seen Franzel taunting him that his love for Breite is self-delusion: 'Joseph! — Joseph! Bauernweib wird halten! — Is sich wahre Liebe doch bluß eine Sach' wie Sturm, und übermorgen is sich vorüber wie Krankheit!' (90). Joseph finally understands that his steady labour and monotonous mode of life are unacceptable: 'Ganzen Tag an der Kette liegen — und für Eich schuften — und nich mal abends sullen bissel Freiheit kosten!' (103); also that he cannot tolerate monogamy: '[a]uf Schritt und Tritt dieses liebende Weib auf die Fersen!' (112). At this point one major cognitive interest of the drama emerges, its function as a tragedy of feminine greatness.[47] For Breite too recognizes her error.

She draws back from the brink of suicide. Her inner, moral overcoming of her own tragic circumstances emerges in a fierce, renewed will to live on — for the sake of the unnamed boy — and a majestic aura which culminates in her assuming control of farm and family. She recognizes Joseph's true Gypsy nature: 'Mit Gewalt feste machen, was flüchtig is und doch nimmeh kann mir gehier'n — nee! — das gewiß nee! Asu verblendet wull'n m'r nimmeh sein' (114). Joseph receives the role commensurate with his constitution: he may stay for the sake of his fatherhood, but otherwise come and go to Franzel as he pleases (114). Joseph must accept her contempt and his folly (112) with gritted teeth: 'Haß wider Haß! Ich finde meine Wege' (115).

There are plenty of clichés here from the literary tradition. The musically gifted, erotically fascinating, and licentious Franzel is a familiar stereotype, as is her mother (also abandoned by her Gypsy man, 86). When Franzel accuses Joseph: '"Du Abtrünniger!"' (91), we recognize the well-worn factoid of Gypsy anthropology, that Gypsies may never marry outside their race.[48] When she wields a sharp dagger to defend herself against unwanted attentions, we also recognize her descent from Bizet's (and Mérimée's) sexually free Carmen.[49] But there is also something new here. As Wolfgang Neuber argued in relation to the central figure of Hauptmann's first novel *Mathilde*,[50] the mainspring of Breite's tragedy is a Darwinian feature: her attraction to the strongest, most promising male in her immediate environment. Her tragic error is thus precisely the same as that of Joseph, to mistake the seriousness of crossing the racial divide. As the maid Tine says: 'A andrer is 'r!' (106). Her tragic greatness — despite the authority she assumes at the conclusion — is also fundamentally Darwinian: the heroic affirmation of her biological role as mother.[51] Thus whilst Joseph is sexually rejected he is also kept on site to perform his necessary work on the farm. Finally, on Joseph's side, we can see that he too has fatally misunderstood his own Gypsy nature, so that the tragedy can justly be said on both sides to have its origin in the issue of race. This was perhaps the cause of Ploetz's enthusiasm for the drama.[52]

Breite's unnamed Gypsy-German boy is the first appearance in Hauptmann's *œuvre* of the miscegenation theme. Swept carefully into the background of the drama, the problem of mixed race is central to the novel *Einhart der Lächler* and the *Habakuk* variants preceding it. In these texts Hauptmann's lifelong fascination by the Gypsy motif unfolds to its full extent, in particular the relation of race and aesthetic gift. One inspiration is doubtless his friendship, dating from around 1900, with Otto Mueller (1874–1930), the well-known expressionist painter and member of *Die Brücke*. Mueller, having begun with portraits of himself and his wife Maschka, restricted himself after around 1903[53] almost exclusively to treatments of the Gypsy motif, in particular expressively stylized, archaic, frankly erotic nudes in arcadian landscapes. He is perhaps best known for the *Zigeunermappe* (1927), which features a more realistic yet also more mystical perspective. 'Ottitschko' Mueller, as he was called in a Gypsifying diminutive, cultivated the legend of his own German-Gypsy descent.[54] He made several visits with Maschka to the Hauptmanns in Schreiberhau, sketched and painted Carl Hauptmann himself,[55] and received visits from them.[56] There is evidence that Hauptmann based *Einhart* and the *Habakuk* fragments on Mueller's striking personality,[57] and this line has traditionally dominated interpretation. More recently, it has been suggested that autobiographical features dominate.[58] But to focus emphatically either on Mueller or the author is to elide the text's drastically foregrounded twin themes of Gypsy–German miscegenation and aesthetic creativity. Mueller, after all, was in 1907 only at the beginning of a career and at best only just settled in a mature style, whereas Einhart's life is told from cradle to grave and his style analysed from early to late. *Einhart* is thus neither biographical nor autobiographical novel. Rather, it treats the relation of race and art. As we have seen, Hauptmann's fascination with the Gypsies long pre-dates the friendship with Mueller.

We can see this by comparing the *Habakuk* fragments with the finished article. They tend for a start to the incident-filled and comic (rather than humoristic) *Schelmenroman* rather than the more sophisticated *Künstlerroman*, and so offer less room for the reflectivity characteristic of the final product. The first, for example, briefly mentions the hero's bourgeois origin and conflict with his father before rapidly moving on: to episodic tableaux of a night in the tramps' hostel (again recalling Ostwald's *Vagabonden*) and study at art academies in two cities, separated by more tramping. Thus Habakuk's inner development as painter competes with the need for interesting incident (and vice versa), and the racial issue is only later touched on (271). The second version is much darker, opening with a scene almost Zolaesque in its grim rendering of *milieu*,[59] as Habakuk is brutally beaten by anti-Gypsy apprentices and staggers through a violent downpour to the much more realistically depicted, reeking tramps' hostel. Filled with 'alte, grauhaarige Lumpenleute', 'wollhaarige [. . .] oder kahlhäuptige [. . .] Wandergreise [. . .]', 'junge [. . .] Arbeitsscheue [. . .]', and the odd 'jüngerer frischer Arbeitsmann' (*Habakuk*, 278), this is even more reminiscent of Ostwald. The second version manages just one brief stay at the academy, before Habakuk, criticized by the professor, prepares to move on. *Einhart der Lächler* by contrast develops the genealogical theme far more amply than *Hakakuk*[2] in the accommodating frame of the *Künstlerroman*, whilst like *Hakakuk*[1] reducing the space devoted to *milieu*.

Thus the entire first book (of five), in a skilful variation of the *Bildungsroman* scheme reminiscent of the treatment of mixed descent in *Buddenbrooks* (Hanno) or *Tonio Köger*, is devoted to the relation of Einhart's racial inheritance and character. His mother Luisa is 'eine Zigeunerin von Blut', brought up in a prosperous bourgeois household, but in fact bought by her childless parents from the breast of a Gypsy woman begging at the door (*Einhart*, I, 5). Although never beautiful, she has the dualistic character evident in the behaviour of the Gypsies in 'Fahrendes Volk', 'im Blicke [. . .] manchmal etwas Demütiges oder auch Wildes' (5). As an 'achtlos versöhnende, hinlachende Demütige' (5), she has both the authentic, distancing contempt of the abject outsider for the conventional, and, in her 'Augen voller verzehrender Sehnsucht' (5), also the outsider's consuming yearning for something beyond the here and now.[60] Both qualities are passed on to Einhart. However, Luisa — not her Gypsy name of course — is presented as unrealized, having failed to live out her fate, acquiescing instead in a falsely comforting bourgeois existence which offers no outlet for development (16–17). Einhart's father by contrast is a stiff Prussian bureaucrat, ironically working in the communication business as a senior postal official, 'ein gewichtiger Ordnungsmann' (3) with a fiercely trimmed moustache and domineering manner. Hauptmann has him appear in the philistine's uniform of the 'Schlafrock' (7). He has banished 'alles Phantastische' (13) from the house. He likes to talk a kind of Darwinistic language, with a constantly recurring refrain of fitness: '"Werde etwas Tüchtiges! — Der Mensch muß etwas Tüchtiges sein! — Jeder muß ein würdiges Mitglied der Menschengesellschaft werden!"' (38; compare 16). The marriage, once fuelled by intense sexual desire, is burnt out (6), the relationship 'eine monotone Dissonanz' (3). As with Luisa (named, no doubt, after the Prussian queen), so too the Gypsy inheritance of her children is buried beneath a thick cosmetic layer of authentically German-sounding names — Katharina, Johanna, Einhart, Rosa, Emma (6) — the nomenclature designed to suggest the seamless continuity of Germanic descent (16) which his own father ('ein berühmter Altertumsforscher', 15) had once studied. In the beautiful daughters true Gypsy qualities — '[d]er Feuerbrand der alten, treibenden Natursehnsucht, die Atemnot in engen Räumen, die Lust ins Unbestimmte hinaus, wie Vögel ziehen nach südlichen Paradiesen' (17) — are buried. But all this Gypsy inheritance too is stifled by bourgeois comfort and indolence (17). They remain all their lives curiously one-sided hybrids, 'phlegmatische [. . .] Zigeunerfräulein' (7), all, even Rosa (the most Gypsylike and closest to Einhart, 24–28),[61] ending as bourgeois matrons (II, 134–36).[62] None of this, however, is true of Einhart. Despite his odd name, the mark of his father's attempt to imprint archaic Germanness on his hybrid children, Gypsy blood is stronger in Einhart than in all the rest. This, more than anything, determines his fate. It is already clear at the outset that he is a born artist, for Einhart *sees*, he has the visionary sight intrinsic to the Gypsy blood, the blood of the race which by breeding and constitution is always looking beyond the horizon of the here and now for something that will satisfy its never-ending yearning: 'wär eben nicht unter dem Namen Einhart ein rechter Nimmersatt von Traum und Verachtung, ein unheilbar Unbürgerlicher, einer, dem es aus langem Wandertum der Urväter mit heißen Purpurbildern im Blute umging, verborgen gewesen' (17). With this not only is the conflict with his father established, but also Einhart's essential artistry and even his later, visionary aesthetic stance. This 'brennendes Feuer, eine ohne Absicht ungebändigte, ziellos aufquellende Lebenssucht' (18) inevitably drives Einhart from his home and sets him on the traditional learning path of the *Künstlerroman*.

Unsurprisingly, his first encounter on the journey to himself is on a hot June night with Gypsies encamped at the edge of the city. This is clearly a successor to the primal scene of his own journey to authorship which Hauptmann had painted in 'Fahrendes Volk'. Like that scene, it has its roots in a personal encounter.[63] But it is much more elaborate. The handsome, 'apollinisch-jüdischer' (29) (!) Pavo, a descendant, no doubt, of Grellmann's and Brentano's Michaly, is playing haunting violin music as 'das schöne, sonngebräunte Volk' (29) performs a wild dance by the fire. Sensing his affinity with the 'seltsame Horde' (29) — every face wears 'ein ewiges Lächeln' (35) — Einhart is inevitably attracted (35). Unlike Rosa with Pavo, he dances the night away with the beautiful Franziska (36), 'inbrünstig, wie im Gottesdienst' (36).[64] She will later grant him a night of pleasure (71–72) before fading from his consciousness. The dance recurs as a schoolbook sketch (45–46). Dance is clearly the visceral-corporeal language in which Hauptmann's familiar pantheistic monism is here transmitted to Einhart. Equally significant, Pavo's image now lives in him (70–71).[65] It recurs partly as a motif of his later painting (130–31; compare 145–47), but, more importantly, as the model of the blood-rooted gaze of the Gypsy artist into the unknown:

> Der junge Zigeuner [. . .] war ihm im Sinn gelegen, und er sah ihn als Geigenspieler in jener Wundernacht voll Rausch. Er sah ihn deutlich wieder vor sich auf einem Kissen sitzen, wie deren in den Wagen gelegen, den heißen Glutblick inbrünstig sehnend und verzehrend in die Weite. Einhart hatte viele Male eine Frage in sich, wohin das Rabenauge jenes Verächters und Träumers gerichtet wäre? (131–32)

It is just this creative gaze that the artist Einhart must cultivate in the rest of the novel, and it is a Darwinistic version of this aesthetic education with which he now engages: 'in den richtigen Kämpfen um ein Leben [. . .] mit Hunger und Durst anzueignen, was aufbaut' (134). So it is that the sixteen-year-old runs away with the Gypsies, only to be hauled back at the next town by a gendarme to face his irate and bemused father (78). Looking back from the perspective of book two, Einhart is able to understand that this, his first Gypsy encounter, is no more than an '"erste[r] Ausflug [. . .] ins Freie"' (131). The narrator leaves us in no doubt that the Gypsy blood henceforth dominates in Einhart, as his ruthlessly unsentimental urge to wander indicates: 'Nun also konnte er ins Unbestimmte vorwärtsgehen. Daß er eine Heimat und Eltern hatte, kam ihm jetzt nicht in den Sinn' (66; compare 74, 96). But like the narrator of 'Fahrendes Volk' he must also learn that there is more to being an artist than being *only* a Gypsy.

Thus his wanderings, after an accommodation reached with his father, lead him first (like Mueller) to a lithographer's apprenticeship, then to the academy in a large city. The academy of course cannot hold him. But he remains in the city until his peaceful death as a recognized master in old age, with occasional retreats to rural sites — the mountains, the coast, a village on the heath remarkably like Worpswede, a grand tour from Antwerp to Paris and Florence — which are prompted mainly by existential catastrophe. It is difficult to reconstruct concrete developments in Einhart's aesthetic. Some, to be sure, retrace Mueller's development, and may indeed contain descriptions of paintings Mueller subsequently destroyed during his so-called lost decade.[66] In particular a description through Einhart's eyes, prior even to his lithographer's apprenticeship, of two Gypsy girls languidedly passing the afternoon by a rural lake (61–62) reads like the *ekphrasis* of a Mueller, as does an early portrait of a whirling, veiled dancer in strangely thin colours (117–18),[67] for which he adopts the oddly transparent, flat, and dull yet resonant 'Leimfarben' (226) typical of Mueller. Otherwise, it is merely made clear that Einhart always reacts against official aesthetics. These rarely transcend tired allegorical or naturalistic renditions of the empirical world (101–05) to grasp what Einhart envisages: '"Seelenhaftes"' (140). In this light it can be argued that Einhart never moves beyond a kind of proto-expressionist or *Blauer Reiter* version of mythifying, still figurative art. Actual works are described in principle, in terms of motif and general intention, not in detail of execution, and Hauptmann's focus is mainly on the inner development.

As so often in novels of development, it is erotic encounters with women in varying degrees of sensuality and spirituality which mark the stations of that inner development. One, the spinster Reseda, discloses a new dimension of spirituality following his sensual encounter with the blowsy Dorothea. His mother's traumatic passing[68] and a period of retreat teach Einhart about death's necessary place in the economy of life. From this trauma he returns stronger, 'neu inniger [. . .], saugender, verzehrender, so wie die Mutter einst' (187). More significant: the majestic (237), priestess-like (243) industrialist's wife Frau Rehorst introduces him to a first synthesis of spirituality and sensual beauty. Obsessed with her, he paints images which emphasize her transcendent qualities (252–53) against a contrastive group background. But she is not the one. Like Luisa she is unrealized. Life has never yet prompted the release of her innate potential (229; 257). Einhart does re-kindle the dead fire of her soul (260), and indeed feels his own Gypsy fire renewed (272). But the carnival reveals this relationship's intrinsic limit. In Gypsy costume (Einhart is Pavo, complete with violin, 301), they self-consciously emulate the ecstatic dance of Einhart and Franziska at the Gypsy camp ten or more years ago.[69] This, however, merely occasions a sudden panic attack, which reveals that Frau Rehorst has left her bourgeois cage too late. She, the narrator judges, is too weak to orientate herself in the great desert of the soul that is authentic life (308). At last Einhart finds his female soulmate in the seamstress Johanna (not his sister). She is a kind of artist, no doubt, but her chief qualification is that she shares both his existential stance and endless depth of gaze (II, 50). At the same time Einhart finds a masculine equivalent in Poncet. This zoologist[70] shares his sense of self-consuming and self-renewing life. Both love fire (II, 47). The motif of Johanna and Einhart together — she as the melody of life, he watching over her (61) — comes to dominate Einhart's production. He has now found 'die eigene Kunst' (59). But tragedy ensues as art conflicts with eros and life. As a direct result of his newly attained aesthetic maturity Einhart becomes lost in his art. Neglected, Johanna tragically betrays him with Poncet, who is unable to resist the existential imperative of 'die Rätselblume des Hungers nach dem Weibe' (95). There is no sense of moral condemnation at this presumably Darwinian outcome. The three indeed live for a time in a kind of reversed parody of Joseph's uneasy relation with Breite and Franzel. At last, however, Johanna, her hold on life loosened by the erotic conflict, weakens and dies. There is a consolation. The smile of the artist race transfigures her face in death (129). Otherwise this, Einhart's only authentic (if childless) love, marks a turning point. He now understands 'die Mythe von der Erlösung durch die Liebe' (93). A recognized master, he returns in his best years to a style which features simple, childlike humans in an idyllic landscape (167–68). There is a coda. The young widow Verena — another unrealized woman — arouses Einhart's Gypsy passion one last time. As with Frau Rehorst his Gypsy lust for life revives her will to live. But here too there is error and a lesson. When Verena gives herself to another,[71] Einhart must learn that she has loved him only as a father (230). At the end, as the aged Einhart gazes into the fire, the deepest monistic truths are revealed.

He grasps that what he has loved has always been 'das Fest der Mühsal, den Glanz der irdischen Dinge' (244), and that the goal of life is quite simply the unadorned affirmation of life: 'daß unser tiefstes Leben nur Leben will ohne Rest und ohne Spiegel' (244). He too smiles on his last journey (245–46).

There are several curious links with German Darwinism and racial hygiene in this novel. Einhart's development mirrors the general Nietzschean-Darwinian trend in his focus on the affirmation of life as the highest value. During his brief apprenticeship with the (Pietistic) lithographer, Einhart's rebellious attitude expresses the standard Nietzschean critique of the Christian ethic as life-denying: 'Aber alles, was der Meister so hinstellte, als müßte man nicht leben, sondern erst sterben, um es zu erlangen, machte ihn rundweg übermütig' (91–92). It is surely no coincidence that his only intellectual peer and true friend in the novel is the zoologist Poncet, who is in authentically Nietzschean style alienated from his discipline — the phylogenetic study of the laws of life — by abstraction and system (II, 48). The racial hygiene conflict between the ontogenetic care of the weak and the phylogenetic health of the race is also thematized, mirrored in the opposition of a village pastor and Frau Rehorst. In the mountains, on a retreat after his mother's death, Einhart by chance encounters the pastor at a meeting of the local council in the tavern. Astonishingly, when the issue of 'Gemeindearmenpflege' (I, 205) arises, the pastor adopts a radical Social Darwinist position:

> 'Armut, meine Herren,' sagte er gerade, als Einhart eingetreten, 'ist meist verdorbenes Blut. Armut ist meist Sünde der Väter bis ins vierte oder zehnte oder bis ins tausendste Glied. Man muß die Armut nicht pflegen. Man muß sie bekämpfen, wie einen Feind. Es gibt solche, die nur immer mitleidig sind. Das ist eitel Schwäche. Das fördert nur das Übel, dem wir steuern sollen. Überlassen Sie ein jeder [*sic*] der Zentralstelle — usw.' (205)

However, this Pastor is, it should be noted, a target of satire — as is official Christianity elsewhere in Hauptmann.[72] He later self-righteously interrogates Einhart about the purity of his Christian faith (212–13). To this Frau Rehorst's charitable work provides the sympathetic foil. She accepts and affirms the physical and spiritual wounds inflicted on the workers in Rehorst's factory by the merciless progress of capitalist industry (258). But her counter-selective 'Wohlfahrtseinrichtungen' (258) — even if they are at one level only a psychological compensation for her dead marriage — heal those wounds, so that the workers may carry on (257). Thus as in Darwin the struggle for existence *also* fosters the growth of social virtues: 'die ersten Knospenkeime sozialer Menschlichkeit' (258). A limited counter-selection is justified, so that in this respect Frau Rehorst — and Hauptmann's implicit author — occupies a position more or less like that of Ploetz. Despite his artistic egocentricity her stance is also sympathetic to Einhart.[73]

It is against this background that Hauptmann creates what amounts in Einhart to a racially hybrid aesthetic.[74] The one, insistent, unremittingly foregrounded argument of Einhart's progressive development is that his aesthetic development is determined by his psychophysical Gypsy inheritance, urging him to ever new visionary horizons. In the encounter with Reseda, it is his Gypsy character, the 'Drang nach etwas Wunderbarem' (150–51), which spurs him, the 'rechte [. . .], vogelfreie [. . .]

Zigeuner' (I, 150), on. As he dances with the fake Gypsy Frau Rehorst, he is 'ein Zigeuner durch und durch' (I, 301). In retreat at the Worpswede-like artist colony, he is 'noch immer ein Zigeuner. Den Sinn für die offnen Erdenräume, für Wälder und Heiden, hatte er nicht verloren' (II, 7). Indeed, on this account he does not fit in with that unique lifestyle and aesthetic: 'Er hatte es noch immer aus dem Wandervolke, die treibenden Süchte, die wie Krankheiten ihn manchmal plötzlich überfielen und versehrten' (22). When he finally grasps the true function of art, this is merely an affirmation of what was always his inheritance: 'So [. . .] war es Einhart im Blut immer lebendig gewesen' (163). Even when settled — and he only rents his house (166) — we hear 'Meister Einhart war ein rechter, loser Zigeuner' (170). His last visions — motifs of his final series of paintings (243) — are prompted by his dreaming Gypsy gaze at the camp fires on the steppes, 'als wenn er hineingestellt wäre, ein alter Zigeuner, in die weite Steppe und hätte irgendwo da sein Wanderzelt aufgeschlagen' (197). At the end he seems indeed to shed any remaining vestiges of *gadjo* identity, his skin 'jetzt noch vollends richtig bronzen gebrannt' (197), his hands 'fein und dürr wie braune Zigeunerhände' (197). But surely the most telling indicator is the narrator's forthright genealogical assertion of the identity of blood and creative insight as the origin of Einhart's intuitive gift:

> Das Blut ist von lange her und fließt wie ein ewiger, roter Strom mit allen Geheimnissen und ihrem Sinn beladen durch die Lebensgefilde. Es braucht nicht erst von Auge und Ohr ins Blut. Das Blut enthüllt es aus der Tiefe hinaus ins Leben. So werden allein auch Weisheitsbringer und Schönheitsbringer, wenn sie aus der Ewigkeit jenes roten Stromes schöpfen, und die dunklen Blumen des Schicksals brechen, die an dessen Ufern blühen. (I, 307–08)

This innate — racial — philosophy of course is also the reason for his rejection of the proto-Worpswede aesthetic (II, 10). On the one hand Einhart, like Max Nordau,[75] believes that artists are loners (II, 28), and rejects collectives in any case. More fundamentally, he cannot share their naturalistic and self-consciously Germanic vision. They — we think of Modersohn — 'priesen Heimat und Scholle, verherrlichten den Frieden der Ackerdienste und Feierstunden, und ließen die weite Welt sich im kleinen Moorgraben spiegeln mit den moosigen Baumästen zusammen, und mit dem ziegenhütenden Weidekind' (II, 29). Einhart by contrast dreams not of 'Heimat' (29) but of the 'Wundersee seiner eigenen Ausschau, darin diese ganze Welt sich in Menschlichkeit spiegelt' (29). In Einhart we can see the ultimate potentialization of the tradition of the Gypsy artist launched in 1817 by Clemens Brentano: the artist no longer as metaphorical Gypsy, but a Gypsy down to his very 'Keimplasma'.[76]

But if this is a frankly racial aesthetic, the manifesto of a particular kind of art characteristically produced by those in whom Gypsy blood rules, then Hauptmann has produced a very paradoxical book. This is in part on account of his own emergence from the racial hygiene movement. Whilst its acceptance of counter-selective measures (through Frau Rehorst) clearly echoes Ploetz's mitigated version of racial hygiene, this novel nevertheless flouts the cardinal principle of racial purity, instead parading the hybrid Einhart as 'gesunden Blutes' (I, 96). Indeed, whilst it might be said that Gypsies as a race are rarely thematized in the standard texts of the early racial hygiene movement — Ammon,[77] Schallmeyer, Ploetz — or their liberal predecessors — Vogt, Büchner, Haeckel (and still less by Darwin) — it should be recalled that this job no longer needed to be done. The Gypsies had long since been anathematized by Cesare Lombroso, who finds them as descendants of the Pariahs (*Verbrecher*, I, 171) to be members of an inferior race and 'geborene [. . .] Verbrecher und Spitzbuben' (III, 316). And surely Max Nordau, Lombroso's radical champion on the cultural scene around 1900, would have judged Einhart, despite his freedom from physiological malformation or nervous symptoms, and despite his sound refusal to join a school, to be *a priori* disqualified for the task of producing healthy art. The contrast between Hauptmann and Jensen could scarcely be more pronounced.

But if Hauptmann produces here a counter-discourse to the racial hygiene doctrine (at least so far as the artist is concerned), then he has also produced an image of the Gypsy which drastically contradicts the traditional orthodox view of German civil society. Gypsies, we know, were by now in the great tradition of anti-Gypsyism definitively, in a pernicious cultural secularization of the biblical term, viewed as a 'plague',[78] and the denunciatory term 'Plage' — with its variation 'Unwesen' — had passed into the official language of a series of Prussian, Bavarian, and finally Imperial German laws. Only eighteen months prior to the publication of *Einhart der Lächler*, on 17 February 1906, the Prussian government had issued the draconian *Anweisung zur Bekämpfung des Zigeunerunwesens*, first of a long series of ever more severe measures eventually culminating in the *Gesetz zur Bekämpfung von Zigeunern, Landfahrern und Arbeitsscheuen* of 1926.[79] All were designed to make life in Germany impossible for Gypsies — and other *a priori* criminalized vagabonds — by imposing on them an unfulfillable system of total police control, echoes of which we can detect in the efficiency with which the local gendarme catches up with young Einhart on his flight with the Gypsies (I, 78). By 1899 Gypsies had their very own chapter — as 'grosse [. . .] Landplage' — in Hanns Gross's standard work *Handbuch der Untersuchungsrichter als System der Kriminalistik*.[80] In the same year Alfred Dillmann, Director of the Munich Police, had founded his *Münchner Nachrichtendienst im Bezug auf die Zigeuner*[81] with its central register — echoes of which we can see in the pastor's reference to the 'Zentralstelle' (*Einhart*, I, 205) — of all known Gypsies in German lands. By 1905 Dillmann had collected enough information to publish his notorious *Zigeunerbuch*,[82] a widely circulated police handbook, with its Lombrosoesque photographs and full descriptions of over three thousand alleged Gypsy felons. By 1929, of course, the Munich *Nachrichtendienst* was to become the *Zentralbüro für die Bekämpfung der Zigeunerplage*, and so in 1936, following the introduction of the National Socialist race laws, to be transformed into Robert Ritter's *Rassenhygienische und bevölkerungsbiologische Forschungsstelle*, source of authority for Romany transportation to the death camps. This is the grand narrative, the journey from institutionalized anti-Gypsyism to the state crime of industrialized genocide, into which Hauptmann's curiously innocent, strangely complicit, unapologetically racist *apology* of the Gypsies fits.

Musik, the last play of the expressionist trilogy *Die goldnen Straßen*, documents just how strongly Hauptmann even after the *opus magnum* of *Einhart* identified with the

Gypsy motif in the racial connotations we have so far described. In this, the last of a series of late plays which attempt to delineate the golden paths towards authentic self-realization, Hauptmann focuses once more — semi-autobiographically — on an artist figure. Here it is the emblematically named Josua, cathedral organist and gifted composer, who — in a remarkable thematic parallel to the hero of Hans Pfitzner's beautiful, exactly coeval opera *Palestrina* — is frozen in creative agony prior to writing his greatest work. The play is framed by mirror-image yet contrastive scenes depicting Josua in visionary communication with the spirits of music. In the opening scene he struggles vainly (with obvious resonances of Hoffmann's Kreisler) to transcribe the voices within onto paper (*Musik*, 9–16); in the last (54–59) he triumphantly succeeds in externalizing that vision as an awe-inspiring work on the Creation. The interest of the play is thus directed at the creative struggle, and it is here that we meet again two of Hauptmann's earliest poetic figures, both from 'Fahrendes Volk': the Graf di Santa Rocca and a *Zigeunerin*. They, along with Josua's bourgeois-philistine mother and his virginal-unrealized bride Georginel embody the chief vectors of the creative conflict.

Both the Graf and the Gypsy girl have, as ever in Hauptmann, a contrastive function in the system of the work. We encounter the Graf as Josua, deep in crisis after his initial artistic failure, intensifies the crisis by failing to perform his professional-bourgeois duties. Filled with contempt for bourgeois art, he has taken drink in order to be able to play a (to him) banal requiem mass. Drunk, he has vomited during the performance and been ignominiously replaced by his student. It is in this abject and contemptible state, shunned by his mother, as he slinks out of the cathedral, that he encounters the Graf (27–32) — as a figuration of his possible future. The Graf has retained all his familiar qualities from the days of *Sonnenwanderer*. We hear a little more about his biography. He has been a rich playboy, genuinely a count by birth, whose dissolute lifestyle has finally brought him low (28). Despite a promise on his mother's grave he has failed to change his life (37). Now, his lust for life sated, his weakness overcome, not 'Büßer' but 'Überwinder' (31), he merely wanders and waits for the death which, as ever in Hauptmann, is a transfiguring merger (30) with the life-principle.[83] But he is still, significantly, the same dusty colour as the earth (32) and still, most importantly, a musician and a composer. He sings the same bawdy song he once sang outside the Mecklenburg tavern (35). 'Bruder' (32), says Josua to him. But he is the wrong kind of musician. He too, admittedly, has only the healthy laughter of contempt for the music of death — the requiem mass just performed in the cathedral (30). But his own music as he tramps along the dusty roads, like that of Josua in his current state, never leaves the confines of his own imagination or his private world:

> 'Wenn ich meine Chausseen haste . . . die nach der großen Fata Morgana endlich doch hinführen . . . da greife ich kühn hinein . . . auf imaginäre Tasten natürlich . . . da rast sich mein staubgrauer Leib wegelang aus wie im Wahnsinn . . . da tumultuieren aus mir bacchantische Töne . . . was so ein gehetzter, einstiger Lüstling aus tiefster Inbrunst noch kann . . . da gell ich . . . gluckse . . . pfeife . . . flöte . . . schrei ich mich aus . . . (Er lacht) jauchze . . . orkane die Schöpfung an (31)

Josua, in a moment of self-misunderstanding, decides to take this 'staubgrauer Heiland' (32) home to his mother and Georginel, in an attempt to compensate his shame and explain his vulnerability to bourgeois norms. Thus begins, however, a kind of Faustian descent into an artificial paradise of still more alcohol, as the pair, now accompanied by the Gypsy girl, instead of heading home, end up in a cellar tavern. Here, Josua has drunkenly crowned the now equally drunken Graf with a laurel wreath — ironic, Tasso-like symbol of aesthetic mastery, symbol of grave misrecognition of this unrealized artist. As Josua, awakening, marks his perilous regression with a grotesque (naturalistic) performance of animal noises (38), even the Graf, casting off the wreath (42), leaves in disgust.

It is thus not the Graf but the Gypsy girl who — *ex negativo* — saves Josua from himself. She too bears a close resemblance to the abject creatures of *Sonnenwanderer*. Although young, she has a child and is thus no longer beautiful, her big, horsey teeth (36) betraying the naked appetite of the *Naturvolk*.[84] As in the earlier tale, she wants only to sell her body to Josua (38–39). But she makes the mistake of crooning a coarse, would-be seductive song, 'Blümlein der Nacht' (39).[85] Precisely this, the 'herumgesudeltes Melos' (39) of the 'Steppenhuhn' (39), the travesty of authentic aesthetic beauty sung by the wreck of a once-beautiful woman, wrenches Josua violently from his stupor and at once transports him to the other extreme of ethereal vision (40). He leaves almost at once to begin transcribing *his* version of the Creation (by contrast to that of the Graf, 31). She, again like her predecessor in 'Fahrendes Volk', heaps darkly sexual insults on him in return (40), and finally runs off in fear of Josua's 'magic' aura (45). Josua, then, is saved for his own aesthetic mission not by the failed Graf, but by the intervention of a member of the aesthetic *Naturvolk* — albeit without her exercising agency.

But this is not all. Hauptmann's last Gypsy has a further role to play — in Georginel's life. She is in fact not presented in a wholly negative light. 'Man erjagt es niemals . . . man lebt . . . und lebt . . . und fühlt kaum das Leben . . .' (26), she whines as Georginel, preoccupied, declines to have her palm read at the cathedral door. This *Zigeunerin*, unlike her predecessors in *Sonnenwanderer*, is more than a mere representative of the aesthetic *Naturvolk*. She is also another of Hauptmann's unrealized women, who through force of circumstance or character fail to take control of their life. Moreover, her song may be false, but she is also open to the transforming power of authentic music, as Josua's student plays some of Beethoven's six small variations in G-flat: 'Huuh [. . .] selig machst du mich mit deinem Getön . . . aaach . . . ganz sinnlos machen mich deine Klänge . . . ich wullt die Welt jitzt neu umarmen . . . spiele nicht weiter . . .. ich muß sunst heulen vor Glick' (42). It is this latent potential of the Gypsy which leads to another, quite different transformation — of Georginel. For the bourgeois child-woman Georginel is in her own way equally unrealized, unready in her sexuality, and so unfitted for the role of Josua's mate. During the long night of Josua's journey to himself she has faithfully watched alone, like a wise virgin, for his return. At last, despite their brief encounter, an internalized, visionary memory of the Gypsy changes her self-understanding. She appears exactly as seen at the cathedral door, with the child on her back (53). Her words (26) too have stuck in Georginel's mind: 'Luß dir wahrsagen . . . scheenes

Frailein . . . man erjagt es niemals . . . und lebt und lebt . . . und fühlt kaum was Leben . . .' (53). Georginel however now assents to the life of aesthetic *Bohème* which fate has prepared for her: 'ich . . . ich fühle die süße Umstrickung . . . ich will leben . . . ich will helfen und tun . . . ich will Schmach und Schmerzen in meine Trauertücher verhüllen mit Demut' (53). Recognizing in the Gypsy an anticipatory mirror-image of her own fate, Georginel begs the Virgin for guidance: 'deiner Magd Seele ist wie ein gähnender Brunnen' (53). Assuming the Madonna pose, the Gypsy reveals her answer: the child (54). Fading, she bespeaks the fate of the artist's wife in Hauptmann's monistic and frankly patriarchal world: 'Die Welt ist hart . . . die Erde aus Steinen . . . die Menschen aus Staub . . . flüchtig ist der Menschen Bestimmung . . . ewig ist die verklärte Gestalt' (54). These Gypsy words, a last internalized aesthetic testament of the *race*, finally commit Georginel, now grown into acceptance of her role, to Josua. He for his part works the image of her as maternal bringer of life in death into the climax of his musical cosmogony: 'Georginel . . . Menschenfrühling . . . ewig zum Opfer geschmückt' (57). One last time, then, the aesthetic potential of the Gypsy race — albeit appropriated by the agency of the occidental consciousness — exercises its transformative power.

Notes to Chapter 7

1. See Eberhard Berger, 'Vorrede', in *Carl Hauptmann: Sämtliche Werke. Wissenschaftliche Ausgabe mit Kommentar*, ed. by Eberhard Berger, Hans-Gert Roloff, and Anna Strolka, 16 vols + 1 Supplementary vol. (Stuttgart, Bad Cannstatt: frommann-holzboog, 1997, in progress), Supplementary vol.: *Carl Hauptmann: Chronik zu Leben und Werk*, ed. by Eberhard Berger and Elfriede Berger (2001), pp. 7–8 (p. 7). This edition is henceforth cited as *SW*.
2. See for example *Chronik*, p. 87, 13 May 1897; also Carl Hauptmann's letter to Paul Zech of 17 April 1917, in *Carl Hauptmann: Leben mit Freunden. Gesammelte Briefe*, ed. by Will-Erich Peuckert (Leipzig: Paul List, 1928), pp. 266–70.
3. See Hauptmann to Karl Zeiss on 5 April 1917 (*Leben mit Freunden*, pp. 264–65).
4. See Walter Delabar, 'Carl Hauptmanns Künstlerroman *Einhart der Lächler*: Eine erste Orientierung', in *Carl Hauptmann 1858–1921. Internationales Symposium: Beiträge*, ed. by Miroslawa Czarneck and Hans-Gert Roloff (Berlin: Weidler, 2004), pp. 93–104 (p. 94).
5. See *Carl Hauptmann und seine Worpsweder Künstlerfreunde: Briefe und Tagebuchblätter*, ed. by Elfriede Berger, 2 vols (Berlin: Schütze, 2003).
6. In *SW* VII/1 (1999), 1–107 (pp. 74–85).
7. *SW* VII/1, 219–88 (pp. 283–88).
8. Cited here from the 1st edn, *Ephraims Breite: Schauspiel in fünf Akten* (Berlin: S. Fischer, 1900).
9. Cited here from the 1st edn (Leipzig: Wolff, 1918). Gypsies also appear in the unpublished 'Märchenkomödie' *Der Wolkenbruch oder Fräulein Kätchens Blendlaterne* (1916). Compare *Chronik*, pp. 237–38.
10. Cited here from the first edn: *Einhart der Lächler: Roman*, 2 vols (Berlin: Marquardt, 1907).
11. *SW* IX/1 (2004), 260–73, 274–83.
12. See Kelly, *The Descent of Darwin*, pp. 8, 57–74.
13. *Die Bedeutung der Keimblättertheorie für die Individualitätslehre und den Generationswechsel* (Jena: J. Hossfeld, 1883).
14. *Die Metaphysik in der modernen Physiologie: Eine kritische Untersuchung* (Dresden: L. Ehlermann, 1893). For the reviews see *Chronik*, pp. 61–64.
15. On Ploetz, Hauptmann, and the racial hygiene movement see Kelly, *Descent of Darwin*, pp. 106–07, and especially Weindling, *Health, Race and German Politics*, esp. pp. 63–64, 74–76, 141–54; also Richard Weikart, *From Darwin to Hitler: Evolutionary Ethics, Eugenics and Racism in Germany* (Basingstoke: Palgrave-Macmillan, 2004), esp. pp. 43–58. Ploetz, like all racial

hygienists a decided opponent of alcohol, appears in literary history only as the original of the figure Alfred Loth, in Gerhart Hauptmann's *Vor Sonnenaufgang* (1889). See on this Ritchie Robertson, 'Modernism and the Self 1890–1924', in *Philosophy and German Literature 1700–1990*, ed. by Nicholas Saul (Cambridge: Cambridge University Press, 2002), pp. 150–97 (p. 160).

16. Robert Ritter, *Ein Menschenschlag: Erbärztliche und erbgeschichtliche Untersuchungen über die — durch 10 Geschlechterfolgen erforschten — Nachkommen von 'Vagabunden, Jaunern und Räubern'* (Leipzig: Georg Thieme, 1937). On Ritter and Justin see Kenrick and Puxon, *Gypsies under the Swastika*, pp. 16–25.
17. See Weindling, *Health, Race and German Politics*, p. 70.
18. His friend Ferdinand Simon married Frieda Bebel. See *Chronik*, p. 57.
19. See Weindling, *Health, Race and German Politics*, pp. 1–10, 11–60.
20. Bénédict-Augustin Morel (1809–73), *Traité des dégénérescences physiques, intellectuelles et morales de l'espèce humaine et des causes qui produisent ces variétés malidives* (Paris, 1857). On Morel and Lombroso, also on Lombroso's reception in Germany, see Mariacarla Gadebusch Bondio, *Die Rezeption der kriminalanthropologischen Theorien von Cesare Lombroso in Deutschland von 1880–1914* (Husum: Matthison, 1995), pp. 38, 94–95; also the standard work in English: Daniel Pick, *Faces of Degeneration: A European Disorder, c.1848–1918* (Cambridge: Cambridge University Press, 1989), esp. pp. 109–52.
21. *Der Verbrecher (homo delinquens) in anthropologischer, ärztlicher und juristischer Beziehung.* In deutscher Bearbeitung von Dr. M. O. Fraenkel. Mit Vorwort von A. von Kirchenheim, 3 vols, 2nd edn (Hamburg: Verlagsanstalt/Königliche Buchhandlung 1894); *L'uomo delinquente in rapporto all'antropologia, giurisprudenza e alla discipline carceraria* (Torino, 1876). Lombroso, as Gadebusch Bondio notes, was no less a committed socialist than Ploetz, and indeed a practising Christian (Bondio, pp. 38, 47). Max Nordau's *Entartung* (1892–93) is of course dedicated to Lombroso and presents itself as the extrapolation of Lombroso's degenerative theory to the realm of cultural production (*Entartung* (1894), I, pp. vii–viii, 30–62). It should perhaps also be pointed out that Nordau (originally Salomon Südfeld) was Jewish and later a Zionist supporter of Theodor Herzl.
22. *Die Tüchtigkeit unsrer Rasse und der Schutz der Schwachen: Ein Versuch über Rassenhygiene und ihr Verhältnis zu den humanen Idealen, besonders zum Socialismus* (Berlin: S. Fischer, 1895).
23. Ludwig Büchner too joined in this discussion. His *Darwinismus und Sozialismus. Oder: Der Kampf um das Dasein und die moderne Gesellschaft* (Leipzig: Günther 1894) insists that innate inequality invalidates social democracy, but recognizes the moral inequity of mass, capitalistically organized society, and offers a range of measures in inheritance law to create a level playing field for the individual's struggle for existence.
24. This was a common theme, developed most fully by Nordau, who applies the term degeneracy diplomatically only to the ruling elite (*Entartung*, I, 5, 7–10).
25. Later Ploetz is less drastic. In a pamphlet of 1911 he argues that the needy should be cared for as much as ever, since this increases the degree of social cohesion and so strengthens the race overall in its global struggle for existence (A.P., *Ziele und Aufgaben der Rassenhygiene: Referat erstattet auf der xxxv. Tagung des deutschen Vereins für öffentliche Gesundheitspflege zu Elberfeld* (Braunschweig: Vieweg, 1911), pp. 23–24.
26. Compare the view of a more sinister figure in the movement, Otto Ammon who, appealing to Wallace, argued in this context for: 'die *Strafrechtspflege* [. . .], die von Hause aus nichts ist, als eine *Anstalt zur Reinigung des menschlichen Keimplasmas von gemeinschädlichen Anlagen*', in: Ammon, *Die natürliche Auslese beim Menschen: Auf Grund der Ergebnisse der anthropologischen Untersuchungen der Wehrpflichtigen in Baden und anderen Materialien* (Jena: Gustav Fischer, 1893), p. 324.
27. He rejects war — with exceptions — as a means of ensuring the race's fitness or expanding its habitat, since war tends to function counter-selectively, by extinguishing the fit and preserving the unfit (*Tüchtigkeit*, p. 63; *Ziele*, p. 26).
28. East Aryans would include for example Hindus, who have a lesser cranial capacity (pp. 131–32).
29. Later Ploetz is far more negative about the potentially regressive consequences of mixing other than related races: 'Der Umstand, daß bei dem Mischlingen allzu verschiedener Blutmassen besonders Intelligenz und Charakter leiden sollen, also Dinge, die erst spät in der

Stammesentwicklung gewonnen worden, erinnert an die Tatsache, daß, wenn man verschiedene Varietäten bei Haustieren kreuzt, oft bei den Nachkommen Eigenschaften hervortreten, die früher vorhandenen stammesgeschichtlichen Stadien angehören' (Ploetz, *Ziele und Aufgaben der Rassenhygiene* (1911), p. 17).

30. It should be noted that in Germany there were strident counter-arguments, including those of Wilhelm Schallmeyer. Schallmeyer's *Vererbung und Auslese in ihrer soziologischen und politischen Bedeutung* (Jena: Gustav Fischer 1910; 1st edn 1903), which won the Krupp Prize for an essay on the application of the laws of evolution to society in 1903 (Weindling, pp. 112–23), vehemently attacked the 'Propagandisten des Arier- und Germanenevangeliums' (374) from Gobineau on as based on prejudice; most races were for him irreducibly mixed; and strict racial purity would lead to incestuous degeneration (pp. 374–83).
31. *Tüchtigkeit unsrer Rasse*, pp. 10–11, 15, 43. He also praises the 'hellsehender Dichter [. . .] Gerhart Hauptmann' (p. 197).
32. *Metaphysik*, p. 301, Note. See Friedrich Nietzsche, *Also sprach Zarathustra*, in *Werke*, ed. by Karl Schlechta, 6 vols (Munich: Hanser, 1980) III, 277–561 (p. 301). On the centrality of this principle for nineteenth-century anthropology see Wolfgang Riedel, *'Homo natura': Literarische Anthropologie um 1900* (Berlin and New York: de Gruyter, 1996).
33. The MS, as Dr Wolfgang Trautwein, Director of the *Stiftung Archiv der Akademie der Künste* at Berlin, informs me, is regrettably untraceable in the archive.
34. In *Leben mit Freunden*, pp. 259–60.
35. On the origin of this idea see Nicholas Saul, 'The Pursuit of the Subject: Literature as Critic and Perfecter of Philosophy 1790–1830', in *German Philosophy and Literature*, pp. 57–101.
36. Carl Hauptmann, *Aus meinem Tagebuch*, ed. by Will-Erich Peuckert, 3rd edn (Leipzig: List, 1928; 1st edn 1900), p. 93.
37. The situation recalls strongly the first Gypsy encounter in Freytag's *Die verlorene Handschrift*. Hauptmann venerated this novel of Germans and Gypsies, in particular the semi-mythical figure of Ilse. See Berger, *Chronik*, pp. 21–22 and Chapter 5. This kind of meeting can be argued to be the primal scene of Gypsy–*gadjo* intercultural encounter. Another example (and there are many others), is Brachvogel, *Friedemann Bach*, II, 252–53.
38. There is a tell-tale resemblance to the narrator's mortifying yet eroticizing description of the beautiful Gypsy girl in the frame of Stifter's *Der Waldbrunnen*: 'zwei Mädchen — sie mochten kaum zwei Jahre auseinander sein — eine jede schlank wie Rahel am Brunnen, mit schwarzen, mandelförmigen Augen und weißen Zähnen — die jungen braunen Brüste nur halb in zerfetzten Tüchern verborgen und um die Kniee graue, schlotternde Lumpen' (p. 75; compare *Waldbrunnen*, p. 2). See too Hauptmann following an encounter with Gypsies in Hungary in December 1904: 'Wunderherrliche Menschen, schöne Griechen im Strassenstaube' (*Chronik*, p. 145).
39. To take two examples from later nineteenth-century Gypsy anthropology which Hauptmann may have known, we find Emil Reinbeck noting how Gypsy woman are classically beautiful when young yet age and become ugly with astonishing rapidity (Reinbeck, pp. 53–54); and the (rather more original) Richard Liebich, who also notes: 'wie das weibliche Geschlecht bei den Zigeunern sich schnell entwickelt, ebenso schnell altert es und zeigt nach kurzer Blüte als Frucht abschreckende Häßlichkeit' (Liebich, p. 22; compare p. 46).
40. This fiction derives from a genuine encounter of Hauptmann's on a bicycle tour through Mecklenburg on 20–21 June 1895 (*Chronik*, p. 70).
41. See Hans Ostwald, *Vagabunden: Ein autobiographischer Roman*, ed. by Klaus Bergmann (Frankfurt a.M. and New York: Campus, 1980; 1st edn *Vagabonden*, Berlin: Bruno und Paul Cassirer, 1900).
42. *Chronik*, p. 46 (summer 1888); compare *Metaphysik in der modernen Physiologie*, Note, 304); also 'Der gemeine Verbrecher', in *Aus meinem Tagebuch*, pp. 44–45.
43. *Genio e follia* (1873). For an example of the German reception Nordau, *Entartung*, pp. 43–44.
44. See Hauptmann's letter to Karl Theodor Strasser of 3 September 1917 (*Leben mit Freunden*, pp. 274–76 (p. 275)). This did not stop him reviving the Graf di Santa Rocca shortly thereafter in *Musik*.
45. Compare the beautiful Gypsy girl ('Fahrendes Volk', p. 77); Joseph (*Ephraims Breite*, pp. 17, 115);

Habakuk (*Habakuk*[1], 260, 265; *Habakuk*[2], pp. 274, 279); and Einhart (*Einhart der Lächler*, I, 18, 33, 50, 121, passim).

46. Hauptmann signed up to Haeckel's *Monistenbund* in December 1905 (*Chronik*, p. 159).
47. The women of Hauptmann's circle were deeply impressed. See Martha Jaschke to Lotte Hauptmann: 'Großartig, dem ganzen Charakter der Breite würdig — sie tödtet sich nicht!' (*Chronik*, p. 103; March 1899).
48. The 'fellachisch' nose of one of the Gypsy girls in 'Fahrendes Volk' (77) is also an allusion to the legendary Egyptian origin of the Gypsies.
49. See Georges Bizet, *Carmen* (1875). Oper in vier Aufzügen, von Henri Meilhac und Ludovic Halévy nach der Novelle von Prosper Mérimée. Deutsche Übersetzung von Julius Hopp. Übersetzung der Dialoge von Wilhelm Zentner, ed. by Wilhelm Zentner (Stuttgart: Reclam, 1977), p. 29 (I/8). Hauptmann — following Nietzsche perhaps — was an admirer of Bizet's *Carmen*, which he thought of as deeply tragic (*Chronik*, p. 139; October–November 1903). On Nietzsche and Carmen see Friedrich Nietzsche, *Der Fall Wagner: Ein Musikanten-Problem* (1888), in *Werke*, IV, 901–38. Wagner's moralizing, says Nietzsche more or less seriously, represents 'das *verarmte Leben*, der Wille zum Ende, die große Müdigkeit' (903), whereas Bizet's pure fatalism and naked erotic hatred of the sexes are wholly liberating.
50. Wolfgang Neuber, 'Zwischen Darwinismus und Metaphysik oder: Lieber licht und gesund als dunkel und krank. Zu Carl Hauptmanns Roman *Mathilde*', in *Carl Hauptmann 1858–1921*, pp. 105–23 (pp. 112–23).
51. See Barbara Becker-Cantarino, 'Die "neue Frau" und die Frauengestalten Carl Hauptmanns', in *Carl Hauptmann 1858–1921*, pp. 47–66 (pp. 55–58). It is interesting to speculate that it was *Ephraims Breite* as well as *Die Metaphysik in der modernen Physiologie* which attracted Otto Weininger's interest and their correspondence (*Chronik*, pp. 110, 115; 30 December 1900, 24 May 1900).
52. See *Chronik*, p. 98 (5 July 1898).
53. Little remains from 1900–10 following his destruction of numerous early works. See Christiane Lange, '"Mueller von Mueller". Anmerkungen zu einem nahezu zerstörtem Frühwerk', in *Otto Mueller*, ed. by Johann Georg Prinz von Hohenzollern, Mario-Andreas von Lüttichau (Munich, Berlin, London, and New York: Prestel, 2003), pp. 12–25.
54. Tanja Pirsig's full account of Mueller's biographical relations with Gypsies disproves it; see Tanja Pirsig, 'Otto Mueller: Mythos und Wahrheit', in *Otto Mueller*, pp. 124–62.
55. The works are lost.
56. *Chronik*, pp. 126, 135, 147, 158, 161, 202; 196. For a full overview of the biographical relations see Tanja Pirsig, 'Die Familie Hauptmann und Otto Mueller', in *Otto Mueller*, pp. 26–45; for a full treatment of the biographical relation of the Hauptmanns and Mueller's iconography, see Tanja Pirsig's master's dissertation: *Carl und Gerhard Hauptmann und die bildenden Künste* (Bonn, 1998).
57. *Chronik*, p. 141 (January 1904). Also (for example) the article 'Carl Hauptmann' in *Kindlers Literaturlexikon*, VII, 376–78 (p. 377).
58. See Delabar, p. 96; also S. Weindling, 'Das autobiographische Element in Carl Hauptmanns *Einhart der Lächler*', *German Quarterly*, 28 (1955), 122–26.
59. Hauptmann detested Zola's aesthetic. See *Aus meinem Tagebuch*, pp. 95–96.
60. Compare Hauptmann's notation after an encounter with Hungarian Gypsies in December 1904: 'Man muß in der Kunst sein wie der Zigeuner, der nie genug hat, und von seinen Werken immer denken, nun endlich bei dem neuen kommt die Erlösung' (*Chronik*, p. 146).
61. This is why Rosa, for example, runs home from the wild Gypsy dance (p. 36).
62. Note the parallel with the family structure in Mörike's *Maler Nolten* (I, 168) — although nasty Ernestine is missing.
63. In Rheinsberg. See *Chronik*, p. 116 (8 June–24 August 1900).
64. See — both on the general significance of the dance revival in the avant-garde around 1900 as indicator of a new psychophysical paradigm and on the mediation of dance and literature — Gabriele Brandstetter, *Tanz-Lektüren: Körperbilder und Raumfiguren der Avantgarde* (Frankfurt a.M.: Fischer, 1995).
65. The male, notably, is the bearer of the aesthetic tradition.

66. Two such paintings are known only as background images in photographs taken by Wilhelm Bölsche of the Hauptmanns at home. See *Otto Mueller*, pp. 29–30.
67. See *Otto Mueller, Die Tänzerin*, 1903 (pp. 19, 22), *Tänzerin (Maschka, tanzend)*, Fig. 9, 1903 (p. 23); and, especially *Tänzerin mit Schleier, von einem Mann beobachtet*, Fig. 11, 1903 (p. 24).
68. From cancer of the bowel (I, 174), intended perhaps as a physiological symbol — or consequence — of her self-consuming frustration.
69. Einhart is around thirty at the beginning of the next book (II, 5).
70. Poncet is 'seines Faches ein Mann, der nach den Gesetzen des Lebens der Vielen suchte' (II, 48).
71. A union celebrated by a Gypsy orchestra (II, 224).
72. Like the 'Landstreicher' Einhart believes in *one* Jesus (p. 213), i.e. as one form of religion among others.
73. Compare: 'Seine Freiheit zu bilden, war gewachsen. Auch seine Andacht vor dem Geheimnis allenthalben war groß geworden, und seine mitleidigen Gefühle für die Übermenge derer, die in den Vorhöfen ihrer Sehnsuchten grau in grau wie die zerlumpten Bettelleute vor den Türen der Osterkirchen hoffnungslos harren.' (II, 163)
74. After *Ephraims Breite* Hauptmann displays a generally positive attitude to racial mixing, and he treats the problem of German–Jewish miscegenation in this light (if tragically) in *Ismael Friedmann* (1913). See on this especially the unfinished letter of 1913 in *Leben mit Freunden*, pp. 189–90.
75. Membership of an aesthetic movement is for Nordau a sign of degenerative weakness. See *Entartung*, I, 55–59.
76. It may be that Hauptmann's uncomfortable synthesis of racial hygiene and humanistic cosmopolitanism was influenced by the liberal-Humboldtian — and anti-Darwinian — anthropologist Adolf Bastian. Hauptmann was for a time enthused by the discipline of cultural anthropology, and in late 1889 had planned a year-long expedition with Bastian to Brazil to research the Bakairi tribe. Its purpose was to confirm the developmental implications of his psychophysical theory by examining the social behaviour and cultural artefacts of archaic tribes (*Chronik*, pp. 50–51, 84; *Leben mit Freunden*, pp. 34–35). Hauptmann's *Fragment* on the culture of the inhabitants of Togo — presumably experienced at an exhibition in Berlin — perhaps gives a hint of the embryonic theory (*Aus meinem Tagebuch*, pp. 84–85). On Bastian and the anti-Darwinian tradition of liberal cultural anthropology see H. Glenn Penny, *Objects of Culture: Ethnology and Ethnographic Museums in Imperial Germany* (Chapel Hill: University of North Carolina Press, 2002).
77. Compare Otto Ammon, *Die natürliche Auslese beim Menschen*, whose extreme Aryanism does not prevent him defending for example the high gifts of the Jewish race (p. 310).
78. So far as I can tell the term was first given currency in ostensibly scholarly discourse by August Friedrich Pott: *Die Zigeuner*, where he refers to them as 'eine arge Landplage und Noth der Regierung' (p. viii). See thereafter in official discourse Emil Reinbeck in *Die Zigeuner*, p. 64. For an overview see Hehemann, *'Bekämpfung des Zigeunerunwesens'*, pp. 153–243, 243–403; also *Zigeuner. Roma, Sinti, Gitanos, Gypsies*, ed. by Rüdiger Vossen, pp. 64–86; and Lucassen, *Zigeuner*, pp. 168–213.
79. See Hehemann, pp. 261–71. A good indicator of the sustained pressure to intensify the control is the legal dissertation of Richard Breithaupt, *Die Zigeuner und der deutsche Staat: Ein Beitrag zur deutschen Rechts- und Kulturgeschichte* (Würzburg: C. J. Becker, 1907), especially the conclusion, pp. 84–87.
80. 3d edn (Graz: Leuschner & Lubensky, 1899), pp. 333–56 (p. 333).
81. See Hehemann, pp. 233, 285–94.
82. *Zigeunerbuch herausgegeben zum amtlichen Gebrauch im Aufrage des K.B. Staatsministeriums des Innern vom Sicherheitsbureau der K. Polizeidirektion München*, ed. by Alfred Dillmann (Munich: Wild, 1905). See for an account of this agency's effectiveness Block, *Die Zigeuner*, pp. 197–201.
83. Compare 'Erlöser Tod' in *Sonnenwanderer* (*SW* VII/1, 18–24).
84. The older Gypsy women of 'Fahrendes Volk' also have characteristically large, predatory teeth (*SW* VII/1, 78).
85. Compare this image with that of the 'Nachtblumen aus Indiens Gärten' (*SW* VII/1, 78) applied

by the narrator of 'Fahrendes Volk' to the younger Gypsy girls. Arnim's *Isabella von Ägypten* seems a likely inspiration of an image Hauptmann clearly liked. There Bella is described as being 'doch in Europa wie die fremde Blume, die sich nächtlich nur erschließt, weil dann in ihrer Heimat der Tag aufgeht' (Achim von Arnim, *Erzählungen*, ed. by Gisela Henckmann (Stuttgart: Reclam, 1991), pp. 34–154 (p. 145)).

CHAPTER 8

❖

Saar, Alscher, and the Beginning of the End

In this concluding chapter the liberal Austrian aristocrat Ferdinand von Saar (1833–1906) and the Banat (Rumanian-) German writer Otto Alscher (1877–1944) can stand despite their contrasting perspectives for the fundamental trends in Germanophone representation of the Gypsy. Either side of 1900, as the First World War brought the nineteenth century to its retarded close, two linked shifts occur: the post-Darwinian Social Darwinist racial paradigm grows to dominate the presence of Gypsy culture in literature and anthropology, and the long epochal trend to the aesthetic recuperation of the Gypsy, after its last hurrah in the work of Carl Hauptmann, fades. Let us take Saar first.

'. . . degenerierende Menschen, denen die Arbeitsscheu im Blute steckt': Gypsies and Atavism in Saar's *Die Troglodytin*

Ferdinand von Saar's grim little 'Novelle aus Österreich' of 1887[1] is a fine example of how far the doctrine of the Gypsy as Lombrosian degenerate and workshy criminal penetrated, despite sympathies to the contrary, even into the discourse of a liberal aristocrat. Although Gypsies, as will be seen, play a key role in the argument, this story tends to foreground the Gypsy less than issues of race, labour, and sexuality which affect a mixed German–Slav population in the Moravian part of the Austrian Empire during the war years 1865–66. At last, however, these very issues bring the Gypsies to the fore.

Here a markedly subjective German narrator, Pernett, is driven to recall an extraordinary incident which even today troubles him. In younger years as an assistant forester he has encountered a beautiful and sexually alluring young Slav girl, Maruschka Kratochvilova, from a proletarian family fallen on hard times. He repeatedly happens upon this seemingly workshy girl in the forest — once even, in an emblematic scene echoing Kleist's 'Schrecken im Bade', stumbling across her whilst bathing. An erotic bond, it is clear, exists between them. Perhaps it is racially conditioned: he, the German, resists it, she, the Slav, does not. Later she forms a liaison with Lali, slow-witted son of the nationalistic Slav *Bürgermeister*, much to the latter's chagrin. Fatal crimes follow. When his affair is broken up, Lali vengefully sets on fire the house of a junior forester who had connived at the affair, but then betrayed it. His responsibility never comes out, and he is sent away to the army, later to die in the Austro-Prussian War of 1866. Maruschka, however, despite her acknowledged innocence, is decided by the commune to be a bad influence and condemned for a year to the workhouse. There she becomes addicted to alcohol and loses her looks. Unreformed, she returns, and in a fit of drunken vengeance destroys the house of the *Bürgermeister* — also by fire. A further attempted — almost successful — seduction of the narrator ensues at the scene, and she escapes. But before justice can track her down a grotesquely swollen woman's body is found in a forest river. Unrecognizable, it is taken to be hers.

Now this tale can be taken as a Lombrosian story of degeneration and (in this sense) just desserts.[2] The narrator is highly sensitive to social and economic conditions. He scrupulously registers a wide range of variation in this respect, from the peasants, foresters, and aristocrats, to the 'ländliches Proletariat' which the 'herrschaftliche Industrien' (iron works; 'Troglodytin', 102) have produced, to the 'Maschinenschlosser und Modelltischler' who reside in a trim, English-style 'Arbeiterkolonie' (103),[3] and, finally, hidden away in decrepit hovels in the nether reaches of the town, the 'niedrige Löhner und Handlanger' (103). It is from the latter that the Kratochvil family proceeds. Whereas the residents of the model colony are well-paid and intelligent (indeed, beginning to concern themselves with socialist politics (103)), Kratochvil has become addicted to alcohol, lost his work at the blast furnace, lost other work as a tile fabricator, and the family has been evicted. Abandoned by the community, whose duty it would have been under the 'Heimatsrecht' to care for them, reduced by disease, they scrape a living by petty thievery (103–04). As a consequence of this socio-economic and ethical downward slide the family is thought of in the Germanic community as in the process of degenerating. In that community, dominant yet in the minority, racial thinking in any case obtains. The senior demesne forester stokes a political-racial rivalry between the would-be autonomous peasant Slav town-dwellers and the cultivated German aristocrats (107–08), who are already in dispute over forest ownership rights. Pernett's fellow assistant forester, in keeping with the latest 1860s anthropological thinking,[4] is more radical. He bleakly comments: 'es sind nun einmal degenerierende Menschen, denen die Arbeitsscheu im Blute steckt. [. . .] Das scheint, wie gesagt, auf rein physischen Gesetzen zu beruhen, die selbst dem äußeren Zwange spotten' (118–19). This evidently Lombrosian theory of inherited idleness is offered as an explanation for the girl's failure to retain the seasonal job which Pernett finds for her (119–20). Her ostentatious displays of sexuality fit equally well into this diagnosis, so much so that the assistant even suggests she earn her living as a prostitute in nearby Brünn (121). The girl's failure to change after a year of the workhouse, her concomitant addiction to drink, and her final criminal act of revenge, seem only to confirm the theory.

And yet, as Virginia Lewis has argued, the text contains counter-indicators which tend to refute easy racial prejudices, promote nurture over (degenerating) nature, and undermine the proffered theory of the assistant forester. The senior demesne forester, for all his pro-German propaganda, is, we are carefully informed, in fact himself a Slav, who has merely identified after long years of service with the Germanic community (108). The German narrator, who so severely manages his own sexuality, is in fact all but seduced by Maruschka and in the end about to succumb to the temptation — only to be saved by the arrival of the fire brigade (135). That Germans are corruptible by money is shown by the junior forester, who connived at the affair of Lali and Maruschka. That the offspring of the degenerate family *can* resume work and better themselves is shown by Maruschka's brother. This boy, once (despite his own physical beauty) workshy enough to maim his hand and so be excused labour in the fields (106), finally becomes chief minder of the local geese, and dramatically improves the family's financial position (106). Indeed lack of education is suggested as an equally plausible reason for the family's failure to work. Even the prejudiced senior forester has noted that the *Bürgermeister*, despite his wealth and position, has allowed his slow-witted son to grow up '"wie das liebe Vieh"' (108). And the narrator himself notes that the Kratochvil children grew up 'selbstverständlich ohne Schulunterricht in äußerster Verwahrlosung' (105), so that Maruschka's last, heated insistence, '"Oh, was hab' ich dort [im Arbeitshaus] ausgestanden! Ich will nicht arbeiten, ich mag nicht arbeiten, ich kann nicht arbeiten"' (134), in this light acquires a quite different complexion.

That said, there remains in this multi-layered text one, perhaps sinister, layer of signification still to be peeled away, which Lewis (despite her interest in ethnic minorities and stereotypes) has not explored, but which bears on the central problem of degeneration and is indeed foregrounded in the title. The Kratochvil family is of course jokingly known in the community as 'Troglodyten' (105), because this connotes two things: the remarkable domicile which the homeless family is compelled to construct — a semi-permanent, cave-like dwelling set half-buried in the earth — and the family's alleged degeneration or atavistic regression, as is implied, to the age of cave-dwellers at a pre-historic stage of evolution.[5] Now Saar's story, in addition to its keen observation of *milieu*, is also replete with allusions to mythical and elemental symbols, which are designed to reinforce stereotypical interpretation. The forest, for example, is clearly that traditional half-cultural, half-natural contact zone familiar from fairytale in which sexual experiments can be played out. Fire, the ancient symbol of uncontrollable sexual passion, is repeatedly linked with Maruschka (her red headscarf, the red field poppies in her hair, the fire she sets). So too is water. When discovered in the bath, she adopts the chaste, yet seductive posture of (Botticelli's) water-born Venus (114), she lives by the stream, and returns Melusine-like to the water at her death. But it is the archetypal symbol of the earth which is most heavily charged in Saar's story, as symbol of regression. The family's return to the earth is often highlighted. The senior forester, for example, scorns their 'verpestete Erdhöhle' (108). It is the symbol of the earth which links Maruschka and her family with the Gypsies. For when the homeless Kratochvils build their remarkable substitute for a home, they do so by reference neither to ethnic majority nor to ethnic minority, neither on a Slavic nor on a Germanic site, but on a Gypsy site and on a Gypsy model. Thus as the family sinks to its lowest social — and evolutionary — level it finds an existential niche only by copying the behaviour of the abject Gypsy race. As chance would have it, the 'Landplage' (104) of wandering Gypsies has visited the town and recently vacated its allocated site in a poor meadow by the river. There they have erected 'eine Reihe löcheriger Zelte' (104). On their departure in the spring the Gypsies, as is their wont, leave behind 'eine geräumige Erdvertiefung, welche die Bewohner eines weitläufigen Zeltes zu besserem Wetterschutz mochten gegraben haben' (104) and some tent poles. Adapting in true Darwinian fashion to their new niche, the Kratochvils have observed 'das braune Volk' (104), colonized the ruins of this (as the narrator observes) merely 'annähernd menschliche [. . .] Behausung' (104), and rebuilt it in more or less Romany style. It should be noted that Saar's description of the Gypsy-style tent is wholly authentic. Grellmann in 1787 devotes several pages to describing variants on this typical construction of the east European Romanies.[6] Martin Block describes closely similar 'halbunterirdische Erdhütten'[7] in 1936. Whilst Saar, then, takes care to construct, and then deconstruct, the framework of degenerative theory with which to interpret the socio-economic phenomenon of the pauperized Kratochvils, he also takes care to suggest through the tent symbolism — and at the level of narrative authority — that the Gypsies, too, represent the post-evolutionary survival of an earlier stage of human development. To this level the Kratochvils, on the pejorative interpretation, have regressed. But whereas it is clear that the Kratochvils, on Saar's critical interpretation of prejuduce, *can* be recuperated into some higher level on the evolutionary scale (by working and by learning, it would seem), what of the Gypsies? Saar leaves them where they are in the phylogenetic order, and the text does not redeem them from the slur of atavistic degeneration.

'Sterbende sind wir!' Otto Alscher and the Beginning of the End

Alscher is an even more depressing phenomenon than the silencing of cultural liberalism in Saar. This writer and journalist, farmer and naturalist was never as widely read as Jensen, Saar, or even Carl Hauptmann. Yet he knew Romany culture extremely well — thanks no doubt to his upbringing in Orschowa in the multicultural Banat zone in Siebenbürgen between Austria-Hungary, Romania, and Serbia, and his extensive travels in a part of the continent densely populated by settled and travelling Gypsies. Romany culture plays a central role in Alscher's conventionally modernist anti-modern advocacy of the counter-civilized, naturalistic life, and conversely his stories attack the entrenched anti-Gypsyism of Germanic cultures.[8] Trained as a graphic artist in Vienna and briefly a member of the literary circle *Jung Tirol* in Innsbruck, Alscher from around 1905 published widely both in Banat German journals and supra-regional established literary organs such as *Der Brenner* and *Die Aktion*, and Romany figures feature almost as frequently and prominently in his early *œuvre* as they do in that of Carl Hauptmann, from the fugitives in his first novel *Ich bin ein Flüchtling* (1909) to the hybrid Gypsy-Hungarian hero of the second, *Gogan und das Tier* (1912), and the almost wholly Romany-centred short story collection *Zigeuner* (1914). Alscher's apology for the Romanies, if it never attains the sophistication of Hauptmann, nevertheless both echoes and intensifies the profound ambiguity of that writer's racist yet tsiganophile stance. Finally, as we shall see, Alscher attacks it. For all this he paid a heavy price. Whilst Hauptmann never had to face the challenge of National Socialist ideology,

Alscher later, guided perhaps by some naive political analogy of his established naturalism, allowed himself to become associated with National Socialism and wrote incriminating journalistic works. He died in a Rumanian internment camp after the end of the war.[9] In what follows we shall see in two typical literary works, *Ich bin ein Flüchtling* and *Zigeuner*, how Alscher constantly struggles — and fails — to temper his underlying, frankly brutal interpretation of Darwin and Social Darwinism as dominating principles of the natural and social world with received elements of Romantic individualism and communitarianism.

Zigeuner, Alscher's first collection of tales, is a good place to start. It is not so much disparate as loosely structured. The stories themselves are extremely varied in theme, form, matter, and perspective. But four will give the characteristic flavour of Alscher's philosophy. 'Der Zigeuner und sein Gott' (*Zigeuner*, 93–99) is a set of anecdotes which exposes the village Gypsy's dry and pragmatic sense of humour in contrast with the Rumanian's dull-wittedness and the orthodox clergy's hypocrisy. 'Ohnmacht' (*Zigeuner*, 80–92) is a grim, rather Social Darwinist tale of a village Gypsy who has been paid in kind for his labour with a vast sack of corn meal, and, with forty kilos on his back, must struggle home against both the elements and the aggression of the Rumanian peasants. The even more Darwinian tale of knowledge and self-overcoming 'Das Mädchen im Walde' (*Zigeuner*, 124–37) again features abject village Gypsies, a brother and sister working as swineherds at the bottom of the social scale. One of the pigs has been taken, and the superstitious brother, fearful on the one hand of his Rumanian boss and on the other of the werewolf, decides to trek two days' distance to the town to buy a pistol and a magic bullet from a wise woman. Only grudgingly does he leave his sister the axe, as her sole means of defence during his long absence. She, however, despite her physical weakness and genuine terror, learns to use her intelligence to keep the beast at bay, and at last kills it in brutal, despairing single combat. By testing herself ruthlessly under new conditions she adapts to survive, demystifies the threat (it is simply a big grey wolf), and acquires a wholly new self-confidence. 'Die Geschlechter' (*Zigeuner*, 100–15) is a psychopathological study of a village Gypsy whose passion for his wife, in a way impenetrable to his own, limited intelligence, compels him to use primeval violence to defend his possession of her. This tale however also typifies how Alscher attempts to soften his unremitting Social Darwinism with sentimental ideas. The (unnamed) man has struck down his wife's woman friend, who had begun to influence her judgement against him, and reduced the woman to a mental cripple. Returning unrepentant from a year in prison, torn between yearning and cynical despair, he is unable to face his wife. After a sleepless night he decides to follow the simplest solution — kill her and flee. But as he is about to swing the axe the cry of the child she has borne him in his absence changes everything, and the need to ensure the survival of wife and offspring becomes his chief aim.

If that gives a taste of Alscher's conflicted world-view, then three other stories give a sense of the collection's intended balance and direction. The opening tale, emblematically entitled 'Rasse' (*Zigeuner*, 7–18), amounts to an attack on Carl Hauptmann and a farewell to the aesthetico-cultural category of *Zigeunerromantik*. For this is the sole tale which, in addition to abject Gypsies, centrally features an artist, and a sophisticated metropolitan German artist at that. This expressionist painter strongly resembles Hauptmann's Einhart or his *sujet* the tsiganophile Otto Mueller, as he undergoes an intercultural-aesthetic crisis. The backstory places him in the Berlin art world. Sated like Einhart or Mueller by the Worpswede scenery (*Zigeuner*, 9), he recalls the wilder, more nervous, more dynamic — in short '"verflucht schön"' (9) — landscape in a Hungarian work at the Berlin Secession. Once in the Carpathians, however, he finds himself overwhelmed by the richness of the motifs and unable to paint — until he encounters a village Gypsy girl. She is another Gypsy staggering under a burden (in this case a water carrier). But this pubescent, still androgynous girl masters her burden aesthetically, transforming struggle into something like an erotic and swaying dance (10). Significant for him is her posture, her head fixed in sovereign pride. Most significant is her gaze, drinking 'in entsagungsreicher Härte das Rätsel des Horizontes' (10). Thus as substitute for the expressive nature he seeks, the Gypsy girl becomes his new *sujet*. Their relationship unfolds in two phases. In the first he paints her obsessively, until at last (11) he imagines that as an artist he has exhausted her semantic potential, and turns to another *sujet*, a mountain path emerging in the mist (another kind of gaze into the infinite), and returns to landscapes. In the second phase, however, he discovers that there is more to this than meets the eye. For if he is satisfied, she is not. She returns. This time he again attempts to capture her in aesthetic representation (11). But now he realizes crushingly that his attempted profile in charcoal and indeed all his other Gypsy pictures are hermeneutic failures, renditions of blank space (14–15). And yet there seems still to be hope, for that failure prompts another kind of communication. When he touches her to change the direction of her fascinating, but incomprehensible gaze, it begins to glow — with a clearly recognizable, nascent erotic desire — and he (and she) at last grasp that communication is physical, not aesthetic. They exchange passionate kisses (17). But for the painter there is another surprise in store. For the Gypsy girl's erotic gaze immediately hardens into a blade stabbing at him, and her expression turns into something savage ('wildfremd', 18), wholly transcending the 'Heimlichkeiten seines Wesens' (18). He releases her mechanically from his embrace. She for her part is now wholly indifferent to him, assuming a relaxed pose, chattering ceaselessly to herself in incomprehensible *Romanes* 'wie nur je ein Weib mit einem Manne, der ihm keine Illusionen mehr zu wecken vermag' (18), and her gaze is released to focus once more on the infinite horizon, 'nach etwas Unbekanntem forschend' (18). He for his part picks up his charcoal 'wie eine zwecklose Arbeit, von der man gleich anfangs weiß, daß man sie doch zu keinem rechten Ende bringen wird' (18).

This, then, is a tale of two failures. The first is the failure of aesthetic cognition (at least of the received aestheticist-expressionist kind exemplified by Carl Hauptmann) to cross intercultural boundaries. Focalized as it is through the German artist's eye, his *gadjo* productions are argued signally to fail to meet the gaze of the Gypsy, to render the inner life of the child of nature for the civilized consciousness. Communication *is* possible between them, but not through the meta-language of art, still less through ordinary language. It is possible only through the language of the body, which is presented here as primal. *This* communication is however not intercultural but interracial. Hence Alscher's term 'Rasse', used positively here to connote both something like the English 'pedigree' and to signal the girl's status as de-individualized representative of a Darwinian species variety. Some of this the artist grasps. However he ultimately fails to grasp the second communication lesson: that he is merely the object of a behavioural rite of passage, instinctively enacted by a girl, experimenting, but only experimenting, with her nascent sexuality before — like any Gypsy girl — finally refusing the *gadjo* embrace until she discovers a more racially suitable male. Thus even the physical communication of the races is doomed. 'Rasse', then, is an odd tale to set at the entrance to a collection of interculturally motivated stories. Romanies are presented as a manifestation of nature wholly beyond *gadjo* categories, with wholly non-aesthetic, nakedly Darwinian priorities. The tale's purpose, then, is to sweep away aestheticizing preconceptions and clear the intercultural ground before engaging — on new terms — with the other.

'Rasse', as the first tale, had marked its recognition of the Gypsy girl's ultimate creaturely identity with the image of her as an animal scenting something new, the scent of sexual or other prey. Her nostrils quiver and flare 'als seien sie die eines Tieres, das unter einer unbekannten Witterung erbebt' (18). The last tale, 'Witterung' (*Zigeuner*, 151–63), takes up precisely this image as concluding, triumphant legitimation of Alscher's Darwinistic naturalism. It is again a tale of sexual conquest, which moves significantly from the *gadjo* to the Gypsy, the social to the natural sphere. In an isolated village, sunk in a narrow and gloomy ravine in the mountains, almost bereft of a reason for existence, the benighted inhabitants are somehow celebrating 'Kirchweih'. That they manage to generate even a semblance of celebration is mainly, says the narrator, thanks to the participation of the local Gypsies (153–54), as musicians and dancers. Even on the stones of this sterile valley they manage to to kick up the trademark dust of the wandering race. Onto this bleak primal scene stumble a boy and a girl, he a shepherd, she the miller's daughter, both seldom in the village, both handsomer than usual in this ugly community, each bent on sexual fulfilment and escape. Their mutual attraction is confirmed, but his lack of social graces prevents any closer communication. Clumsily rejecting a transparent invitation to visit with her aunt on her way home, the boy finds himself perched rather foolishly alone on a tree bole as night falls, pondering his lost chance. But then something deeper in him, released perhaps by the night, makes possible another opportunity: 'Da hebt er die Nase, riecht, wittert' (161). What the boy scents is the 'Priboi' (161), an alpine flower which flourishes in the forest where he works, and which the girl emblematically was wearing today in her hair. Transformed, conscious only of bodily sensation, the boy realizes that she is returning alone to the mill, and begins jubilantly to hunt what has now become his sexual prey: 'Ein Mädchen allein in Nacht und Einsamkeit. | Er möchte jubeln' (162). Closing in on her, he also undergoes a reverse *metanoia*, moves ever closer to his animalistic forebears. Yet there is no hint of moral disapproval or censuring of behavioural atavism:

> Aber dick und unbewegt ist die Dunkelheit, und da lächelt er vor sich hin, sein Schritt wird leicht und weich, als rühre ihn ein Mitleid an. Jetzt sieht er sie

dicht vor sich. Es straffen sich alle seine Sehnen, jäh schnellt er auf sie hin, als hole er zugleich zum Schlage aus, um das, was ihn bedrückt, zu zerhauen.

Und wie ein Fuchs, der ein Kaninchen anspringt, nur rasch, damit es ja nicht in den engen, den allzu engen Bau schlüpfe, huscht er durch die glatte Stille der Nacht. (163)

This is the tale's conclusion. The boy's urgent, tensed presence wholly elides the girl's perspective. The shift of modality in sexual pairing, the characteristically violent and reductive language of sexual conquest, are celebrated and valorized as the natural triumph of the sexual hunting instinct over the civilized mating rituals of the village dance. The openness of the ending wills the reader to share the primal thrill of the hunt, so that narrator and reader escape from the polluting embrace of civilization to what is presented as the freedom and natural order of the world outside.

The title story, 'Zigeuner' (*Zigeuner*, 29–43), is the *locus classicus* of Alscher's statements on the Gypsy race. It is one of the first attempts after Victor von Strauss to re-centre the vocality of the Gypsy representation, ventriloquize the Gypsy voice, and so give the Gypsy perspective on *gadjo* civilization. Yet it too, despite all apologetic elements and despite Alscher's deep-seated naturalism, promulgates at last an intercultural pessimism. Here he deploys a Borrow-like narrator, well-informed about Romany culture, competent in the language, sympathetically disposed, who uses these advantages to establish his presence among the Gypsies and interrogate their perspective of the *gadjo* other. This man knows that in Siebenbürgen there are four tribes of wandering Gypsies, the Tschale, the Kukuya, the Leila and the Aschani. One day, as spring awakens and in turn wakes peasant and overwintering Gypsy alike to resume their natural behavioural patterns, he falls in with the Gypsy girl Yula on the way to join her people, the Leila. He admires the ineradicable yearning for the infinite which her alien gaze bespeaks, and wins her trust with his command of *Romanes*. She in turn is mystified by the *gadjo* culture of the peasants, who see spring not as the occasion to wander, but as the start of another job. Once in their camp, he is besieged by children keen to inspect the strange 'ray' (35), but is at first ignored by the men, until they notice that he understands their (critical) talk of him. At that point the shy Gypsies change their received behaviour pattern and attempt cross-cultural communication. Culture and luxury, explains the narrator, are indeed, as the Romanies had always suspected, absurd, in that both the characteristic *gadjo* hunger for these goods, and the compulsion to work to obtain them, proceed only from the desire to keep up with others in society and are conditioned by fear of rejection (36). This, the Romany elder Giza concludes, is why the *gadje* heartlessly reject the Gypsy hunger for food. They simply do not recognize it as a need (37). Once the Gypsies, so Giza tells the narrator for his part, had admired the *gadje* as gods. They had hoped that the *gadje* spirits would enrich them too. At last, frustrated, they developed envy. But even this envy was stillborn, as they realized that the 'Urmen', the spirits or fairies of the *gadje*, did not make them happy. Now they realize there exists a deeper sense of solidarity: '"Ihr habt vielleicht keine guten Urmen, — ihr seid nicht anders wie wir [. . .] ihr seid nicht anders wie wir!"' (39). At this, a tremendous wave of exaltation passes through the assembled Gypsy community, a tumult of confused responses arises in which it seems to the narrator '[a]ls würde eine erst so fremde Stimme immer bekannter, um zuletzt in eines Freundes Stimme herzliche Vertrautheit überzugehen' (39). 'Noch nie hat sich mir dieses Volk so offenbart, wie die Männer vom Stamme der Leila' (40), he confesses. Stirred by the nobility of the Leila, he recognizes with admiration the (ancient topos of the) 'Rest von Brahminenstolz im Pariablute' (40).[10] And yet this shared hermeneutic triumph over otherness almost immediately fades into insignificance. The naive Yula follows him on his way to the nearby village inn, lamenting the fact of his separation from the Romanies. Here, as in 'Rasse', a (now chaste) kiss for a moment bridges the divide between Gypsy and *gadjo*. He promises to her delight to return tomorrow. But by then, to his consternation, the Gypsies have gone, clearly choosing to foreclose any initial promise of intercultural communication. The tale closes by way of explanation with his helpless, resigned, and racist reproach:

> 'Ihr Ghetto? . . . Ja, es ist ihr Ghetto, das sie wandern heißt, ihnen Ruhelosigkeit gibt, jedes Heimatgefühl mitnimmt und Mißtrauen einimpft wider alle, die zufrieden sind.
>
> Denn ihr Ghetto ist nichts als das Leidensbewußtsein ihres Pariablutes . . . Ihr Ghetto ist nichts als der Verfolgungswahn einer ganzen Rasse'. (43)

A gloomy verdict from a committed tsiganophile, seemingly abandoning the wandering Gypsies to their fate.

If the collection *Zigeuner* comes to a wholly pessimistic conclusion about any possibilities, aesthetic or otherwise, of integrating the Romanies into 'civilized' culture, the earlier novel *Ich bin ein Flüchtling* (1909) makes the grim Social Darwinist basis of this tragic pessimism entirely clear. This is the story of two settled Rumanian Gypsy brothers, Mitre and Ion, whose simple wants are not met by the harsh environment in which they live, and who are remorselessly driven to the legal, cultural and existential margin, where they come to the realization (as the title implies), that their proper existential status in the order of being is *as* refugee. When we meet them, staggering as Alscher's Gypsies so often do under the burden of their loaded rucksacks on their way home (*Flüchtling*, 1), they are leading a blameless subsistence life in a Rumanian Banat border village. As settled Gypsies, they do indeed have a sense of belonging to place: 'Sie waren Zigeuner, und doch hatten sie eine Heimat. Seit den Tagen ihrer Urgroßeltern ansässig, hatten sich die Enkel an die Scholle gewöhnt' (141). The crude aggression of Arkan, a Rumanian peasant (106), leads however to conflict, and the Gypsies, uninformed yet sceptical about their status under the law, inured to institutionalized anti-Gypsyism, take flight first in the homely forest (13), then across the Hungarian border (19–20). They never manage to leave this border area, crossing and re-crossing it in desperate search of home. The measure of their desperation is a compensatory fantasy of discovering easy wealth, and they fall in with a band of rogueish Rumanian treasure hunters (20–21).[11] This, however, coupled with the death of Ion's daughter back at the village, his consequent moral despair, and the lack of papers which would enable them to work, only leads them into a life of crime. The state and the city, it turns out, are encroaching on the land of the villagers. There is a dispute over the title to a villager's land, and the treasure hunters strike a blow for the country against the city by raiding the 'Forstamt', stealing the large sum of money stored there, and appropriating the official maps which prove the ownership (the law, inevitably, is on the side of the city). It comes to an emblematic violent confrontation between villagers and gendarmes, which leaves many dead in the village square. Before fleeing across the border once more to Rumania, the Gypsies are persuaded to commit one last crime. But their burglary is discovered, and Ion kills (or seems to kill) a gendarme (111, 113), so that he is from now on unambiguously a fugitive from the law. Across the border there remains only one choice. The settled Gypsies encounter wandering Gypsies, and are admitted temporarily to the tribe on condition that they re-acculturate themselves. They thus cross another, *inner* border, which now formalizes their outsider status: 'Sie hatten sich über die Grenze der allgemeinen Menschheit hinausbegeben — und waren frei geworden' (150). The scenes with these Gypsies, for a time, prefigure the events in the story 'Zigeuner', as the wandering Gypsies, roused by spring (151), prepare to move. They are presented as very different, as more authentic than the acculturated Mitre and Ion. In their faces is inscribed the characteristic 'zügellose [. . .] Rassenunstetheit' (153). Their history of alienation in the technology-dominated west and acceptance of institutionalized persecution is presented in familiar terms (155–65), and there is a strong sense that Mitre and Ion are now recuperating their racially defined authenticity, as they espouse 'der unverlorene Grundton ihrer Rasse zum Wandern' (160) and accept the status of 'vogelfrei [. . .], freilich nicht für den Einzelnen, sondern für den Staat und die Gesellschaft' (161). But all this leads merely to more tribulations and ultimate disaster. They cheat and are cheated by peasants. They are forbidden entry to a city to obtain treatment for a sick woman, who dies.[12] The crisis comes when the past catches up with Ion and Mitre, and they are denounced at the wake by one of their *gadjo* former accomplices. Ion is condemned to fifteen years' imprisonment, Mitre to two. The novel ends with a coda: Mitre rejoining his 'Wanderzigeuner'. From now on the Romanies accept their impotence and draw their conclusions: '"Nur als Flüchtige sind wir stark, leben können wir nur als Zerstreute. Die Heimatlosigkeit ist unser Krieg, unser Kampf ist das Flüchten! [. . .] Sterbende sind wir! [. . .] O lei! Rom muli!"' (246). As Mitre flees in despair, hoping against hope, the Gypsy voices seem to him 'wie der Notschrei von Menschen, die im Ertrinken sind' (249). On this note the novel ends.

There is much that is clumsy and unsubtle in this first novel.[13] But there is also much to commend, notably in its strong rendition of the Gypsy standpoint. The Gypsies' incomprehension and fear of *gadjo* culture, especially the law, is powerfully evoked, and the trial scene, presented entirely through Mitre's bewildered and abject consciousness (231–35), is a telling antidote to (for example) Hebbel's unsympathetic treatment of the same situation.[14] At times Alscher can recall Hoffmann and even Kafka in this context, as, for example, when a wronged Gypsy is mercilessly sent from room to room of the *Gemeindehaus*, only to discover the correct officer asleep, and then to be humiliatingly evicted (180–84). The episode in which a village community comes into conflict with the authorities over the ownership of a parcel of land features the thoroughly Kafkaesque figure of a 'Landvermesser', who carries similar connotations of the abuse of knowledge and power (97–100).

That said, the tragic, racially based Social Darwinism of Alscher's novel is a categorial framework for treating the phenomenon of the Romanies which finally leaves them no place to go. In this context the key reference is the climactic courtroom scene. For here the arguments presented by the prosecutor are designed precisely to refute the sentimental tsiganophilia which the defence — *and* Alscher's sympathetic narrator — have presented in the Gypsies' favour. The defence argues that Ion and Mitre have been corrupted by the Rumanian thieves, and at last blames 'die Zivilisation [. . .], welche zwar verlangt, daß sich der Zigeuner ihr unterordne, die aber durch nichts die Abneigung dieses Volkes vor dem Fremden zu vermindern sucht, sie im Gegenteil stets fühlen lasse, daß sie Paria seien' (233). To this, in words which echo those of the rebarbative Pastor in Hauptmann's *Einhart, der Lächler*[15] or Alfred Ploetz's utopian racial hygiene, the prosecution responds with pure Social Darwinism. Natural science (to which the defence has alluded) teaches us '"daß der natürliche Vorgang unter den Lebewesen ein fortwährender Kampf ist, zum Zwecke der Schaffung besserer Lebensmöglichkeiten"' (234). At the level of micro-organisms we find the principle: '"Das Starke verschlingt immer das Schwächere, verdrängt es, und das Lebensfähigste siegt"' (234). The same process regulates human relations. Indeed, history teaches us '"die Unmöglichkeit eines praktischen Altruismus, weil dieser nichts weiter erzielt, als die Züchtung des Schwachen, des sozial Kranken"' (234). The lesson in this case is therefore clear:

> 'In unserem Staate ist der Zigeuner ein rückständiges, die Zivilisation hinderndes Wesen. Da sich aber unser Staat natürlich zu entwickeln gedenkt, muß er auch alles Kranke in sich ausmerzen. Es ist eine heilige Pflicht der Regierung, jede wilde Wucherung am Leibe der Gesellschaft zu bekämpfen. Und der Zigeuner ist nichts als eine wilde Wucherung . . . . Ob das nun schwachen Gemütern brutal erscheint, — das Gesetz ist verpflichtet, der Gesellschaftsunmöglichkeit der Wanderzigeuner Herr zu werden!' (234)

True, Alscher does not restrict the relevance of his Darwinistic analysis to the Gypsies. Arkan, the Rumanian peasant whose aggression began their inevitable downfall, is clearly presented as a degenerate, born criminal type in Lombroso's style: 'eine hagere Gestalt mit knochigen Zügen, quadratisch niederer Stirn und einem übergroßen Kinn' (3). And the prosecutor, let us note, attacks only the wandering, not the settled Gypsies. But the burden of Alscher's argument is that the settled Gypsies too are being forced by institutionalized anti-Gypsyism back to their original lifestyle; and that the wandering Gypsies either bring their fate upon themselves by accepting the ghetto or can do nothing about it.

Either way: with friends like these, who needs enemies? As the long nineteenth century ground to its catastrophic end, it seemed that tsiganophile energies, in literature and anthropology, were losing logical force in the discursive contest, and that the discourse of race as determinant of culture was gaining ground in equal measure. Thomas Mann's references to Gypsies are self-consciously formulated as clichés. He likes to talk conventionally of artists as (Bohemian) Gypsies,[16] and he sites the Gypsy question *stricto sensu* at the margin of (for his interest) weightier intellectual considerations. Race is however never quite marginalized. The 'Zigeuner im grünen Wagen', whom Tonio Kröger in 1903 rejects, but who are part of him,[17] are intended to connote only the social disreputability of the Bohemian, merely metaphorical race of artists. Yet Kröger's aesthetic gift is explicitly linked with the Southern racial provenance of his mother. The same, in a minor variation, is true of *Der Tod in Venedig* (1912). The 'Zigeunertum' which the classically self-disciplined, self-censoring author Aschenbach in *Der Tod in Venedig* (1912) heroically overcomes, but which still defeats him,[18] is intended only as a symbol of ethical and cultural dissoluteness. Yet Mann's protagonist is presented as inheriting his aesthetic difficulties through his (genuinely) Bohemian mother. Hugo von Hofmannsthal's Gypsy, in the first version of *Der Turm* (1924), is equally negative. This nameless Romany girl is the loyal consort of Olivier, the scum of human society risen to its surface, amoral representative of the lowest in human nature, proponent of chaos in human affairs, and opponent of the messianic Sigismund. She is pregnant with his issue. Magician, charismatic dancer, prophetess, emblematically beautiful apostle of the material and corporeal, she finally murders Sigismund by cutting his lifeline with a poisoned knife, and so destroys a burgeoning utopia.[19]

The professional anthropologists are no better. Let me end with two very different examples from the epoch. Victor Areco's *Das Liebesleben der Zigeuner*[20] (1912) certainly purports to be a serious cultural anthropological study. The text follows only after the reader has been subjected to a stern motto taken from the report of the Royal National Statistical Office for Hungary in 1905, no less: 'Die Zigeuner bedeuten in ihrem heutigen Zustand ein beträchtliches nationalökonomisches Defizit' (Areco, p. i); and a preface claiming that the volume is based on extensive fieldwork, personal experience, and scholarly reading (pp. xi f.). Thus prepared, the reader discovers that Areco in truth upholds the bad Gypsy anthropological tradition of rewriting, adding to that dismal narrative only yet more *piquant* elements calculated to please. Thus an extensive parade of familiar authorities, from Rüdiger and Grellmann to Borrow, Pott, Vaillant, Reinbeck, Liebich, Wlislocki,[21] the criminal judge Gross,[22] and even Mérimée,[23] is followed by a digest of official Romany history in the west. Into this unshakable edifice of fact are embedded judgemental commonplaces masquerading as lapidary insights: 'Unstet und arbeitsscheu ziehen sie von Land zu Land' (1). 'Ein seltsames Volk, ohne Vergangenheit, ohne Zukunft' (1). '*Zigeuner bleibt Zigeuner, wo immer er auch wohnt*' (25–26). 'Er [der Zigeuner] hat vom Werte eines kultivierten Ich in den allerseltensten Fällen auch nur eine Ahnung' (89). 'Überhaupt haftet [. . .] den Zigeunern ein eigentümlicher, fast widerlicher, stechender, in geschlossenen Räumen besonders auffallender Geruch an' (93). 'Die Verlotterung der Zigeuner ist eben nicht aufzuhalten und dies wird das Ende dieser Parias auch sein' (246). That done, Areco adds the specialized part of his dissertation. By comparison with 'Kulturvölker' (30), he notes in his opening gambit, Gypsies are agreed to display 'sexuelle [. . .] Ungebundenheit und d[ie] Aberrationen des Geschlechtstriebes' to an horrific degree (32). This, he continues (succumbing once more to literary contamination),[24] is doubtless thanks to the 'fast magische Anziehungskraft' (44) of their bodies — although the erotic charisma of Romany women, we learn (yet again), falls dramatically on their reaching a certain age (48). To their highly-sexed nature is owed also their preference for skimpy and brightly-coloured clothing — red, Areco solemnly assures us on scientific evidence, is the most sexually provocative colour (66–68). Still more salaciously, the oppression suffered by Gypsies in eastern territories makes them especially susceptible to the sexual aberrations of sadism and masochism (84). These insights, and many more of equal dignity, are substantiated with lengthy pseudo-factual descriptions over 330 pages of annotated text.

If Areco attempts with the instruments of official positivistic cultural anthropology to institutionalize the familiar Orientalist image of the erotically charismatic Gypsy and continues to propagate the idea of the nation's inevitable decline, then Martin Block's *Die Zigeuner: Ihr Leben und ihre Seele* (1936) is (in retrospect at least) an even more sinister performance. As a work it flatters at first sight to deceive. Although presented for the popular market with numerous lavish illustrations, it *is* a scholarly work of cultural anthropology, based on legitimate methods, including extensive fieldwork in Rumania. Its motto, '. . . und ich habe sie dort zurückgelassen, von wo ich hergekommen, um euch dies zu erzählen', proclaims in *Romanes* and German by contrast to Areco's the solidarity of a certain shared experience and situation. Block, rare amongst Gypsy anthropologists, recalls that the vast body of literature on the Romanies is by reason of its provenance questionable: 'Alles stammt, mit Ausnahme von ganz wenigen kleineren Schriften, von *Nichtzigeunern*' (Block, 8). A full account is thus given of the fieldwork method he has adopted (following his chief authority Wlislocki)[25] to remedy this defect (10–19). He has won the confidence of Romanies, shared their life, overcome the problems of distance and deception, and, at the risk of going wholly native, gained sympathetic insight: 'Um es kurz zu sagen, man muß eben praktischer Schauspieler sein, der sich in die Rolle des Zigeuners so hineinlebt, daß er etwas vom Zigeunertum verspürt, ohne aber in dessen Umwelt hineinzuwachsen' (11). At one level of discourse, then, the tone is sympathetic and conciliatory: 'Die Zigeuner sind Menschen wie wir, und doch sind sie anders als wir' (1). They fascinate the *gadje*, because they have remained a 'Naturvolk' (1, 66), childlike and alien in the midst of their culturally advanced host nations (2, 9, 194), and so are a worthy object of study in their difference. Some prejudices are dismissed. Gypsies are (correctly) noted to be sexually conservative and prudish about the state of nakedness (65–66, 139). The short-lived quality of Gypsy beauty is explained as due to the large number of childbirths each mother faces in her life (62). The allegedly characteristic Gypsy odour is due to poverty (63). At last integration, 'sich in den Organismus unserer Kultur einzugliedern' (211) of at least settled Gypsies emerges as Block's aim. He searches constantly for qualities such as family solidarity, national pride, selflessness, and honour (at least in respect of fellow Gypsies) (212), which will build sympathy with the Gypsies' Germanic hosts. In the chapter 'Der Staat und die Zigeuner' (194–205), Block is on this account deeply concerned to balance. Noting the extraordinary rigour of the Gypsy legislation in Prussia and Bavaria since 1880 (197–203), he nevertheless approves its strategic tendency, by means of a system of seamless police control (including draconian finger-printing regulations), to make the Gypsies settle or evict them altogether. That concession made, he notes however that no Gypsy, especially if he is loyal to the wandering lifestyle (201–02), could possibly fulfil the letter of these laws. In practice, he smoothly observes: 'So streng ist man aber nicht'

(202). Given that the Gypsies' delicts are usually minor (204), he ends with a plea for judicious and latitudinarian application of the law (203).

A clue to the less palatable subtext of this work is however given in the chapter 'Rasse und Rassenpflege der Zigeuner' (58–67). Here the old prejudices are re-packaged in terms of the new racial 'science'. So for example anthropometric data, just as in the work of the racial hygienist Otto Ammon,[26] are used to distinguish a purer and nobler type of Gypsy, characterized by a long head, regular oval features, small chin, and aquiline nose, from a coarser type, with a round head, snub nose, and prominent jaw (60). This racial hygiene approach permits a revalorization of some features of Gypsy behaviour in wholly new terms. What is tactfully called 'das Aufnehmen fremder Kinder' (64) is re-legitimated as a healthy instinctive drive for the preservation of the Gypsies 'als Rasse' (64), in that an admixture of new blood (as had been held from Gobineau on) would protect the race against degeneration:

> [. . .] fremdes Blut muß es sein. Ohne sich dessen bewußt zu werden, beugen sie dadurch dem Untergang ihrer Rasse vor, die nicht den Vorzug hat wie die unsrige, eine große Mischungsbasis gehabt und aus mehreren einander verwandten Rassen sich zusammengesetzt zu haben. (65)

From this perspective the Gypsies seem to Block to be model Social Darwinist eugenicists *avant la lettre*:

> Dieses Volk sieht stets auf gesunden Nachwuchs, kranke Kinder stoßen sich durch Tod von selbst aus ihrem Stammeskörper aus, ebensowenig duldet es Verbrecher unter sich. Vater-, Mutter-, Kindes- oder Lustmörder würden rücksichtslos aus dem Stamme entfernt werden. Moralisch kranke, asoziale, oder nach Zigeunergesetz unsozial handelnde Stammesgenossen werden durch zeitweiligen oder bei Unverbesserlichkeit lebenslänglichen Ausschluß aus dem Stamme bestraft. Auf diese Weise hält sich die Rasse gesund und lebensfähig. (65)[27]

Tragically, this concern for preserving intrinsic racial quality emerges as Block's most powerful argument for the toleration and integration of the Gypsies. He notes that settled Gypsies in Germany (if not the criminal vagrants) possess a German passport, have even fought and died for the fatherland, and hang above their beds a portrait of the (deceased) President Hindenburg or of Chancellor Adolf Hitler (197). He supports on these grounds the case for the pioneering recognition of the Romanies as a nation ('Volk', 210–11), and prints photographs of the Woiwod Gh. Niculescu (elected chief of the Rumanian Gypsies) at the Gypsy Congress in Bucharest in 1935, with the Romany flag and posters of King Michael under the aegis (or in the shadow) of a large, paternal-seeming Hitler.[28] At last, whilst leaving the question of the Gypsies' future open: 'Ein ewiges Volk? Die Welt wird umgebaut. Kein Mensch kennt die Schicksale der Völker' (213), he notes that Gypsies are '[u]ns weitläufig verwandt, mit eigener indogermanischer Sprache' (213) and 'ein verhältnismäßig rassereines Volk, das seit Jahrtausenden bis heute seinem Volkstum treu geblieben ist' (213). Thus for all his sympathy and solidarity with the Romanies, Block chooses as his chief argument to plead for their continued well-being the very body of racial hygiene arguments which was soon to be used for their destruction; and by the same logic envisions Adolf Hitler as their protector. One year after his well-intentioned study there appeared Robert Ritter's *Ein Menschenschlag: Erbärztliche Untersuchungen über die — durch 10 Geschlechterfolgen erforschten — Nachkommen von Vagabunden, Jaunern und Räubern*, the work which did indeed, in a sense probably unintended by Martin Block, apply the 'science' of racial hygiene to decisions affecting the future of the Gypsies in Germany. But with that the die was cast.

Alscher and Block, writer and anthropologist, Social Darwinist racists both, represent the last stations in our reconstruction of the Gypsy story in the second half of the long nineteenth century. Looking back, patterns have become clear. The relation of Germans and Gypsies has rarely or never been simple. True, the mainstream tradition of social anti-Gypsyism and its legislative correlate, rooted in the settled people's mistrust of the immigrant and the institutionalization of their outsider status, has been plain at every juncture, and this has been a structural given in every episode of the intercultural story. Official German cultural anthropology has with few exceptions tended to reinforce that criminalized image, which remains traceably constant across the paradigm shifts, from the rogueish vagabond of the seventeenth century (Thomasius), to the feminized, infantilized, and racialized Indian other of the eighteenth (Grellmann), and the degenerate tribe of the long Darwinian nineteenth (Lombroso and after). It is no coincidence that judicial officers such as Liebich and Gross feature large as anthropological authorities in this story. But that is not the whole story. Lay anthropologists, notably (for all his errors) Liszt, to an extent at least advocate a self-reflexive critique of established norms. Nor is it chance that the major critic of official German Gypsy anthropology should be an artist. Whilst it is true that some distinguished writers, notably Hebbel, unashamedly propagate the established discourse of criminalization well into the second half of the nineteenth century, the fact is, that to criticize that discourse was the major role of those Germans who write the Gypsy even in the racist nineteenth century. Widely read *Gründerzeit* authors such as Raabe and Keller and less read ones such as Strauss take up the tsiganophile tradition of Brentano, Arnim, and Liszt, abandon the univocal, germanocentric presentation of the Gypsy, attempt to give the silenced Romany a voice in the host culture, indeed present a critique of Germanic identity formation which radically questions the epistemological, cultural, and legal basis of anti-Gypsyism. Despite all differences, Freytag's and May's celebrations of the noble Gypsy's aid in German identity and nation formation uphold the imaginary link of Gypsy and German destiny. In the age of nationalist and imperialist self-definition these seekers after home still find in the homeless Gypsies an irresistible source of cultural self-valorization. That said, there is a notable modulation in this relationship after the founding of the empire and the establishment of Darwinian orthodoxy in the anthropological field. May's celebration of the Gypsies, we saw, is either predicated on a trivialized, Cooper-esque notion of the Gypsies as noble savages, who (in a process to which May assents) are doomed to extinction, or it revives the older, tsiganophobe tradition of the counterfeit Gypsy. Freytag's Gypsies are little more than the illiterate, pre-cultural foil required for his celebration of German nation and German episteme. With the conservative turn in the last quarter of the century the relation of German and Gypsy in literature becomes tragically mixed, and grimly Darwinian arguments from natural selection determine the Gypsy image. Jensen's, Saar's, Hauptmann's, and Alscher's Gypsies are all presented in more or less authentic ethnocentric detail and with more or less evident sympathy. Yet Jensen's Gypsy image is at bottom nothing but the Romantic sheen on a Darwinian understanding of racial destiny, which unsentimentally validates the final absorption of the 'amphibious' Gypsies into the Germanic racial pool. Saar, even as he criticizes the concept, offers up the Gypsies as a model of cultural degeneracy. Hauptmann, despite his occasional proclivity to defend the persecuted Gypsies in *milieu*-style presentations at the margins of his discourse, in fact limits his cognitive interest to that remarkable synthesis of Romanticism and racial hygiene. Alscher, finally, attacks both the aestheticist ideology of Hauptmann's Romantic racism and institutionalized anti-Gypsyism, but can offer as an alternative only the negation of civilized values and an icy Social Darwinist condemnation of the Gypsies' failure to adapt.

The same pattern applies to our other cognitive interest, the Orientalist model and German cultural history. It is on the one hand clear from our investigation of the Gypsies in the German nineteenth century that that they are consistently represented under the sign of German Orientalism. It also clear that Said is correct in his assertion that German Orientalism, like any other variety, has been an intellectual weapon for exercising epistemological and political power over the Gypsies. Nineteenth-century Germans tended to regard the Gypsies through a model of inner-directed Orientalism. It is, finally, clear that German Orientalism directed at the Gypsies, like all Orientalisms, has been fundamentally a discourse about Germans, and that this interest is especially virulent in the epoch of Germanic struggles for cultural and political identity. To this is owed the remarkable extent to which German writers of this epoch present Gypsy agents as crucial in the constitution of German political and cultural selves, as if the encounter with the Romany other is an indispensable rite of passage for becoming a true German.

On the other hand it is also the case that our investigation has confirmed the limits of Saidian Orientalism. Many scholars have by now attacked its paradoxically uniformitarian, ideologically one-dimensional stance. The art historian John Mackenzie[29] refuted the all too easy parallelism of imperial political hegemony and Orientalism, and pleaded for the primacy of pluralist eclecticism in nineteenth-century aesthetics. Russell Berman, pre-eminently, noted in controversy with the late Suzanne Zantop[30] that German Orientalism, far from being dualistic, in fact encompassed a heterophilic strand of profoundly *non*-Orientalist hermeneutic sensitivity to eastern cultural otherness — a phenomenon which he explains in terms of Germany's coming late to empire, and which, as he points out, also has deep implications for the undifferentiated Foucauldian understanding of western rationality underlying Said's theory.[31] This stance has gained support. Ritchie Robertson supported it in studies devoted to the Jewish question in Germany,[32] and most recently Todd Kontje has argued for at least four varieties of German Orientalism.[33] Our studies of German-Gypsy Orientalism in the nineteenth century also confirm the trend to differentiation. We have seen that Gypsies *can* be represented in German realist literature with vulgar-Orientalist contempt (Hebbel) as the excluded other, pillar of the (clearly still fragile) German self-understanding. But we have also seen Germans attempting sensitively to give voice to the silenced Romanies (Strauss). We have seen Germans positively (if pessimistically) identifying *themselves* with features of the Gypsy condition (Immermann). In the most self-conscious of the social realists (Raabe, Keller), we have seen the intellectual foundations of German Orientalism ruthlessly deconstructed and a general questioning of *any* identity construction derived from that premise. Finally, in an ultimate combination of opposites, we have seen Germans both identify with and attempt to give voice to the silenced Romanies *and* denounce them as doomed dwellers in a wandering ghetto (Alscher). Thus beyond the polar opposite, tsiganophile and tsiganophobe, tendencies described lies in fact a spectrum of radically variable positions; even if those positions finally prefigure what was to come after 1938. The trend of German–Gypsy relations, as with all contingent necessities, is clear from the late nineteenth century on. But if our reconstruction of the presence of the Gypsies in nineteenth-century German literature and anthropology has shown anything, it has also shown that there is no pre-programmed, 'mounting frenzy of exterminationist' anti-Gypsyism[34] in Germany, not even in those writers who foreground their interpretation of Social Darwinism.

Notes to Chapter 8

1. Citations are from Ferdinand von Saar, *Novellen aus Österreich*, ed. with afterword by Karl Wagner, 2 vols (Vienna, Munich: Deuticke, 1998), II, 101–36 (pp. 118–19).
2. In what follows I am influenced by Virginia Lewis, 'Work and Freedom in the Minority Community: Ferdinand von Saar's *Die Troglodytin*', in *The German Mosaic: Cultural and Linguistic Diversity in Society*, ed. by Carol-Aisha Blackshire-Belay (London: Greenwood, 1994), pp. 11–20.
3. Saar is thinking of New Lanark or Saltaire.
4. There is an unfortunate minor discrepancy here, since Lombroso's *L'uomo delinquente* only appeared in 1876. But Morel's *Traité des dégénérés* appeared in 1857.
5. A contemporary anglophone parallel is offered of course by R. L. Stevenson. In *The Strange Case of Dr Jekyll and Mr Hyde* (1886), Stevenson has the degenerated Hyde described as 'troglodytic' and 'ape-like'. See Robert Louis Stevenson, *The Strange Case of Dr Jekyll and Mr Hyde and Other Tales*, ed., with Introduction and Notes by Roger Luckhurst (Oxford: Oxford University Press, 2006), pp. 1–66 (pp. 16, 20).
6. Grellmann, *Historischer Versuch* (1787), pp. 72–76.
7. Block, *Die Zigeuner*, pp. 83–84. (p. 83). Compare the descriptions of Otto Alscher, whose work is treated below: *Ich bin ein Flüchtling: Roman* (Berlin: Egon Fleischel, 1909), pp, 151, 233, and *Zigeuner: Novellen* (Munich: Albert Langen, 1914), p. 29.
8. I have gratefully used the biobliographical information in Axel Goodbody, 'A Life among Gypsies and Wolves: Otto Alscher's Quest for an Alternative to Modern Civilisation', *German Monitor*, 57 (2003), 181–208, esp. pp. 180–89. Thanks too to Dr Goodbody for lending Otto Alscher, *Ezählungen*, ed. by Horst Fassel (Munich: Landsmannschaft der Banater Schwaben, 1995). Fassel's afterword (*Erzählungen*, pp. 416–32) offers further biographical details and a full bibliography.
9. See Goodbody, pp. 188–89.
10. The narrator's allusion to 'Brahminenstolz' and 'Paria' is of course another literary topos, probably referencing Goethe's 'Paria', possibly also Stifter's 'Narrenburg'. See Chapter 3.
11. Compare Ion's continued digging after Veta's grave is finished (pp. 213–14).
12. She (perhaps inevitably) is buried by a Roman *limes* fort (pp. 212–13).
13. Notably the narrator's interventions. Perhaps the worst instance of this is where, ninety pages

into the plot, the narrator disingenuously observes that the Gypsies could have resolved all their problems by simply presenting themselves before the law and telling the truth of the encounter with Arkan (p. 92).

14. See Chapter 4.
15. See Hauptmann, *Einhart*, I, 205.
16. See Thomas Mann, *Betrachtungen eines Unpolitischen* (1919), in Thomas Mann *Gesammelte Werke*, 13 vols (Frankfurt a.M.: Fischer, 1974), XII, 7–589: 'Der Künstler ist und bleibt Zigeuner' (p. 403).
17. See Thomas Mann, *Tonio Kröger*, in *Gesammelte Werke*, VIII, 271–338, here pp. 275, 279, 291, 317.
18. See Thomas Mann, *Der Tod in Venedig*, in *Gesammelte Werke*, VIII, 444–525, here pp. 456, 523.
19. See Hugo von Hofmannsthal, *Der Turm: Ein Trauerspiel in fünf Aufzügen*, in Hofmannsthal, *Gesammelte Werke*, ed. by Bernd Schoeller, Rudolf Hirsch, 10 vols (Frankfurt a.M.: Fischer, 1979), III, 255–381, here pp. 349, 365–69.
20. Citations are from Victor Areco, *Das Liebesleben der Zigeuner* (Das Liebesleben aller Zeiten und Völker, III) (Leipzig: Leipziger Verlag, 1912).
21. Areco, pp. 133, 253.
22. Areco, pp. 43, 93.
23. Areco, pp. 23, 29.
24. The interference is of course from Goethe's novel of adultery *Die Wahlverwandtschaften*.
25. Block, pp. 12–13. See on Wlislocki the caustic Ruch, pp. 191–315, esp. pp. 191–261.
26. Compare Ammon, *Die natürliche Auslese beim Menschen*, esp. ch. 6: 'Die natürliche Auslese und die seelischen Anlagen', pp. 176–89, which distinguishes between '*Langköpfe* germanischer Abkunft als die Träger des höheren Geisteslebens, als die von der Natur berufenen Inhaber herrschender Stellungen' (185), and 'Rundköpfe' (185), suitable for agriculture, subordinate technical tasks, and 'meist fügsame Unterthanen' (185).
27. Compare Block, p. 203.
28. Illustrations 94 and 96, facing p. 192.
29. MacKenzie, *Orientalism, History, Theory and the Arts*.
30. Russell Berman, *Enlightenment or Empire*, esp. pp. 10–11, 235; Zantop, pp. 1–16. See too Pizer, pp. 159–81, esp. pp. 159–60.
31. Russell Berman, *Enlightenment or Empire*, pp. 233–35.
32. Robertson, *'Jewish Question'*, esp. pp. 428–65.
33. Kontje, *German Orientalisms*, esp. pp. 1–14.
34. Robertson, *'Jewish Question'*, p. 3.

BIBLIOGRAPHY

❖

Sources

ALSCHER, OTTO, *Ich bin ein Flüchtling: Roman* (Berlin: Egon Fleischel, 1909)
——*Zigeuner: Novellen* (Munich: Albert Langen, 1914)
——*Ezählungen*, ed. by Horst Fassel (Munich: Landsmannschaft der Banater Schwaben, 1995)
AMMON, OTTO, *Die natürliche Auslese beim Menschen: Auf Grund der Ergebnisse der anthropologischen Untersuchungen der Wehrpflichtigen in Baden und anderen Materialien* (Jena: Gustav Fischer, 1893)
ANON., 'Zigeuner', in *Kleines Brockhaus'sches Lexikon für den Handgebrauch*, 4 vols (Leipzig: Brockhaus, 1856), IV/3, p. 801
ARNIM, ACHIM VON, 'Von Volksliedern', in *Des Knaben Wunderhorn*, 3 vols (Munich: dtv, 1966), pp. 233–57
——*Isabella von Ägypten, Kaiser Karls des Fünften erste Jugendliebe: Eine Erzählung*, in von Arnim, *Erzählungen*, ed. by Gisela Henckmann (Stuttgart: Reclam, 1991), pp. 34–154
BECHER, JOHANNES R., 'Romeo und Julia auf dem Dorfe: Nach der gleichnamigen Erzählung von Gottfried Keller', in Johannes R. Becher, *Romane in Versen* (Berlin: Aufbau, 1946), pp. 7–20
BISCHOFF, FERDINAND, *Deutsch–Zigeunerisches Wörterbuch* (Ilmenau: Voigt, 1827)
BIZET, GEORGES, *Carmen* (1875). Oper in vier Aufzügen, von Henri Meilhac und Ludovic Halévy nach der Novelle von Prosper Mérimée. Deutsche Übersetzung von Julius Hopp. Übersetzung der Dialoge von Wilhelm Zentner, ed. by Wilhelm Zenter (Stuttgart: Reclam, 1977)
BLOCK, MARTIN, *Die Zigeuner: Ihr Leben und ihre Seele, dargestellt auf Grund eigener Reisen und Forschungen* (Leipzig: Bibliographisches Institut, 1936)
BORROW, GEORGE, *The Zincali: An Account of the Gypsies in Spain* (London: Dent, n.d.; 1st edn 1841)
BRACHVOGEL, A. E., *Friedemann Bach*, 3 vols, 2nd edn (Berlin: Otto Janke,1859; 1st edn 1858)
BREITHAUPT, RICHARD, *Die Zigeuner und der deutsche Staat: Ein Beitrag zur deutschen Rechts- und Kulturgeschichte* (Würzburg: C. J. Becker, 1907)
BRENTANO, CLEMENS, *Die mehreren Wehmüller und ungarischen Nationalgesichter*, in Brentano, *Sämtliche Erzähllungen*, ed. by Gerhard Schaub (Munich: Goldmann, 1991), pp. 142–88
BÜCHNER, DR. LOUIS [LUDWIG], 'Das Schlachtfeld der Natur oder der Kampf um's Dasein', *Die Gartenlaube: Illustriertes Familienblatt*, 6 (1861), 93–95
——*Darwinismus und Sozialismus. Oder: Der Kampf um das Dasein und die moderne Gesellschaft* (Leipzig: Günther, 1894)
CERVANTES DE SAAVEDRA, MIGUEL, *The Little Gypsy Girl* (*La gitanilla*), in Cervantes, *Exemplary Stories*, trans. by C. A. Jones (Harmondsworth: Penguin, 1972), pp. 19–84
DARWIN, CHARLES, *The Origin of Species by Means of Natural Selection* (London: Murray, 1901) (based on the sixth edn, 1872; 11st edn, 1859)
——*The Descent of Man and Natural Selection in Relation to Sex* (based on the 2nd edn, 1874 (London: Murray, 1901)

——*Über die Entstehung der Arten im Thier- und Pflanzenreich durch natürliche Züchtung oder Erhaltung der vervollkommneten Rassen im Kampfe um's Dasein.* Nach der 2. Auflage mit einer geschichtlichen Vorrede und andern Zusätzen des Verfassers für diese deutsche Ausgabe aus dem Englischen übersetzt und mit Anmerkungen versehen von H. G. Bronn (Stuttgart: Schweizerbart, 1860)

——*Über die Entstehung der Arten durch natürliche Zuchtwahl oder die Erhaltung der begünstigten Rassen im Kampfe um's Dasein.* Nach der 4. engl. Ausgabe übers. von J. V. Carus (Stuttgart: Schweizerbart, 1867)

DEVRIENT, EDUARD, *Die Zigeuner.* Romantische Oper in vier Akten (1832), in Edward Devrient, *Dramatische und dramaturgische Schriften*, 10 vols (Leipzig: Weber, 1846–69), III, 337–443

DILLMANN, ALFRED, *Zigeunerbuch herausgegeben zum amtlichen Gebrauch im Aufrage des K.B. Staatsministeriums des Innern vom Sicherheitsbureau der K. Polizeidirektion München* (Munich: Wild, 1905)

FABRI, FRIEDRICH, *Bedarf Deutschland der Colonien? Eine politisch-ökonomische Betrachtung* (Gotha: Perthes, 1879)

FONTANE, THEODOR, *Gesammelte Werke*, ed. by Peter Bramböck, 5 vols (Munich: Nymphenburger, 1979)

FREYTAG, GUSTAV, *Soll und Haben: Roman in sechs Büchern*, 86th edn (1st edn 1855; Leipzig: S. Hirzel, 1916)

——*Die verlorene Handschrift: Roman in fünf Büchern*, 38th edn, 2 vols (1st edn 1864; Leipzig: S. Hirzel, 1904)

GOBINEAU, ARTHUR GRAF, *Versuch über die Ungleichheit der Menschenrassen*, trans. by Ludwig Schemann, 4 vols (Stuttgart: Frommann, 1939–49) [*Essai sur l'inégalité des races humaines*, 4 vols (Paris: Firmin Didot, 1853–54)]

GOETHE, JOHANN WOLFGANG VON, *Sämmtliche Werke*, Weimarer Ausgabe, 133 vols (Weimar: Böhlau, 1887–1914)

——*Werke*, Hamburger Ausgabe, ed. by Erich Trunz, 14 vols (Hamburg: Beck, 1948–60)

GRAFFUNDER, H., *Ueber die Sprache der Zigeuner: Eine grammatische Skizze* (Erfurt: F. W. Otto, 1835)

GRELLMANN, HEINRICH MORITZ GOTTLIEB, *Historischer Versuch über die Zigeuner betreffend die Lebensart und Verfassung[,] Sitten und Schicksale dieses Volks seit seiner Erscheinung in Europa, und dessen Ursprung*, 2nd edn (Göttingen: Dieterich, 1787; 1st edn, Leipzig 1783)

GROLMAN, FERDINAND LUDWIG ALEXANDER VON, *Wörterbuch der in Teutschland üblichen Spitzbuben-Sprachen, in zwei Bänden, die Gauner- und Zigeuner-Sprache enthaltend*, 2 vols (Gießen: C. G. Müller, 1822)

GROSS, HANNS, *Handbuch der Untersuchungsrichter als System der Kriminalistik*, 3rd edn (Graz: Leuschner & Lubensky, 1899; (1st edn 1893)

HARDENBERG, FRIEDRICH VON, *Novalis: Schriften*, Historisch-kritische Ausgabe, ed. by Paul Kluckhohn, Richard Samuel, Hans-Joachim Mähl, and Gerhard Schulz, 7 vols (Stuttgart, Berlin, Cologne, and Mainz: Kohlhammer, 1960–)

HARTMANN, EDUARD VON, *Philosophie des Unbewussten*, 6th edn (Berlin 1874; 1st edn 1869)

HAUPTMANN, CARL, *Die Bedeutung der Keimblättertheorie für die Individualitätslehre und den Generationswechsel* (Jena: J. Hossfeld, 1883)

——*Die Metaphysik in der modernen Physiologie: Eine kritische Untersuchung* (Dresden: L. Ehlermann, 1893)

——*Ephraims Breite: Schauspiel in fünf Akten* (Berlin: S. Fischer, 1900)

——*Einhart der Lächler: Roman*, 2 vols (Berlin: Marquardt, 1907)

——*Musik: Ein Spiel in vier Akten* (Leipzig: Wolff, 1918)

——*Leben mit Freunden: Gesammelte Briefe*, ed. by Will-Erich Peuckert (Leipzig: Paul List, 1928)

—— *Sämtliche Werke.* Wissenschaftliche Ausgabe mit Kommentar, ed. by Eberhard Berger, Hans-Gert Roloff, and Anna Strolka, 16 vols + 1 Supplementary vol. (Stuttgart: Bad Cannstatt: frommann-holzboog, 1997, in progress)

—— *Carl Hauptmann und seine Worpswede Künstlerfreunde: Briefe und Tagebuchblätter*, ed. by Elfriede Berger, 2 vols (Berlin: Schütze, 2003)

HEBBEL, FRIEDRICH, *Sämtliche Werke: Historisch-kritische Ausgabe*, ed. by Richard Maria Werner, 16 vols (Berlin: Behr, 1904–07)

—— *Werke*, ed. by Gerhard Fricke, Werner Keller, and Karl Pörnbacher, 5 vols (Munich: Hanser, 1965)

—— *Tagebücher*, ed. by Karl Pörnbacher, 3 vols (Munich: dtv, 1984)

HEGEL, G. W. F., *Werke*, ed. by Eva Moldenhauer and Karl Magnus Michel, 20 vols (Frankfurt a.M.: Suhrkamp, 1970)

HEISTER, CARL VON, *Ethnographische und geschichtliche Notizen über die Zigeuner* (Königsberg: Gräse und Unzer, 1842)

HERDER, JOHANN GOTTFRIED, *Werke*, ed. by Martin Bollacher et al, 10 vols (Frankfurt a.M.: Deutscher Klassiker Verlag, 1985–2000)

HOFMANNSTHAL, HUGO VON, *Gesammelte Werke*, ed. by Bernd Schoeller and Rudolf Hirsch, 10 vols (Frankfurt a.M.: Fischer, 1979)

IMMERMANN, KARL, *Werke*, ed. by Harry Maync, 4 vols (Leipzig, Vienna. Bibliographisches Institut, n.d.)

JENSEN-HEYCK and PETERSEN papers, Landesbibliothek Schleswig-Holstein (Kiel), shelfmark Cb 28, Cb 29

JENSEN, WILHELM, *Die braune Erica: Novelle*, 2nd edn (Berlin: Paetel, 1873; 1st edn 1868)

—— *Unter heißerer Sonne* (Berlin, Vienna: Ullstein, n.d.; 1st edn 1869)

—— *Gradiva: Ein pompejanisches Phantasiestück* (Dresden, Leipzig: Reißner, 1903)

KELLER, GOTTFRIED, *Sämtliche Werke und ausgewählte Briefe*, ed. by Clemens Heselhaus, 3 vols (Munich: Hanser, 1958)

—— *Sämtliche Werke*, ed. by Thomas Böning, Gerhard Kaiser, and Dominik Müller, 7 vols (Frankfurt a.M.: Deutscher Klassiker Verlag, 1985–96)

KÖRNER, THEODOR, *Sämtliche Werke*, 2 vols (Berlin: Bibliographische Anstalt/A. Warschauer, n.d.)

KOGALNITCHAN, MICHAEL VON, *Skizze einer Geschichte der Zigeuner, ihrer Sitten und ihrer Sprache, nebst einem kleinen Wörterbuche dieser Sprache.* Aus dem Französischen übersetzt und mit Zusätzen begleitet von Fr. Casca. (Stuttgart: J. F. Cast, 1840)

LIEBICH, RICHARD, *Die Zigeuner in ihrem Wesen und in ihrer Sprache: Nach eigenen Beobachtungen dargestellt* (Leipzig: Brockhaus, 1863)

LISZT, FRANZ, *Die Zigeuner und ihre Musik in Ungarn*, trans. by Peter Cornelius (Pesth: Heckenast 1861); in Liszt, *Gesammelte Schriften*, 4 vols (Leipzig: Breitkopf & Härtel, 1910), III. [*Des Bohémiens et leur musique en Hongrie* (1859)]

LOMBROSO, CESARE, *Genio e follia in rapporto alla medicina legale, alla critica ed alla storia* (Roma: Fratelli Bocca, 1882; 1st edn, 1873)

—— *Der Verbrecher (homo delinquens) in anthropologischer, ärztlicher und juristischer Beziehung* In deutscher Bearbeitung von Dr. M. O. Fraenkel. Mit Vorwort von A. von Kirchenheim, 3 vols, 2nd edn (Hamburg: Verlagsanstalt/Königliche Buchhandlung 1894) [*L'uomo delinquente in rapporto all'antropologia, giurisprudenza e alla discipline carceraria* (Torino, 1876)]

MANN, THOMAS, *Gesammelte Werke*, 13 vols (Frankfurt a.M.: Fischer, 1974)

MAY, KARL, *Werke.* Historisch-kritische Ausgabe für die Karl May-Stiftung, ed. by Hermann Wiedenroth (Bargfeld: Bücherhaus, 1993–)

—— *Der Gitano: Ein Abenteuer unter den Carlisten*, in *Der Beobachter an der Elbe*, 2 (1874–75), no. 52

—— *Die Juweleninsel* (Vienna, Heidelberg: Karl May Taschenbücher im Verlag Carl Ueberreuter, 1952)

—— *Zepter und Hammer* (Vienna, Heidelberg: Karl May Taschenbücher im Verlag Carl Ueberreuter, 1952)

MIKLOSICH, FRANZ, *Über die Mundarten und die Wanderungen der Zigeuner Europas* (Vienna: Karl Gerold's Sohn, 1872)

MÖRIKE, EDUARD, *Sämtliche Werke*, ed. by Jost Perfahl, 2 vols (Munich: Winkler, 1976)

MOREL, BÉNÉDICT-AUGUSTIN, *Traité des dégénérescences physiques, intellectuelles et morales de l'espèce humaine et des causes qui produisent ces variétés malidives* (Paris, 1857)

MÜLLNER, ADOLPH, *Die Schuld: Trauerpiel in vier Akten*, 4th edn (Tübingen: Cotta, 1821; 1st edn 1815), pp. 1–204

NIETZSCHE, FRIEDRICH, *Werke*, ed. by Karl Schlechta, 6 vols (Munich: Hanser, 1980)

NORDAU, MAX, *Entartung*, 2 vols, 3rd edn (Berlin: Carl Duncker 1896; 11st edn 1892–93)

OSTWALD, HANS, *Vagabunden: Ein autobiographischer Roman*, ed.by Klaus Bergmann (Frankfurt a.M. and New York: Campus, 1980) (1st edn *Vagabonden*, Berlin: Bruno und Paul Cassirer, 1900)

PLOETZ, ALFRED, *Die Tüchtigkeit unsrer Rasse und der Schutz der Schwachen: Ein Versuch über Rassenhygiene und ihr Verhältnis zu den humanen Idealen, besonders zum Socialismus* (Berlin: S. Fischer, 1895)

—— *Ziele und Aufgaben der Rassenhygiene: Referat erstattet auf der xxxv. Tagung des deutschen Vereins für öffentliche Gesundheitspflege zu Elberfeld* (Braunschweig: Vieweg, 1911)

POTT, AUGUST FRIEDRICH, *Die Zigeuner in Europa und Asien: Ethnographisch-linguistische Untersuchung, vornehmlich ihrer Herkunft und Sprache, nach gedruckten und ungedruckten Quellen*, 2 vols (Halle: Heynemann, 1844–45)

—— *Die Ungleichheit menschlicher Rassen hauptsächlich vom sprachwissenschaftlichem Standpunkte, unter besonderer Berücksichtigung von des Grafen Gobineau gleichnamigem Werk. Mit einem Ueberblicke ueber die Sprachverhältnisse der Völker. Ein etymologischer Versuch* (Lemgo and Detmold: Meyer, 1856)

RAABE, WILHELM, *Sämtliche Werke*, ed. by Karl Hoppe, 20 vols + 5 suppl. vols (Göttingen: Vandenhoeck & Ruprecht, 1951–)

REINBECK, EMIL, *Die Zigeuner: Eine wissenschaftliche Monographie nach historischen Quellen bearbeitet. Herkommen, Geschichte und eigenthümliche Lebensweise dieses räthselhaften Wandervolkes, von seinen ersten Auftritten im fünfzehnten Jahrhundert bis auf diese Zeit* (Salzkotten, Leipzig: Sobbe, 1861)

RITTER, ROBERT, *Ein Menschenschlag: Erbärztliche und erbgeschichtliche Untersuchungen über die — durch 10 Geschlechterfolgen erforschten — Nachkommen von 'Vagabunden, Jaunern und Räubern'* (Leipzig: Georg Thieme, 1937)

RÜDIGER, JOHANN CHRISTOPH CHRISTIAN, 'Von der Sprache und Herkunft der Zigeuner aus Indien', in *Neuester Zuwachs der teutschen, fremden und allgemeinen Sprachkunde in eigenen Aufsätzen*, 1. Stück (Leipzig, 1782), 37–84

SAAR, FERDINAND VON, *Novellen aus Österreich*, ed. by with afterword by Karl Wagner, 2 vols (Vienna and Munich: Deuticke, 1998)

SCHALLMEYER, WILHELM, *Vererbung und Auslese in ihrer soziologischen und politischen Bedeutung* (Jena: Gustav Fischer 1910; 1st edn 1903)

SCOTT, SIR WALTER, *Guy Mannering, or the Astrologer*, ed. by P. D. Garside (Edinburgh: Edinburgh University Press, 1999)

SHAKESPEARE, WILLIAM, *Most Excellent and Lamentable Tragedie, of Romeo and Juliet*, ed. by John Dover Wilson (Cambridge: Cambridge University Press, 1977; 1st edn, 1955)

—— *The Tempest*, ed. by Sir Arthur Quiller-Couch and John Dover Wilson (Cambridge: Cambridge University Press, 1977; 1st edn, 1921)

STEVENSON, ROBERT LOUIS, *The Strange Case of Dr Jekyll and Mr Hyde and Other Tales*, ed. with Introduction and Notes by Roger Luckhurst (Oxford: Oxford University Press, 2006), pp. 1–66

STIFTER, ADALBERT, *Sämmtliche Werke*, ed. by August Sauer and others, 25 vols (Prag/ Reichenberg, 1904–)
——*Gesammelte Werke*, ed. by Max Stefl, 6 vols (Wiesbaden: Insel, 1959)
——*Die Narrenburg*, ed. by Christian Begemann (Vienna: Residenz, 1996)
STORM, THEODOR, *Sämtliche Werke*, ed. by Karl Ernst Laage and Dieter Lohmeier, 4 vols (Frankfurt a.M.: Deutscher Klassiker Verlag 1987–88)
STRAUSS, DAVID FRIEDRICH, *Der alte und der neue Glaube*, 2nd edn (Bonn: Emil Strauss, 1873; 1st edn, 1872)
STRAUSS UND TORNEY, VICTOR VON, *Mitteilungen aus den Akten betreffend den Zigeuner Tuvia Panti aus Ungarn und Anderes von Victor Strauss*, ed. by Lulu von Strauss und Torney (Berlin and Vienna: Meyer & Jessen, 1912), pp. 17–107
TETZNER, THEODOR, *Geschichte der Zigeuner; ihre Herkunft, Natur und Art* (Weimar, Ilmenau: Voigt, 1835)
THOMASIUS, JAKOB, *Dissertation de Cingaris* (Leipzig, n.p., 1652)
——*Gründliche Historische Nachricht von denen Ziegeunern, Darinnen nebst andern Merckwürdigkeiten dieses Volcks insonderheit desselben Ursprung und erstes Vaterland, Ankunfft, Fortpflantzung und Ausbreitung in Teutschland und andern Europäischen Ländern aus bewährten Geschicht-Schreibern kürtzlich gezeiget und erwiesen wird.* Aus dem Lateinischen des hochberühmten Jacobi Thomasii in das Teutsche übersetzt (Frankfurt a.M. and Leipzig: n.p., 1748)
VOGT, CARL, *Vorlesungen über den Menschen*[,] *seine Stellung in der Schöpfung und in der Geschichte der Erde*, 2 vols (Gießen: Rieker, 1863)
WLISLOCKI, HEINRICH VON, *Aus dem inneren Leben der Zigeuner*, in von Wlislocki, *Ethnologische Mittheilungen* (Berlin: E. Felber, 1892)
——*Zur Ethnologie der Zigeuner in Südosteuropa: Tsiganologische Aufsätze und Briefe aus dem Zeitraum 1880–1905*, ed. by Joachim S. Hohmann, Studien zur Tsiganologie und Folkloristik, 12 (Frankfurt a.M.: Peter Lang, 1994)
Ziegeuner, in *Zedlers Grosses vollständiges Universal-Lexikon aller Wissenschaften und Künste*, 62 vols (Leipzig and Halle: Johann Heinrich Zedler, 1732–), LXII (1749), 520–44
WOLFF, PIUS ALEXANDER, *Preciosa: Schauspiel in vier Aufzügen* (Leipzig: Reclam, n.d.)
WOLZOGEN, CAROLINE VON, 'Die Zigeuner', in *Taschenbuch für Damen* (Stuttgart: Cotta 1802), pp. 84–152

Secondary Literature

A Catalogue of the Gypsy Books Collected by the Late Robert Andrew Scott MacFie [. . .] *Sometime Editor and Secretary of the Gypsy Lore Society* (Liverpool: University of Liverpool, 1936)
ACTON, THOMAS, *Gypsy Politics and Traveller Identity* (Hatfield: University of Hertfordshire Press, 1997)
AGNEW, VANESSA, 'Ethnographic Transgressions and Confessions in Georg Forster's *Voyage Round the World*', in *Schwellen: Germanistische Erkundungen einer Metapher*, ed. by Nicholas Saul, Daniel Steuer, and Frank Möbus (Würzburg: Königshausen & Neumann, 1999), pp. 304–15
ASHCROFT, BILL, 'Caliban's Language', in Ashcroft, *On Post-Colonial Futures: Transformations of Colonial Culture* (London and New York: Continuum, 2001), pp. 81–102
ASHCROFT, BILL, GARETH GRIFFITHS, and HELEN TIFFIN, eds, *The Post-Colonial Studies Reader* (London, New York: Routledge, 1995)
BALDENSPERGER, FERNAND, 'L'entrée pathétique des tziganes dans les lettres occidentales', *Revue de littérature comparée*, 18 (1938), 587–603
BARKHOFF, JÜRGEN, GILBERT CARR, and ROGER PAULIN, eds, *Das schwierige 19. Jahrhundert: Festschrift für Eda Sagarra zum 65. Geburtstag* (Tübingen: Niemeyer, 2000)

BECKER-CANTARINO, BARBARA, 'Die "neue Frau" und die Frauengestalten Carl Hauptmanns', in *Carl Hauptmann 1858–1921*, 47–66

BEER, GILLIAN, *Darwin's Plots: Evolutionary Narrative in Darwin, George Eliot and Nineteenth-Century Fiction* (Cambridge: Cambridge University Press, 2000) (1st edn 1983)

BEGEMANN, CHRISTIAN, 'Natur und Kultur: Überlegungen zu einem durchkreuzten Gegensatz im Werk Adalbert Stifters', in *Adalbert Stifters schrecklich schöne Welt: Beiträge des Internationalen Kolloquiums zur Adalbert-Stifter-Ausstellung (Universität Antwerpen 1993), Acta Austriaca-Belgica*, 1 (1996), 41–52

——*Die Welt der Zeichen: Stifter-Lektüren* (Stuttgart: Metzler, 1995)

BERGER, EBERHARD, 'Vorrede', in *Carl Hauptmann: Sämtliche Werke. Wissenschaftliche Ausgabe mit Kommentar*, ed. by Eberhard Berger, Hans-Gert Roloff, and Anna Strolka, 16 vols + 1 Supplementary vol. (Stuttgart: Bad Cannstatt: frommann-holzboog, 1997, in progress), Supplementary vol.: *Carl Hauptmann: Chronik zu Leben und Werk*, ed. by Eberhard Berger and Elfriede Berger (2001), 7–8

BERGER, HEIDI, 'Das Zigeunerbild in der deutschen Literatur des 19. Jahrhunderts', Ph.D. thesis (University of Waterloo, Waterloo, Ontario, 1972)

BERMAN, NINA, *Orientalismus, Kolonialismus und Moderne: Zum Bild des Orients in der deutschsprachigen Literatur um 1900* (Stuttgart: Metzler, 1997)

——'The Appeal of Karl May in the Wilhelmine Empire: Emigration, Modernization, and the Need for Heroes', in Todd Kontje, ed., *A Companion to Gernman Realism, 1848–1900* (Rochester, NY: Camden House, 2002), pp. 283–305

BERMAN, RUSSELL, *Enlightenment or Empire: Colonial Discourse in German Literature* (Lincoln, NB and London: University of Nebraska Press, 1998)

——'*Effi Briest* and the End of Realism', in Todd Kontje, ed., *A Companion to German Realism* (Rochester, NY: Camden House, 2002), pp. 339–64

BERND, CLIFFORD A., *Theodor Storm's Craft of Fiction: The Torment of a Narrator* (Chapel Hill: University of North Carolina Press, 1963)

——*Poetic Realism in Scandinavia and Central Europe 1820–1895* (Columbia, SC: Camden House, 1995)

BLACKBOURN, DAVID, *The Long Nineteenth Century: A History of Germany, 1780–1918* (New York and Oxford: Oxford University Press, 1998)

BHABHA, HOMI, *The Location of Culture* (London and New York: Routledge, 1994)

——'Signs taken for Wonders', in Bill Ashcroft, Gareth Griffiths, and Helen Tiffin, eds, *The Post-Colonial Studies Reader* (London: Routledge, 1995), pp. 29–35

BOA, ELIZABETH, '*Hermann und Dorothea*: An Early Example of *Heimalliteratur*?', *Publications of the English Goethe Society*, 69 (2000), 20–36

BÖHLER, MICHAEL, 'Clemens Brentanos *Die mehreren Wehmüller und ungarischen Nationalgesichter*. Kunst. Kommerz und Liebe im Modernisierungsprozeß', *Aurora*, 54 (1994), 145–66

BÖHME, HARTMUT and GERNOT BÖHME, *Das Andere der Vernunft: Zur Entdeckung von Rationalitätsstrukturen am Beispiel Kants* (Frankfurt a.M.: Suhrkamp, 1985)

BRANDSTETTER, GABRIELE, *Tanz-Lektüren: Körperbilder und Raumfiguren der Avantgarde* (Frankfurt a.M.: Fischer, 1995)

BREGER, CLAUDIA, *Ortlosigkeit des Fremden: 'Zigeunerinnen' und 'Zigeuner' in der deutschsprachigen Literatur um 1800* (Cologne, Weimar, and Vienna: Böhlau, 1998)

BRENNER, PETER J., 'Die Einheit der Welt: Zur Entzauberung der Fremde und Verfremdung der Heimat in Raabes *Abu Telfan*', *Raabe-Jahrbuch* (1989), 45–62

BREWSTER, PHILIP, 'Onkel Ketschwayo in Neuteutoburg: Zeitgeschichtliche Anspielungen in Raabes *Stopfkuchen*', *Raabe-Jahrbuch* (1983), 96–118

BROWN, MARILYN, *Gypsies and Other Bohemians: The Myth of the Artist in Nineteenth-Century France* (Ann Arbor: University of Michigan Research Press, 1985)

BROWNE, JANET, *Charles Darwin*. 2 vols (London: Pimlico, 2002–3; 1st edn 1996, 2002)

COOKE, PAUL, *Representing East Germany since Unification: From Colonization to Nostalgia* (Oxford and New York: Berg, 2005)

DANCKWORTT, BARBARA, 'Franz Mettbach — Die Konsequenzen der preußischen "Zigeunerpolitik" für die Sinti von Friedrichslohra', in Barbara Danckwortt, Thorsten Querg, and Claudia Schöningh, eds, *Historische Rassismusforschung: Ideologen — Täter — Opfer*. Mit einer Einleitung von Wolfgang Wippermann (Hamburg: Argument,1995), pp. 273–95

DELABAR, WALTER, 'Carl Hauptmanns Künstlerroman *Einhart der Lächler*: Eine erste Orientierung', in *Carl Hauptmann 1858–1921. Internationales Symposium: Beiträge*, ed. by Miroslawa Czarnecka and Hans-Gert Roloff (Berlin: Weidler, 2004), pp. 93–104

DENKLER, HORST, *Wilhelm Raabe: Legende — Leben — Literatur* (Tübingen: Niemeyer, 1989)

DURING, SIMON, *Foucault and Literature: Towards a Genealogy of Writing* (London and New York: Routledge, 1992)

DÜRR, VOLKER C., 'Idealistische Wissenschaft: Der (bürgerliche) Realismus und Gustav Freytag's Roman "Die verlorene Handschrift"', *Zeitschrift für deutsche Philologie*, 120 (2001), 3–33

EBHARDT, WILHELM, *Die Zigeuner in der hochdeutschen Literatur bis zu Goethes 'Götz von Berlichingen'* (Erlangen: Buchdruckerei des Werraboten Otto Fischer, 1928)

FASOLD, REGINA, 'Theodor Storms Verständnis von "Vererbung" im Kontext des Darwinismus-Diskurses seiner Zeit', in *Storm-Lektüren: Festschrift für Karl Ernst Laage zumn 80. Geburtstag*, ed. by Gerd Eversbegr, David A. Jackson, and Eckart Pastor (Würzburg: Königshausen & Neumann, 2000), pp. 47–58

FISCHER, SABINE and MORAY MCGOWAN, eds, *'Denn du tanzt auf einem Seil': Positionen deutschsprachiger MigrantInnenliteratur* (Tübingen: Stauffenburg, 1997)

FOHRMANN, JÜRGEN and HARRO MÜLLER, 'Einleitung: Diskurstheorien und Literaturwissenschaft', in *Diskurstheorien und Literaturwissenschaft*, ed. by Jürgen Fohrmann and Harro Müller (Frankfurt a.M.: Suhrkamp, 1988), pp. 9–22

FOUCAULT, MICHEL, *L'ordre du discours* (Paris: Gallimard, 1971)

——'What is an Author?', in *Modern Criticism and Theory*, ed. by David Lodge and Nigel Wood, 2nd edn (London: Longman, 2000) (1st edn, 1988), pp. 174–87

FRANK, GUSTAV, *Krise und Experiment: Komplexe Erzähltexte im literarischen Umbruch des 19. Jahrhunderts* (Wiesbaden: Deutscher Universitätsverlag, 1998)

FRASER, ANGUS, *The Gypsies* (Oxford: Clarendon Press, 1992)

FREUD, SIGMUND, 'Der Wahn und die Träume in W. Jensens *Gradiva*' (1907), in Freud, *Studienausgabe*, ed. by Alexander Mitscherlich and others, 14 vols (Frankfurt a.M.: Fischer, 1982), X, 9–85

FRIEDRICHSMEYER, SARA ANN, 'Romantic Nationalism: Achim von Arnim's Gypsy Princess Isabella', in *Germanness: Cultural Productions of Nation*, ed. by Patricia Herminghouse and Magda Mueller (Providence, RI and Oxford: Berghahn, 1997), pp. 51–65

GADEBUSCH BONDIO, MARIACARLA, *Die Rezeption der kriminalanthropologischen Theorien von Cesare Lombroso in Deutschland von 1880–1914* (Husum: Matthison, 1995)

GEULEN, EVA, *Worthörig wider Willen: Darstellungsproblematik und Sprachreflexion in der Prosa Adalbert Stifters* (Munich: Iudicium, 1992)

GLASER, HORST ALBERT, *Die Restauration des Schönen: Stifters 'Der Nachsommer'* (Stuttgart: Metzler, 1965)

GÖTTSCHE, DIRK, *Zeitreflexion und Zeitkritik im Werk Wilhelm Raabes* (Würzburg. Königshausen & Neumann, 2000)

——*Zeit im Roman: Literarische Zeitreflexion und die Geschichte des Zeitromans im späten 18. und im 19. Jahrhundert* (Munich: Fink, 2001)

——'Der koloniale "Zusammenhang der Dinge" in der deutschen Provinz: Wilhelm Raabe in postkolonialer Sicht' (unpublished typescript, to appear in *Raabe-Jahrbuch*, 2005–06)

GOODBODY, AXEL, 'A Life among Gypsies and Wolves: Otto Alscher's Quest for an Alternative to Modern Civilisation', in *German Monitor*, 57 (2003), 181–208

GREIPL, PETER, 'Drei bisher ungedruckte Stifter-Briefe', in Walter Hettche, ed., *Stifter-Studien: Ein Festgeschenk für Wolfgang Frühwald zum 65. Geburtstag* (Tübingen: Niemeyer, 2000), pp. 255–59

GUBSER, MARTIN, *Literarischer Antisemitismus: Untersuchungen zu Gustav Freytag und anderen bürgerlichen Schriftstellern des 19. Jahrhunderts* (Göttingen: Vandenhoeck & Ruprecht, 1998)

GUTHKE, KARL S., 'Gottfried Keller und die Romantik: Eine motivvergleichende Studie', *Der Deutschunterricht,* 11 (1959), 14–30

——'Hebbels "Blick in's Weite": Eurozentrik und Exotik', in *Resonanzen. Festschrift für Hans Joachim Kreutzer zum 65. Geburtstag*, ed. by Sabine Doering, Waltraud Maierhofer, and Peter Philipp Riedl (Würzburg: Königshausen & Neuman, 2000), pp. 363–73

HAHN, MARCUS, *Geschichte und Epigonen: '19. Jahrhundert'/'Postmoderne', Stifter/Bernhard* (Freiburg im Breisgau: Rombach, 2003)

HANCOCK, IAN, *The Pariah Syndrome* (Ann Arbor: Karoma, 1987)

——*We are the Romany People/Ame sam e Rromane dzene* (Hatfield: University of Hertfordshire Press/Centre de récherches Tsiganes, 2002)

HASUBEK, PETER, 'Karl Immermann: *Die Epigonen*', in *Romane und Erzählungen zwischen Romantik und Realismus,* ed. by Paul Michael Lützeler (Stuttgart: Reclam, 1983), pp. 202–30

HEHEMANN, RAINER, *Die 'Bekämpfung des Zigeunerunwesens' im Wilhelminischen Republik und in der Weimarer Republik, 1871–1933* (Frankfurt a.M.: Haag + Herchen, 1989)

HEIN, JÜRGEN, *Dorfgeschichte* (Stuttgart: Metzler, 1976)

——ed., *Gottfried Keller: Romeo und Julia auf dem Dorfe. Erläuterungen und Dokumente* (Stuttgart: Reclam, 1977)

HERTLING, G. H., 'Mignons Schwestern im Erzählwerk Adalbert Stifters: *Katzensilber, Der Waldbrunnen, Die Narrenburg*', in *Goethes Mignon und ihre Schwestern. Interpretation und Rezeption*, ed. by Gerhard Hoffmeister (New York: Lang, 1993), pp. 165–97

HETTCHE, WALTER, 'Nach alter Melodie: Die Gedichte von Julius Rodenberg, Wilhelm Jensen und Paul Heyse zum 70. Geburtstag Wilhelm Raabes', *Raabe-Jahrbuch* (1999), 144–56

HOHMANN, JOACHIM S., *Geschichte der Zigeunerverfolgung in Deutschland* (Frankfurt a.M.: Campus, 1981)

HÖLZ, KARL, *Zigeuner, Wilde und Exoten: Fremdbilder in der französischen Literatur des 19. Jahrhunderts* (Berlin: Erich Schmidt, 2002)

HOLUB, ROBERT C., *Reflections of Realism: Paradox, Norm and Ideology in Nineteenth-Century German Prose* (Detroit: Wayne State University Press, 1991)

HUNTER-LOUGHEED, ROSEMARIE, *Adalbert Stifter: Der Waldbrunnen. Interpretation und Ursprungshypothese* (Linz: Adalbert-Stifter-Institut des Landes Ober-Österreich, 1988)

JACKSON, DAVID A., *Theodor Storm: Dichter und demokratischer Humanist* (Berlin: Erich Schmidt, 2000)

JEZIORKOWSKI, KLAUS, *Literarität und Historismus: Beobachtungen zu ihrer Erscheinungsfrom im 19. Jahrhundert am Beispiel Gottfried Kellers* (Heidelberg: Winter, 1979)

KELLY, ALFRED, *The Descent of Darwin: The Popularisation of Darwinism in German 1860–1914* (Chapel Hill: University of North Carolina Press, 1981)

KENRICK, DONALD and GRATTAN PUXON, *Gypsies under the Swastika* (Hatfield: Gypsy Research Centre: University of Hertfordshire Press, 1995)

KETELSEN, UWE-K., 'Wilhelm Jensen — oder der Typus des Berufsschriftstellers in der zweiten Hälfte des 19. Jahrhunderts', *Raabe-Jahrbuch* (1996), 28–42

KLOTZ, VOLKER, '*Die Juweleninsel* — und was daraus werden könnte: Lese-Notizen zu den Erstlingsromanen nebst einigen Fragen zur Karl-May-Forschung', *Jahrbuch der Karl-May-Gesellschaft* (1979), 262–75

——'Machart und Weltanschauung eines Kolportagereißers: Karl Mays *Das Waldröschen*', *Text + Kritik: Sonderband Karl May* (1987), 60–89

KLUGE, GERHARD, 'Kommentar', in *Clemens Brentano, Sämtliche Werke und Briefe, historisch-kritische Ausgabe*, ed. by Jürgen Behrens, Wolfgang Frühwald, and Detlev Lüders, 36 vols (Frankfurt a.M.: Suhrkamp/Stuttgart, Berlin, Cologne, and Mainz: Kohlhammer, 1975–), XIX, 658–96

KOCH, ECKEHARD, '"Der Gitano ist ein gehetzter Hund": Karl May und die Zigeuner', in *Jahrbuch der Karl-May-Gesellschaft* (1989), pp. 178–229

KONTJE, TODD, *German Orientalisms* (Ann Arbor: University of Michigan Press, 2004)

KRAUSNICK, MICHAIL, 'Images of Sinti and Roma in German Children's and Teenage Literature', in *Sinti and Roma. Gypsies in German-Speaking Society and Literature*, ed. by Susan Tebbutt (New York and Oxford: Berghahn, 1998), pp. 107–28

KREUZER, INGRID, 'Hebbel als Novellist', in *Hebbel in neuer Sicht*, ed. by Helmut Kreuzer (Stuttgart, Berlin, Cologne, and Mainz: Kohlhammer, 1969; 1st edn, 1963), pp. 150–63

KRISTÉVA, JULIA, *Powers of Horror: An Essay on Abjection*, trans. by Leon S. Roudiez (New York: Columbia University Press, 1982)

KUGLER, STEFANI and DAGMAR HEINZE, 'Von der Unmöglichkeit, den Anderen zu lieben: Caroline von Wolzogens *Die Zigeuner* und Caroline Auguste Fischers *William der Neger*', in *Das Subjekt und die Anderen. Interkulturalität und Geschlechterdifferenz vom 18. Jahrhundert bis zur Gegenwart*, ed. by Herbert Uerlings (Berlin: Erich Schmidt, 2001), pp. 135–54

KUGLER, STEFANI, *Kunst-Zigeuner: Konstruktion des 'Zigeuners' in der deutschen Literatur der ersten Hälfte des 19. Jahrhunderts* (Trier: Wissenschaftlicher Verlag, 2004)

KURZKE, HERMANN, *Romantik und Konservatismus: Das 'politische' Werk Friedrich von Hardenbergs (Novalis) im Horizont seiner Wirkungsgeschichte* (Munich: Fink, 1983)

LANDFESTER, ULRIKE, '"Da, wo ich duldend mich unterwerfen sollte, da werde ich mich rächen" — Mignon auf dem Weg zur Revolte', *Internationales Jahrbuch der Bettina von Arnim-Gesellschaft*, 4 (1990), 71–97

LANGE, CHRISTIANE, '"Mueller von Mueller": Anmerkungen zu einem nahezu zerstörtem Frühwerk', in *Otto Mueller*, ed. by Johann Georg Prinz von Hohenzollern and Mario-Andreas von Lüttichau (Munich, Berlin, London, and New York: Prestel, 2003), pp. 12–25

LEWIS, VIRGINIA, 'Work and Freedom in the Minority Community: Ferdinand von Saar's *Die Troglodytin*', in *The German Mosaic: Cultural and Linguistic Diversity in Society* ed. by Carol-Aisha Blackshire-Belay (London: Greenwood, 1994), pp. 11–20

LORENZ, CHRISTOPH F., 'Karl Mays kleines Welttheater', *Mitteilungen der Karl-May-Gesellschaft*, 42 (1979), 31–33

——'Von der *Messingstadt* zur *Stadt der Toten*: Bildlichkeit und literarische Tradition von *Ardistan und Dschinnistan*', *Text + Kritik: Sonderband Karl May* (1987), 222–43

——'*Scepter und Hammer*' and '*Die Juweleninsel*', in *Karl-May-Handbuch*, ed. by Gerd Ueding and Klaus Rettner, 2nd edn (Würzburg: Königshausen & Neumann, 2001), pp. 305–12

LUCASSEN, LEO, *Zigeuner: Die Geschichte eines polizeilichen Ordnungsbegriffes in Deutschland 1700–1945* (Cologne, Weimar, and Vienna: Böhlau, 1996)

MCHAFFIE, M. A., and J. M. RITCHIE, 'Bee's Lake or the Curse of Silence: A Study of Theodor Storm's *Immensee*', *German Life and Letters*, 15 (1962), 36–48

MACKENZIE, JOHN M., *Orientalism, History, Theory and the Arts* (Manchester: Manchester University Press, 1995)

MAHR, JOHANNES, '"Tausend Eisenbahnen hasten . . . Um mich: Ich bin nur die Mitte!" Eisenbahngedichte aus der Zeit des deutschen Kaiserreichs', in *Technik in der Literatur: Ein Forschungsüberblick und zwölf Aufsätze*, ed. by Harro Segeberg (Frankfurt a.M.: Suhrkamp, 1987), pp. 132–73

MANNONI, OCTAVIO, *Prospero and Caliban: The Psychology of Colonization* (Ann Arbor: University of Michigan Press, 1950)

MAYALL, DAVID, *Gypsy Identities 1500–2000: From Egipcyans and Moon-Men to the Ethnic Romany* (London: Routledge, 2003)

MICHLER, WERNER, *Darwinismus und Literatur: Naturwissenschaftliche und literarische Intelligenz in Österreich, 1859–1914* (Vienna: Böhlau, 1999)

MINDEN, MICHAEL, 'Problems of Realism in Immermann's *Die Epigonen*', *Oxford German Studies*, 16 (1985), 66–80

MODE, HEINZ and SIEGFRIED WÖLFFLING, *Zigeuner: Der Weg eines Volkes in Deutschland* (Leipzig: Koehler & Amelang, 1968)

NAUMANN, URSULA, *Adalbert Stifter* (Stuttgart: Metzler, 1979)

NEUBER, WOLFGANG, 'Zwischen Darwinismus und Metaphysik oder: Lieber licht und gesund als dunkel und krank. Zu Carl Hauptmanns Roman *Mathilde*', in *Carl Hauptmann 1858–1921*, pp. 105–23

NEUMANN, GERHARD, 'Der Körper des Menschen und die belebte Statue: Zu einer Grundformel in Gottfried Kellers *Sinngedicht*', in *Pygmalion: Geschichte des Mythos in der abendländischen Kultur*, ed. by Mathias Meyer and Gerhard Neumann (Freiburg im Breisgau: Rombach, 1997), pp. 555–91

——'"Zuversicht". Adalbert Stifters Schicksalskonzept zwischen Novellistik und Autobiographie', in *Stifter-Studien: Ein Festgeschenk für Wolfgang Frühwald zum 65. Geburtstag*, ed. by Walter Hettche (Tübingen: Niemeyer, 2000), pp. 162–87

OESTERLE, GÜNTER, '"Zigeunerbilder" als Maske des Romantischen', in *'Zigeunerbilder' in der deutschsprachigen Literatur*, ed. by Wilhelm Solms and Daniel Strauß (Heidelberg: Dokumentations- und Kulturzentrum Deutscher Sinti und Roma, 1995), pp. 47–64

——, and INGRID OESTERLE, 'Die Affinität des Romantischen zum Zigeunerischen oder die verfolgten Zigeuner als Metapher für die gefährdete romantische Poesie', in *Hermenautik — Hermeneutik: Literarische und geisteswissenschaftliche Beiträge zu Ehren von Horst Peter Neumann*, ed. by Holger Helbig and others (Würzburg: Königshausen & Neumann, 1996), pp. 95–118

OESTERLE, INGRID, 'Peripherie und Zentrum — Kunst und Publizistik — Wahrnehmungsgrenzfall "große Stadt": Die Aufzeichnungen Friedrich Hebbels in Paris', in *Das schwierige neunzehnte Jahrhundert: Festschrift Eda Sagarra zum 65. Geburtstag*, ed. by Jürgen Barkhoff, Gilbert Carr, Wolfgang Frühwald, and Roger Paulin (Tübingen: Niemeyer, 2000), pp. 187–206

OKELY, JUDITH, *The Traveller-Gypsies* (Cambridge: Cambridge University Press, 1983)

OPPERMANN, HANS, *Wilhelm Raabe* (Hamburg: Rowohlt, 1970)

PASTOR, ECKHART, *Die Sprache der Erinnerung: Zu den Novellen von Theodor Storm* (Frankfurt a.M.. Athenäum, 1988)

PAULIN, ROGER C., *The Brief Compass: The Nineteenth-Century German Novelle* (Oxford: Clarendon Press, 1985)

PENNY, H. GLENN, *Objects of Culture: Ethnology and Ethnographic Museums in Imperial Germany* (Chapel Hill: University of North Carolina Press, 2002)

PFOTENHAUER, HELMUT, 'Die Wiederkehr der Einbildungen: Kellers *Pankraz, der Schmoller*', in Helmut Pfotenhauer, *Sprachbilder: Untersuchungen zur Literatur seit dem achtzehnten Jahrundert* (Würzburg: Königshausen & Neumann, 2000), pp. 175–86

PICK, DANIEL, *Faces of Degeneration: A European Disorder, c.1848–1918* (Cambridge: Cambridge University Press, 1989)

PIRSIG, TANJA, *Carl und Gerhard Hauptmann und die bildenden Künste*, MA thesis (Bonn, 1998)
——'Die Familie Hauptmann und Otto Mueller', in *Otto Mueller*, pp. 26–45
——'Otto Mueller: Mythos und Wahrheit', in *Otto Mueller*, pp. 124–62
PIZER, JOHN, 'Wilhelm Raabe and the German Colonial Experience', in *A Companion to German Realism 1848–1900*, ed. by Todd Kontje (Rochester, NY: Camden House, 2002), pp. 159–82
PLUMPE, GERHARD, ed., *Theorien des bürgerlichen Realismus: Eine Textsammlung* (Stuttgart: Reclam, 1997)
——'Einleitung' in *Bürgerlicher Realismus und Gründerzeit 1848–1890*, ed. by Edward McInnes and Gerhard Plumpe (Munich: Hanser, 1996), pp. 17–83
PRATT, MARY LOUISE, *Imperial Eyes: Travel Writing and Transculturation* (London and New York: Routledge, 1992)
RADCLIFFE, STANLEY, 'Raabe and the Railway', *New German Studies*, 2 (1974), 133–44
REEMTSMA, KATRIN, *Sinti und Roma: Geschichte, Kultur, Gegenwart* (Munich: Beck, 1996)
RICŒUR, PAUL, *The Rule of Metaphor: Multi-disciplinary Studies of the Creation of Meaning in Language* (Toronto and Buffalo: University of Toronto Press, 1977)
RIEDEL, MANFRED, 'Vom Biedermeier zum Maschinenzeitalter: Zur Kulturgeschichte der ersten Eisenbahnen in Deutschland' (1961), reprinted in *Technik in der Literatur: Ein Forschungsüberblick und zwölf Aufsätze*, ed. by Harro Segeberg (Frankfurt a.M.: Suhrkamp, 1987), pp. 102–31
RIEDEL, WOLFGANG, *"Homo natura": Literarische Anthropologie um 1900* (Berlin and New York: de Gruyter, 1996)
ROBERTSON, RITCHIE, *The 'Jewish Question' in German Literature 1749–1939: Emancipation and its Discontents* (Oxford: Oxford University Press, 1999)
——'Modernism and the Self 1890–1924', in *Philosophy and German Literature 1700–1990*, ed. by Nicholas Saul (Cambridge: Cambridge University Press, 2002), pp. 150–97
ROHSE, EBERHARD, '"Transzendentale Menschenkunde" im Zeichen des Affen: Raabes literarische Antworten auf die Darwinismusdebatte des 19. Jahrhunderts', *Raabe-Jahrbuch* (1988), 168–210
RUCH, MARTIN, *Zur Wissenschaftsgeschichte der deutschsprachigen 'Zigeunerforschung' von den Anfängen bis 1900* (Diss., Freiburg im Breisgau, 1986)
RUDOLPH, ANDREA, *Genreentscheidung und Symbolgehalt im Werk Friedrich Hebbels* (Frankfurt a.M.: Peter Lang, 2000)
SAGARRA, EDA, *A Social History of Germany 1648–1914* (London: Methuen, 1977)
SAID, EDWARD W., *Orientalism: Western Conceptions of the Orient* (Harmondsworth: Penguin, 1978)
——*Culture and Imperialism* (London: Vintage, 1993)
SAMMERN-FRANKENEGG, FRITZ RÜDIGER, *Perspektivische Strukturen einer Erinnerungsdichtung: Studien zur Deutung von Storms 'Immensee'* (Stuttgart: Heinz, 1976)
SAMMONS, JEFFREY, *Wilhelm Raabe: The Fiction of the Alternative Community* (Princeton: Princeton University Press, 1987)
——*The Shifting Fortunes of Wilhelm Raabe: A History of Criticism as Cautionary Tale* (Columbia, SC: Camden House, 1992)
——'Wilhelm Raabe's and Wilhelm Jensen's Scandinavian Fiction: A Contrast in Nationalisms', in *Studies in German and Scandinavian Literatuire after 1500. A Festschrift for George C. Schoolfield*, ed. by James A.Parente and Richard Erich Schade (Columbia, SC: Camden House, 1993), pp. 116–28
——*Ideology, Mimesis, Fantasy: Charles Sealsfield, Friedrich Gerstäcker, Karl May, and Other German Novelists of America* (Chapel Hill and London: University of North Carolina Press, 1998)

SAUL, NICHOLAS, 'Aesthetic Humanism: German Literature 1790–1830', in *The Cambridge History of German Literature*, ed. by Helen Watanabe-O'Kelly (Cambridge: Cambridge University Press, 1997), pp. 202–71

——'Leiche und Humor: Clemens Brentanos Schauspielfragment "Zigeunerin" und der Patriotismus um 1813', *JFDH* (1998), 111–66

——'The Pursuit of the Subject: Literature as Critic and Perfecter of Philosophy 1790–1830', in *German Philosophy and Literature 1700–1990*, ed. by Nicholas Saul (Cambridge: Cambridge University Press, 2002), 57–101

——and SUSAN TEBBUTT, 'Gypsies, Utopias and Counter-Cultures in Modern German Culture', in *Counter-Cultures*, ed. by Steve Giles and Maike Oergel (Zurich: Lang, 2003), pp. 43–60

——'Half a Gypsy: The Case of Ezra Jennings in Wilkie Collins's *The Moonstone* (1868)', in *The Role of the Romanies: Images and Self-Images of "Gypsies"/Romanies in European Cultures*, ed. by Nicholas Saul and Susan Tebbutt (Liverpool: Liverpool University Press, 2004), pp. 119–30

——'"*Poëtisirung* d[es] Körpers": Der Poesiebegriff Friedrich von Hardenbergs (Novalis) und die anthropologische Tradition', in *Novalis — Poesie und Poetik*, ed. by Herbert Uerlings (Tübingen: Niemeyer, 2004), pp. 151–69

——'Zum Zusammenhang von Hebbels früher Erzähl- und Reiseprosa: Kunst, Leben und Tod im Übergang zur Moderne', *Hebbel-Jahrbuch* (2004), pp. 72–89

——'Hackl's *Abschied von Sidonie* and the Romany Holocaust Remembered', *Bulletin of The Center for Holocaust Studies at the University of Vermont*, 9.2 (2005), 1–3, 8

SCHAMA, SIMON, *Landscape and Memory* (London: HarperCollins 1995)

SCHAUB, GERHARD, 'Mitidika und ihre Schwestern: Zur Kontinuität eines Frauentyps in Brentanos Werken', in *Zwischen den Wissenschaften: Beiträge zur deutschen Literaturgeschichte. Bernhard Gajek zum 65. Geburtstag*, ed. by Gerhard Hahn, Ernst Weber, and others (Regensberg: Pustet, 1994), pp. 304–17

SCHIVELBUSCH, WOLFGANG, *Geschichte der Eisenbahnreise: Zur Industrialisierung von Raum und Zeit im 19. Jahrhundert* (Munich, Vienna, and Frankfurt a.M.: Hanser, 1977)

SCHMIDT-STOLZ, REGINE, *Von Finkenrode nach Altershausen: Das Motiv der Heimkehr im Werk Wilhelm Raabes als Ausdruck einer sich wandelnden Lebenseinstellung, dargestellt an fünf Romanen aus fünf Lebensabschnitten* (Bern: Peter Lang, 1984)

SCHRADER, HANS-JÜRGEN, 'Brentanos *Die mehreren Wehmüller*: Potenzieren und Logarithmisieren als Endspiel', *Aurora*, 54 (1994), 119–44

SJØGREN, CHRISTINE OERTEL, 'The Frame of "Der Waldbrunnen" Reconsidered: A Note on Adalbert Stifter's Aesthetics', *Modern Austrian Literature*, 19.1 (1986), 9–25

SPRENGEL, PETER, *Darwin in der Poesie: Spuren der Evolutionslehre in der deutschsprachigen Literatur des 19. und 20. Jahrhunderts* (Würzburg: Königshausen & Neumann, 1998)

STADLER, ULRICH, *'Die theuren Dinge': Studien zu Bunyan, Jung-Stilling und Novalis* (Bern and Munich: Francke, 1980)

STAFFORD, FIONA J., *The Last of the Race: The Growth of a Myth from Milton to Darwin* (Oxford: Oxford University Press, 1994)

STERN, J. P., *Idylls and Realities: Studies in Nineteenth-Century German Literature* (London: Methuen, 1971)

STREITFELD, ERWIN, 'Aus Adalbert Stifters Bibliothek: Nach den Bücher- und Handschrift enverzeichnissen in den Verlassenschaftsakten von Adalbert und Amelie Stifter', *Raabe-Jahrbuch* (1977), 103–48

STRUCK, WOLFGANG, 'See- und Mordgeschichten: Zur Konstruktion exotischer Räume in realistischen Erzähltexten', *Raabe-Jahrbuch* (1999), 60–70

SWALES, ERIKA, *The Poetics of Scepticism: Gottfried Keller and 'Die Leute von Seldwyla'* (Oxford and New York: Berg, 1994)

SWALES, MARTIN, 'Gottfried Keller's *Romeo und Julia auf den Dorfe*', in *Zu Gottfried Keller*, ed. by Hartmut Steinecke (Stuttgart: Klett, 1984), pp. 56–67

SZONDI, PETER, 'Das Naive ist das Sentimentale: Zur Begriffsdialektik in Schillers Abhandlung' (1972), in Szondi, *Lektüren und Lektionen: Versuche über Literatur, Literaturtheorie und Literatursoziologie* (Frankfurt a.M.: Suhrkamp, 1972), pp. 47–99

TEBBUTT, SUSAN, ed., *Sinti and Roma: Gypsies in German-Speaking Society and Literature* (New York and Oxford: Berghahn, 1998)

TRUMPENER, KATIE, 'The Time of the Gypsies: A "People without a History" in the Narratives of the West', *Critical Enquiry*, 18 (1992), 843–84

UERLINGS, HERBERT, *Poetiken der Interkulturalität: Haiti bei Kleist, Seghers, Müller, Buch und Fichte* (Tübingen: Niemeyer, 1997)

VOSSEN, RÜDIGER, *Zigeuner: Roma, Sinti, Gitanos, Gypsies zwischen Verfolgung und Romantisierung. Katalog zur Ausstellung 'Zigeuner zwischen Romantisierung und Verfolgung — Roma, Sinti, Manusch, Calé in Europa' des Hamburgischen Museums für Völkerkunde* (Frankfurt a.M., Berlin, and Vienna: Ullstein, 1993)

WALKER, ALAN, *Franz Liszt*, 3 vols (New York: Knopf, 1983–96)

WATANABE-O'Kelly, Helen, ed., *Cambridge History of German Literature* (Cambridge: Cambridge University Press, 1997)

WEHLER, HANS-ULRICH, *Bismarck und der Imperialismus* (Cologne and Berlin: Kiepenheuer und Witsch, 1969)

—— *Das deutsche Kaiserreich 1871–1918* (Göttingen: Vandenhoeck & Ruprecht, 1973)

WEHNERT, JÜRGEN, 'Auswahlbibliographie zu Karl May', *Text + Kritik: Sonderband Karl May* (1987), 279–96

WEIGEL, SIGRID, 'Der schielende Blick: Thesen zur Geschichte weiblicher Schreibpraxis', in *Die verborgene Frau: Sechs Beiträge zu einer feministischen Literaturwissenschaft*, ed. by Inge Stephan and Sigrid Weigel, 3rd edn (Hamburg: Argument, 1988; 1st edn, 1976), pp. 82–137

WEIKART, RICHARD, *From Darwin to Hitler: Evolutionary Ethics, Eugenics, and Racism in Germany* (New York and Basingstoke: Palgrave Macmillan, 2004)

WEINDLING, PAUL, *Health, Race and German Politics between National Unification and Nazism, 1870–1945* (Cambridge: Cambridge University Press, 1989)

WEINDLING, S., 'Das autobiographische Element in Carl Hauptmanns *Einhart der Lächler*', *GQ* 28 (1955), 122–26

WILLEMS, WIM, *In Search of the True Gypsy: From Enlightenment to Final Solution* (London, Portland, OR: Frank Cass, 1997)

WINGERTSZAHN, CHRISTOPH, *Ambiguität und Ambivalenz im erzählerischen Werk Achim von Arnims* (St Ingbert: Röhrig, 1990), pp. 96–120

WIPPERMANN, WOLFGANG, *Geschichte der Sinti und Roma in Deutschland: Darstellung und Dokumente* (Berlin: Pädagogisches Zentrum, 1993)

WYSLING, HANS, 'Und immer wieder kehrt Odysseus heim: Das "Fabelhafte" bei Gottfried Keller', in *Gottfried Keller: Elf Essays zu seinem Werk*, ed. by Hans Wysling (Munich: Fink, 1990), pp. 151–62

YOUNG, ROBERT J. C., *Colonial Desire: Hybridity in Theory, Culture and Race* (London and New York: Routledge, 1995)

ZANTOP, SUZANNE, *Colonial Fantasies: Conquest, Family and Nation in Precolonial Germany, 1770–1870* (Durham, NC, and London: Duke University Press, 1997)

ZIMMERMANN, MICHAEL, *Rassenutopie und Genozid: Die nationalsozialistische 'Lösung der Zigeunerfrage'* (Hamburg: Christians, 1996)

—— *Verfolgt, vertrieben, vernichtet: Die nationalsozialistische Vernichtungspolitik gegen Sinti und Roma* (Essen: Klartext, 1989)

INDEX

For Product Safety Concerns and Information please contact our EU representative GPSR@taylorandfrancis.com Taylor & Francis Verlag GmbH, Kaufingerstraße 24, 80331 München, Germany

Printed and bound by CPI Group (UK) Ltd, Croydon, CR0 4YY
08/06/2025
01896999-0019